Warfare in History

THE

BATTLE OF HASTINGS

SOURCES AND INTERPRETATIONS

Warfare in History

General Editor: Matthew Bennett
ISSN 1358–779X

THE
BATTLE OF HASTINGS

SOURCES AND INTERPRETATIONS

EDITED AND INTRODUCED BY

Stephen Morillo

THE BOYDELL PRESS

This collection first published 1996
The Boydell Press, Woodbridge

ISBN 0 85115 593 6 hardback
ISBN 0 85115 619 3 paperback

The Boydell Press is an imprint of Boydell & Brewer Ltd
PO Box 9, Woodbridge, Suffolk IP12 3DF, UK
and of Boydell & Brewer Inc.
PO Box 41026, Rochester, NY 14604-4126, USA

British Library Cataloguing-in-Publication Data
Battle of Hastings: Sources and
Interpretations. – (Warfare in History:
Sources & Interpretations Series; Vol. 1)
I. Morillo, Stephen   II. Series
942.021
ISBN 0–85115–593–6
ISBN 0–85115–619–3 pbk

Library of Congress Cataloging-in-Publication Data
The Battle of Hastings : sources and interpretations / edited and
introduced by Stephen Morillo.
    p.   cm. – (Warfare in history ; v. 1)
Includes bibliographical references.
ISBN 0–85115–593–6 (hardback : alk. paper).
ISBN 0–85115–619–3 (pbk. : alk. paper)
    1. Hastings, Battle of, 1066 – Sources. [1. Great Britain –
History – William I, 1066–1087 – Sources.]   I. Morillo, Stephen.
II. Series.
DA196.B32   1995
942.02'1–dc20   95–14358

The paper used in this publication meets the minimum requirements
of American National Standard for Information Sciences –
Permanence of Paper for Printed Library Materials, ANSI Z39.48–1984

Printed in Great Britain by
St Edmundsbury Press Ltd, Bury St Edmunds, Suffolk

CONTENTS

GENERAL EDITOR'S PREFACE

Every generation of historians can labour under the delusion that it alone has achieved an objective assessment of the past. Previous attempts at research and analysis stand to be shot at by an apparently wiser and more sophisticated breed, perhaps unaware that they are creating their own orthodoxies to be undermined in turn. Military historians have had a particularly poor reputation for being 'old-fashioned'. Military history has been seen as the playground of retired professional soldiers seeking intellectual stimulation in their prolonged years of retirement. Worse still, the bloody conflicts of the twentieth century have rendered it an unattractive area to many. It can seem out of tune with the times, out of touch with current concerns and growth areas of historical research such as gender studies or the history of sexuality.

Even those historians who have tackled military themes have appeared happier to deal with them from a 'War and Society' point of view. That is to say, frequently exploring the implications of a range of military activities for the population and economy of a particular country, region or location, whilst leaving out the actual fighting. It is the intention of the 'Sources and Interpretation' volumes of the *Warfare and Society* series, to reintegrate the operational, tactical, technical and equipment aspects of the conduct of warfare, whilst not ignoring its impact on wider society. In this context, it becomes just as acceptable to study the history of particular campaigns or battles, as to investigate the social structures which made war-fighting possible.

In the first volume of the series, Stephen Morillo tackles head-on the 'decisive battles' school of old military historians, such as J.F.C. Fuller and his imitators, and explains how he is a 'new' man. A 'new military historian' takes into account a wider range of social, economic, cultural, intellectual and, yes, gender factors, when drawing his or her conclusions. Yet as a commentator s/he does not draw back from attempting to analyze and elucidate an event as ephemeral as a battle. Even the day-long conflict fought on a ridge a few miles north of Hastings on 14 October 1066, enshrined as it is in historiography as a pivotal event in English history, marked on the map by the great abbey built on the site, described in numerous contemporary accounts, and remarkably, celebrated pictorially in the Bayeux Tapestry, unique by its survival, can still only, at this great distance in time, be dimly perceived. Not that this has prevented a great deal of apparent certitude from historians of the last three centuries, combined with rationalist or nationalist prejudices.

The volume is divided into fifty pages on sources and almost 200 pages of interpretation, the latter concisely compiled from a great deal more commentary. In them, Dr Morillo seeks to draw attention to both material and method. The assumptions of one generation are held up and challenged by the scrutiny of another. As befits the most recent commentator, he has the last word, when he tells us that Hastings was a most 'unusual' battle. This had been evident to William of Poitiers, duke William's contemporary, but was a point that many later historians missed in their eagerness to draw lessons from the event. This series is intended to help the reader look at the past afresh, and challenge assumptions about military history. If it can help to bring about a resurgence of interest in the discipline, and perhaps win it a wider respectability in the eyes of historians then it will have succeeded in its aim.

Matthew Bennett
February 1996

PREFACE

The idea for a book focused on Hastings and designed as a teaching tool originated in conversations between Robert Easton, Richard Abels and myself, and I took up the editing task at their suggestion. I'd like to thank them not only for providing the idea, but for many useful suggestions along the way. In addition to discussing with me possible selections, Richard also read drafts of the main introduction and the short introductions to each selection, providing much useful criticism and commentary, as did his wife Ellen. My own wife Kim gave the introduction a thorough editorial going over, much improving its readability. Matthew Bennett suggested useful refinements to the list of selections. While the final choice of sources and secondary articles with all its inevitable faults and omissions was mine, I am indebted to all these people for improving both the selections and the original material. I also owe major thanks to Ezra Ball and Carl Muma in the Wabash Media Center for help in producing the maps. Without their hardware and software expertise, my job as designer would have been much more onerous. A final thank you and a dedication goes to all those students, past and future, with whom I share a passion for history and a dedication to learning and teaching. I hope you find this volume both useful and enjoyable.

Stephen Morillo
Wabash College
September 1994

INTRODUCTION

In one sense, a book on the battle of Hastings hardly needs justification. Hastings was a 'Decisive Battle'.[1] Its date is one of the most famous in history – one of only two memorable dates in English history, according to the witty historical parody by Sellar and Yeatman, *1066 and All That*.[2] The dramatic story of that year's events has been rendered as popular history,[3] as an historical novel by an authority on the period,[4] and in numberless historical accounts going right back to the days of the Conquest. Academic warriors continue to refight the battle today with nearly as much ferocity, at times, as was shown by the Anglo-Saxons under King Harold and the Normans and their allies under Duke William on Saturday, October 14th, nearly a millennium ago. The battle had momentous consequences, and so interpreting the battle matters for interpreting what came after. As Sellar and Yeatman say with only a touch of hyperbole:[5]

> The Norman Conquest was a Good Thing, as from this time onwards England stopped being conquered and thus was able to become top nation.

This volume is designed in part as a guide into these ongoing academic debates about the campaign and battle of 1066.

But in another sense a volume dedicated to one event in one year may need some justification as a teaching tool. Teachers of surveys, especially, often find the pressure of 'coverage' makes detailed examination of events difficult. Yet teachers also recognize the benefits of close examination: students are able to come to grips with the primary sources, to see and join in the scholarly debates that details can ignite, and to feel the personal side of history – often its most exciting face – more intensely. I shall return to the more specific question of 'Why Hastings?' below. But this volume is also designed as a focused package of primary sources and secondary articles suitable for classroom use as well as for the interested reader.

The purpose of the volume as a teaching and learning tool has guided its organization. First, this introduction is intended to provide a brief survey of the context of the campaign and battle: a sort of roadmap with some key features marked 'what to look out for'. While the historical context is one part of such a survey – what Europe was like in 1066, the main events of the year, the consequences of the Conquest, and the place of the battle in history – the historiographical setting is just as important. What have the main points of contention been in interpreting the battle? How have views of the battle changed through time? Sketching answers to such questions

---

[1] A concept discussed further below.
[2] W.C. Sellar and R.J. Yeatman, *1066 and All That. A Memorable History of England* (New York, 1931).
[3] David Howarth, *1066: The Year of the Conquest* (London: Collins, 1977).
[4] Hope Muntz, *The Golden Warrior* (New York, 1949).
[5] Sellar and Yeatman, *1066*, p. 17.

provides help in understanding the primary sources and the scholarly articles which make up the bulk of this book.

Part I of the book contains all the significant primary sources for the battle. While the information we have about Hastings is meagre by comparison with many late medieval and early modern battles, the fight is richly documented for its time. The accounts presented here are all nearly contemporary with the battle,[6] and show us the events from several points of view and in two different media, since the Bayeux Tapestry tells the story pictorially.

Part II presents a selection of secondary sources, divided into sections on the armies of the two societies that met that day; the campaign; and the battle. The literature generated by Hastings is vast, and any selection is bound to be subjective – undoubtedly another editor would have made different choices. But I hope that the selections presented here represent a fair sampling of the perspectives and approaches that historians have taken in interpreting the events preserved for us in the primary sources.

History

Latin Christendom in 1066 was in the midst of a multifaceted transformation, as the work of generations of peasants and merchants, churchmen and warriors laid the foundations for the twelfth and thirteenth century flowering of high medieval civilization. The violence and political fragmentation of the age after Charlemagne, exacerbated by Viking, Magyar and Saracen invasions, had called forth differing responses across the continent, but all pointed at some sort of reconstruction of order and authority. The end of the invasions, the slow spread of agricultural improvements and stable peasant culture, and renewed population growth all contributed to an economic revival that, from about the year 1000, provided new tools and resources to authority builders. England and Normandy, connected to an emerging North Sea-Baltic maritime trade system, had certainly profited from this revival; England's economy in 1066, particularly, was relatively monetarized for the time.[7]

Most of the authority builders in this rude but vigorous civilization were members of the warrior elite that dominated society. Virtually every political unit in Europe was run by a warleader and his band of supporters for their own benefit. But conceptions of public duty and the public good had never entirely disappeared from this world's political conceptions, and began by the middle of the eleventh century to exert more influence over this predatory ruling class. England's centralized Carolingian-style monarchy, under both Anglo-Saxon and Danish kings, was perhaps more advanced than most in its range of claims to public power. But even a classic warleader such as William the Bastard, duke of Normandy, who built his government on

---

6   The one possible exception is the *Carmen de Hastingae Proelio*: see selection 6 and note 31 below. There are short descriptions of the battle in William of Malmesbury and Orderic Vitalis; both are mainly derived from earlier accounts. The long and detailed *Roman de Rou* by Wace, though claiming an oral tradition directly connected to the battle, is now generally considered unreliable.

7   The literature on the evolution of Europe after 1000 and for the general topics that follow is voluminous, and this essay will not attempt a full bibliographic guide. Good recent introductions with bibliographies include Malcolm Barber, *The Two Cities: Medieval Europe, 1050–1320* (London, 1992) for the medieval world and Marjorie Chibnall, *Anglo-Norman England, 1066–1166* (Blackwell, 1986) for conquest-era England.

a network of kinship relations among his bellicose supporters, could use the conception of public good imbedded in the Peace of God to justify restrictions on private warfare among his followers. Leaders like William found such concepts, harnessed to greater monetary resources and used in conjunction with the military power of the elite, vital in enhancing their own power. In building their own power, they laid the unplanned foundations of medieval states. The combination of Norman and English governmental powers created by William's conquest of the kingdom would create one of the most precocious and centralized of those states.

The influence of the Church in spreading Christian teachings was crucial in maintaining and spreading ideas of public good, as the example of the Peace of God shows. And the Church itself was the exceptional, non-warrior political force, though its membership was closely connected by family ties and ties of lordship, landholding and mutual interest to those of the warrior elite. In 1066 the political centre of the Church, the papacy, was only beginning to assert its independence through the continuing propagation of the Gregorian reform movement. A century and a half later, the ideology of reform had carried the papacy to a position of spiritual and above all political leadership in the Latin west, a position often in conflict with secular leadership. But in 1066 Pope Alexander III needed allies and reform was a potential tool of ambitious secular leaders. In this complicated setting, aggressive diplomacy on the part of one such leader, Duke William, gained papal approval for his planned invasion of England, sealed by a papal banner under which the Duke's army would fight.

Why did William aim at England in the first place? Simple greed is a part, but only a part, of the answer. William had a fortunate congruence of opportunity, motive and means in 1066 which form the immediate background to the campaign and battle.

Edward the Confessor, king of England, was childless. He had come to the throne in 1042, succeeding his half-brother Hardacnut, whose father Cnut had conquered England in 1016 from Edward's father Ethelred and married Edward's mother. Edward had therefore spent most of his youth in exile in Normandy at the court of William's father Robert; he maintained connections to Normandy after he came to the throne. It is neither clear nor likely that Edward had designated William as his heir, as the Norman duke claimed when Edward died, but it is possible.

The only other surviving member of the English royal family in 1066 was Edgar Atheling, a young boy in 1066 whose family had until recently been in exile in Hungary. The kingship instead fell, probably through Edward's designation and certainly by the choice of the Anglo-Danish ruling class, to Harold Godwinson. Harold was the eldest son and heir of Earl Godwin, and thus head of the most powerful family in England. He took over a kingdom with substantial economic and military resources (see selection 7 below). He was crowned shortly after Edward died at the end of 1065.

The fallout of an incident that had taken place in 1064 complicated Harold's accession, however. The circumstances are not entirely clear, but whether on a diplomatic mission for Edward to Normandy or by accident, Harold had found himself shipwrecked in Ponthieu and imprisoned by Guy, the local count. William freed Harold and made him his guest; Harold joined William on several military campaigns. Sometime during his stay, Harold took an oath recognizing William's right to the throne of England. Whether Harold gave the oath freely, as the Norman chroniclers later claimed, or was coerced, making the oath invalid, as Harold's supporters would argue, has remained unclear, though coercion is likely. But William's ability to portray Harold as an oath-breaker proved instrumental in his gaining papal sanction for his invasion. It certainly constituted the key pretext for William's expedition.

With motive in hand, William could put opportunity and means to use. William had become duke as an illegitimate minor, and had survived a troubled minority only with the help of his overlord the king of France. But once he gained his footing he mastered the turbulent Norman warrior class and established himself as a warleader of note (see selection 9 below). For much of his early rule he fought on the defensive against both the king, who found his former ward becoming disturbingly powerful, and against the count of Anjou, the ruler of a rival principality to the southwest of Normandy. But in 1060 both king and count died. A minor and a succession dispute respectively left Normandy temporarily free of external threats and gave William the opportunity to pursue foreign adventures designed to enrich the warrior class he led. His Norman soldiery was informally organized (see selection 8 below) but loyal; augmented substantially by mercenaries from a wide area (but especially from Brittany, Flanders and France) attracted by the duke's money and reputation, they gave William the means he needed to stalk his ambitions in England.

Thus we come to the events of 1066. The diplomatic manoeuvring of late winter gave way to military preparations in spring and early summer. William began to gather an invasion fleet and army at a camp near the mouth of the Dives river and in neighbouring ports. Harold repulsed a raid by his exiled brother Tostig and in May, in expectation of William's coming, mobilized troops in the counties of southern England and based his fleet on the Isle of Wight. The fleet and army waited all summer and on September 8, having exhausted their provisions, went home. William's force, having waited either for a favourable wind or by plan, left the Dives area a few days later, but could not cross the Channel; instead west winds blew it up the Channel to St Valéry, at the mouth of the Somme, where it waited another two weeks for the weather to change. It was now late in the campaign season and as yet nothing had really happened.

Something then did happen, but from a totally unexpected quarter. Harald Hardraada of Norway, one of the most famous warriors in all Christendom, landed in northern England with a large fleet and support from the rebel Tostig. The invaders defeated an Anglo-Saxon force under the northern earls Edwin and Morcar at Gate Fulford and headed for York. Gathering his army, Harold Godwinson marched rapidly north and surprised the invaders at Stamford Bridge. After a bloody fight, he won a complete victory, killing Hardraada and Tostig. But as he rested at York he learned that William, having at last got the favourable winds he had been praying for, had crossed with his army to Pevensey and set about ravaging Harold's ancestral lands in Sussex. Harold raced back to London by forced marches, waited a scant two weeks there to rest and receive reinforcements for his tired and depleted army, and then headed towards William.

It is not clear whether Harold intended at this point to surprise William as he had Harald and Tostig, or whether he planned to bottle William up on the Hastings peninsula and starve him out. In the event, William learned of Harold's approach and forced the issue himself. On Saturday, October 14, the two armies met on a hill north of Hastings, and after a long hard fight William emerged not only victorious but master of the kingdom, as Harold and his brothers all died in the contest, depriving the remaining English resistance of effective leadership. Marching east along the coast, William survived a bout with dysentery at Dover to make a destructive westward-looping approach on London, where the leading men of the kingdom submitted to him. He was crowned king on Christmas day, 1066.

William's stated intention was to rule as his Anglo-Saxon predecessors had, and this conservative attitude does seem to have guided his actions at first. But the problems of pacifying the kingdom in the five years after Hastings inevitably caused some transformations in the governance of the realm – the private castles, unknown before the conquest, that soon controlled the countryside were the most visible sign of change – and the replacement of one ruling class with another worked longer term transformations on the kingdom. Over the next century a synthesis of Anglo-Saxon and Norman elements of law, administration, and culture took place, creating a cross-Channel Anglo-Norman realm that was in many ways more than the sum of its parts. England's new connection to the continent, expanded even more under the Angevin Henry II, drew it away from the Scandinavian world and firmly into the Franco-centric medieval cosmos. For England, for France, and for Latin Christendom as a whole, the long-term consequences of the battle were significant.

Historiography

The long view: theories and contexts

Because Hastings had such momentous consequences, it is easy to sound hyperbolic in assessing the place of Hastings in history. This is particularly true because the concept of 'decisive battles' is so fraught with historiographical dangers. A closer examination of the ways in which Hastings was decisive reveals some of these problems. For the sake of comparison with other 'decisive battles' I shall use J.F.C. Fuller's *Military History of the Western World*,[8] which is organized around chapters on what he saw as the decisive battles in western history. (His account of Hastings is selection 14 below.) I shall limit the comparison to those battles in his first two volumes (through Waterloo), to allow for long term consequences to enter the discussion.

In the most trivial sense, Hastings was decisive in that one side won convincingly over the other – there is no Pyrrhus here, exclaiming 'One more such victory and I am lost.' But battles decisive in this sense were not uncommon in ancient and medieval warfare: when the rare set-piece battle did occur, it often ended in a clear victory. Hastings is in thinner company as a battle that effectively decided the larger war that included it, but there are still plenty of examples of this sort of decisiveness, including Napoleon's final defeat at Waterloo and Hannibal's final defeat at Zama, where the Romans ended the Second Punic War, for example.[9]

In fact, it is long term consequences that set Hastings apart. The Anglo-Norman synthesis made possible by William's victory created a new set of structures or parameters in English history. In effect, it set England on a new historical path, one with ramifications for a much broader area of the world. Furthermore, it seems reasonable to say that the synthesis that resulted from Hastings would not have happened otherwise, nor was the chance for something similar to happen likely to repeat itself. I shall elaborate on this idea in a moment; but first, how does this sort

---

[8] J.F.C. Fuller *A Military History of the Western World*, 3 vols (Minerva Press, 1954).

[9] Though Hastings stands apart from battles such as Waterloo and Zama by coming at the beginning of the war, rather than at the end of a long conflict.

of decisiveness compare to other great battles? The short answer is that it is exceedingly rare.

There are plenty of battles that in fact changed very little in the long or short term. The Duke of Marlborough's masterpiece at Blenheim in 1704 was a notable victory capping a brilliant campaign, but it hardly changed the course of history. Even more common on Fuller's list are battles that changed little by themselves, but instead stand as symbols of a longer military process. The Roman victory over the Macedonians at Pydna in 168 BC, which sealed Roman control of the Greek world, did not cause the Roman Empire; rather, it stands as an example of a Roman expansionism which depended on battlefield victories as little as not infrequent battlefield defeats slowed it, as Hannibal could attest after Cannae. The Siege of Constantinople in 1453 (several sieges sneak into Fuller's list of battles) is another example of this sort, as the rest of the Byzantine Empire had long since fallen to the Turks. Similarly, there are battles that altered the immediate political configuration of an area, but not the underlying dynamics, so that it is likely that the consequences of the battle would have come about in some form anyway. The Crusader States became a tenuous proposition militarily long before Saladin defeated the Kingdom of Jerusalem's forces at Hattin in 1187, for example.

Closer to the sort of impact I have suggested for Hastings but still not quite comparable were those battles commonly thought to have preserved or protected a set of developments just getting underway. Thus Salamis, the great naval battle in 480 BC where the Greek world escaped domination by the Persian empire, and the siege of Constantinople in 717, linked by Fuller with Poitiers in 732 as the places where the expansion of Islam was halted.[10] While significant, battles that preserve rather than create possibilities are probably less responsible for the consequences that follow than those which open new paths.

In fact, taken on the terms of this historical game of 'what if', only one other battle on Fuller's list can really be compared to Hastings: Alexander's victory over Darius' Persians at Arbela in 331 BC from which the Hellenistic world emerged. Just as Alexander's fusion of Greek and west Asian civilizations, setting *poleis* in the context of Persian monarchy, created a cultural matrix that shaped political and intellectual developments for centuries in the eastern Mediterranean, so William's fusion of Saxon and Norman proved creative in lasting ways. To take probably the most important facet of the Anglo-Norman synthesis, the combination of a conquering king and a new military ruling class with Anglo-Saxon courts, legal traditions and royal powers laid the foundations for the development of the English common law tradition and related developments pointing to 'constitutionalism' (via Magna Carta) and representative government.[11]

Stating the consequences of Hastings in this way, however, should raise questions about the view of history the sentence implies. The developments sketched above were only made possible by Hastings (whereas before they were, if not impossible, then far less likely), not predetermined by the outcome of the battle. The particular path that developments took after 1066 was influenced by a vast cast of historical actors (including Henry II and John in particular), and cannot be separated from a larger background of economic growth, intellectual developments such as the pro-

---

[10] The usual formulation is that these battles did something like 'preserve the western tradition', a notion clearly loaded with Eurocentric assumptions.

[11] See Chibnall, *Anglo-Norman England*, Part III, and the literature cited there.

gress of Roman Law, and the birth of representative institutions in most of medieval Europe.[12] And in no way could William be thought to have intended such long term developments: his conservative attitude to his new kingdom has already been mentioned.[13]

What this reveals is that we must carefully examine histories of 'decisive battles' for the philosophical and cultural assumptions which lie behind the very concept. Large set piece encounters have attracted the attention of historians since ancient times – they seem to epitomise the heroic, the glorious, and the fascinatingly terrible in war, and in obeying the dramatic unities of time, place and action lend themselves to dramatic treatments by their chroniclers.[14] But they were also exceedingly rare events in warfare until the modern era. There were good reasons for this. Battle was risky, and so to be entered into only when the odds were overwhelmingly in one's favour (in which case one's opponent would presumably be seeking desperately to avoid it) or as a last resort. And in many times and places, battle furthered the aims of war only indirectly. Raiding and plundering, much the most common activity in most war, could be an end in itself; and if conquest of territory were the aim, plundering also served as one tool in capturing enemy strongholds, along with sieges. Capturing strongholds was the only sure way to conquest, and victory in battle did not always assure the surrender of fortifications. Armies were therefore built as much for ravaging and siege work as for battle, which affected how they could fight on the battlefield.[15]

Thus, excessive focus on the battlefields of history distorts our picture of warfare as a whole. Furthermore, the notion that the set piece confrontation, no matter how rare, was the ultimate test of an army and the most truly warlike of military actions may be culturally bound. Victor Davis Hanson claims that the idea and practice of 'decisive battles' – face-to-face fights at the point of edged weapons – originated in the phalanx warfare of Greek city states, and descended thence to become 'the western way of war', in contradistinction to other traditions which emphasize indirection, missile fire, and avoidance of such ultimate tests of human nature as decisive battle presents.[16]

Certainly emphasis on battles became part of the western historiographical tradition, especially among the writers of popular military history, often retired military men: that 'disproportionately huge crowd of narrower-minded writers, for whom "military historian" was the most complimentary title that could be found, military

[12] See Brian M. Downing, *The Military Revolution and Political Change* (Princeton, 1992), for an interesting study of the varied fates of medieval representative institutions in the context of early modern political and military developments.

[13] In this sense Arbela and Alexander were clearly the more significant, since Alexander consciously attempted to initiate and guide the revolutionary synthesis that followed his victory.

[14] Herodotus, Thucydides and Caesar are but the most prominent examples of ancient historians who placed set-piece battle descriptions prominently in their histories.

[15] The late Roman military writer Vegetius takes avoidance of battle and living off one's enemy's land as two of his most basic strategic principles. See Flavius Vegetius Renatus, *Epitoma rei militaris*, ed. C. Lang (Stuttgart, 1967); translation of Books I–III available in T.R. Phillips, *Roots of Strategy* (Harrisburg, 1985).

[16] Victor Davis Hanson, *The Western Way of War* (New York, 1989); John Keegan, *A History of Warfare* (New York, 1993), takes up the theme in the context of his global and temporally sweeping survey of war in human history.

enthusiast or even war maniac the more apposite', as one recent historian has put it.[17] The problem with such an emphasis, though, is not just with the distortion it created in our picture of warfare. It is also that the narrowness of vision often extended to the philosophy of history behind the dramatic story. The history of great battles was the history of military politics, a history shaped by the lives and actions of Great Men. 'Great Man' history has a long and venerable pedigree, but is no longer a very respectable philosophic peg for the hanging of theories of history.[18]

Yet it is still an easy peg to get hung up on, even if unintentionally. Hastings had important consequences; Hastings was thus a decisive battle; William won at Hastings (earning the mark of the Great Man, the enduring nickname, even if his is not 'the Great' but only 'the Conqueror', demoting him from the very top ranks of greatness); William was thus responsible for (may even have planned) the consequences of his actions. The unconscious train of thought is hard to resist – but it is fundamentally wrong, about William and about history. For it is here that we must remember the utter unpredictability of long-term (and even most short-term) developments, and that history is much more than the lives of Great Men.

The 'new military history' that has begun redrawing our picture of premodern warfare draws widely on methods and perspectives that began challenging the Great Men much earlier in other fields of historical enquiry. From social history comes closer attention to the experiences of the common fighting men of an army, and indeed of the women and even children who almost always accompanied armies on campaign as camp followers.[19] Economic and environmental history both have influenced the new logistical studies that have exposed the material limits within which armies operated: their dependence on the agricultural cycle, on the weather, their vulnerability to disease – the latter the biggest killer in armies until World War I.[20] Institutional historians have explored the relationship of a societies' armed forces to its administrative capacities and socio-political structures.[21] Cultural historians have brought new insight to the study of warrior culture and the *mentalité* of warfare.[22] Even 'Cliometrics' – the historical analysis of numerical and statistical data –, though given scant reliable material to work on much before the nineteenth century, has set to work where it can.[23]

---

[17] Geoffrey Best, *War and Society in Revolutionary Europe, 1770–1870* (Fontana History of War and European Society, 1982), p. 7; thanks to Richard Abels for this reference.

[18] John Keegan, *The Face of Battle* (New York, 1976), pp. 53–72, discusses this issue in more detail.

[19] Keegan, *Face of Battle*, is the seminal study of the common man's experience of war, which Hanson's *Western Way of War* extends to the study of Greek warfare. See e.g. Rosalind Hill, 'Crusading Warfare: a camp-follower's view 1097–1120', *Anglo-Norman Studies* 1, 75–83 and M. Chibnall, 'Women in Orderic Vitalis', *The Haskins Society Journal* 2 (1990), 105–121, for women's varied relationships to war and military society.

[20] See e.g. John Gillingham, 'William the Bastard at War', in C. Harper-Bill et al., *Studies in Medieval History presented to R. Allen Brown* (Woodbridge, 1989) and 'Richard I and the Science of War', in Gilingham and Holt, eds, *War and Government in the Middle Ages. Essays in Honour of J.O. Prestwich* (Woodbridge, 1984); Bernard Bachrach, 'Some Observations on the Military Administration of the Norman Conquest', *Anglo-Norman Studies* 8 (1985), 1–26; and selection 10 below.

[21] See e.g. Richard Abels, *Lordship and Military Obligation in Anglo-Saxon England* (Berkeley, 1988); H.J. Hewitt, *The Organization of War under Edward III* (Manchester, 1966); and S. Morillo, *Warfare under the Anglo-Norman Kings, 1066–1135* (Woodbridge, 1994).

[22] See e.g. Maurice Keen, *Chivalry* (New Haven, 1984); Duby, *The Legend of Bouvines*, trans. C. Tihanyi (Berkeley, 1990).

[23] See selections 7 and 10 below.

As a result, our knowledge of military systems and the practices of warfare has expanded significantly in the last twenty-five years, and the place in warfare of battle, decisive or not, has been put in much better perspective. In fact, the new military history has focused on other aspects of war almost to the exclusion of battle history. But the drama of the face-to-face conflict is still compelling and great battles are still an important part of the history of warfare, especially for battles as decisive as Hastings. A close focus on Hastings can be valuable, therefore, as an entry into the battle's own context. Hastings should be seen not as a typical act of medieval warfare (which it was not), but as part of a larger process that extended from the mobilization of Normandy to the Harrying of the North, William's destructive campaign in late 1069 that crushed the last major hope of resistance to the new Norman order in England. This process, with its multiple themes of state building and its relation to military force, of conquest, resistance and synthesis, and of cultural encounter and the literary construction of events after they have happened, is very typical of the age,[24] and raises problems common to much historical investigation. Close examination of the sources and interpretations that surround Hastings can thus be a valuable practical exercise.

But on a more theoretical level, if a Great Man theory of history will not suffice to explain the significance of Decisive Battles, how should we see their place in the much richer, more nuanced history that new perspectives have revealed to us? Chaos theory may provide a very good intellectual tool for conceptualizing the problem. It is my sense that human history is a chaotic system.[25] In a chaotic system, small inputs can create very large perturbations. Because tiny changes in the initial conditions of a chaotic system can create huge differences in later conditions, such systems are in principle unpredictable – we can never know enough about the initial state of the system to predict accurately what the system will look like at a later time. Chaotic systems are not random – there are normal laws of cause and effect at work, making changes in such a system explainable after the fact even if they aren't predictable. Nor are chaotic systems patternless: we may not be able to predict subsequent states of any individual bit of the system, but we can often discern repeating tendencies and broad parameters within which the system tends to stay unless it is seriously disturbed. Within such parameters, the unpredictability of events that the complexity of a chaotic system creates is one way of seeing the role of chance or contingency in history:[26] that is, the sort of explainable but not predictable factors long recognized even in military history ('for want of a nail . . .'), but not often given sufficient emphasis, perhaps because Luck and Great Men don't mix.

There is a tension between thematic description of the parameters of a system – the history of the 'long dureé', of what Braudel called 'the structures of everyday life' – and the narrative tracing of any bit of the system's contingent path within the parameters. But it is the creative tension of a balancing act and not the tension of

---

[24] Robert Bartlett, *The Making of Europe. Conquest, Colonization and Cultural Change, 950–1350* (Princeton, 1993) puts these themes at the center of his interpretation of the making of a European world.

[25] For an excellent discussion of this theory and its implications for history, see George A. Reisch, 'Chaos, History and Narrative', *History and Theory* 30 (1991), 1–20. A somewhat different approach to the same problem which reaches similar conclusions follows in the same volume: Donald N. McCloskey, 'History, Differential Equations, and the Problem of Narration', 21–36.

[26] Stephen Jay Gould, *Wonderful Life. The Burgess Shale and the Nature of History* (New York, 1989), is a wonderful investigation of the role of contingency in history; see especially pp. 277–291.

incompatibility, for narrative without theme is mere chronicle, while theme without narrative is ahistorical.[27] The balance is certainly struck in the history of truly decisive battles: those most contingent of events whose effects alter the parameters of possibility.[28] In this context, the 'great men' of history such as William the Bastard do not control and predict the uncontrollable and unpredictable. Rather they are those best able to take advantage of the chances thrown their way and make things happen; and even then, only the subsequent, unpredictable course of events can place their actions at a retrospectively recognizable turning point in the broad path of possibility. John Gillingham recognizes this when he says that the first Norman king should be known as William the Lucky Bastard.[29]

Such a view of history warns us not to read more into Hastings than is actually there. Hastings was a significant, decisive battle, but much of its significance is retrospective. Understanding what went on that Saturday in 1066 requires that we try to see the event as the participants did, in the context of its past and present but not its future.

Moving in for a closer look

If we want to get a sense of what an historical event meant at the time it happened we must turn to the sources, and getting at the sources is one of the great advantages for students of examining a single event closely. Hastings is especially interesting in this respect. The primary sources for the battle are limited enough in number to be manageable, and rich enough to let us see what went on in some detail. And they raise interesting problems of interpretation because of their variety of style and point of view.

Variety in style means that not all the sources can be read in the same way. Most obviously, the Bayeux Tapestry, a pictorial telling of the story of 1066, cannot be read at all in the literal sense (except for its short captions). Perhaps as a result, the problem of interpreting the authorship, point of view and meaning of the Tapestry has generated much debate.[30]

But there is variety among the written sources as well, mostly in terms of literary intent and quality. The Anglo-Saxon Chronicles, at one end of the literary spectrum, consists of year-by-year entries of notable events, and so makes no pretence of providing an overall theme, a unified story, or a consistent point of view. It was not even one chronicle, but a related set of annals compiled at various monastic centres around England, each reflecting the local interests of its place of compilation. While the monk of Worcester who created a Latin version of the Chronicles, the *Chronicon ex Chronicis* of 'Florence' of Worcester, perhaps paid a bit more attention to style, his work shares with its source its essentially annalistic character.

---

[27] Cf. McCloskey, 'History, Differential Equations', pp. 23–6.

[28] Such an analysis describes neatly Duby's *Legend of Bouvines*, in which he traces not only the chance outcome of the battle and how it reflected and was molded by the cultural structures within which it took place, but the structures of memory and culture generated by the event through succeeding centuries.

[29] See selection 9 below; I explore these issues myself further in an article to be published elsewhere: S. Morillo, 'Unfavorable Winds: The Conqueror's Crossing and Theories of History'.

[30] The bibliography of Domesday is voluminous; see, e.g., D. Bernstein, *The Mystery of the Bayeux Tapestry* (Chicago UP, 1986); N.P. Brooks and H.E. Walker, 'The authority and interpretation of the Bayeux Tapestry', *ANS* 1 (1978), 1–34; S.A. Brown, 'The Bayeux Tapestry: Why Eustace, Odo and William?', *ANS* 12 (1989), 7–28, and the bibliographies and notes therein.

At the other end of the literary spectrum stand the *Gesta* of William of Poitiers and the *Carmen de Hastingae Proelio*. Though very different from each other, both are consciously 'literary' works, aimed at an audience which expected entertainment as well as history. William of Poitiers based his history of the deeds of William duke of Normandy on classical models. Since the publicist saw the Duke as a new and greater Caesar, he was ready to draw parallels to the Duke's actions (and even descriptions of them) from his sources. Such practices, while not intended to deceive his audience, can present us with a distorted picture of what actually happened. On the other hand, the focus and narrative depth of this literary production show us the year's events in far more detail than the bare entries of the Anglo-Saxon Chronicle do. The same is true of the *Carmen*, though this work is not prose but poetry, raising a different set of interpretive issues. But though the provenance of the work has been questioned,[31] it is not questioned as a source because it is poetry, which could be a medium for narrative just as prose could.

Another way in which the *Carmen* differs from William of Poitiers is in point of view. It is often claimed that the winners write history. The Anglo-Saxon Chronicle is proof that this is not entirely true. But with Hastings it is also a simplification, since the winning force was not homogeneous. William of Poitiers (and William of Jumièges), both Normans, were clearly writing to glorify Duke William. But if the traditional attribution of the *Carmen* to Guy of Amiens is correct, we have in the poem a source from Ponthieu, taking Eustace of Boulogne as its focus, if not quite its hero – that is, a view of the battle from the winning side, but from outside the winners' inner circle.

Thus a close examination of Hastings allows the student and the interested reader to delve into the complexities of medieval sources and see firsthand the problems raised in interpreting them. Similarly, a close look at Hastings, where the sources are accessible and the issues are well known, brings to life the academic debates exemplified in the secondary articles in this collection. These demonstrate the fact, often disturbing to students, that there is no 'one correct history', no one textbook truth. History is a process, an approach to a better understanding of the past; and debates, reinterpretations, and the search for new evidence are all part of that process – a part shown clearly in these articles.

Finally, it could be argued that if an event is typical or representative of the common occurrences of its time, then close examination of the event may give us a feel for much beyond the event itself. Hastings, though, was not a typical event. However common warfare was in eleventh century Europe, battles were rare events in warfare. And Hastings was not even a typical battle.[32] So we must be careful about taking Hastings as representative of its age. But if we understand the ways in which it was unusual, then we gain, even if indirectly, knowledge about the 'usual' of its time, and we gain a clearer view of the battlefield itself.

---

[31] See the introduction to selection 6 below; the editors' introduction to *The Carmen de Hastingae Proelio of Bishop Guy of Amiens*, ed. C. Morton and H. Muntz (Oxford UP, 1972), makes the most complete case for accepting the traditional attribution of the poem. The modern attack on this attribution comes from R.H.C. Davis, 'The *Carmen de Hastingae Proelio*', *EHR* 93 (1978), 241–61. See Davis, L.J. Engels, et al., 'The *Carmen de Hastingae Proelio*: a discussion', *ANS* 2 (1979), 1–20 for an exchange on the poem's provenance and references to the literature it has generated.

[32] See selection 18 below for more on this point. See Morillo, *Warfare under the Anglo-Norman Kings* for a detailed elaboration of the points in this selection and for a study of normal patterns of warfare.

Views of the battlefield

By now, views of the battlefield abound, though the lines of sight are cluttered with contentious issues. It may seem redundant, especially in a volume dedicated to descriptions of the battle, to add another in this introduction. But I hope by presenting a predominantly visual rather than verbal overview of the day's events to set the stage as clearly as possible and where possible to indicate points of academic debate. I have therefore encapsulated the battle in a series of maps with explanatory captions.

This view of the battlefield is as much an interpretation as any written or pictorial account, and I have leaned towards presenting my own interpretation rather than attempting a vague synthesis of the range of views exemplified in the rest of this volume. But the main sequence of events is in fact generally agreed on; it is the details, the emphasis, and the speculation about possibilities and probabilities that continues to generate heat. One advantage of presenting a series of maps is that the broad outlines will tend to outweigh the details of interpretation in such a format.

But reading the primary sources will make clear (if it is not obvious immediately) how much speculation must go into even a basic reconstruction of the battle. For instance, we know roughly when the battle started, and we know about when it finally ended. We know the major stages of the fighting between those times. But assigning a sequence of intermediate times to the main events, as I have been rash enough to do here, must be a matter of educated guesswork, at best. It is nonetheless a useful exercise, for it highlights the large periods of time which any reconstruction of the battle must account for and which our sources don't give much detail about. The long afternoon of October 14, 1066 – could the soldiers on both sides have been fighting continually through this time? – is thrown into particular relief by this method.

We also know the basic disposition of troops on either side. But once one tries to figure out where all those troops were at each stage of the battle, the paucity of the information in our sources again becomes clear. The positions presented here should be seen again as impressions and educated guesses, and the size and shape of the units as symbols, not as exact representations to scale of the armies' positions.

With these caveats in mind, the drama of the day is ready to unfold.

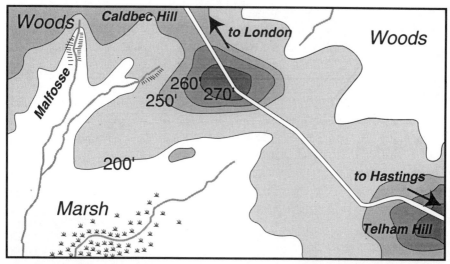

The Stage. The battle took place on the road out of the Hastings peninsula, before it joins the main road to London and Dover (see also the maps with selection 6 below). Marshes and woods on either side of the high ground along which the road ran restricted the possible field of battle on its flanks.

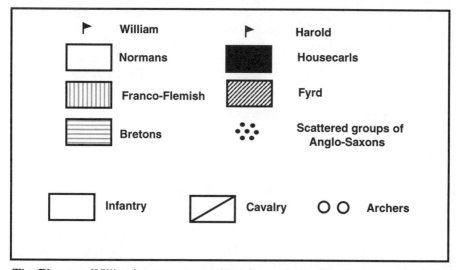

The Players. William's army was a mixed force of Normans, Bretons, Flemings, and other Frenchmen, and included infantry, archers, and cavalry. Harold's army was more homogeneous: Anglo-Danish in composition, all subjects of the king, and all fighting on foot, even though many (especially the housecarls) rode to the battlefield. Harold's army lacked archers. Was this because archers were not usually part of English forces, or had the archers available to Harold been used at Stamford Bridge, and been left behind in the forced marches from York to London and on to Hastings?

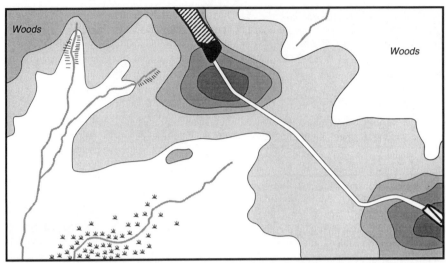

8 am: Initial sighting. Warned of Harold's advance by scouts, William's forces advance from Hastings in the early morning; the leading units probably came over Telham Hill about 8 am. At that point, they probably sighted the vanguard of the Anglo-Saxon army coming out of the woods on Caldbec Hill and emerging onto the ridge across the road. Harold's intentions at this point are subject to much debate. Had he intended to march on Hastings and surprise William's army (as he had Harald at Stamford Bridge) but found himself surprised by William's rapid advance? Was he establishing a blockading position to bottle up William on the peninsula, but meaning to avoid battle? Or did he intend to fight a defensive battle in this tactically well-chosen position? Whatever he intended, the latter possibility would at least open the engagement.

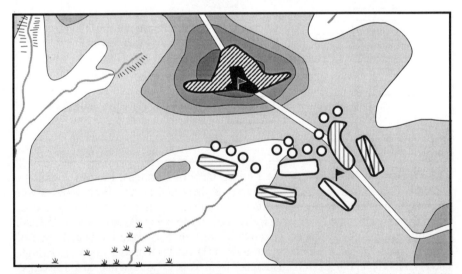

8:30 am: Deployment. While Harold's army spread out along the crest of the hill that blocked Duke William from the rest of England, the Duke's army moved into the valley between Telham Hill and Harold's army, with the Normans in the centre, the Bretons on the left and the Franco-Flemish forces on the right. Harold's army formed a shield wall that could have been anywhere from three or four to ten or twelve ranks deep – the size of both armies is open to debate, and estimating depth from probable size or size from probable depth (both of which have been tried) is essentially circular reasoning. The housecarl core of the army mostly gathered around Harold's standard in the centre of the line, but some probably formed the first few ranks for some distance out to the flanks, stiffening the fyrdmen behind them.

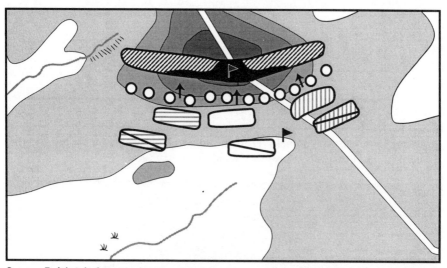

9 am: Initial infantry attack. William opens the battle by sending his archers forward; firing up the hill, their attack proves ineffective. The Duke's heavy infantry then advances up the hill.

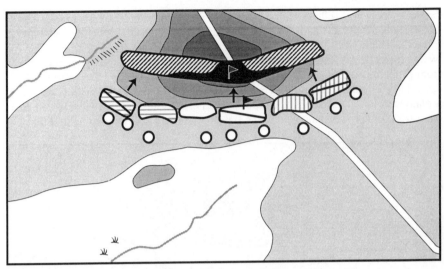

9:30 am: Initial cavalry attack. William's infantry makes little impression on the shield wall, and the cavalry move up the hill to try their luck.

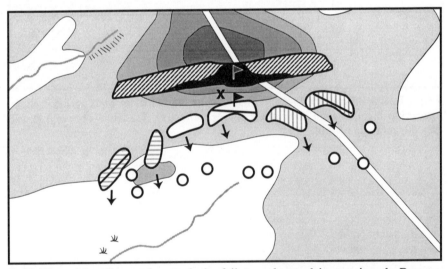

9:45: The crisis. The cavalry attack also fails to make much impression; the Bretons on the left, in particular, seem to have run into difficulties. A retreat that turns increasingly panicky starts on the left and spreads through the whole army, which thinks William has fallen (he may have had a horse killed under him in the first attack). The battle was probably ready for resolution – like most medieval battles, in under an hour. The problem: the English do not launch the counter-attack which could have swept the field. Why not? Were they tactically incapable because of their all-infantry army? Did Harold miss his chance? Or did an attack start, but get halted in the centre by the deaths of Harold's brothers Gyrth and Leofwine (at the 'X'? was William involved?) who were leading it?

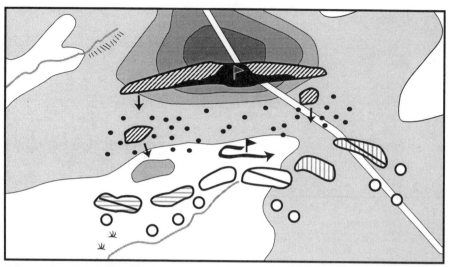

10 am: William rallies his troops. Pursued not by the entire English army but only by groups on the wings and scattered individuals, William's army falls back. William himself, baring his head and riding along the lines to show he still lived, rallies his army from the brink of defeat.

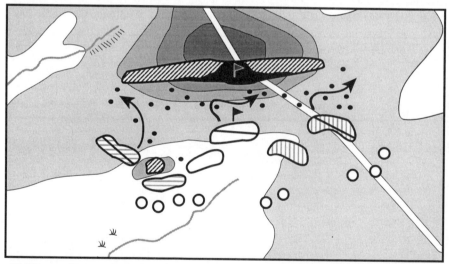

10:30 am: Counterattack. The rallied Normans and their allies turn on their pursuers; the cavalry has an easy time with the scattered groups who have left the shield wall. Perhaps a smaller group which kept its cohesion is not overrun instantly but is trapped on a hill surrounded by its enemies. The success of this counterattack poses a question: was the entire retreat a planned ruse – the first 'feigned flight' of the day?

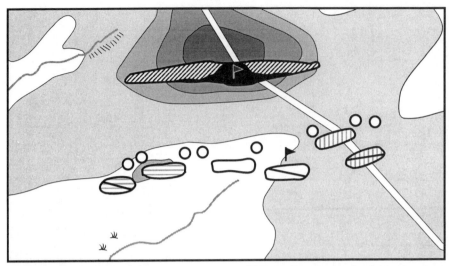

11 am: Regrouping. Weakened somewhat by the loss of those who left the shield wall and perhaps by the loss of crucial leadership, Harold's army is nonetheless still formidable and still in possession of a strong defensive position. William's army, having survived its panic, regroups and rests after the morning's fighting. Neither side has gained a clear advantage, though Harold has probably lost his best chance for an attack on William and will be forced into a defensive fight the rest of the day.

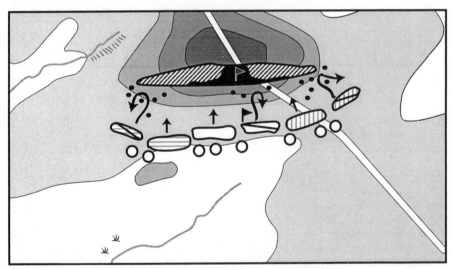

12 noon – 6 pm: 'An unknown sort of battle . . .' If the above timing is close to correct, we must now account for a long period of time about which we know little. William of Poitiers calls it 'an unknown sort of battle, in which one side launched attacks and manoeuvres, the other stood like rocks fixed to the ground.' Duke William probably alternated infantry and cavalry attacks with further periods of rest and regrouping. Inspired by the earlier course of the battle, did his cavalry also engage in a number of feigned flights, drawing more English off the hills, especially from the wings of Harold's army? In any case, by late afternoon no decision had been reached.

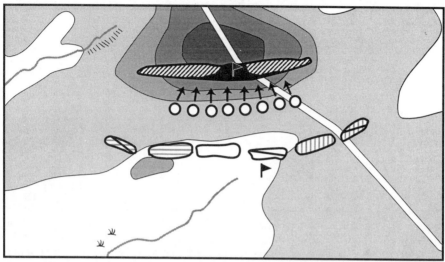

7 pm: Final archery attack. Regrouping for what had to be the final attack of the day, win or lose, William again sends his archers forward. Perhaps they attempted high angle plunging fire this time, disrupting the shieldwall more than before. Most importantly, was Harold himself mortally wounded at this point by an arrow in the eye?

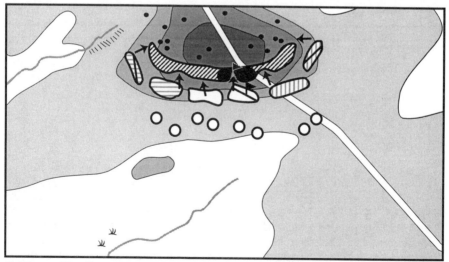

7:30 pm: The final attack. William's army advances again up the hill, and finally breaks through the defenses of the shield wall. Harold, whether already wounded or not, was cut down at his standard, and with his death the English army began to break up.

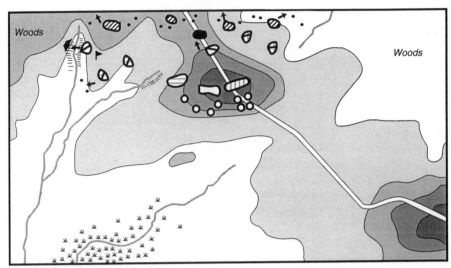

8 pm: The pursuit. In the growing darkness, the Normans and their allies pursue the defeated English, but the fall of night (and, undoubtedly, the exhaustion of the victors) cuts short any lengthy chase. It is possible that some Norman cavalry got into trouble at the 'Malfosse', riding in the darkness into a steep ravine where a group of Saxons made a last stand, though the sources are not clear on this episode.

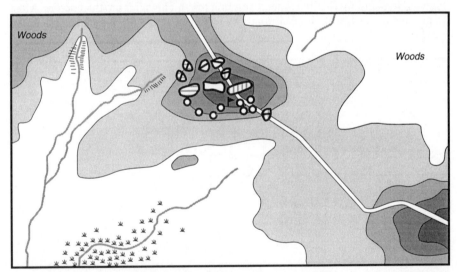

9 pm: William in possession of the field. By this time, William and his army are in possession of the field; Harold's body has been recovered and arrangements are being made to deal with the dead and wounded. One of the longest battles in medieval history has come to a decisive end.

While key turning points in the battle provide grist for many of the discussions Hastings continues to generate, some of the ongoing issues relate to the campaign or to broader questions about the battle. It may be useful to note some of these.

That the Normans won the battle is, as Allen Brown notes in his discussion of the battle (selection 17 below), perhaps the only universally agreed on fact. Why did they win? This is the question that has probably created the most argument over the last two centuries. Ironically, however, it seems to have generated little controversy before the nineteenth century. At the risk of oversimplifying, the answer to contemporaries was that God was on William's side, and with God's help the Duke outfought King Harold. That judgement hadn't changed much by the end of the eighteenth century. God could be thought of as luck, and outfighting could be called better generalship, and the verdict was roughly the same. David Hume's balanced account of the battle shows this (see selection 12 below).

It was the nineteenth century that brought controversy to the question. Corrosive constructs of nationalism, racism, and class etched their politicized patterns into the history of the battle, and two armed camps emerged to claim the field as their own. E.A. Freeman (see selection 13 below) represents the 'pro-Saxon' side. In this view, the Anglo-Saxons were the true Englishmen, practitioners of Germanic proto-democracy and virtue, temporarily conquered by 'foreigners' whose influence would be absorbed and subsumed with the reemergence in later centuries of true Englishness. The loss in 1066, in this view, was a product of bad luck, sneaky despicable Norman tactics, and above all of heroic tragedy: Harold and his army, faced by two near-simultaneous invasions, were simply asked to do too much in too little time. J.H. Round led the counterattack.[33] His 'pro-Norman' view saw the English kingdom and military as outmoded if not degenerate, and invested in the Normans all the aristocratic virtues of martial spirit, nobility, and natural superiority that the English supposedly lacked. The outcome of Hastings was, from this perspective, natural and inevitable.

Almost no one would argue in those terms anymore, but a modern version of this division survives to the present. Political and national character are replaced by military technology and organization as the essential indicators of superiority. The Normans, in this view, with their modern 'feudal system' based on a heavy cavalry whose stirrups made them invincible to hapless infantry, were bound to ride down the English, still clinging anachronistically to the old Germanic mode of militias fighting on foot.[34] This argument links intimately to the problem of the effect of the Norman Conquest: was the Anglo-Norman realm more Anglo or more Norman in its makeup? From Round forward, the inevitability of Norman victory has been followed by 'the introduction of feudalism into England'. The debate over feudalism and the larger issue of the settlement is voluminous and well beyond the scope of this volume. But views of the battlefield colour views of the aftermath, as this debate shows.

If there is a trend in this debate, it is towards seeing Normandy and England before 1066 as less different than had been thought (see selections 7 and 8 below), and the settlement as more a matter of synthesis than dominance for one side or the other. So too the result of Hastings has come again to seem less clear cut, and more the result of some combination of generalship and luck. But even here the scope of generalship and its balance with luck leaves ample room for disagreement.

---

[33] For Round's attack, see 'Mr Freeman and the Battle of Hastings', *Feudal England* (London, 1909), 332–98.
[34] See Morillo, *Warfare under the Anglo-Norman Kings*, Ch. 5, for a detailed discussion of the Stirrup Theory and an alternative explanation for the patterns of warfare the stirrup supposedly explains.

That William outgeneralled Harold on the field of Hastings would probably win majority (but not unanimous) consent from historians today, though how decisively would be contested. One of the most interesting recent debates extends the question of generalship back into the campaign, and looks at the timing of William's invasion. The long-held view was that William was ready to sail by early August, but was then held up by unfavourable winds for almost two months, his project nearly coming to grief as a result. More recently, the delay has been interpreted as an intentional ploy on William's part. Great Man versus chaotic system? The debate is taken up below (see selections 9–11).

No doubt other issues will continue to be raised in coming years. History is always an unfinished project, because the stories we tell about the past must of necessity include their share of speculation about probabilities, plausibilities, and the unknowable. I hope with this collection of sources and articles to welcome you to an ongoing discussion and invite you to join it yourself.

Part I. SOURCES

The campaign and battle of Hastings are unusually well documented for a medieval battle, particularly for one so early. The following six selections give all the significant primary accounts of the events; they present various points of view, and are the basis for most of what we know about the battle. There are one or two other accounts, principally in Orderic Vitalis, William of Malmesbury and Wace, but those are derived predominantly from one or another of the sources presented here or are unreliable. There are indirect ways of learning more about the battle, as the secondary selections will demonstrate, but walking the battlefield (highly recommended) is the best way of getting a feel for what happened that Saturday in 1066.

1. William of Poitiers, *Gesta Willelmi*

The longest prose account of the Hastings campaign is from the *Gesta Willelmi ducis Normannorum et regis Anglorum*, 'The Deeds of William, duke of the Normans and king of the English', of William of Poitiers. It is an extremely valuable account not only because of its length, but because William of Poitiers was a Norman who served duke William first as a soldier and then as a military chaplain and priest. His knowledge of military affairs is clear, and though he did not accompany the duke on the 1066 campiagn, he clearly had access to those who had. He wrote his account around 1071, only a few years after the events he narrates. His account of the 1066 campaign is thus both contemporary and generally reliable. But he is not unbiased: he writes as a Norman and an enthusiastic admirer of his duke, and he adopts heroic rhetoric and classical models in extolling the deeds he narrates. He is therefore less reliable for the actions and especially motivations on the Anglo-Saxon side of the conflict, and in general his presentation and interpretation of events should be approached critically.

See William of Poitiers, *Histoire de Guillaume le Conquérant*, ed. Raymonde Foreville (Paris, 1952), for a scholarly edition of the original.

About the same time, Edward, king of the English, who had already appointed William as his heir, and who held him in the same affection as a brother or son, gave more serious evidence of his intentions than before. He decided to anticipate the implacable decree of death, whose approaching hour this man, who aspired to heaven by the saintliness of his life, now felt. In order to confirm his promise by an oath, Edward sent to William Harold, the most prominent of his subjects in wealth, honour and power, and whose brother and nephew had already been given as hostages to ensure this succession. This was a measure of the utmost wisdom because its authenticity and authority would restrain the dissensions among the whole English nation, if – as might be expected from the vagaries and perfidy of their behaviour – they had tried to rebel against it.

Harold, as he was on his voyage to carry out this mission, and had already escaped the dangers of the crossing, landed in Ponthieu, where he fell into the hands of count Guy. He and his attendants were captured and thrown into prison, a misadventure which a man of his standing would willingly have exchanged for shipwreck. For the lure of gain has led certain nations in Gaul into an accursed practice, barbarous and totally foreign to Christian justice. They set ambushes for rich or powerful men, throw them into prison, and submit them to outrages and tortures. Overcome with misfortunes, and almost on the verge of death, they are only released on the payment of a huge [sum of money].

Duke William, informed of the fate of the man who had been sent to him, hastily despatched an embassy and snatched him from prison by prayers and threats, and went to meet him with due honour. Guy behaved well: without being persuaded to do so by the lure of gain or the constraint of force, he led him in person to the castle of Eu, and presented to the duke a man whom he could freely have tortured, killed or sold. As a suitable reward, William gave him vast and rich lands, and added large sums of money as well. As for Harold, William brought him into Rouen, the capital of his principality, with all honour; here his varied hospitality and attention restored and made joyful the men who had suffered such hardship on the way. William doubtless congratulated himself on having a guest of such distinction, an ambassador from his relation and dear friend: he hoped that he would be a faithful mediator between himself and the English, for whom he was second only to the king.

At a gathering at Bonneville, Harold took an oath of faithfulness to him according to the sacred rite of the Christians. And, as highly respected men of the utmost sincerity have related, who were witnesses to the event, in the last item in the oath that was drawn up, he pronounced, clearly and of his own free will, these words: that he would be the agent [vicarius] of duke William at the court of king Edward for as long as the king lived; that he would try with all his authority and power, to ensure for him the possession of the kingdom of England on Edward's death; and that meanwhile, he would hand over the castle of Dover, fortified under his direction and his own expense, to a garrison of the duke's knights; that he would deliver, at the same time, in various places in the kingdom, other castles to be fortified in the duke's orders; and that he would also provide abundantly for the provisioning of the garrisons. The duke, having received Harold as a vassal, and before he had taken this oath, conferred on him, at his request, all the lands he held, with full powers. For it was feared that Edward, who was already ill, would not live much longer. After this, because he knew that Harold was bold and eager for new glory, he provided him and

4

his company with weapons, armour and the finest horses, and took them with him to fight in Brittany. He treated him as a guest and ambassador, but now made him almost one of his companions, in order to strengthen the ties between them by doing him honour. For Brittany had treacherously begun an armed rebellion against Normandy.

The prime mover of this audacious enterprise was Conan, son of Alan. When he came of age, he proved to be ferocious in the extreme: once free of the guardianship he had long endured, he seized Eudo, his uncle on his father's side, loaded him with chains, threw him into prison, and began to exercise power over the province which his father had left him, with extreme violence. Then, renewing his father's rebellion, he wanted to be the enemy, not the vassal, of Normandy. William, who was his overlord by ancient right (just as he was lord of the Normans), placed a castle called St James on the frontier with Brittany, for fear that famished raiders would come and ravage the defenceless churches and the people of the most remote area of his lands. For Charles [the Simple], king of France, had bought the peace and friendship of Rollo, the first duke of the Normans, and ancestor of the future dukes, by giving him his daughter Gisela in marriage and Brittany in perpetual servitude. The Franks, unable to resist with their swords the Danish axes any longer, had obtained this treaty with prayers, as the pages of their annals bear witness. For this reason, the counts of Brittany could never entirely shake off the yoke of Norman domination, although they tried several times to do so with all their might. Alan and Conan, more closely related to the rulers of Normandy, were all the more proud and arrogant in opposing them. The boldness of Conan was such that he did not hesitate to announce the date on which he was going to attack the Norman frontier. This man, by temperament violent and at an impetuous age, was greatly helped by the fidelity of a widely-dispersed region which had more warriors in it than one would have believed.

For in these parts, one single warrior begets fifty, having ten or more shared wives, in the barbarian fashion: it is a custom derived from the ancient Moors, ignorant of divine law and chaste morals. This multitude devote themselves principally to arms and horsemanship, and hardly study farming or morals. They live chiefly on milk, very little on bread. Fat pastures nourish their flocks in vast spaces where the harvest is almost unknown. When they are not at war, they live by rapine and brigandry, or civil strife, or exercise themselves in these ways. They go into battle with eager haste, and in the struggle they strike out furiously. They are used to repulsing their enemy, and only yield with difficulty. Victory and glory won in combat are greeted with great rejoicing and pride; they like to despoil these whom they have killed, regarding it as an honour and a pleasure.

Without taking the least notice of these terrible customs, duke William, remembering the day on which Conan had announced his attack, set out in person to meet him on enemy territory. The latter, fearing the imminence of a thunderbolt, fled headlong, abandoning the siege of Dol, a castle in his own lands. This castle, opposed to the rebellion, remained faithful to the just cause. Its defender, Rivallon, tried to retain Conan, recalling him ironically, begging him to wait for another two days, saying that this would be long enough to arrange his ransom. Conan, terrified and miserable, heeded his fear instead, and fled even further off. The fearsome commander who pursued him would have chased the fugitive, if he had not realised the obvious danger of leading a large army across deserted, starved and unknown country. If anything remained of the previous year's produce, in this deprived land, their inhabitants had hidden it in a safe place, along with their flocks. Therefore, fearing that the goods of the Church might be sacrilegiously pillaged, if the army came across them, he led them back, exhausted by the lack of provisions; he also assumed that Conan would soon beg for his crime to be pardoned, and submit to his mercy. But hardly had he crossed the frontier of Brittany when he learnt that Geoffrey of Anjou, with a large force, had joined Conan and that the two of them were preparing to give battle the next day. He showed himself all the more eager to engage in combat, because he deemed it more glorious to defeat two enemies, both redoubtable in themselves, in one combat. From such a victory he would derive many advantages.

However, Rivallon, on whose territory the army had encamped, did not cease to complain. He would prefer to have been delivered from his enemy without the damage caused by so doing ruining his whole fief. If the duke settled down to await the enemy in such an unfertile and exhausted place, it would be totally ruined. It made no difference to the peasants whether they were ruined by the deeds of the Norman army or by those of the Bretons; they would still lose the fruits of the year's labours. The expulsion of Conan had so far brought Rivallon fame, rather than the ruin of his goods. The duke replied that he must consider whether a hasty departure would be misinterpreted, and promised to pay in gold compensation for any damage. From then on, he forbade his soldiers to take grain or animals. They obeyed this order so strictly that one grain of corn would have repaid all the harm done. The duke waited in vain for battle; the enemy continued to flee even further off.

When he returned to his quarters, the duke, having detained his very dear guest Harold for some time, sent him home loaded with presents, worthy of the rank of the two of them, both of him on whose behalf he had been sent and of him whose honour he had thus increased. In addition, one of the two hostages, his nephew returned with him, freed as a mark of respect to his person. Thus, Harold, we address these brief reproaches to you. What inspired you to dare, after these good deeds, to despoil William of his inheritance and to fight against him, you who by a sacrosanct oath of word and hand, had recognised as master of both yourself and your nation? What you should have repressed, you wickedly encouraged. The favourable breeze which swelled your black-hearted sails on the return voyage was impious, the calm sea which bore you was impious in allowing itself to carry you to the other shore, O most shameful of men. The harbour which received you was ill-starred, you who were going to drag your country into the most disastrous shipwreck.

Suddenly news came that England had lost its king, Edward, and Harold had been crowned in his place. This foolish Englishman did not await a public election, but on the day of mourning when the good king was buried and the whole nation lamented, he broke his oath and seized the throne by acclamation, thanks to the support of some iniquitous partisans. He received an unholy consecration at the hands of Stigand, who had been deprived of the office of priest by the just zeal of a papal anathema. Duke William, having consulted his men, decided to avenge this offence and regain his inheritance by force of arms, despite many who used clever arguments to dissuade him from such an arduous enterprise, as being well beyond the power of the Norman forces. In those days Normandy had among its councillors besides bishops and abbots, outstanding laymen, the light and ornament of the gathering, whose reputation they much enhanced: Robert, count of Mortain; Robert, count of Eu, brother of the bishop of Lisieux, Hugh; Richard, count of Evreux, son of archbishop Robert; Roger de Beaumont; Roger de Montgomery; William Fitz Osbern; Hugh, viscount [of Avranches]. Thanks to their wisdom and efforts, the land remained unharmed. With them to look after it, the Roman republic would not have needed two hundred senators, if it had retained its ancient power until today. In the discussions, however, we know that they all yielded to the wisdom of the prince, as if he had known in advance, by divine inspiration, what needed to be done and what needed to be avoided. To those who act piously, God has given wisdom, writes a man who is learned in divine matters.

With admirable prudence, William ordered the provision of ships, arms, men and supplies, and all other things necessary for war; almost all Normandy was devoted to the task, and it would take too long to describe the preparations in detail. Equally, he made arrangements for the government and security of Normandy in his absence. Numerous soldiers from outside the duchy arrived to offer their help, partly motivated by the famed generosity of the duke, but all fully confident in the justice of his cause.

He forbade all forms of pillage, and fed at his own expense 50,000 soldiers while contrary winds detained them for a month at the mouth of the river Dives. His moderation and prudence lay in the fact that he paid most of the expenses of his soldiers and guests, and would not allow anyone to take anything whatsoever. The inhabitants of the countryside around grazed their herds of cows or sheep in safety, both in the fields and on the open pasture. The corn awaited the reaper's scythe untouched, without being trampled by the soldiers or cut down by foragers. However weak or defenceless, any man could pass through countryside, singing as he rode, watching, but not fearing, the squadrons of soldiers.

At this time the see of St Peter at Rome was occupied by pope Alexander, the most worthy of all to rule over the universal church. Whoever consulted him received a just and salutary answer. He had been bishop of Lucca, and had no ambition for a higher rank, but the urgent council of several persons whose authority was respected by the Romans, supported by the agreement of a large assembly, had raised him to his present standing as primate, to preside over, as their head and master, all the bishops throughout the world. He deserved this election by his sanctity and the purity of his teaching. In later years his virtues shone from east to west: just as the sun, by the laws of nature, follows an unchanging course, so he followed the truth throughout his life, condemning iniquity wherever he could, without compromise.

Having sought the approval of the pope and informed him of the enterprise he was undertaking, the duke received through his favour a standard, which was a sign of the protection of St Peter, as a result of which he was able to march more confidently and safely against his adversary. He had recently formed a friendly alliance with Henry, son of the emperor Henry and grandson of Conrad; under the terms of this, Germany would lend him military assistance against any enemy, should he request it. The Danish king, Svend, had sworn a pact with him after various negotiations; but he showed himself to be the faithful ally of the duke's enemies, as you will see later when you read of the disasters that befell him.

Harold, meanwhile, prepared to give battle by sea or land, drawing up a huge army on the shore, and sending out spies in secret. One of these was captured, and as he tried to disguise the reason for his presence using the story he had been briefed to tell, the duke showed his magnanimity in these words: 'What need has Harold to buy the devotion and labour, for gold and silver, of men like you who come to spy on us? Our determination, our preparations – are there any more certain indications he would like, other than my actual presence? Take this message to him from me: he can live for the rest of his days in peace, if within a year from now, he has not seen me in the place which he regards as his most secure refuge.'

Stunned by such a rash promise, many of the Norman magnates did not hide their mistrust. Inspired by cowardice, they exaggerated in discussions the strength of Harold's army and the weakness of their own. According to them, Harold had distributed large sums and thus won over leaders and powerful kings; he had a numerous fleet and seamen expert in nautical matters, who had often endured the dangers of the sea and naval battles; his kingdom, both for numbers of soldiers and financial resources, was much superior to the duke's domains. Who could therefore hope that within the allotted time, the space of a year, the ships could be built and rowers could be found? Who did not fear that this expedition would not reduce a prosperous country to the most miserable state? Who dare to say that even the forces of a Roman emperor could bring such a difficult enterprise to a successful conclusion?

But the duke rallied the waverers with the following speech: 'We know Harold's wisdom, and fear it, but nonetheless it makes us hopeful. He spends his money in vain: he dissipates his gold without making his position any stronger. He is not stout-hearted enough to promise the least part of my lands. As for me, I shall promise and distribute as I choose both my own lands and those which are said to be his. For there is no doubt that whoever is bold enough to dispose of his enemy's possessions as though they were his own will overcome his enemy. The problem of shipping will not prevent us, because we shall soon have enough vessels. Let them learn what, if fortune favours us, we shall soon demonstrate: that it is the valour rather than the number of soldiers which wins battles. Besides, he will be fighting to keep his ill-gotten gains: we simply lay claim to what we have been given and have acquired by good deeds. It is this fundamental certainty on our side, which, putting aside every danger, will assure us triumph, honour and glory.'

For this wise and faithful man knew that almighty God, who desires no evil, would not let a just cause fail, particularly when he considered that he did not aim so much to increase his personal power and glory as to reform Christian practices in this land.

Now the whole fleet, so carefully prepared, set sail from the mouth of the Dives and neighbouring ports, where it had waited so long for a south wind in order to cross, and was carried by the west wind towards the anchorage of Saint Valéry. There too, through prayers, offerings and vows the prince entrusted himself to the assistance of Heaven; he had not been dissuaded by contrary winds, terrible shipwrecks or the cowardly desertion of several of those who had given their word. Dealing with his problems by wise behaviour, he buried those who had drowned, hiding the fact as far as possible and burying them secretly. Increasing his supplies each day, he warded off famine. By a variety of encouragements, he regained those who had been overcome with fear, and put heart into the waverers. He fought using holy prayers, and went as far as bringing the body of St Valéry, a confessor most acceptable to God, out of the cathedral in order to ensure that the contrary wind became a favourable one. All the warriors who were departing with him took part in this demonstration of humility.

At last the long-awaited breeze arose: they gave thanks to heaven with voice and hand, and all shouted together to encourage each other. They left shore as quietly as possible and set out very eagerly on this voyage whose outcome remained uncertain. Their haste was such that while someone called a man at arms, someone else his companion, most of them, heedless of their subordinates, companions or even vital equipment, were only fearful of being left on shore, and hastened on board. The duke, however, urged any laggards whom he saw to embark as quickly as possible.

Because he feared that they might make a landfall before dawn on the shore towards which they were sailing, and might be at risk in a dangerous or unknown anchorage, he made a crier announce that once they were on the open sea, they should wait for a while, and all the ships should anchor around his, until a fire was lit at his masthead and they heard a trumpet call as signal to resume their voyage.

Ancient Greece has passed down the story of the vengeance of Agamemnon of the house of Atreus who set out to redeem his brother's marital honour with a thousand ships: we bear witness, that William went to reclaim his royal crown with a greater number. Men tell how Xerxes linked the famous towns of Sestos and Abydos, separated by the sea, with a bridge of ships. We for our part proclaim how – and it is true – William reunited under the single governance of his power the whole extent of Norman and English land. William, whom no-one has yet surpassed, has adorned his country with magnificent trophies and made it illustrious with the greatest triumphs: we think that he is the equal of Xerxes, who was conquered by a stronger enemy, and deprived of his fleet, and indeed that he surpasses him in courage.

The ships set sail again after their nocturnal halt; the one which the duke was in was so swift that it left the others far behind it, as if it wished to respond by its speed to the man who urged it on to victory with all his zeal. In the morning, a rower, ordered to see from the top of the mast if any ships were coming after them, declared that he could see nothing on the horizon but sea and sky. They anchored at once, and to prevent his companions from becoming fearful and dismayed, the intrepid duke had a plentiful and cheerful meal, as if he was in his own hall, served with spiced wine, asserting that the other ships would not be long in arriving, guided by God to whose keeping he had entrusted them. Virgil, the prince of poets, whose songs in praise of the Trojan Aeneas, ancestor and glory of early Rome, would not have thought the self-control which William showed at this feast unworthy of his pen. When the watch was asked again what he could see, he shouted that he could see four ships; at the third question, he declared that there were so many that it seemed like a forest rigged with sails. At that point the duke's hope changed to joy: how he praised divine mercy from the bottom of his heart, we leave to the imagination.

Borne by a favourable breeze to Pevensey, he disembarked with ease and without having to fight his way ashore. Harold, indeed, had withdrawn to Yorkshire to fight his own brother Tostig and the king of Norway, Harold. It was hardly astonishing that his brother, driven by wrongs done to him and wishing to recover his confiscated lands, should invoke foreign aid against him; Harold's sister, too, morally quite unlike him, used vows and advice to oppose him, because he was a man soiled by luxury, a cruel homicide, proud of his wealth and plunder, an enemy of justice and goodness. This woman, as wise as any man, who recognised goodness and cherished it in her way of life, intended that the man whom her husband Edward had chosen by adopting him as his son should rule over the English: William the wise, just and strong.

War between duke William and Harold of England. The rejoicing Normans, once they had landed, occupied Pevensey, where they built their first camp, and built another at Hastings, providing a refuge for themselves and a shelter for their boats. Marius and Pompey the great, both distinguished by their intelligence and energy, deserved their triumphs, one for bringing Jugurtha to Rome in chains, the other for forcing Mithridates to drink poison: but even they, when they led an entire army into enemy territory, were afraid to expose themselves to danger by taking one legion and leaving the main body of their troops. It was their custom, like the generals of today, to send out scouts, rather than to go themselves, more anxious about their own safety than wishing to leave such duties to their army. But William, taking no more than twenty-five knights, boldly explored the lie of the land and its inhabitants. He came back on foot because the paths were so difficult, and laughed at having to do so; and – the reader may laugh at this – he earned yet more praise by carrying on his shoulders not only his own hauberk, but also that of one of his companions, famous for his strength and courage, William Fitz Osbern.

A rich inhabitant of these parts, Norman by birth, Robert, son of the lady Wimarc, sent a message to his lord and relative the duke at Hastings, in the following words: 'King Harold, having fought his own brother and the king of Norway, who was regarded as the most valiant warrior under heaven, has killed both of them in one battle, destroying their powerful armies. Encouraged by this success, he is returning to meet you by forced marches, at the head of a very numerous and strong army: against him, your men will be no more use, in my opinion, than as many vile curs. You are reputed to be a clever man; until now you have managed your affairs in peace and war with wisdom. Now you should act with caution, and beware of hurling yourself into a danger from which you cannot escape. I advise you to remain behind your fortifications and to refrain from giving battle for the time being.' But the duke replied to the messenger: 'Take my thanks to your master for his advice, in which he counsels prudence, though it would have been better put in less insulting words. Tell him that I will not hide behind ditches and palisades, but will engage Harold's army as soon as possible: I would not despair of crushing him and his men, with God's help, because my troops are so bold, even if I had only ten thousand warriors instead of the sixty thousand I have brought.'

One day, when the duke was inspecting the guard who protected the ships, a monk sent as an ambassador by Harold, was announced to him as he came from the ships. He went at once to find him, and cunningly said: 'There is no-one closer to William, count of the Normans, than I, his seneschal. You will have no way of speaking to him except through me: tell me what message you bring. He will be glad to learn of it through me, because no-one is dearer to him than me. Afterwards you can come and talk to him as you wish.' Once he had learnt the purpose of the embassy through what the monk told him, the duke at once made arrangements that he should be received as a guest and treated with every respect. Meanwhile, he and his men debated how to reply to the message.

The next day, seated amidst his magnates, he had the monk summoned, and said: 'I am William, by grace of God prince of the Normans. What you told me yesterday, please repeat in the presence of these men.' The messenger said: 'This is the message that King Harold sends to you. You have invaded his lands, whether from self-confidence or boldness, he does not know. He remembers that King Edward at first resolved to make you heir to the kingdom of England and that he himself gave you his pledge in Normandy. Equally, he knows that this kingdom belongs to him by right, because the same king, his lord, gave it to him on his deathbed. Now, since the time when Saint Augustine came to this land, the common custom of the nation is that a donation made by a dying man is held as valid. He therefore asks you and your men to leave the land which is his by right. Otherwise he will break the oath of friendship and the articles which he confirmed to you in Normandy, and the responsibility will be entirely yours.'

When he heard Harold's message, the duke asked the monk if the latter would take his own ambassador safely to Harold. He promised to look after the messenger's safety just as he would his own. At once, the duke instructed a monk from Fécamp to carry a message promptly to Harold. 'It is neither boldness nor injustice, but mature reflection and the quest for justice which have led me to cross to this land, of which King Edward, my lord and relative, made me the heir, as Harold himself admits, because of the high honours and numerous benefices which I and my ancestors have conferred on him and his brother, as well as their men, and because, of all the men of his race, he believed me to be the most worthy and capable of supporting him in his lifetime, and of governing the kingdom after his death. He would not have done this without the agreement of his magnates, by the advice of archbishop Stigand, earl Godwin, earl Leofric, and earl Siward: all of them subscribed under oath that they would receive me as lord after the death of Edward and would never during his lifetime attempt to seize the kingdom by plotting against me. He gave as hostages Godwin's son and grandson. Finally, he sent Harold himself to Normandy, so that, he and I both being present, he would swear what his father and the other men already named had sworn in my absence. But, on his voyage towards me, he was in danger of being taken prisoner and I rescued him by strength and wisdom. Harold made himself my vassal by doing homage, and gave me surety in writing for my claim for the kingdom of England. I am ready to plead my case in a court wherever he pleases, either by English law or by Norman law. If, according to the verdict of law, either Normans or English decide that the kingdom belongs to him legitimately, let him possess it in peace. But if they decide that it should be restored to me, let him hand it over to me. However, if he rejects the proposal, I do not think that it is just to make my men fight his men and die as a result, because they have no part in our quarrel. I am ready to wager my head against his [in single combat] that I have a better right to the English kingdom than him.'

Such were the words of the duke: we have chosen to set them before everyone's eyes, rather than our own version, because we want to ensure for him eternal fame. It is a good illustration of his wisdom, justice, piety and boldness. The force of his argument, when considered (and Cicero, the best of the Roman orators, could not have weakened it) demolishes the arguments of Harold. In short, he was ready to abide by whatever judgment customary law decreed. He refused to condemn his enemies the English to die because of his personal quarrel. His wish was to decide the matter in single combat, at the risk of his own head.

As soon as the monk gave this message to Harold, who was approaching, he went pale with astonishment and remained silent for a long time, as if struck dumb. The messenger asked for an answer, not once but several times; at first he replied: 'We will continue our advance' and then 'We will march on to victory.' The messenger insisted on another reply, saying: 'The duke does not want the armies to be destroyed, but wishes for a single combat.' For this intrepid and good man preferred to renounce a just claim rather than cause the death of many men. He was sure that Harold's head would fall, because he was less brave and had an unjust cause. Finally Harold, raising his eyes to heaven, exclaimed: 'Let the Lord decide today between William and myself according to justice!' Blinded by his desire to rule, forgetful in his haste of the injustice of his cause, he chose, to his own ruin, his conscience as just judge.

In the meanwhile, trusted soldiers, sent out as scouts on the duke's orders, announced the imminent arrival of the enemy, because the king in his fury had hastened his march, particularly because he had learnt of the devastation around the Norman camp. He intended to surprise them and to crush them in a nocturnal or surprise attack. And in case they took to flight he had armed a fleet of seven hundred boats to ambush them on the sea. The duke hastily ordered all those who were in the camp to arm themselves, for many of his companions had gone foraging that day. He himself attended the mystery of the Mass with the greatest devotion, and took communion of the body and blood of our Lord, strengthening both body and soul. He humbly placed around his neck the relics whose protection Harold had forfeited when he broke the oath which he had sworn on them. Two bishops were with him, Odo of Bayeux and Geoffrey of Coutances; with them were a number of clergy and some monks. They gathered and prepared to fight the enemy with prayers. The duke put on his hauberk reversed to the left: anyone else would have been terrified, but the duke laughed this off as pure chance instead of taking it as a sinister happening.

The speech with which he rallied the courage and eagerness of his troops, although brief due to the circumstances, was doubtless a fine one, although it has not come down to us in all its splendour. He reminded the Normans that under his command they had always been victorious in many and great dangers. He reminded everyone of their country, their noble deeds and their great name. 'Now you must prove with your hands the stuff of which you are made, the spirit that inspires you. Now it is no longer a matter of living and ruling but of escaping with your lives from imminent danger. If you fight manfully, victory, honour, and riches will be yours; otherwise you will be slain or as captives, you will serve the whims of a most cruel enemy, and will be remembered for ever with shame. There is no way of escape: on the one hand, an army and an unknown and hostile countryside bar the way, on the other, a navy and the sea. Men should not be frightened by numbers. On many occasions the English, defeated by the swords of their enemies, have perished; most of the time, they have been conquered and have had to surrender to the enemy. They have never distinguished themselves by great deeds of arms. Men inexperienced in battle can be easily overcome by the courage and skill of a few. Above all, divine help will not be lacking for a just cause. If such a band are daring, and do not yield, victory will soon be theirs to celebrate.'

He advanced with his troops in the following highly advantageous order, behind the banner which the pope had sent him. In the vanguard he placed infantry armed with bows and crossbows; behind them were also infantry, but more steady and armed with hauberks; in the rear, the cavalry squadrons, in the midst of which he took his place with the elite. From this position he could command the whole army by voice and gesture. If an author from antiquity had described Harold's army, he would have said that as it passed rivers dried up, the forests became open country. For from every part of the country large numbers of English had gathered. Some were moved by affection for Harold, all by love of their country, which they wished to defend from strangers, even though the cause was unjust. Considerable help had been sent from the land of the Danes, to whom they were related. But, frightened of attacking William, whom they feared more than the king of Norway, on equal terms, they camped on higher ground, a hill close to the forest through which they had come. They immediately dismounted and went on foot, drawn up one close to the other. The duke and his men, in no way frightened by the difficulty of the place, began slowly to climb the steep slope.

The terrible sound of the trumpets announced on both sides the beginning of the battle. The Normans boldly and swiftly launched the attack. Just as when speakers plead a case of theft before a judge, the plaintiff opens the proceedings. So the Norman infantry advanced closer, provoking the English, and causing wounds and death with their missiles. The latter resisted bravely, each according to their means. They threw javelins and all sorts of darts, the most lethal of axes and stones fixed to pieces of wood. Under this deadly hail you might have thought that our men would be crushed. The mounted warriors came to the rescue, and those who had been in the rear found themselves in front. Disdaining to fight from a distance, they rode into battle using their swords. The great war-cries, here Norman, there barbarian, were drowned by the noise of battle and the groans of the dying. So for a time both sides fought fiercely. The English were greatly helped by the higher position which they held; they did not have to march to the attack, but remained tightly grouped. Their numbers and the strength of their army, as well as their weapons of attack, which penetrated without difficulty shields and other pieces of armour were also to their advantage. So they resisted vigorously or repulsed those who dared to attack them at close quarters with swords. They even wounded those who threw spears at them from a distance. So, frightened by such ferocity, the infantry and Breton mounted warriors both retreated, with all the auxiliary troops who formed the left wing. Almost the whole of the duke's army yielded – in saying this, no shame is intended for the unconquered Norman race. The armies of Rome in her majesty, even when they contained royal contingents and however accustomed they were to victory on land or sea, sometimes retreated when they learnt that their leader had been slain, or believed that he had been. The Normans believed that their duke and lord had been killed. Their retreat was not a shameful flight, but a sorrowful withdrawal.

The prince, seeing the greater part of the enemy camp setting out in pursuit of his men, hurled himself in front of the fugitives, and stopped them by striking them or menacing them with his lance. Then, having uncovered his head and taken off his helmet, he shouted: 'Look at me! I am alive, and will be the victor, with God's help! What madness induces you to flee? What avenue of retreat is open to you? Those whom you could have slaughtered like sheep have driven you back and are killing you! You are deserting victory and inextinguishable glory to lose yourselves in flight and eternal shame! By fleeing, none of you will escape death.' With these words, they regained courage. At their head he hurled himself forward and with the lightning of his sword he devastated the enemy nation which had rebelled against him, their lawful king, and deserved to be slaughtered.

Strengthened in their resolve, they attacked with increased vigour the enemy army which, despite having sustained very great losses, did not seem any less in number. The English confidently resisted with all their strength, striving above all to prevent a breach in their line opening under the assault. Their extraordinarily tight formation meant that those who were killed hardly had room to fall. Even so, some breaches opened under the sword-blows of the most doughty fighters. They were made by the men of Maine, the French, Bretons, men from Aquitaine, but above all by the Normans, with unequalled courage. A certain young Norman, Robert, son of Roger of Beaumont, nephew and heir of Hugh, count of Meulan, through his mother Adeline, was fighting that day for the first time; he carried out an exploit which deserves everlasting praise. At the head of the battalion at the right wing which he commanded, he attacked and brought down the enemy with great boldness. We cannot, nor do we intend to, narrate everyone's exploits as they merit. The most fertile writer, if he had been eyewitness of this war, would have great difficulty in describing each small detail, and we wish to hasten to finish the praise of Count William in order to celebrate the glory of King William.

Seeing that it would be impossible for them to overcome, without great loss to themselves, such a numerous enemy which offered a cruel resistance, the Normans and their allies turned their backs, pretending to take flight. They remembered how, a little earlier, flight had led to the success they desired. Among the barbarians, who hoped that they were victorious, there was the greatest rejoicing. They urged each other on with cries of triumph while they abused our men and threatened to hurl themselves as one man on them. As before, several thousands were bold enough to rush forward, as if on wings, to pursue those who they took to be fleeing, when the Normans suddenly turned their horses' heads, stopped them in their tracks, crushed them completely and massacred them down to the last man.

Having twice used this trick with the same success, they attacked with the greatest vigour the rest of the army, which still inspired fear, and which was very difficult to surround. Then an unusual kind of combat ensured, one side attacking in bursts and in a variety of movements, the other rooted in the ground, putting up with the assault. The English weakened, and, as if they admitted their wrongdoing by defeat itself, they now undertook their punishment. The Normans shot arrows, wounded and transfixed men; the dead as they fell, moved more than the living. Even the lightly wounded could not escape, but perished under the dense heap of their companions. So fortune concurred in William's triumph by hastening it.

There took part in this battle Eustace, count of Boulogne; William, son of Richard, count of Evreux; Geoffrey, son of Rotrou, count of Mortagne; William Fitz Osbern; Aimery, viscount of Thouars; Walter Giffard, Hugh of Montfort, Ralph of Tosny, Hugh of Grandmesnil, William of Warenne, and a great number of others, outstanding for their eminence as soldiers and fame, whose names should be written in history books among those of the bravest warriors. As for William, their leader, he surpassed them in both courage and wisdom, and should rightly be placed above some of the Greek and Roman leaders so highly praised in the records, and treated as the equal of others. His leadership in the battle was noble, preventing men from fleeing, inspiring courage in others, sharing danger, more often ordering his men to follow him than to advance. From this it is clear that his courage opened the way for his soldiers and encouraged their boldness. A not inconsiderable part of the enemy army lost heart merely at the sight of this astonishing and frightening horseman, before they had sustained any injury. Three horses were killed under him. Three times he intrepidly leapt to the ground and hastened to avenge the death of his warhorse. This shows his quickness, his strength of mind and body. The fury of his sword pierced shields, helmets and hauberks; he struck down several soldiers with his shield alone. His soldiers were astonished to see him fight on foot: many, already wounded, found new courage from his example. Some indeed, weak from loss of blood, leaned on their shields and fought manfully; others, unable to do more, encouraged their fellows to follow the duke fearlessly by shouts and gestures, lest they should let victory slip through their hands. He helped and rescued many of his men.

William would have been no more afraid to meet Harold, whom the poets compared to Hector or Turnus, in single combat, than Achilles or Aeneas, the ancient adversaries of the two heroes. Tydeus, attacked by fifty men, used a rock to defend himself; William, his equal, scarcely less well-born, did not fear to meet a thousand single-handed. The author of the *Thebaid* or *Aeneid*, who, after the fashion of poets, make great deeds even greater in their books, would have found the real exploits of this man a better subject for verse, and nearer to the truth. And if they had risen to the greatness of the topic, they had made him the subject of their songs, the beauty of their style would have earned him a place among the gods. But our feeble prose, which only proposes in humble fashion for the benefit of rulers, to relate his piety in worshipping the true God – who alone is great, eternal to the end of time and beyond, must come shortly to the end of the true story of this battle, which he won justly and bravely.

At the close of the day, the English realised that they could no longer resist the Normans. They knew that they had been reduced in number by the death of many of their troops. The king himself, his brothers, and the leading men of the kingdom had been killed: those who remained were at the end of the struggle; and there was no hope of relief. They saw that the Normans were hardly weakened at all by the death of those who had been killed, and, as if they drew on new strength by fighting, they threatened them more fiercely than at the beginning. The duke in his fury spared no-one who opposed him, as if his valour as a soldier would only be satisfied by victory. So they fled, and left the field as quickly as they could, some seizing horses, others on foot, some by road, others across country. Some, covered in blood, struggled to flee, or were too weak to do so. The desire to escape alive gave strength to some. Many died in the depths of the forests: their pursuers found corpses all along the roads. The Normans, although they did not know the countryside, pursued them eagerly, slaughtering the fleeing rebels, setting the seal on their victory. Amidst the dead, the horses' hooves trampled all those who lay in their path.

However, those who fled regained confidence when they found a deep valley and numerous ditches. For this race, descendants of the ancient Saxons, the most ferocious of men, were always ready to cross swords. They would not have retreated except in face of an invincible force. They had just defeated with ease the king of Norway, at the head of a numerous, battle-hardened army. At the head of his victorious standards, the duke, seeing troops suddenly gathered and believing them to be newly arrived reinforcements, did not turn aside or halt; more fearsome, armed with the butt of his spear than those who brandished long javelins, he restrained by his manly voice count Eustace, who had turned back with fifty mounted soldiers and was getting ready to sound the retreat. The latter whispered in the duke's ear the advice that he should turn back, predicting instant death if he continued. While he said this, Eustace was struck between the shoulders by a blow whose sound and force showed themselves by blood flowing from his nose and mouth: half dead, he only escaped with the help of his companions. The duke, disdaining fear and failure, attacked and overcame his adversaries. In this conflict some of the most famous Norman warriors fell, because the difficulty of the lie of the land meant that they could not show their usual courage.

Having thus achieved his victory, the duke returned to the battlefield, found a scene of carnage which he could only look at with pity, even though the victims were wicked men and it is glorious and praiseworthy to kill a tyrant. The ground was covered with corpses for a vast distance, stained with blood: they were the flower of the nobility and youth of the English. Beside the king, two of his brothers were found: he himself, stripped of all marks of his rank, was recognised not by his face, but by certain signs; he was carried to the duke's camp, where the duke entrusted William Malet with the duty of burying him, but refused to hand over his body to his mother, who offered to pay its weight in gold. He was aware that it would not have been fitting to accept gold in exchange: and he also thought that it would not have been fitting to allow a man to be buried in accordance with his mother's wishes who by excessive greed had been responsible for the deaths of many who would never be properly buried. They said in jest that he should be made guardian of the shore and sea which, in his anger, he had earlier occupied.

2. William of Jumièges, *Gesta Normannorum Ducum*

Like William of Poitiers, William of Jumièges was a contemporary of the events of 1066, writing his 'Deeds of the dukes of the Normans' in about 1070. And though he had access to less detailed information about the campaign than did William of Poitiers and was a monk with no military training, he was also a Norman, writing from a Norman point of view, with obvious pride in Norman military achievements. The selection presented here on the campaign of 1066 comes from the seventh book of the *Gesta*. The work as a whole was probably more widely known than William of Poitiers', being copied and interpolated by several later chroniclers including Orderic Vitalis.

Reprinted, by permission, from *English Historical Documents*, ed. D.C. Douglas and G.W. Greenaway (London: Methuen, 2nd edn, 1981), II.228–30.
See William of Jumièges, *Gesta Normannorum Ducum of William of Jumièges, Orderic Vitalis and Robert of Torigni*, ed. E. Van Houts, 2 vols (Oxford 1992, 1995).

Edward, king of the English, being, according to the dispensation of God, without an heir, sent Robert,[1] archbishop of Canterbury, to the duke with a message appointing the duke as heir to the kingdom which God had entrusted to him. He also at a later time sent to the duke, Harold[2] the greatest of all the counts in his kingdom alike in riches and honour and power. This he did in order that Harold might guarantee the crown to the duke by his fealty and confirm the same with an oath according to Christian usage. When Harold set out on his mission, he was borne along by the wind until he reached Ponthieu, and there he fell into the hands of Guy, count of Abbeville,[3] who straightway threw him with his retinue into prison. When the duke heard of this he sent messengers, and by force caused him to be released.[4] Harold thereupon sojourned with the duke for some time, and performed fealty to him in respect of the kingdom with many oaths.[5] After this the duke sent him back to the king with many gifts.

In due course King Edward completed the term of his happy life, and departed from this world in the year of the Incarnation of our Lord 1065.[6] Then Harold immediately seized the kingdom, thus violating the oath which he had sworn to the duke. So the duke at once sent messengers to Harold urging him to desist from this mad policy, and to keep the faith which he had pledged with his oath. Harold, however, not only disdained to listen to this message, but seduced all the English people away from obedience to the duke. In these days a star with three long rays appeared. It lit up the greater part of the southern sky for the space of a fortnight, and many thought that this portended a great change in some kingdom.

Prince William was thus compelled to watch the strength of Harold increasing daily at a time when it was the duke who should have been crowned with a royal diadem. He therefore hastily built a fleet of three thousand ships. At length he brought this fleet to anchor at St Valery in Ponthieu where he filled it with mighty horses and most valiant men, with hauberks and helmets.[7] Then when a favourable wind began to blow, he set sail, and crossing the sea he landed at Pevensey where he immediately built a castle with a strong rampart. He left this in charge of some troops, and with others he hurried to Hastings where he erected another similar fortress. Harold, rejecting caution, advanced against this, and, after riding all night, he appeared on the field of battle early in the morning.

But the duke had taken precautions against night-attacks by the enemy, and as the darkness approached he had ordered his men to stand by until dawn. At first light, having disposed his troops in three lines of battle, he advanced undaunted against the terrible enemy. The battle began at the third hour of the day, and continued amid a welter of carnage and slaughter until nightfall. Harold himself, fighting amid the front rank of his army, fell covered with deadly wounds. And the English, seeing their

1   Robert, abbot of Jumièges, bishop of London, 1044, archbishop of Canterbury, 1051,
2   The Anglo-Saxon Chronicle is silent as to this famous mission and the date.
3   Guy of Ponthieu. An analogy may be found in the description of the dukes of Normandy as counts of Rouen.
4   *missis legatis, violenter illum extorsit.*
5   *facta fidelitate de regno plurimis sacramentis.*
6   Edward died 5 January 1066.
7   The rhetoric exactly summarises the significance of the equipment. It was on the specially armed mounted knight that William relied.

king dead, lost confidence in their own safety, and as night was approaching they turned and fled.

The most valiant duke, returning from the pursuit and slaughter of his enemies, came back to the field of battle in the middle of the night. At first dawn, having despoiled the corpses of his enemies and buried the bodies of his dear comrades, he took the road which leads to London. They say that in this battle many thousands of the English perished, and that Christ thus recompensed them for the foul and unjust murder of Alfred, brother of King Edward.[8] At length the most fortunate lord of battle, who was equally eminent in counsel, avoided the city, and taking a by-way to Wallingford, he there brought his troops safely across the river, and bade them at that place lay out a camp. It was from there that he advanced against London. When the advance guard of his army reached the central square of the city, they found there a large company of rebels who were ready to offer a fierce resistance to them. The Normans, therefore, engaged and inflicted upon the city a great mourning on account of the large number of young men and citizens whom they slew. At length the Londoners saw that they could hold out no longer. So they gave hostages and submitted themselves and all their possessions to their hereditary lord,[9] to their most noble conqueror.[10] His triumph was thus completed after so many dangers, and his wonderful virtues even our praise has not been able adequately to extol. He was chosen king by all the magnates both of the Normans and of the English on Christmas day; he was anointed with the holy oil by the bishops of the kingdom; and he was vested with the royal crown in the year of the Incarnation of our Lord 1066.

[8]　Alfred came to England from Normandy in 1036, and was brutally murdered. It is probable that Godwine was implicated in the crime, and this formed a constant part of the Norman propaganda against Godwine's son, Harold.
[9]　The emphasis on the hereditary title is noteworthy.
[10]　*nobilissimo victori suo*. Is this the earliest application of the name to William?

3. The Anglo-Saxon Chronicle

The Anglo-Saxon Chronicle was in fact a group of related but distinct vernacular annals compiled year to year and edited in different monastic centers. For the period 1042–1079, three different versions survive (designated 'C', 'D' and 'E'), and the entries from each for the year 1066 are presented here. Though none of these versions were particularly closely connected to King Harold (note that only version 'D' gives significant attention to Hastings, 'C' and 'E' being apparently more concerned with the northern battles at Fulford and Stamford Bridge), all share an Anglo-Saxon point of view and see the events of that year as calamitous. The contrast with the Norman historians is striking and instructive. The decline of English as an educated language after the Conquest eventually doomed the writing of the Anglo-Saxon Chronicle, but version 'E' continued to be written until 1154, and the various versions influenced Latin chroniclers like Florence of Worcester.

Reprinted, by permission, from *The Anglo-Saxon Chronicle*, ed. Dorothy Whitelock with D.C. Douglas and S.I. Tucker (Eyre and Spottiswode, 1961). Copyright © Dorothy Whitelock and David Douglas, 1961.

C

1066[1] In this year Harold came from York to Westminster at the Easter following the Christmas that the king died, and Easter was then on 16 April. Then over all England there was seen a sign in the skies such as had never been seen before.[2] Some said it was the star 'comet' which some call the long-haired star, and it first appeared on the eve of the Greater Litany, that is 24 April, and so shone all the week. And soon after this Earl Tosti came from overseas[3] into the Isle of Wight with as large a fleet as he could muster, and both money and provisions were given him. And then he went away from there and did damage everywhere along the sea-coast wherever he could reach, until he came to Sandwich. When King Harold, who was in London, was informed that Tosti his brother was come to Sandwich, he assembled a naval force and a land force larger than any king had assembled before in this country, because he had been told as a fact that Count William from Normandy, King Edward's kinsman,[4] meant to come here and subdue this country. This was exactly what happened afterwards. When Tosti found that King Harold was on his way to Sandwich, he went from Sandwich and took some of the sailors with him, some willingly and some unwillingly, and then went north to [. . . . . .][5] and ravaged in Lindsey[6] and killed many good men there. When Earl Edwin and Earl Morcar[7] understood about this, they came there and drove him out of the country; and then he went to Scotland, and the king of Scots[8] gave him protection, and helped him with provisions, and he stayed there all the summer. Then King Harold came to Sandwich and waited for his fleet there, because it was long before it could be assembled; and when his fleet was assembled, he went into the Isle of Wight and lay there all that summer and autumn; and a land force

D

In this year King Harold came from York to Westminster at the Easter following the Christmas that the king died, and Easter was then on 16 April. Then over all England there was seen a sign in the skies such as had never been seen before.[20] Some said it was the star 'comet' which some call the long-haired star; and it first appeared on the eve of the Greater Litany, that is 24 April, and so shone all the week. And soon after this Earl Tosti came from overseas into the Isle of Wight with as large a fleet as he could muster and both money and provisions were given him. And King Harold his brother assembled a naval force and a land force larger than any king had assembled before in this country, because he had been told that William the Bastard[21] meant to come here and conquer this country. This was exactly what happened afterwards. Meanwhile Earl Tosti came into the Humber with sixty ships and Earl Edwin came with a land force and drove him out, and the sailors deserted him. And he went to Scotland with twelve small vessels, and there Harold, king of Norway,[22] met him with three hundred[23] ships, and Tosti submitted to him and became his vassal; and they both went up the Humber until they reached York. And there Earl Edwin and Morcar his brother fought against them; but the Norwegians had the victory. Harold, king of the English, was informed that things had gone thus; and the fight was on the Vigil of St Matthew.[24] Then Harold our king[25] came upon the Norwegians by surprise and met them beyond York at Stamford Bridge with a large force of the English people; and that day there was a very fierce fight on both sides. There was killed Harold Fairhair[26] and Earl Tosti, and the Norwegians who survived took to flight; and the English attacked them fiercely as they pursued them until some got to the ships. Some were drowned,

E

In this year the minster of Westminster was consecrated on Holy Innocents' Day,[39] and King Edward died on the eve of the Epiphany,[40] and was buried on the Feast of the Epiphany[41] in the newly consecrated church at Westminster. And Earl Harold succeeded to the realm of England, just as the king had granted it to him, and as he had been chosen to the position. And he was consecrated king on the Feast of the Epiphany.[42] And the same year that he became king he went out with a naval force against William,[43] and meanwhile Earl Tosti came into the Humber with sixty ships; and Earl Edwin[44] came with a land force and drove him out and the sailors deserted him, and he went to Scotland with twelve small vessels, and Harold, the Norse king,[45] met him with three hundred ships, and Tosti submitted to him; and they both went up the Humber until they reached York. And Earl Morcar and Earl Edwin fought against them, and the Norse king had the victory.[46] And King Harold was informed as to what had been done, and what had happened, and he came with a very great force of Englishmen and met him at Stamford Bridge,[47] and killed him and Earl Tosti and valiantly overcame all the invaders. Meanwhile Count William landed at Hastings on Michaelmas Day,[48] and Harold came from the north and fought with him before all the army had come, and there he fell and his two brothers Gyrth and Leofwine; and William conquered this country, and came to Westminster, and Archbishop Aldred consecrated him king, and people paid taxes to him, and gave him hostages and afterwards bought their lands. And[49] Leofric, abbot of Peterborough, was at that campaign and fell ill there, and came home and died soon after, on the eve of All Saints. God have mercy on his soul. In his day there was every happiness and every good at Peterborough, and he was

1   'C' omits the number of this annal. 'E', having omitted the number 1065, returns to the true date. As in the previous annal, 'D' combines 'C' and 'E'.
2   Halley's comet.
3   Florence: 'from Flanders'. Gaimar says that most of Tosti's men were Flemings, and that they landed at *Wardstane* and harried there, and then went to Thanet, where they were joined by Copsi (Tosti's subordinate when he was earl of Northumbria) with 17 ships from Orkney. Having caused great damage in *Brunemue* and elsewhere, they went to the Humber. After their defeat by Edwin and Morcar, the Flemings deserted Tosti (ll. 5159–5188). On the course of Tosti's raid, see F.M. Stenton, *Anglo-Saxon England*, pp. 578f., where *Brunemue* is taken to refer to the mouth of the Burnham river in Norfolk.
4   See note 21. Note the difference of emphasis. 'C' may imply that William had some claim to the throne.
5   Florence, who is following the 'C' version, omits the reference to this unnamed place.
6   Florence: 'where he burnt many villages'.
7   Earls respectively of Mercia and Northumbria.
8   Malcolm Canmore.

20   Halley's comet.
21   See note 4. Note the difference of emphasis. 'C' may imply that William had some claim to the throne.
22   Harold Hardrada.
23   Florence: 'more than 500'.
24   i.e. 20 September.
25   The note of enthusiasm in 'D' should be remarked.
26   An error for Hardrada.

39   28 December 1065.
40   5 January 1066.
41   6 January 1066.
42   6 January 1066.
43   This, in 'E' only, perhaps refers to a skirmish off the south-east coast.
44   He had succeeded his father, Ælfgar, as earl of Mercia.
45   Harold Hardrada.
46   The battle of Fulford took place on Wednesday, 20 September 1066.
47   The battle of Stamford Bridge took place on Monday, 25 September.
48   29 September.
49   What follows in 'E' is a Peterborough addition.

C

was kept everywhere along by the sea, though in the end it was no use. When it was the Feast of the Nativity of St Mary,[9] the provisions of the people were gone, and nobody could keep them there any longer. Then the men were allowed to go home, and the king rode inland, and the ships were brought up to London, and many perished before they reached there. When the ships came home, Harold, king of Norway, came by surprise north into the Tyne with a very large naval force – no small one: it could be [. . . . . .] or more.[10] And Earl Tosti came to him with all those he had mustered, just as they had agreed beforehand, and they both went with all the fleet up the Ouse towards York.[11] Then King Harold in the south was informed when he disembarked that Harold, king of Norway, and Earl Tosti were come ashore near York. Then he went northwards day and night as quickly as he could assemble his force. Then before Harold could get there Earl Edwin and Earl Morcar assembled from their earldom as large a force as they could muster, and fought against the invaders[12] and caused them heavy casualties, and many of the English host were killed and drowned and put to flight, and the Norwegians remained masters of the field. And this fight was on the eve of St Matthew the Apostle, and that was a Wednesday. And then after the fight Harold, king of Norway, and Earl Tosti went into York[13] with as large a force as suited them, and they were given hostages[14] from the city and also helped with provisions, and so went from there on board ship and settled a complete peace, arranging that they should all go with him southwards and subdue this country. Then in the middle of these proceedings Harold, king of the English, came on the Sunday[15] with all his force to Tadcaster, and there marshalled his troops, and then on Monday[16] went right on through York.

D

and some burned, and some destroyed in various ways so that few survived and the English remained in command of the field. The king gave quarter to Olaf, son of the Norse king, and their bishop and the earl of Orkney[27] and all those who survived on the ships, and they went up to our king and swore oaths[28] that they would always keep peace and friendship with this country; and the king let them go home with twenty-four[29] ships. These two pitched battles were fought within five nights. Then Count William came from Normandy to Pevensey on Michaelmas Eve,[30] and as soon as they were able to move on they built a castle at Hastings.[31] King Harold was informed of this[32] and he assembled a large army and came against him at the hoary appletree.[33] And William came against him by surprise before his army was drawn up in battle array. But the king nevertheless fought hard against him, with the men who were willing to support him, and there were heavy casualties on both sides. There King Harold was killed and Earl Leofwine his brother, and Earl Gyrth his brother, and many good men, and the French remained masters of the field, even as God granted it to them because of the sins of the people. Archbishop Aldred and the citizens of London wanted to have Edgar *Cild* as king, as was his proper due; and Edwin and Morcar promised him that they would fight on his side; but always the more it ought to have been forward the more it got behind, and the worse it grew from day to day, exactly as everything came to be at the end. The battle took place on the festival of Calixtus the pope.[34] And Count William went back to Hastings, and waited there to see whether submission would be made to him. But when he understood that no one meant to come to him, he went inland with all his army that was left to him, and that came to him

E

beloved by everyone, so that the king gave to St Peter and him the abbacy of Burton and that of Coventry which Earl Leofric, who was his uncle, had built, and that of Crowland and that of Thorney. And he did much for the benefit of the monastery of Peterborough with gold and silver and vestments and land, more indeed than any before or after him. Then the Golden City became a wretched city. Then the monks elected Brand, the provost, as abbot, because he was a very good man and very wise, and sent him to the atheling Edgar[50] because the local people expected that he would be king, and the atheling gladly gave assent to it. When King William heard about this he grew very angry, and said the abbot had slighted him. Then distinguished men acted as intermediaries and brought them into agreement, because the abbot was of good family. Then he gave the king 40 marks of gold as settlement. And he lived a little while after this – only three years. Then all confusions and evils came upon the monastery. May God take pity on it!

9 8 September.
10 The text is corrupt. Florence, who is close to 'C', reads: 'with a powerful fleet, more than 500 large ships'.
11 Florence says they landed at Riccall. Gaimar says they left their ships at 'St Wilfrid's'.
12 Florence: 'on the northern bank of the R. Ouse, near York'. Simeon of Durham inserts the name Fulford into Florence's account, and Gaimar gives this name also.
13 On Sunday, 24 September.
14 According to Florence, they were given 150 hostages, and left 150 of their men as hostages in York when they went to their ships.
15 24 September.
16 25 September.

27 Florence: 'Paul, who had been sent off with part of the army to guard the ships'.
28 *Id.*: 'and gave hostages'.
29 *Id.*: '20'.
30 28 September, but 'E' has 29 September.
31 Florence, who has mainly followed 'C; until this ends, and who then for the battle of Stamford Bridge is close to 'D', seems independent of the Chronicle for his account of the battle of Hastings.
32 According to Gaimar (ll. 5252–5255), he entrusted his booty to Archbishop Aldred and left Mærleswein in charge when he went south. On Harold's actions, see F.M. Stenton, *Anglo-Saxon England*, pp. 583f.
33 The only narrative contemporary description of the battle; cf. the Norman accounts, *E.H.D.*, II, Nos 3 and 4, and see also the chapter by Sir Frank Stenton on 'The Historical Background' in *The Bayeux Tapestry: A comprehensive Survey* (London, 1957).
34 Saturday, 14 October.

50 Son of the atheling Edward who died in 1057.

C

And Harold, king of Norway, and Earl Tosti and their divisions were gone inland beyond York to Stamford Bridge, because they had been promised for certain that hostages would be brought to them there out of all the shire. Then Harold, king of the English, came against them by surprise beyond the bridge, and there they joined battle, and went on fighting strenuously till late in the day. And there Harold, king of Norway, was killed and Earl Tosti, and numberless men with them both Norwegians and English, and the Norwegians[17] fled from the English. There was one of the Norwegians there who withstood the English host so that they could not cross the bridge nor win victory. Then an Englishman shot an arrow, but it was no use, and then another came under the bridge and stabbed him under the corselet. Then Harold, king of the English, came over the bridge and his host with him, and there killed large numbers of both Norwegians and Flemings, and Harold let the king's son Hetmundus[18] go home to Norway with all the ships.[19]

D

afterwards from overseas, and ravaged all the region that he overran until he reached Berkhamstead.[35] There he was met by Archbishop Aldred and Edgar *Cild*, and Earl Edwin and Earl Morcar, and all the chief men from London. And they submitted out of necessity after most damage had been done – and it was a great piece of folly that they had not done it earlier, since God would not make things better, because of our sins. And they gave hostages and swore oaths to him, and he promised them that he would be a gracious liege lord, and yet in the meantime they ravaged all that they overran. Then on Christmas Day, Archbishop Aldred consecrated him king at Westminster. And he promised Aldred on Christ's book and swore moreover (before Aldred would place the crown on his head) that he would rule all this people as well as the best of the kings before him, if they would be loyal to him. All the same he laid taxes on people very severely, and then went in spring overseas to Normandy, and took with him Archbishop Stigand, and Æthelnoth, abbot of Glastonbury, and Edgar *Cild* and Earl Edwin and Earl Morcar, and Earl Waltheof,[36] and many other good men from England. And Bishop Odo[37] and Earl William[38] stayed behind and built castles far and wide throughout this country, and distressed the wretched folk, and always after that it grew much worse. May the end be good when God wills!

17 Here the original part of 'C' ends at the foot of a folio, and what follows is on an added page in much later handwriting and language. On this, see B. Dickins, 'The Late Addition to ASC 1066 C', *Proc. Leeds Phil. and Lit. Soc.*, V (1940), pp. 148f.
18 Or 'who was called "Mundus" (the Elegant?)', see B. Dickins, *op. cit.*
19 Here 'C' ends.

35 In what follows, Florence again has points of agreement with 'D', though he is fuller. He adds to the list of those who submitted at Berkhamstead Wulfstan, bishop of Worcester, and Walter, bishop of Hereford, and explains that it was Stigand's uncanonical position that led to Aldred's crowning of William.
36 Florence adds: 'the son of Earl Siward, and the noble leader Æthelnoth the Kentishman'. He puts William's journey in 1067, whereas 'D', using Lady Day reckoning, puts it in 1066.
37 Odo, half-brother of the Conqueror, being the son of Herluin and Herleva, was bishop of Bayeux from 1049 to 1097. He became earl of Kent shortly after 1066.
38 William fitz Osbern, son of Osbern the steward, was given the Isle of Wight and the earldom of Hereford shortly after 1066.

4. Florence of Worcester, *Chronicon ex Chronicis*

The 'Chronicle of Chronicles' was compiled at Worcester by a monk commonly called 'Florence', though after 1118 (and perhaps before) it was the work of a monk named John. For the eleventh century it is a compilation of earlier material, probably including a lost version of the Anglo-Saxon Chronicle, translated into Latin and handled by the compiler with some care and concern for accuracy. It thus gives us a useful point of comparison with the Anglo-Saxon Chronicle, and presents a contemporary view of the events of 1066 filtered through the lens of Anglo-Norman accomodation which followed the Conquest.

Reprinted from *Church Historians of England*, vol. II, part I, ed. and trans. Joseph Stevenson (1853), 294–7.

No fully satisfactory edition of the original exists, but see Florence of Worcester, *Chronicon ex Chronicis*, 2 vols, ed. B. Thorpe (London, 1848–9).

A.D. 1066. On Thursday, the vigil of our Lord's Epiphany [5th Jan.], in the fourth indiction, the pride of the English, the pacific king Eadward, son of king Aethelred, died at London, having reigned over the Anglo-Saxons twenty-three years, six months, and twenty-seven days: the next day he was buried in kingly style, amid the bitter lamentations of all present. After his interment, the subregulus Harold, son of earl Godwin, whom the king had nominated as his successor, was elected king by the chief nobles of all England; and on the same day was crowned with great ceremony, by Aldred, archbishop of York. On taking the helm of the kingdom, he immediately began to abolish unjust laws and make good ones; to patronise churches and monasteries; to pay particular attention and yield reverence to bishops, abbots, monks, and clerks; to show himself pious, humble, and affable to all good men: but he treated malefactors with the utmost severity, and gave general orders to his earls, ealdormen, sheriffs, and thanes to imprison all thieves, robbers, and disturbers of the kingdom; and he himself laboured by sea and by land for the protection of his country.

On the 8th of the kalends of May [24 April] in this year, a comet was seen not only in England, but, it is said, all over the world, and shone for seven days with exceeding brightness. Shortly afterwards earl Tosti returned from Flanders and landed at the Isle of Wight. After making the islanders pay tribute and stipend, he departed and went pillaging along the sea-coast until he arrived at the port of Sandwich. As soon as king Harold, who was then at London, heard this, he assembled a large fleet and an army of cavalry, and he prepared to go in person to the port of Sandwich. When Tosti was informed of this he took some of the shipmen of the place, willing and unwilling, and bent his course towards Lindesey, where he burned many vills and put many men to death. Thereupon Eadwin, earl of the Mercians, and Morcar, earl of the Northumbrians, hastened up with an army and expelled him from that part of the country. Departing thence he went to Malcolm, king of the Scots, and remained with him during the whole of the summer. Meanwhile king Harold arrived at the port of Sandwich, and waited there for his fleet. When it was assembled, he crossed over with it to the Isle of Wight, and inasmuch as king Eadward's cousin William, earl of the Normans, was preparing to invade England with an army, he watched all the summer and autumn for his coming; and in addition distributed a land force at suitable points along the sea-coast. But about the feast-day of the Nativity of St Mary [8th Sept.] provisions fell short, so the naval and land forces returned home.

After this Harold Harvagra,[1] king of the Norwegians, and brother of St Olaf the king, arrived on a sudden at the mouth of the river Tyne, with a powerful fleet, consisting of more than five hundred large ships. Earl Tosti, according to previous arrangement, joined him with his fleet. They hastened their course and entered the river Humber, and then sailing up the river Ouse against the stream, landed at a place called Richale. King Harold, on hearing this, marched in haste towards Northumbria; but before his arrival the two brothers, earl Eadwin and Morcar, at the head of a large army, fought a battle with the Norwegians on the northern bank of the river Ouse near York, on Wednesday, being the vigil of the feast-day of St Matthew the apostle [20th Sept.], and they fought so bravely at the onset that many of the enemy were overthrown. But after a long contest the English were unable to withstand the attacks of

1 Here Florence is in error; Harold Hardrada, and not Harold *Harfagr*, was the ally of Tostig.

the Norwegians, and fled with great loss; and more were drowned in the river than slain in the field. The Norwegians remained masters of the field of carnage, and having taken one hundred and fifty hostages from York, and leaving there one hundred and fifty of their own men as hostages, they went to their ships. Five days afterwards, that is, on Monday, the 7th of the kalends of October [25th Sept.], as Harold, king of the English, was coming to York with many thousand well-armed fighting men, he fell in with the Norwegians at a place called Stamford-bridge, slew king Harold and earl Tosti, with the greater part of their army, and gained a complete victory; nevertheless, the battle was stoutly contested. He, however, permitted Olaf, the son of the Norwegian king, and Paul, earl of Orkney, who had been sent off with a portion of the army to guard the fleet, to return home without molestation, with twenty ships and the remains of the army; first, however, taking hostages and oaths [of submission] from them.

In the midst of these things, and when the king might have considered that all his enemies were subdued, it was told to him that William, earl of the Normans, had arrived with a countless host of horsemen, slingers, archers, and foot-soldiers, having brought with him powerful auxiliaries from all parts of Gaul, and that he had landed at a place called Pefnesea [Pevensey]. Thereat, the king at once, and in great haste, marched his army towards London; and though he well knew that some of the bravest Englishmen had fallen in his two [former] battles, and that one half of his army had not yet arrived, he did not hesitate to advance with all speed into South Saxony against his enemies; and on Saturday the 11th of the kalends of September [22nd Oct.], before a third of his army was in order for fighting, he joined battle with them nine miles from Hastings, where they had fortified a castle. But inasmuch as the English were drawn up in a narrow place, many retired from the ranks, and very few remained true to him; nevertheless from the third hour of the day until dusk he bravely withstood the enemy, and fought so valiantly and stubbornly in his own defence, that the enemy's forces could hardly make any impression. At last, after great slaughter on both sides, about twilight the king, alas! fell. There were slain also earl Girth, and his brother earl Leofwin, and nearly all the nobility of England. Then earl William returned with his men to Hastings.

Harold reigned nine months and as many days. On hearing of his death, the earls Eadwin and Morcar, who had withdrawn themselves and their men from the conflict, went to London and sent their sister queen Algitha to Chester; but Aldred, archbishop of York, and the said earls, with the citizens of London and the shipmen, were desirous of elevating to the throne Eadgar the etheling, nephew of king Eadmund Ironside, and promised that they would renew the contest under his command. But while numbers were preparing to go out to fight, the earls withdrew their assistance and returned home with their army.

Meanwhile earl William was laying waste South Saxony, Kent, South Hampton-shire, Surrey, Middle Saxony, and Hertfordshire, and kept on burning the vills and slaying the natives until he came to a vill called Beorcham. There archbishop Aldred, Wulstan, bishop of Worcester, Walter, bishop of Hereford, Eadgar the etheling, earls Eadwin and Morcar, the chief men of London, and many more came to him, and, giving hostages, surrendered and swore fealty to him. So he entered into a treaty with them; yet, nevertheless, he permitted his army to burn the vills and keep on pillaging. But when the feast of our Lord's Nativity [25th Dec.] drew nigh, he went to London with his whole army in order that he might be made king. And because Stigand, the primate of all England, was accused by the pope of having obtained the pall in an uncanonical manner, he was anointed king at Westminster with great ceremony on Christmas-day (which in that year fell on a Monday) by Aldred, archbishop of York, having previously (for the archbishop had made it a condition) sworn at the altar of St Peter the apostle, in the presence of the clergy and people, that he would defend the holy churches of God and their ministers, and would also rule justly and with royal care the people who were placed under him, and would ordain and maintain right law, and utterly prohibit all spoliation and unrighteous judgments.

5. The Bayeux Tapestry

The Bayeux Tapestry is in fact an embroidered roll almost 20 inches high and originally more than 230 feet long. It is a unique source, presenting a narrative almost as detailed as William of Poitiers', but in a visual format that gives us details that writers could take for granted: the appearance, for instance, of arms, armor, ships and everyday implements and actions. Interpreting its format is by no means straight-forward, however. Reproduction of the Tapestry in a series of photographs tends to make it appear more 'cartoon-like', with a linear development of the story in discrete panels, than it really is. The organic connection of one scene to the next and the possibility of one scene being presented from more than one perspective should be borne in mind when 'reading' this source.

Other aspects of the Tapestry's creation and meaning are equally problematical. It is generally agreed that the Tapestry was produced within a generation of the Con-quest, possibly very soon after 1066, and that it was produced at the behest of someone (Odo of Bayeux is frequently advanced) on the Norman side. But it is also usually thought to have been produced, at least in part, by Anglo-Saxons (the style is more Anglo-Saxon than Norman), and whether the final product pleased those who commissioned it is open to question. Thus, while the value of this source is clear, its meaning and point of view, often, are not so obvious.

Reprinted from Eric Maclagan, *The Bayeux Tapestry* (Harmondsworth, 1949), plates 59–80.

The bibliography of the Bayeux Tapestry is voluminous; see, e.g., D. Bernstein, *The Mystery of the Bayeux Tapestry* (Chicago University Press, 1986); N.P. Brooks and H.E. Walker, 'The Authority and Interpretation of the Bayeux Tapestry', *Proceedings of the Battle Conference on Anglo-Norman Studies* 1 (1978), 1–34; S.A. Brown, 'The Bayeux Tapestry: Why Estace, Odo and William?', *Anglo-Norman Studies* 12 (1989), 7–28. The best modern edition (in full colour) is Sir David Wilson, *The Bayeux Tapestry* (Thames and Hudson, 1985).

1 Scouts from the two forces spot each other

3 Duke William exhorts his knights

2 King Harold is told about Duke William's army

4 The Norman advance boldly . . .

5 . . . and wisely to battle . . .

7 Attacks on the English shield wall

6 . . . against the English army

8 The English resist the Norman attack

9 More attacks

11 . . . brothers of King Harold

10 Here fell Leofwine and Gyrth . . .

12 Both English and French die in battle

12   An isolated group of English holding a hill

14   Eustace: 'Here is Duke William'

13 Bishop Odo, holding his staff, rallies troops

15 The French attack

16 Those with Harold fall

18 . . . is killed

17 Here King Harold . . .

19 And the English turn to flight

20 Final rout of the English

21a The fox and the crow

21b The ploughman

6. The *Carmen de Hastingae Proelio*

The *Carmen* is, with William of Poitiers and the Bayeux Tapestry, the third detailed narrative of the campaign and battle. But it is also the most problematic in terms of provenance. There are basically two positions with regard to the *Carmen*. The first is that it is the work of Guy, bishop of Amiens, who wrote it before May 1068. In this account it is a valuable contemporary source which William of Poitiers used in writing his *Gesta*. The second, more recent, position is that it was composed later (possibly much later) by an unknown author, and is derivative both of William of Poitiers and of other unreliable traditions, and is thus worthless as a source for the events of 1066. If the second position is true, a number of details we think we know of the campaign and battle would lose their foundation as 'fact'. The academic jury is still in some ways deadlocked over this question, but the doubts raised by proponents of the second position have not succeeded in convincingly dislodging the *Carmen* from the canon of sources for the battle, and it is worth comparing to the other sources we have. If the original attribution to Guy of Amiens is correct, the *Carmen* is one of the accounts closest to the events, and gives us a perspective that is continental but not Norman.

Reprinted from *The Carmen de Hastingae Proelio of Bishop Guy of Amiens*, ed. Catherine Morton and Hope Muntz (1972) by permission of Oxford University Press. Copyright Catherine Morton and Hope Muntz (1972).

The editors make the most complete case for accepting the traditional attribution of the poem. The modern attack on this attribution comes from R.H.C. Davis, 'The *Carmen de Hastingae Proelio*', *English Historical Review* 93 (1978), 241–61. See Davis, L.J. Engels et al., 'The *Carmen de Hastingae Proelio*: A Discussion', *Proceedings of the Battle Conference on Anglo-Norman Studies* 2 (1979), 1–20 for an exchange on the poem's provenance and references to the literature it has generated.

The duke said: 'Where is the king?' 'Not far off,' answered the monk. He said to him in his ear: 'You can see the standards! I bear many words which I hold unfit to be repeated, yet I will report what it would be harmful to conceal. He hopes to be able to take you by surprise; by sea and by land he is planning great battles. He is said to have sent five hundred ships to sea to hinder our voyage back. Where he goes he leads forests (of spears) into the open country, and he makes the rivers through which he passes run dry! Perhaps you fear the number? But the greater number[1] lacking greater strength often retires worsted by very few. He has champions with combed anointed hair,[2] effeminate young men, sluggish in the art of war; whatever their number, they may be likened to as many sheep, or to foxes terrified by a thunderbolt.[3] Remember your ancestors, great duke, and may you achieve what your grandfather and your father achieved! Your forefather subdued the Normans, your grandfather the Bretons, your sire laid the neck of the English under the yoke. And what will you do, planning greater things, if not follow them through abundance of valour?'

He kept silence for a little and then, causing himself to delay there, he drew up the armed ranks by a command. He dispatched the foot in advance to open the battle with arrows, and set crossbowmen in the midst so that their speeding shafts might pierce the faces of the English (these wounds given, they might fall back). He hoped to establish the knights in the rear of the foot but the onset of the battle did not allow this; for he perceived companies of the English appearing not far off and could see the forest glitter, full of spears.

Suddenly the forest poured forth troops of men, and from the hiding-places of the woods a host dashed forward. There was a hill near the forest and a neighbouring valley and the ground was untilled because of its roughness. Coming on in massed order – the English custom – they seized possession of this place for the battle. (A race ignorant of war, the English scorn the solace of horses and trusting in their strength they stand fast on foot; and they count it the highest honour to die in arms that their native soil may not pass under another yoke.)

Preparing to meet the enemy, the king mounted the hill and strengthened both his

---

1 We understand *numerus* here as 'a great number', a sense supported by vv. 321–22. Cf. v. 528. There is therefore no need to emend *pluribus*, v. 324.

2 *Milicies* is rare; in the one classical example that we have found (*CIL* iii. 6687) it appears to be only a variant form on *militia* (cf. *amicitia/amicities, avaritia/avarities*). Here, however, and in *EE*, p. 20, it apparently has a specialized sense, 'omnes enim erant nobiles, omnes plenae aetatis robore ualentes, omnes cuiuis pugnae satis habiles . . . Talis itaque milicies . . . intrat pelagus.' *Milicies* here cannot mean all Canute's forces, nor in the *Carmen* is the combed and anointed *milicies* likely to have included the fyrd – *rustica gens*, as they are later called. It seems rather that we have in these two passages an attempt to distinguish a king's picked private troops, the Housecarls, who were required to have just those qualities enumerated in the *EE*, and who groomed themselves carefully – especially their hair – before battle. It is possible that the rarity of this word (and its seeming limitation in the eleventh century to the bodyguard of a Scandinavian or semi-Scandinavian king) was due to the elimination by this time, except in the north, of the sort of sworn brotherhood of warriors (*comitatus, antrustions, gardingi*) kept by early Germanic kings. Elsewhere we have found *milicies* only in Gower's Latin works. In two instances it is used of the king's knights (*Vox clamantis* i. 1265; 'Verses on Henry IV', in T. Wright, *Political Poems and Songs* ii. 1. 15); in the one other example it means the second estate: 'Clerus, Milicies, et Agricultures' (*Vox clamantis* iii, cap. 1).

3 *P., C.*, and *G.* evidently took the MS. *Vt* as 'like', 'as'. Sheep are not, however, much like foxes, and *M.* suggested *Aut.* We prefer *Vel*, written *Vl* in the MS., a simpler corruption.

wings with noble men. On the highest point of the summit he planted his banner, and ordered his other standards to be set up. All the men dismounted and left their horses in the rear, and taking their stand on foot they let the trumpets sound for battle.

The humble and God-fearing duke led a more measured advance and courageously approached the steeps of the hill. The foot-soldiers ran ahead to engage the enemy with arrows (against crossbow-bolts[4] shields are of no avail!). The helmeted warriors hastened to close ranks; on both sides the foemen raged with brandished spears. As a wild boar standing wearied by the hounds defends himself with his tusks and with foaming jaws scorns to submit to weapons, fearing neither his opponent nor the spears that threaten death, so the great throng of the English contended dauntlessly. Meantime, while the battle hung in ominous suspense and the dread scourge of death in war was pending, a player, whom his most valiant soul greatly ennobled, rode out before the countless army of the duke. He heartened the men of France and terrified the English, and, tossing his sword high, he sported with it. A certain Englishman, when he saw a lone man out of so many thousands move off at a distance, juggling with his sword, was fired with the ardour proper to a soldier's heart – heedless of life, he sprang forward to meet his death. The mummer, surnamed Taillefer,[5] as soon as he had been reached, pricked his horse with the spurs; he pierced the Englishman's shield with his keen lance and hewed the head from the prostrate body with his sword. Turning his eyes on his comrades, he displayed this trophy and showed that the beginning of the battle favoured them. All rejoiced and at the same time called upon the Lord.[6] They exulted that the first blow was theirs, both a tremor and a thrill ran through brave hearts and at once the men hastened to close shields.

First the bands of archers attacked and from a distance transfixed bodies with their shafts and the crossbow-men destroyed the shields as if by a hail-storm, shattered them by countless blows.[7] Now the French attacked the left, the Bretons the right;[8] the duke with the Normans fought in the centre. The English stood firm on their ground in the closest order. They met missile with missile, sword-stroke with sword-stroke; bodies could not be laid down, nor did the dead give place to living soldiers, for each corpse though lifeless stood as if unharmed and held its post; nor would the attackers have been able to penetrate the dense forest of Englishmen had not guile reinforced their strength.

The French, versed in stratagems, skilled in warfare, pretended to fly as if defeated.

---

[4] The four-sided bolts fired from crossbows. The diminutive derivative *quadrellum* gives the Old French *quarrel*:

'Plus qu'arcbaleste ne poet traire un quarrel'
(*Chanson de Roland* (ed. J. Bédier), v. 2265).

Although the words *quadrata iacula* are used only of crossbow-bolts, the bolts themselves are often referred to by various more general words for 'arrow' or 'dart', both in classical Latin (cf. Vegetius, *De Re Militari*, ii. 15 end; iii. 21; iii. 24 end) and in medieval. A good example of this variety occurs in the several accounts of the death of Richard I. In most, the shaft that struck him is called *sagitta*, but it also appears as *quoddam quarellum* (and shot from an *arcubalista*) in John of Oxenedes (*RS* xiii. 102); *quadratum telum* (again from an *arcubalista*) in Gervase of Canterbury (*RS* lxxiii. 91); *jaculum balistae* in the Bermondsey annalist (*Annales Monastici* iii. 448–49); and *spiculum* in the Margam annalist (ibid. i. 26).

[5] Taillefer. The *Carmen* is the only eleventh-century source to name him.

[6] Apparently a reference to the Norman battle-cry, 'Dex aïe'.

[7] The matter of vv. 411–12 expands that of v. 382.

[8] Cf. vv. 429–30. 'Right' and 'left' are given in both passages from the point of view of the subject in each case: French and Bretons here, the *Rustica . . . gens* there.

The English peasantry[9] rejoiced and believed they had won; they pursued in the rear with naked swords. (The unwounded gone, the maimed sank down and the once dense wood was thinned!) When they saw[10] that the ground was weakening the duke's left wing, that a wide road lay open for penetrating the right, charging headlong, each[11] wing of the English vied to be first to slaughter the scattered enemy in various ways. But those who feigned flight wheeled on the pursuers and forced them, held in check, to flee from death. A great part fell there (but the part in close order stood fast), for indeed ten thousand suffered destruction in that place. As meek sheep fall before the ravening lion, so the accursed rabble went down, fated to die. But the very powerful force that survived in the battle[12] attacked more furiously and counted their losses nothing. The English people, prevailing by their number, repulsed the enemy and by their might compelled him to run – and then the flight which had first been a ruse became enforced by valour. The Normans fled, their shields covered their backs!

When the duke saw his people retreat vanquished, he rushed to confront the rout. He rebuked and felled them with his hand, and with his spear he checked and marshalled them.[13] Raging, he himself bared his head of the helmet.[14] To the Normans he showed a furious countenance – to the French he spoke words of entreaty: 'Where are you flying? Where does it avail you to go to die? O France, nobler than all the kingdoms of the earth, – you, who had been the victor – how can you bear to be seen vanquished? You fly from sheep, not men, and fear without cause; what you are doing is most shameful! The sea lies behind: the sea-voyage back is formidable, wind and weather against you. It is hard to return home, hard and long the voyage; here no way of escape remains for you! You will fight to conquer, if you want only to live!'[15] He spoke, and at once their faces grew red

---

9   *Rustica . . . gens* is probably to be taken literally. Although Harold has been said to have strengthened his wings with noble men (v. 374), most of these forces will have been shire levies. The French were on William's right (v. 413); the Bretons, on his left, are known to have been in difficulties.

10   The subject of *Conspicit* is the *Rustica . . . gens* of v. 425. For the inversion of the temporal conjunction *ut*, cf. v. 747. *Cornu tenuare sinistrum* we understand to mean that the terrain of battle broke up the Breton force into small and separate groups. Cf. Ovid, *Remedia amoris* 445:

> Grandia per multos tenuantur flumina rivos

and *Ars amatoria* i. 761:

> leves Proteus modo se tenuabit in undas.

11   The unexpressed antecedent of *utrumque* is the English *cornu* opposed to each of the duke's *cornua*. It cannot be the French and Bretons who are vying with each other to wipe out the enemy, nor can the contest be between the opposing armies as a whole, for the Bretons are in trouble and the French do not wheel round on their pursuers until v. 433.

12   One of the two examples of hiatus in the poem. Cf. v. 610.

13   *Signa ferendo* (v. 446), the 'movement' – actually a near-rout – of William's troops that he hastened to stem. Cf. Caesar, *De bello Gallico* vi. 37. 4: 'Totis trepidatur castris, atque alius ex alio causam tumultus quaerit; neque quo signa ferantur neque quam in partem quisque conveniat provident.' Although Lewis and Short give no examples of the use of *increpare* with a noun of physical instrument, it is not infrequent: cf. Tibullus i. 1. 30, 'stimulo tardos increpuisse boves'; Statius, *Theb.* iii. 431, 'increpat hasta'; Ovid, *Metam.* xiv. 820–21, 'equos . . . ictu verberis increpuit'. Thus *manu* of v. 446 parallels *hasta* of v. 447, each modifying two verbs. William's use of his lance for signals has already been mentioned (v. 310).

14   Cf. *GG*, p. 190; *BT*, Pl. 68.

15   Vv. 450–59 bear comparison with *EE*, p. 20, where Canute, in much the same predicament, says almost the same things: 'Namque memorabat ille abesse diffugium, in terra scilicet hostes, et a litore longe remotas pupes, ideoque, si non uincerent, quod pariter occumbere deberent.'

with shame. They wheeled,[16] they turned to face the enemy. The duke, as leader, was the first to strike; after him the rest laid on. Coming to their senses,[17] they regained strength by scorning fear. As stubble consumes in flames before the breath of the wind, so, O English horde, you went to destruction before the French. At the appearance of the duke the trembling host fell back, as soft wax melts away in face of fire. With drawn sword he hewed to pieces helms and shields, and even his war-horse slew many.

Harold's brother, Gyrth by name, born of a royal line, was undaunted by the face of the lion; posing a javelin, he hurled it from afar with a strong arm. The flying weapon wounded the body of the horse and forced the duke to fight on foot; but reduced to a foot-soldier, he fought yet better, for he rushed upon the young man like a snarling lion. Hewing him limb from limb, he shouted to him: 'Take the crown you have earned from us![18] If my horse is dead, thus I requite you – as a common soldier!'

He spoke, and wheeled round to the mêlée which had instantly sprung up around him; with the strength of Hercules he withstood his opponents. Some he maimed, some he mutilated, some the sword devoured, very many souls he sent to darkness. When he saw a knight of Maine riding through the slaughter, he signed to him with a sword dyed with brains and gore to come to his aid. But he, dreading to be cut down, refused to save him – terrified of death as a hare before a hound! The duke, like a resourceful warrior, suddenly turned upon him;[19] seizing him furiously by the nasal of the helmet, he tumbled him head over heels to the ground, and rushed to mount the horse thus left to him.

O Ruler of Heaven, thou who art tender and pitiful towards us and by divine will rulest all things, what destruction the surviving band of English suffered! Then pity died and cruelty triumphed, life perished, savage death raged, and the sword ran wild! Where Mars holds sway, no man shows mercy!

When the duke was horsed, he then assailed the enemy more strongly; he attacked, he struck like lightning, he pursued. As he strove to win, as he dyed the field with the blood of the slain, the son of Helloc,[20] a swift and able man, lay in wait, meaning to kill him. But when the javelin was cast, the horse received the blow. It fell to the ground, and the duke was on foot and filled with rage! He wondered how he could defend himself or what to do, for he was stunned to have been robbed of two horses in a single encounter. For a moment this left him confounded, then he made light of

---

[16] *Terga retro faciunt* is a play on the expressions *terga uertere*, 'to flee', and *ora retro facere*, 'to turn away, fall back'. Here the French turn about to *face* the enemy.

[17] *M.*, followed by *G.*, took v. 463 as a single sentence; the punctuation of *P.* (followed by *C.*) shows that he understood *ad corda reuersi* as the idiom 'having come to their senses'. Cf. 'Imperator, versus in arcum pravum, non est adhuc ad cor reversus' (*Flores Hist.* ii. 103); 'Ego permodum ad cor revertens absolutionis beneficium petii humiliter ac devote' (*Pat. Rolls Hen III* (1903), p. 210).

[18] William apparently thought that he had killed Harold himself.

[19] *P* and *C.* punctuate, 'Dux memor, ut miles, subito se vertit ad illum'; *M.*, followed by *G.*, 'Dux memor, ut miles subito se vertit ad illum'. It is surely William who turns toward the other. The knight of Maine has already been characterized as a coward, and is unlikely to have changed his mind and approached a duke beset by English and in a very bad temper.

[20] Helloc's son is otherwise unknown, although a similar incident is recounted by Wace (*RR*, vv. 8809–814). The name is not English and may be an attempt at Havelock. But cf. also 'Haruc' mentioned in *The Chronicle of Æthelweard*, ed. A. Campbell (Nelson's Medieval Texts, 1962), pp. lix, 52.

it; he judged that with courage Fortune would smile on him and further his vows without deceit. Therefore he swore that if his right hand had not lost its cunning, the death of his horse should not go unavenged! Seeing the author of the crime lurking at a distance in the press, he rushed forthwith to destroy him. Cutting through his groin with a thrust of his right hand and a merciless sword-stroke, he spilt his entrails on the ground. And then Count Eustace,[21] sprung from noble ancestors, surrounded by a great band of warriors, hastened to be held first to the duke's aid and became a foot-soldier so that he might depart mounted. There was a certain knight whom the count had reared; what Eustace had done for his commander, that man did for him.

Under such auspices, the count and the duke, joining forces, renewed the battle together wherever the clashing arms glittered most brightly. By the swords of both the field was cleared of English, and a number deserted, tottering and exhausted. As a waning wood falls to the stroke of the axe, so the forest of Englishmen was brought to nothing.

Now the victor, joyful France almost ruled the field; already she was seeking the spoils of war[22] when the duke sighted the king far off on the steeps of the hill, fiercely hewing to pieces the Normans who were besetting him. He called Eustace to him; leaving the conflict in that place to the French, he brought strong aid to those hard pressed. Like a second son of Hector, Hugh, the noble heir of Ponthieu, escorted these two, prompt in service; fourth was Giffard, known by his father's surname:[23] these four bore arms for the destruction of the king.[24] Yet there were many others? These were better than the rest! If anyone doubts this, the true course of the action proves it, for by measureless slaughter Harold was forcing the masters of the field[25] to go

---

[21] Eustace II, count of Boulogne. The *Carmen* is the only source not to particularize him as 'of Boulogne'.

[22] That plundering had begun before the death of Harold is borne out by the Bayeux Tapestry (*BT*, Pl. 71, lower margin).

[23] The four knights who killed Harold are identified by Guy as William, Eustace of Boulogne, Hugh of Ponthieu, and a 'Gilfard', probably Giffard.

[24] That it took several men to kill Harold is supported by FW (1066) and Wace (*RR*, vv. 8859–860). The omission of any description of Harold's death by William of Jumièges and William of Poitiers (who has just said that William would not have feared to meet Harold in single combat) is understandable.

[25] Both *P*. and *C*. have a comma after *tenentes*, indicating that it was read as modifying *cedes*: 'By overwhelming slaughter, holding in itself the decision of battle, Harold was forced to go the way of (all) flesh.' This interpretation, however, required that the text be emended. *P*. would have replaced *Heraldus* with *Heraldum* (the note is missing, but *Heraldus* is the word starred for comment); *cogit(ur)*, the emendation in *C*., is unmetrical.

There are two strong reasons for leaving the text as it stands, in addition to the undesirability of unnecessary emendation. Firstly, it is Harold who is said to have been hewing down the Normans, not the reverse (vv. 533–34), and it was the very success of the four in achieving what these others could not that made them in v. 451 *aliis . . . meliores*. Secondly, *bellica iura* is neither an idiomatic phrase nor even a common combination of words; where it occurs, it means not 'the verdict of battle', but 'the way of war'. Cf.:

Nec querimur caesos: haec bellica jura vicesque
Armorum . . .   (Statius, *Theb.* xii. 552.)

Mox adolescentis vestitus flore juventae,
Armorum studium tractabat, patre jubente,
Sed nec in hoc segnem senserunt bellica jura:
Id quoque posteris cognovit publica cura.

                (Tenth-century poem in praise of King Athelstan, quoted in *GR* i. 145–46.)

Bellica iura must not, therefore, be confused with the singular form *bellico iure* or *iure belli*, 'by right

the way of (all) flesh. The first, cleaving his breast through the shield with his point, drenched the earth with a gushing torrent of blood; the second smote off his head below the protection of the helmet and the third pierced the inwards of his belly with his lance; the fourth hewed off his thigh and bore away the severed limb:[26] the ground held the body thus destroyed.

The flying rumour 'Harold is dead!' spread through the fray and forthwith proud hearts were tamed by fear. The English refused battle. Vanquished, they besought mercy; despairing of life, they fled from death. Two thousand in number the duke sent to Hades then, not counting the other thousands beyond telling. It was evening; already the wheeling heavens were turning day to twilight when God made the duke the victor. Only darkness and flight through the thickets and coverts of the deep forest availed the defeated English. The conqueror, resting meanwhile, passed the night among the dead and waited till day should return. Ever vigilant, the son of Hector pursued the fleeing with slaughter; Mars served as his squire, death raged, his comrade. Till it was fully day he spent the night in varying conflict, not overcome by sleep, nor suffering himself to dream.

After the glorious light of the sun began to shine and cleanse the world of brooding darkness, the duke surveyed the field, and taking up the bodies of his fallen, he buried them in the bosom of the earth. The corpses of the English, strewn upon the ground, he left to be devoured by worms and wolves, by birds and dogs. Harold's dismembered body he gathered together, and wrapped what he had gathered in fine purple linen;[27] and returning to his camp by the sea, he bore it with him, that he might carry out the customary funeral rites.

The mother of Harold, in the toils of overwhelming grief, sent even to the duke himself, asking with entreaties that he would restore to her, unhappy woman, a widow and bereft of three sons, the bones of one in place of the three; or, if it pleased him, she would outweigh the body in pure gold. But the duke, infuriated, utterly rejected both petitions, swearing that he would sooner entrust the shores of that very port to him – under a heap of stones! Therefore, even as he had sworn, he commanded the body to be buried in the earth on the high summit of a cliff; and forthwith a certain man, part Norman, part English, Harold's comrade,[28] willingly did his behest; for he swiftly took up the king's body and buried it, setting over it a stone, and he wrote as epitaph:

---

of conquest', in which the operative word is *iure*, as in *iure hereditario, iure naturali, iure sanguinis*, etc. We have here nothing more than the common medieval idiom *iura tenentes, bellica* merely indicating what kind of rights were possessed: 'Harold was forcing those possessing the rights of war (i.e. the rightful victors) to go the way of (all) flesh.' This view is supported by the statement in vv. 531–34 that the duke had all but won, save for Harold's stubborn resistance. *Actio uera probat* in this passage also bears a quasi-legal meaning; see above, the note to v. 230.

[26] Cf. the description of this incidnet in *GR* ii. 303. *Coxa* may be a euphemism; cf. 'Essai d'interpretation du thème iconographique de la paternité dans l'art byzantin', by S.A. Papadopoulos, in *Cahiers archéologiques: Fin de l'Antiquité et Moyen Age* xviii (Paris, 1969), pp. 120–36.

[27] *Sindon* is used at this period of linen, rather than of cotton, and frequently of both altar-cloths and shrouds. Cf. Petrus Comestor, *Hist. Schol., Exodus* 63. Alan of Lille also speaks of *sindon purpura* (*Planc. Nat., P.L.* ccx. 432C).

[28] I.e. William Malet (cf. *GG*, p. 204 n. 4). The manner in which Malet was part English has not been definitely established. If it could be shown that he had descent from the family of Leofric of Mercia, he would have been a cousin of Harold's queen, and thus connected with him by affinity. *Compater*, at this period, can mean 'godfather', 'connection by spiritual affinity', and 'comrade,

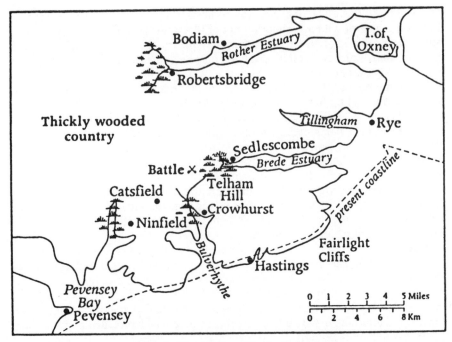

Map 1. The Hastings District in 1066
(Modern place-names are shown for reference)

'By the duke's commands, O Harold, you rest here a king,
That you may still be guardian of the shore and sea.'

The duke, lamenting amidst his people over the buried bones, distributed alms to the poor of Christ. And with the name of duke laid aside, and the king being thus interred, he departed from that place, having himself assumed the royal title.

intimate friend': it is not attested in the sense of 'fellow godfather' until the thirteenth century, and there is no other evidence to support the assertion often met with that Harold and Malet had stood sponsors together. *M.* and *G.* read *Compatit*, in error, for *compatior* is normally deponent and takes its object in the dative (cf. above, v. 69: 'compaciendo sibi').

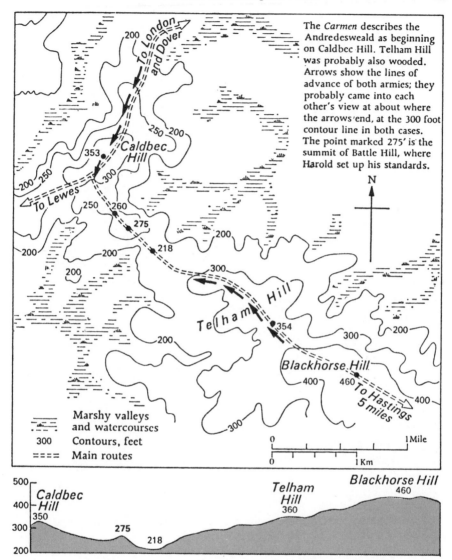

The *Carmen* describes the Andredesweald as beginning on Caldbec Hill. Telham Hill was probably also wooded. Arrows show the lines of advance of both armies; they probably came into each other's view at about where the arrows end, at the 300 foot contour line in both cases. The point marked 275' is the summit of Battle Hill, where Harold set up his standards.

Marshy valleys and watercourses

300 Contours, feet

==== Main routes

Map 2. The Isthmus of the Hastings Peninsula and Battleground

Part II: Interpretations

Given the paucity of primary narratives even for this well covered campaign and battle, reaching a better understanding of the events is often a matter of new interpretations and of discovering new forms of evidence. The selections in this section illustrate both the variety of different sources and interpretive frameworks brought to bear on the issues raised by the primary sources, and the inability of those attempts to solve every problem.

A. Anglo-Saxons and Normans

What sort of armies fought at Hastings? These two articles look beyond the immediate accounts of the campaign and battle to the institutional histories of military service in England and Normandy before 1066. Understanding the two societies before the Conquest not only allows a more accurate impression of the forces on the field in October 1066, but is also necessary in appraising the effect of the Conquest on *both* societies in the century after 1066. What were the key similarities and differences between late Anglo-Saxon England and pre-Conquest Normandy in terms of military organization and social structure? Were the similarities more important than the differences? These issues underlie the articles presented here.

7. Richard Abels, 'Bookland and Fyrd Service in Late Saxon England'

Richard Abels examines the bases of military obligation in eleventh century England in this article. Who served in the Anglo-Saxon *fyrd*, or army, and why did they serve? Central to his argument is the nature of 'bookland' – land held by a royal charter or 'book' (*boc*) – and its relationship to the ties of lordship that linked the Anglo-Saxon warrior class of thegns together. The picture that emerges is of a fairly sophisticated system, subject to regional variation but conforming to a basic pattern throughout the kingdom. An addendum to the article addresses the place of household warriors such as the housecarls in the overall Anglo-Saxon military establishment, and looks more specifically at Harold's army at Hastings in the light of his findings.

Reprinted from *Anglo-Norman Studies* 7 (1984), 1–25. Copyright Richard Abels 1984, 1985,1996.

Bookland and Fyrd Service in Late Saxon England

Richard Abels

Few problems in early English history have generated as much controversy and yet remained so far from being satisfactorily resolved as that of military obligation on the eve of the Conquest. It is not difficult to account for the interest; the topic is, after all, intimately connected with the long and often bitter debate over the origins of English feudalism.[1] Nor must one search long for the source of the uncertainty. Practically every piece of evidence that we possess seems tolerant of two or more plausible interpretations. Starting with the same texts, scholars have thus come to radically different conclusions concerning the nature of military obligation in late Saxon England. Some have contended that *fyrd* service was the duty of peasants, that the *expeditio* of the land-books and Domesday custumals was in fact limited to *ceorls* recruited territorially. The thegn's obligation, they assert, was completely different in origin, following from his rank. Whether he held fifty hides of land or one was irrelevant, for he was a warrior and a king's man by birth.[2] Others have argued that the late Anglo-Saxon *fyrd* was essentially a feudal host of landed aristocrats and their commended thegns, whose obligation to service derived from their possession of land.[3] The one point upon which all seem agreed is that land played a crucial role in the recruitment of the Confessor's army. The precise nature of that role, however, has been at the very core of this controversy.

An earlier version of this paper was presented at the Nineteenth International Congress on Medieval Studies, held at Western Michigan University on 11 May 1984. I am very grateful to Professor J.M.W. Bean, the director of my doctoral studies, whose perceptive criticism led me to rethink and rework a number of my arguments, always to their benefit. I would also like to thank Professor C. Warren Hollister, who was kind enough to read a draft of this piece, for his helpful comments and much appreciated encouragement.

[1] The 'Feudal Revolution' has generated an extensive literature. For the historiography of the controversy see David C. Douglas, *The Norman Conquest and British Historians*, Glasgow 1946; reprinted in *Time and the Hour. Some Collected Papers of David C. Douglas*, London 1977, and C. Warren Hollister, 'The Norman Conquest and the Genesis of English Feudalism', *American Historical Review*, 6, 1961, 641–64; *idem*, '1066: The "Feudal Revolution" ', *American Historical Review*, 73, 1968, 708–23. The debate has been continued most recently by R. Allen Brown, whose book, *The Origins of English Feudalism*, New York 1973, defends and elaborates upon J.H. Round's thesis that the Normans introduced feudalism into England, and John Gillingham, 'The introduction of knight service into England', *ante*, IV, 1981, 53–64, who argues that no such 'feudal revolution' occurred.
[2] Notably F.M. Stenton, *The First Century of English Feudalism 1066–1166*, 2nd edn, Oxford 1961, 115–52.
[3] See, e.g., Eric John, *Land Tenure in Early England*, Leicester 1960, 140–61; *idem, Orbis Britanniae and Other Studies*, Leicester 1966, 128–53; *idem*, in *The Anglo-Saxons*, ed. James Campbell, Ithaca, New York 1982, 168–9, 236–7; H.G. Richardson and G.O. Sayles, *The Governance of Mediaeval England from the Conquest to Magna Carta*, Edinburgh 1963, 22–61. Cf. C. Warren Hollister, *Anglo-Saxon Military Institutions*, Oxford 1982, 59–84, on the personnel of the 'select fyrd'.

The land-books with their reservations of the 'common burdens', the legal compilations, and the Domesday Book custumals all represent military service in late Anglo-Saxon England as rooted in the soil. But was the obligation to render such service territorial, tenurial, or personal? To put it another way, who served in the king's host and why? Fragmentary as the sources are, the answer they give seems clear to me: the obligation to serve the king in arms rested in the eleventh century upon a dual foundation of land tenure and lordship. On the one hand, those who possessed land either in book-right or as a royal loan were obliged to render the military service due from their holdings, just as they owed the payment of geld. On the other hand, those thegns who were personally commended to the king were expected to attend him on campaign if so ordered.

The attempt to characterise these duties as 'Germanic' or 'feudal' is fruitless. Military obligation had evolved and changed as the king's need for and ability to exact armed service from his subjects had changed. Just as English law on the eve of the Conquest was a hodgepodge of archaic custom and royal innovation that varied according to locale, thus preserving if not the reality then at least the memory of independent kingdoms and peoples, so the defence of the realm depended upon a system that had developed organically over the centuries and which reflected the military history of England. Late Anglo-Saxon military obligation looked back to the war bands of seventh-century rulers such as Oswald and Oswiu and to the 'New Model' army of Alfred and his successors, not forward to the *servicia debita* of the Conqueror and his sons. The long and complicated history of the evolution of the process whereby *fyrd* service was fixed to bookland is beyond the scope of the present paper.[4] I wish to emphasise here only that discussions of the *fyrd* need not and should not be conducted in the shadow of Anglo-Norman 'feudalism'.

By the beginning of the eleventh century *fyrd* service was intimately connected with bookland. The legal compilations of the early eleventh century evidence the closeness of this tie. By the reign of Cnut bookland was conceived as land for which one performed *fyrdfaereld*. Thus, II *Cnut* 79 stipulates that if a landowner has 'defended his land on campaign either by sea or land' (*se the land gewerod haebbe on scypfyrde and on landfyrde*), he was both to hold the land undisturbed by litigation during his days, and to have the right to dispose of it as he pleased upon his death.[5] Although this text does not use the term *bocland*, its language leaves no doubt as to the type of tenure acquitted by attendance in the *fyrd*, for free disposal forms the very essence of book-right. One may infer from this, then, that a landholder's title to land possessed in book-right obliged him to 'defend' it in person on the king's campaigns. Conversely, we learn from other laws and the charters that one who deserted the royal host or broke the king's peace while in the field forfeited his land.[6] All land that he

---

[4] The development of the 'common burdens' (the three military obligations, bridge repair, maintenance of fortifications, and *fyrd* service, that were generally reserved in the Old English landbooks) has been discussed by Eric John, *Land Tenure*, 64–79 and Nicholas Brooks, 'The development of military obligations in eighth- and ninth-century England', in *England Before the Conquest*, ed. Peter Clemoes and Kathleen Hughes, Cambridge 1971, 69–84. My views on this subject, which differ considerably from those advanced by John and Brooks, will appear in a future publication.

[5] A.J. Robertson, ed. and trans., *The Laws of the Kings of England from Edmund to Henry I*, 1925; reprint, New York 1974, 214–15.

[6] Penalties for desertion of the *fyrd* are given in V *Aethelred* 28; VI *Aethelred* 35; II *Cnut* 77; Robertson, *Laws*, 86–7, 102–3, 214–15. For an example of forfeiture for breaking the king's peace while on campaign, see John Kemble, ed., *Codex Diplomaticus Aevi Saxonici*, 6 vols, London

held on loan reverted to the lord who had granted it to him, and all his bookland passed back into the king's hand.[7]

The *Rectitudines Singularum Personarum*, a work attributed to the early eleventh century, affords further insight into the relationship between bookland and *fyrd*-service. This tract sets forth the rights and obligations of the lord of an estate and of the various groups of men who dwelled upon it under him.[8] The text begins with the holder of the tenure, termed here a 'thegn':

> Thegn's law. The law of the thegn is that he be worthy of [i.e., entitled to][9] his book-right, and that he do three things in respect of his land: service in the host [*fyrdfaereld*], the repairing of fortresses [*burhbote*], and work on bridges [*brycegeweorc*]. [§ 1.] Also in respect of many estates, further land-dues [*landriht*] arise on the king's order [or summons; *cyninges gebanne*] such as service connected with the deer hedge at the king's residence,[10] and equipping a guardship [*frithscip*], and guarding the coast [*saeweard*], and guarding the lord's person [*haefodweard*], and military guard [*fyrdweard*], almsgiving and church dues, and many other things.[11]

Military service is thus the fundamental obligation of the thegn. But the *Rectitudines* does not connect such service to the 'freedom' of the thegn. Rather, the lord of the estate owes the performance of the 'common burdens' as a condition of holding his land in book-right. Moreover, he owes this service not to some abstract 'state' or 'folk' but to his *lord*, the king.

While the three 'common burdens' may be the most prominent services due from a thegn's bookland, they hardly constitute all the service that the king could require from his thegn in respect of his land. If we examine the duties enumerated in chapter 1 § 1 and compare them with those owed by the *geneat*, enumerated in chapter 2, we find that the relationship between the king and his thegn paralleled in some respects that which existed between the thegn and his *geneat*.[12] It would thus seem that the author of the *Rectitudines* viewed bookland as a privileged but still dependent form

1839–48, no. 1304; catalogued in P.H. Sawyer, *Anglo-Saxon Charters: an annotated list and bibliography*, Royal Historical Society Guides and Handbooks 8, London 1968, no. 927.

7   II *Cnut* 77 § 1. Cf. II *Cnut* 13; Robertson, *Laws*, 180–1.

8   Felix Liebermann, ed., *Die Gesetze der Angelsachsen*, i (Texts), Halle 1903, 444–53; *EHD*, i, 875–9. See the commentary on this text by F.M. Stenton, *Anglo-Saxon England*, 3rd edn, Oxford 1971, 473–6. Cf. H.P.R. Finberg, 'Anglo-Saxon England to 1042', in *idem*, ed., *The Agrarian History of England and Wales*, i, Cambridge 1972, 512–15, 519.

9   *Wyrthe* [or *weorthe*]. The phrase *wyrthe beon* often appears in Anglo-Saxon writs with the meaning of 'to be entitled to' or 'to possess lawfully' some privilege, estate, or office. See, e.g., F.E. Harmer, ed., *Anglo-Saxon Writs*, Manchester 1952, nos 8, 12, 16, 28, 44, 51, 69, 80, *passim*. Cf. Harmer's comments at pp. 63–4, 433, 444, 475–6. See also I *Aethelred* 1 §§ 7, 14 (Roberston, *Laws*, 52–5); 'The London Charter of William the Conqueror', ch. 2 (Robertson, *Laws*, 230–1). Cf. *ASC* 'E', s.a. 1046, Charles Plummer, *Two of the Saxon Chronicles Parallel*, i, 1892; reprint, Oxford 1952, 168. The implication seems to be that one who is deserving of an honour is entitled to it.

10 Cf. *Rectitudines* 2, 3 § 4; Liebermann, i, 445, 446.

11 *EHD*, ii, 875. Liebermann, i, 444.

12 Liebermann, i, 445; *EHD*, ii, 875. The 'geneat's right', which included carrying and riding services, guarding his lord's person, and maintaining his deer hedges, is strikingly similar to the dues owed the king by his thegns in southern Lancashire 'in the time of King Edward'. Cf. *Domesday Book*, i, 269b ('inter Ripam et Mersham').

of tenure. The thegn was the lord of the estate, but he held his land *de rege*,[13] rendering service to the king for it, just as his own man, the *geneat*, held of and rendered service to him.

The *Rectitudines* asserts that a thegn was to 'do three things in respect of his land'. It would be rash, however, to assume from the use of 'do' in the text that thegns were expected to acquit the 'common burdens' through their own labour. Presumably wealthy thegns would not have repaired fortresses and bridges with their own hands or personally discharged their obligations at the king's deer hedge or kept watch on the sea coast. Rather, they would have been responsible for such services. The third chapter of the *Rectitudines*, which enumerates the duties of the cottar, a free tenant endowed with five or more acres, supports this view. The cottar, we are told, must 'acquit his lord's demesne [*werige his hlafordes inland*], if so ordered, by keeping watch on the sea coast [*saeward*] and by working at the king's deer hedge [*aet cyniges deorhege*] and such things according to his condition [*aet swilean thingan, swilc his maeth sy*]'. We hear an echo of this last clause in the Lancashire Domesday's description of the inhabitants and customs of 'the land between the Ribble and Mersey Rivers'. The thegns of this locality, king's men of modest wealth, each living on a hide or so of royal land, were obliged to 'build the king's lodges, and whatever pertained to them, fisheries, woodland enclosures, and stag-beats, just as if they were villagers [*sicut villani*]'.[14] 'Sicut villani' can only mean that thegns ordinarily did not perform such menial labour but could be required to do so by local custom. We are led to conclude from these and similar passages in Domesday Book that thegns and peasants rendered different sorts of service.[15] Although men of thegnly rank sometimes laboured at deer hedges and performed other such manual labour in the service of the king, they were not ordinarily expected to do so. All but the most humble of thegns would have dispatched peasant tenants to take care of these tasks.

Was the labour necessary for the upkeep of fortresses and bridges also performed by peasants? One would assume so, but here the *Rectitudines* proves to be of little value, since neither appears among the obligations of its cottars and *geburs*. The text simply states that the bookholder was responsible for maintaining the bridges and fortifications in his neighbourhood; it does not specify who was to perform the actual work. Domesday Book must be called on to fill the gap. The Domesday survey of Chester relates that the royal reeve was wont in the time of King Edward ('T.R.E.') to call up one man from each hide of that shire for the repair of the city walls, and that the lord of that man was responsible for his appearance. If someone failed to appear, a 40s fine was to be paid, not, however, by the delinquent peasant but by his

[13] Cf. Frank Barlow, *Edward the Confessor*, Berkeley 1970, 147–8. Circuit 1 of Domesday Book, comprising the shires of Kent, Sussex, Surrey, Hampshire, and Berkshire, uses 'N tenuit de rege', as its standard formula for expressing book-right. This, of course, is merely a Norman interpretation of Anglo-Saxon tenurial practice, not unlike the use of the terms *relevatio* and *relevamentum* to describe the Old English heriot in Domesday Book. See, e.g., *Domesday Book*, i, 1, 56, 280b. For an example of a pre-Conquest tenure described as *de rege* in the South Midlands circuit, see *Domesday Book*, i, 151b (Drayton, Bucks.).

[14] *Domesday Book*, i, 269b ('inter Ripam et Mersham').

[15] Domesday Book records that the Bishop of Worcester's tenant at Huddington, T.R.E., held 'as a rustic doing service'. *Domesday Book*, i, 173b. Similarly, the entry for Kempsey refers to *rusticum opus*. Cf. *Domesday Book*, i, 67b (Durnford, Wilts.), where a tenant of the Church of Wilton served his landlord 'as a thegn'.

lord.[16] Apparently, the thegns of Cheshire 'did' *burhbot* in respect of their land by making sure that their peasants answered the reeve's summons, much as the thegn of the *Rectitudines* acquitted himself of his obligation at the king's deer hedge. The Cheshire customal suggests that while the lords of bookland may have owed *burhbot* and the related service of *brycegeweorc* as a condition of their tenure, their peasant tenants actually performed the necessary labour.

The third 'common burden', *fyrdfaereld*, was different. Bookholders were not only responsible for supplying troops to the king, they acquitted their land personally in his host. This, at any rate, is the inference drawn from the military provisions of Cnut's second law code. II *Cnut* 79, as we have mentioned above, states explicitly that landholders defended their land 'on scypfyrde and on landfyrde', and that such service was to be done in full view of the shire. Of course, it is possible that the 'defended' (*gewerod*) of this clause meant no more than 'acquitted the land of its military obligations', but such a possibility seems unlikely in light of the other two laws in this series. Taken together II *Cnut* 77–9 draw a picture of a *fyrd* manned by landholders, in which commended men fought at the side of their lords. Thus if a warrior were to desert his lord out of cowardice while on campaign, he was to lose his life and property (II *Cnut* 77). But if a man were to distinguish himself in battle by falling by the side of his lord, his lord was to remit the payment of his heriot and his heirs were to succeed to his landed estate (II *Cnut* 78). In view of this and the distinctly martial connotation of the word 'thegn' in the texts of the tenth and eleventh centuries, one may reasonably assume that the first requirement of the 'thegn's law' of the *Rectitudines* was that he serve in the *fyrd* 'in respect of his land'.

The later law codes lend support to this construction of the nature of bookland in the *Rectitudines*, indirectly suggesting that bookland was a dependent tenure held directly of the king. According to the dooms, the possession of such a tenure placed a man in a special relationship with the king. In effect, they represent the king as the landholder's own *landhlaford*. For just as a 'landlord' was to be responsible for the good behaviour of those who dwelt under him and entitled to the fines incurred by them,[17] so I *Aethelred* 1 §14 represents the king as possessed of the exclusive right to take *wites* from those who held bookland.[18] The holder of the book was, in fact, so closely associated with the king that he could not be forced to pay compensation or answer for a crime unless a king's reeve was present.[19] What makes this piece of legislation all the more remarkable is how well it dovetails with III *Aethelred* 11, which states that no one but the king should have jurisdiction [*socne*] over a king's thegn.[20] While neither the law codes nor Domesday Book explicitly describes the

---

16 *Domesday Book*, i, 262b.

17 For 'landlords' standing surety for their tenants, see III *Aethelstan* 7 §1; F.L. Attenborough, *The Laws of the Earliest English Kings*, 1922, reprinted New York 1974, 144–5. For the right of a *landhlaford* or *landrica* to the fines incurred within his lands, see, e.g., I *Aethelred* 3 §1 and III *Aethelred* 3 §§2 and 3. Cf. VI *Aethelstan* [the *Iudicia Civitatis Lundoniae*] 1 §1; Attenborough, 156–7. The *landhlaford* is equated explicitly with the holder of bookland in the last law, the clear implication being that the possession of a book conferred regalian rights. Cf. the glosses in the tenth-century supplement to 'Aelfric's Vocabulary': *fundos, bocland vel landrice*. T. Wright and R.P Wülker, eds, *Anglo-Saxon and Old English Vocabularies*, vol. I, 1884, reprinted Darmstadt 1968, 247.

18 Robertson, *Laws*, 54–5

19 Robertson, *Laws*, 54–5.

20 Robertson, *Laws*, 68–9. The first and third codes of Aethelred have points in common. Both appear

king as the personal lord of every bookholder,[21] nevertheless, the two laws cited above strongly suggest that the holder of such tenure enjoyed a relationship to the king analogous to the one created by the act of commendation.

Even the interposition of some other lord between the king and the bookholder did not affect the royal interest and rights over his book. The king continued to assert and exercise his authority over such land, exacting from it the *utwaru* owed him. And just as land held on loan from some lord reverted to that lord if his man made forfeiture,[22] so all bookland passed back into the king's hand, no matter whom the landholder claimed as his chosen lord.[23]

Once the connection between bookland tenure and royal lordship is understood, certain difficulties in the Domesday passages concerning *fyrd* service are resolved, and the basis of military obligation in late Anglo-Saxon England becomes far clearer. But before we examine the two major texts, the customs of Worcestershire and Berkshire, we must offer a caveat. Any study of late Anglo-Saxon institutions must inevitably revolve around Domesday Book, yet the problems of interpretation associated with this work are notorious and extend to the passages dealing with military matters. On the whole the survey is simply unconcerned with detailing the workings of the pre-Conquest *fyrd*. This is quite understandable if, as has been plausibly suggested, the Inquest was undertaken to provide William with a record of his kingdom's wealth and resources at a time when such information was crucial.[24] Just as Domesday Book is silent on the knight-service that the Conqueror expected from his tenants-in-chief, it says little about military arrangements 'on the day that King Edward was alive and dead'. The only aspect of the old *fyrd* that seems to have interested the commissioners was its fiscal side, the customary payments to the king in lieu of such service and the fines owed the king for failure to answer his summons. Nevertheless, the scattered references to *expeditio* in Domesday Book, as ambiguous

---

to have been issued c.996. Patrick Wormald, 'Aethelred the Lawmaker', in *Ethelred the Unready*, ed. David Hill, British Archaeological reports, British ser. 59, 1978, 63–4.

[21] E.g., II *Cnut* 13, 13 § 1, 77, 77 § 1, in which we find bookholders commended to men other than the king. Many of the lesser Domesday Book bookholders were commended T.R.E. to men of local importance, often to more powerful landholders within the same hundred. E.g., Burgraed, father of Eadwine, dominated the lordship pattern within Stodden and Willey Hundreds, Bed., as did Aelmer of Bennington in Broadwater Hundred, Mddlx. Even well endowed landowners occasionally 'bowed' to lords other than the king T.R.E. Thus Aki, who held 16 hides in Hertfordshire, was both a king's thegn and a *homo* of Earl Harold. *Domesday Book*, i, 138, 142.

[22] II *Cnut* 77. Cf. A.J. Robertson, ed., *Anglo-Saxon Charters*, 2nd edn, Cambridge 1956, 62, 66, 88, 168, 178.

[23] E.g., II *Cnut* 13 § 1; Robertson, *Laws*, 180–1: 'And if he [an outlaw] has bookland, it shall be forfeited into the hands of the king without regard to the question of whose man he is'. Cf. II *Cnut* 77, 77 § 1; Robertson, *Laws*, 214–15. The principle that bookland was forfeited to the king and that loanland returned to the lord who had title to it was established by the beginning of the tenth century. See F.E. Harmer, ed., *Select English Historical Documents of the Ninth and Tenth Centuries*, Cambridge 1914, no. 18, pp. 30–2; Sawyer, no. 1445. Cf. Robertson, *Charters*, 62, 66, 88, 168, 178.

[24] As David C. Douglas emphasises, *William the Conqueror: The Norman Impact upon England*, Berkeley, California 1964, 346–56, the making of Domesday Book must be viewed against the backdrop of the threatened invasion by Cnut VI, king of the Danes, in 1085–6. In view of the sequence of events in *ASC*, s.a. 1085, it seems possible that Domesday Book was initiated, at least in part, so that William could better support his mercenary army. On the importance of stipendiary troops in the early Anglo-Norman kingdom, see two important articles by J.O. Prestwich: 'War and Finance', *TRHS*, 5th ser. 4, 1952, 19–43; and 'The military household of the Norman kings', *EHR* 96, 1981, 1–35.

as each alone may be, taken together allow us a glimpse into the nature of military obligation on the eve of the Conquest.

Without any doubt, the Domesday survey of Worcestershire provides the most complete evidence for a study of this topic. The customs of this county read:

> When the king goes against the enemy, should anyone summoned by his edict remain, if he is a man so free that he has his soke and sake, and can go with his land to whomever he wishes, he is in the king's mercy for all of his land. But if the free man of some other lord leads another man to the host in his place, he pays 40s to his lord who received the summons. But if nobody at all goes in his place, he shall pay his lord 40s; but his lord shall pay the entire amount to the king.[25]

Although this passage is primarily concerned with the king's financial interests in the *fyrd*, that is, with the forfeitures that he could claim if someone failed to fulfil his military service, it also illuminates the nature of the obligation to serve the king on campaign and the organisation of the royal host. The text identifies two separate categories of free men who attend the king on expedition. The first is clearly composed of men of considerable rank, for they are described as 'so free' that they not only hold their lands by book-right, indicated in the text by the stock formula for the right of free disposal,[26] but also enjoy rights of jurisdiction, sake and soke, over those who dwell upon their estates. Let us label this group, A. The second category of *fyrdmen* in this shire, B, is also made up of free men, and this is not at all surprising when one remembers that to be 'fyrdworthy', one had to be free.[27] But all similarity between the two groups ends here. In almost every other respect, they seem to differ. The text speaks of A as being summoned to the *fyrd* by the king's edict; B apparently receives no such summons. If a man from group A fails to respond to the king's call, all of his land may be lost to the king; one of group B, on the contrary, faces no more than *fyrdwite*, a money fine of 40 shillings, for neglecting the host, and this money is given, not to the king, but to the man's lord. And while the text makes a point of defining the tenurial privileges enjoyed by A, it never specifically mentions B's rights over the land, a silence which itself eloquently attests B's lesser freedom.

In fact, while A is identified by his free tenure, B seems to be identified more on the basis of lordship. For this group is introduced in the text with a cryptic statement concerning their commendation: they are the free men of 'some other lord' [*cuius-cunque alterius domini*]. But other than whom? The Domesday jurors have handed us a puzzle. The difference in lordship was deemed both worthy of mention, and yet so obvious that it called for no further elaboration. To comprehend its meaning, one must know who the lords of A and B were. It is reasonable to surmise that the lord of group A was in fact the king himself. This would explain why it was unnecessary to name him explicitly in the text; the Worcestershire customs, after all, were royal customs set forth by the local jurors upon the demand and for the benefit of the king.

25 *Domesday Book*, i, 172. On this text see also Frederic Maitland, *Domesday Book and Beyond*, 1897; reprint, New York 1966, 159.

26 J.H. Round, *Feudal England*, 1895; reprint, New York 1964, 20–30; Carl Stephenson, 'Commendation and Related Problems in Domesday', *EHR* 59, 1944, 292ff.

27 F.E. Harmer, ed. and trans., *Anglo-Saxon Writs*, Manchester 1952, no. 61, pp. 249, 475–6 (comments).

Nor need we rest this identification solely upon the logic of this argument. Rather, one should ask who would have been the lord of a man who possessed not only his lands in book-right but the perquisites of justice as well. The answer, of course, is the king, for only he could book land and confer franchises of immunity. Indeed, II *Cnut* 12 describes a grant of jurisdiction as a special honour that a king would bestow upon a favoured subject.[28]

The *fyrdmen* of group B were therefore the men of lords other than the king. The text itself gives some reason to believe that they were in fact commended to members of group A, for their lords are described as the recipients of the king's summons, and this, as one may remember, is a characteristic of the *fyrd* warriors of group A. The Domesday Book survey of this shire and *Hemming's Cartulary*, a work concerned with the lands of the Church of Worcester and ascribed to an English monk of the late eleventh century,[29] lend support to this thesis. When one peruses the folios of the Worcestershire Domesday and the eleventh-century charters relating to the county, at least one great lord stands out: the bishop of Worcester, the lord of the triple hundred of Oswaldslow.[30] In the eleventh century the bishop exercised regalian authority within Oswaldslow, and among the services that he demanded from his tenants was the performance of armed service upon the king's expeditions, whether by land or by sea.[31] While technically this service belonged to the *cyninges utwaru*, the bishop held his lands 'so freely' that he alone answered for the royal service owed from them. As Domesday Book stated:

> The Church of St Mary of Worcester has one hundred called Oswaldslow, in which lie 300 hides. From these the bishop of the same church has by a constitution of ancient times [*a constitutione antiquorum temporum*][32] all the profits of jurisdiction [*redditiones socharum*] and all customary dues pertain-

---

[28] Robertson, *Laws*, 180. Cf. *The (So-Called) Laws of William I* 2 §§3, 4; Robertson, *Laws*, 252–5. Cf. the Domesday customs of Nottinghamshire, *Domesday Book*, i, 280b, which stress the king's authority over those thegns who held their land with sake and soke. Cf. also *Domesday Book*, i, 1 (Dover, Kent). On the meaning of sake and soke, see Maitland, 80–107, 282–3; *Julius Goebel, Felony and Misdemeanour*, 1937; reprint, Philadelphia 1976, 338–78 (an unconvincing attempt to limit sake and soke to the *profits* of justice and to deny the existence of private jurisdiction before the Conquest); N.D. Hurnard, 'The Anglo-Norman Franchises', *EHR* 64, 1949, 289–327, 433–60; Helen Cam, 'The Evolution of the Medieval English Franchise', *Speculum*, 32 (1957), 427–42; reprint, *idem, Lawfinders and Law Makers in Medieval England*, London 1962, 22–43. Only Cam's interpretation takes into account the growing power of the Anglo-Saxon kings during the tenth and eleventh centuries.

[29] *Hemingi Chartularium Ecclesia Wigorniensis*, Th. Hearne, ed., Oxford 1723. For an important discussion of this cartulary, see N.R. Ker, 'Hemming's Cartulary', in *Studies in Medieval History presented to Frederick Maurice Powicke*, 1948; reprint, Oxford 1969, 49–75.

[30] *Domesday Book*, i, 172. Cf. Walter de Gray Birch, ed., *Cartularium Saxonicum*, 3 vols and index, 1885–93; reprint, New York 1964, iii, no. 1136 (Sawyer, no. 1368). For other relevant charters, consult Sawyer, nos 1297–9, 1302, 1305, 1306–75, 1409, 1411, 1412.

[31] Seem, e.g., *Heming*, i, 264; Benjamin Thorpe, *Diplomatarium Anglicum Aevi Saxonici*, London 1865, 450–1. The monk Hemming gives details about the lease of Crowle to Simund, a Danish *miles* of Leofric, earl of Mercia. Simund agreed to perform service *to the monastery* for this land on expedition, by land and by sea ['ut pro ea ipse ad expeditionem terra marique (quae tunc crebro agebatur) monasterio serviret']. Cf. *Domesday Book*, i, 174 (Crowle, Worcs.).

[32] If the *Altitonantis* charter, Birch, no. 1135 (Sawyer, no. 731), is genuine, this immunity is to be dated to Eadgar's reign. See Eric John, 'War and Society in the Tenth Century: The Maldon Campaign', *TRHS* 5th ser. 27, 1977, 192–3 (and references). Cf. R.R. Darlington. *The Cartulary of Worcester Priory*, Oxford 1975, xiii–xviii. Note that the Domesday jurors believed that the immunity dated back to 'ancient times'.

ing therein to the demesne support and to the king's service [*regis servitium*] and his own, so that no sheriff [Hemming's *indiculum* adds here 'or *exactor* of royal service'[33]] can have any claim there for any plea or any other cause. Thus the whole county witnesses.[34]

The landholders of Oswaldslow thus 'defended' their land to the bishop rather than to the king or to one of his officers. The exclusion of the sheriff meant that the bishop himself would have been responsible for bringing his complement of *fyrd* warriors into the field, and indeed, in 1066 we find that the bishop had a tenant named Eadric, whom Hemming describes as 'the pilot of the bishop's ship and the leader of the same bishop's military forces owed to the king's service [*ductor exercitus eiusdem episcopi ad servitium regis*]'.[35] Undoubtedly, the bishop of Worcester should be numbered among the lords of the *fyrdmen* of group B.

Although the bishop of Worcester's position in the shire was exceptional, rivalled only by that of the earl of Mercia, there were others 'so free that they had their soke and sake and could go with their land to whomsoever they wished'. Three other churches, Evesham, Pershore, and Westminster, held between them the lordship of four hundreds.[36] St Peter's of Westminster possessed its lands 'as quit and free of all claims as King Edward held in his demesne',[37] and all enjoyed the pleas of their free men and most forfeitures that they might make.[38] As Domesday Book put it in its description of Pershore, the abbot 'has the forfeitures from his 100 hides as he ought to have from his own land . . . and all others enjoy the same from their lands'.[39] The implication seems to be that in Worcestershire book-right ordinarily carried with it sake and soke over the inhabitants of the estate. If this is correct, then a king's thegn like Beworhtwine who, in Hemming's words, had his land 'freely by inheritance, having, that is, the power of giving it to whomsoever he wished, since it was his paternal inheritance, for which he owed service to no man but the king', would also have had jurisdictional rights and, consequently, would have been responsible for the *fyrd* service arising from the lands of his tenants.[40] These pre-Conquest grants of liberty had in fact alienated so much of

[33] *Exactor regalis servitii*. Hemming's version of the Domesday Worcester liberties contains a number of other small differencs. See VCH *Worcestershire* i, London 1901, 288–9. Cf. *Heming*, i, 287.

[34] *Domesday Book* i, 172b.

[35] *Heming*, i, 81. Cf. *Heming*, i, 77, cited by Maitland, 308. Further discussion of the military obligations of the bishop of Worcester can be found in Maitland, 307–9; John, *Land Tenure*, 115–26; *idem*, *Orbis Britanniae*, 149–51. Cf. Stenton, *English Feudalism*, 128 (which does not take into account Hemming's description of the Crowle lease); R. Allen Brown, *Origins of English Feudalism*, London 1973, 54ff.

[36] *Domesday Book*, i, 172 (the county customs); 172b (lands of Worcester); 174b (lands of Westminster); 175–175b (lands of Pershore); 175b–176 (lands of Evesham). See also Harmer, *Writs*, nos 73–106 (pp. 286–372), 115–16 (pp. 407–11).

[37] *Domesday Book*, i, 172 (the county customs); 174b–175 (Pershore, Worcs.). Cf. Harmer, *Writs*, nos 99–100, pp. 363–5.

[38] The county customs, *Domesday Book*, i, 172, state that the king usually reserved the forfeitures arising from breach of the peace, obstruction of justice, forcible entry into a home, and rape (for which there was no monetary compensation, the only amends being *de corpore justicia*). The Church of Worcester was unique in possessing all these forfeitures in its lands. See Harmer, *Writs*, 319. One should note the absence of fyrdwite from this list.

[39] *Domesday Book*, i, 175b (*terra Sanctae Mariae de Persore*, Worcs).

[40] *Heming*, i, 263, cited by Round, VCH, *Worcestershire*, i, 267. Cf. Harmer, *Writs*, nos 85 (pp. 351–2) and 1200 (pp. 364–5).

the profits of royal justice that the sheriff was provoked to complain in the shire return: 'In this county there are twelve hundreds; seven are so quit, the shire says, that the sheriff has nothing in them, and therefore he [the sheriff] says that he loses much in farm [*in firma*]'.[41] The Worcestershire military customs, concerned as they are with the money fines arising from neglect of the *fyrd*, can only be fully appreciated if read in light of this county's jurisdictional arrangements.

An analysis of the Worcestershire customs thus suggests that there were two distinct types of *fyrdmen* in this shire. On the one hand, there were the great landowners, the king's prelates, agents, and shire thegns, all of whom held privileged tenures and seigneurial rights over the lands of other free men. These were the men to whom the king addressed his summonses and writs.[42] On the other hand, there were lesser *fyrdmen* drawn from the lower rungs of free society,[43] men who were commended and sometimes held their land under the jurisdiction of the local magnates.

The gulf between the social and legal status of the two groups helps explain the discrepancy in the penalties they faced for neglect of military service. The *fyrdmen* of group A stood in an especially close relationship to the king. They held their land by book-right, which made them the king's justiciables; they themselves possessed by royal favour rights of jurisdiction; and lastly, they were the king's own men. This threefold tie to the king aggravated their offence. Although the law codes regard simple neglect of the 'common burdens' as emendable by the payment of a *wite*,[44] the *fyrdmen* of group A were guilty of more than mere neglect. They had received a personal summons to attend their royal lord in battle, and their failure to respond was wilful disobedience. Loss of their property was appropriate punishment.[45] As king's thegns they were entitled to their bookland, to use the language of the *Rectitudines*, but their rank also obliged them to 'do three things in regard to their land', one of which was the performance of *fyrd* service.[46] Both the refusal to acquit his land as he ought and his despite of the king's just command called into question a thegn's 'worthiness' to hold the book.[47] It is not surprising that the king should have regarded it as having been forfeited into his hands.[48]

---

[41] *Domesday Book*, i, 172; VCH, *Worcestershire*, i, 282. The sheriff was also excluded from the military matters in these seven hundreds, if we can generalise from the triple hundred of Oswaldslow.

[42] Harmer, *Writs*, 14, 52–4. Cf. *Domesday Book*, i, 262 (Chester), on the lord's receipt of a summons from the royal reeve ordering him to supply men for *burhbot* (repair of walls).

[43] That *ceorls* fought is certain. Domesday Book refers to a number of *liberi homines* who fell in the Battle of Hastings. *Domesday Book*, i, 50; ii, 275b, 409b, 449. (These warriors, however, were not 'ordinary free peasants': each was the lord of cottars and bordars.) Cf. the implication of *ASC* 'C', s.a. 1052. Cf. also the reference to well-armed *ceorls* in the *Northleoda laga*, 10; *EHD*, i, 469.

[44] Cf. II *Cnut* 65, which stipulates a 120 shilling *wite* for the neglect of *burhbot*, *brycebot*, and *fyrdfare*. Cf. VI *Aethelred* 35, which associates the desertion of a *fyrd* personally led by the king with the forfeiture of property. Cf. also V *Aethelred* 28 § 1, which states that he who deserts a *fyrd* led by someone other than the king must compensate the king with a payment of 120 shillings. It is possible that the punishment for neglect of *fyrd* service was increased between the reigns of Cnut and Edward the Confessor.

[45] Cf. *Leges Henrici Primi*, ed. L.J. Downer, Oxford 1972, 116 (13:1).

[46] *Rectitudines* 1; *EHD*, i, 468.

[47] Cf. II *Eadgar* 3 and II *Cnut* 15 §1, both of which stipulate that a thegn who possesses jurisdictional rights is to forfeit his rank and privileges if found guilty of malfeasance. Robertson, *Laws*, 24–5, 180–1. Cf. also VI *Aethelred* 5 §3, which states that a cleric is to be entitled [*wyrthe*] to the rights of a thegn [*thegenrihtes*], and 5 §4, which adds: 'And he who will not do what befits his order shall impair his status before God and man'.

[48] Cf. *Ine* 51.

The situation of the *fyrdmen* of group B was entirely different. They held their tenures either by loan from a lord other than the king, from whom they 'could not recede' (that is, whose permission was needed if they wished to place this land under the protection of another lord),[49] or under his seigneury. A *fyrdman* of this sort was obliged to serve his lord, not the king, and his lord was the one responsible for the *cyninges utwaru* arising from the tenement. Simply put, the king demanded a certain number of *fyrd* warriors from a certain number of hides. Whoever held an estate 'freely' or possessed jurisdiction over it was answerable for those soldiers, the precise identity of whom was a matter of little consequence to the king. A lord was thus quit with the king if he brought his full quota of provisioned warriors on campaign. If one of the *fyrdmen* whom the magnate expected to go remained behind, the lord was expected to find a suitable replacement. The absentee, for his part, was amerced 40 shillings, payable to the man he had wronged, his lord. The king, having received the required complement of warriors from the magnate's lands, stood outside this transaction. But if the lord for some reason was unable to secure a substitute, and the king received less than his due, the lord owed the king compensation for his dereliction. Hence, the 40 shillings that the nobleman exacted from the absent *fyrdman* were turned over by him in full to the king, which meant, in practice, to the sheriff. The failure of the lesser *fyrdman* to accompany his *land-hlaford* was viewed simultaneously as the fault of the lord, for which *wite* had to be paid to the king, and an injury to the lord, for which he was compensated by the wrongdoer.[50]

In a number of ways the Domesday customs of Berkshire resemble those of Worcestershire. The Berkshire text reads in full:

> If the king sent an army anywhere, only one soldier [*miles*] went from five hides, and for his provision or pay [*eius uictum uel stipendium*], four shillings were given him from each hide for his two months of service. The money, however, was not sent to the king but given to the soldiers [*militibus*]. If anyone summoned to serve in an expedition failed to do so, he forfeited all his land to the king. If anyone for the sake of remaining behind promised to send another in his place, and nevertheless, he who should have been sent remained behind, his lord [*dominus eius*] was freed of obligation by the payment of 50 shillings.[51]

Both this and the Worcestershire custumal are concerned with *royal* expeditions and the penalties to be assessed against one who fails to fulfil his obligations to the king. In both shires the penalty varied according to the gravity of the offence. Those who ignored personal summonses to attend the host forfeited all their land to the king. If, however, the man of some lord promised to send another on campaign in his place, and that substitute failed to appear, the lord of the defaulter was liable for a *wite* of 50 shillings, but once this money was tendered to the king, the lord was quit.

The major difficulty presented by the Berkshire passage is in reconciling the 'five-hide rule' with the king's summons. Stenton argued that every landed thegn

---

49   Domesday Book uses the formula, 'X could [or could not] sell or give this land to whom he would [or recede with it to any lord he wished] without the permission of his lord', or a variation upon this. On this formula, see Carl Stephenson, 'Commendation and Related Problems in Domesday', *EHR* 59, 1944, 292ff.

50   Cf. Maitland, 159

51   *Domesday Book*, i, 56b. *EHD*, ii, 929.

received a personal summons to battle because of his rank. In addition, each had the entirely distinct responsibility to see that 'the free men upon his estate served in accordance with local custom', that is, with the 'five-hide rule'.[52] In Berkshire, then, according to Stenton, a landed thegn was obliged to see that one peasant warrior appeared in the host from every five hides of land that he possessed. Hollister countered by asserting that 'the entire Berkshire passage should be regarded as a self-consistent unit which refers neither to thegns exclusively nor to peasants exclusively but rather to warrior-representatives of five-hide districts, whether thegn or peasants'.[53] On Hollister's view, the summons was sent to an important lord, who in turn summoned the 'warrior representatives' from each of the five-hide military units on his estate.[54] The text itself is vague enough to permit either interpretation. It says only: 'If anyone summoned to serve in an expedition failed to go, he forfeited all his land to the king'. Nothing in this implies that every Berkshire thegn received a personal summons from the king. Nor is there any clear indication of the relationship, if any, that existed between the *milites* who served for five hides and those summoned to attend the *fyrd*.

Is it then possible to identify these landholders and relate their obligation for military service to the 'five-hide rule'? The most fruitful approach to this problem lies in examining the Berkshire customs in light of those of Worcestershire. The Berkshire survey, unlike Worcestershire's, is silent about the types of tenures forfeited by those who failed to heed the king's ban. However, since only bookland and royal loanland could be forfeited into the king's hand, it is reasonable to conclude that those who received summonses to serve in the Berkshire hundreds of the royal *fyrd* either held their land by book-right or as a loan from the king. In other words, the primary responsibility for defending the king in battle fell in this shire upon the lords of bookland – the same sort of men as summoned in Worcestershire – and the king's own demesne thegns. The identity of the former is known from the various entries in the Domesday survey; the existence of the latter may be inferred from the Berkshire customs themselves. The customs describe the *heriot*, or 'relief', as the Norman scribe termed it, due from 'the demesne thegns or soldiers of the king' (*taini uel milites regis dominici*) in this shire, and it is quite possible that such men were king's retainers maintained on the royal lands.[55] For what it is worth, their *heriot* consisted of all their weapons along with two horses, one saddled and the other unsaddled. Whatever their obligation to serve may have been, these men at least

---

52 Stenton, *English Feudalism*, 118–22, esp. 119, n. 1; *idem, Anglo-Saxon England*, 583.

53 Hollister, *Military Institutions*, 73.

54 Hollister, *Military Institutions*, 96.

55 *Domesday Book*, i, 56b. The term *dominicus* in Domesday Book most often appears in the context of landholding, to distinguish the 'home-farm' of a lord from the *terra villanorum*, See, e.g., *Domesday Book*, i, 209a (Leighton, Beds.); 209a (Luton); 209b (Houghton). Occasionally, however, it is applied to individuals, e.g., *Domesday Book*, ii, 203 (Rockland, Norfolk, where one Eadwine is said to have been a 'teinus dominicus regis'). The most telling instance occurs in the borough customs of Norwich and Thetford. Here we find that certain burgesses were so much King Edward's own men [*erant ita dominici regis*] that 'they could not recede from him or do homage to another without his permission'. *Domesday Book*, ii, 116, 119. As both Round and Stephenson pointed out, the Domesday formula 'potuit recedere . . . sine licentia domini sui', refers most often to the right of free disposal of land. Those who could not 'give or sell their land or take it where they wished' and those who 'could not turn to another lord' were individuals who held their land on loan from another. Round, *Feudal England*, 20–30; Stephenson, 292ff. The *taini uel milites dominici regis*, then, may have been personally commended to the king and holding *de rege*.

possessed the accoutrements of *fyrd* warriors. The Berkshire thegn with five hides of land, then, was responsible for the appearance of one *miles* in the host, and ordinarily he himself would have served as the *fyrd* warrior. A lord whose estates were rated at more than five hides had to find additional warriors upon the basis of one soldier from every five hides. If he failed to produce the requisite number of *fyrdmen* he, like his counterpart in Worcestershire, would have had to compensate the king with money. If, however, he ignored the summons entirely, his land would then have been at the mercy of the king. Lastly, the small landowner with less than five hides may have had to enter into some arrangement with his neighbours to acquit his land of its military obligations, but in lieu of solid evidence this must remain speculation.[56] What is to be emphasised here is that the Berkshire customs describe a *tenurial* service owed to the Crown by those who held immediately of the Crown.[57] This service was the 'common burden' termed *fyrdfaereld* in the charters of the period. The customs merely define the obligation as it existed in this particular shire on the eve of the Conquest.

The proposed characterisation of *fyrd* service in the Berkshire and Worcestershire Domesday custumals as a tenurial due normally discharged by the landholder himself receives strong support from two entries in the Lincolnshire Domesday survey. The first crops up in the description of a 'manor':

> In Covenham [Ludborough Wapentake] Alsi and Chetel and Turuer had 3.5 carucates of land [assessed] to the geld [*ad geldum*] . . . Chetel and Turuer were brothers, and after their father's death they divided the land, in such wise however that when Chetel was doing the king's service he should have his brother Tutuer's aid.[58]

The second is found in the *clamores* section appended to the account of the shire:

> Siwate and Alnod and Fenchel and Aschil divided their father's land amongst them equally, share and share alike, and held it in such wise that if a royal campaign was necessary [*ita tenuerunt ut si opus fuit expeditione regis*], and Siwate could go, the other brothers assisted him [*alii fratres iuuerunt eum*].

---

[56] Hollister, 73, 79–80. The positive evidence for this, however, is weak. Hollister cited holdings 'in parage' and thegnland tenures as proof, but in the first case one is dealing with a single estate held by coheirs, at least in regard to *utware*, rather than with separate holdings, and in the second the arrangements made for military service were not with the Crown but with an ecclesiastical landlord. Perhaps the most compelling argument for an arrangement whereby lesser land-owners would combine to acquit their military obligations is its resemblance to the well-known Carolingian recruitment system detailed in the capitularies of 806 and 808. Free men endowed with three or four manses were to equip themselves and serve in Charlemagne's host; those with less land were to combine to arm and provision one of their number: a man with three manses would thus aid another with four, the latter performing the actual service. See 'Capitula de causis diversis', ao 806, March, caps 1–2; 'Capitulare missorum de exercitu promovendo', cap. 2; *MGH Capitularis*, i, 1883, nos 48, 49; and the discussion of these texts by F.L. Ganshof, *Frankish Institutions under Charlemagne*, New York 1968, 59–62 (and notes). This may be another example of the Anglo-Saxon monarchs following the lead of the Carolingians, but without English evidence of a more substantial nature, the Frankish material must remain merely suggestive.

[57] Although the military obligations of those who held bookland and those who held loans carved out of the royal demesne may have differed in origin.

[58] *Domesday Book*, i, 354; C.W. Foster and T. Longley, *The Lincolnshire Domesday and the Lindsey Survey*, Publications of the Lincoln Record Society 19, 1924 (repr. 1976), 103.

After him [Siwate], another went, and Siwate with the others assisted him; and thus with respect to them all. Siwate, nevertheless [*tamen*], was the king's man [*homo regis*].[59]

Both of these are concerned with bookland held 'in parage',[60] and reveal how such holdings were acquitted of the king's *utware*. While the exact arrangement whereby the king was provided with a *fyrd* warrior appears to have been private, the military service was clearly the responsibility of the landholder(s). The use of such phrases as 'they divided the land in such wise' or 'they held it in such wise' shows that the Domesday jurors conceived of *fyrd* service as a necessary condition of tenure. Thus, all the brothers owed personal service in the king's host in respect of their land. Because estates held in parage were deemed to constitute a single holding for purposes of the king's *utware* regardless of how many individuals enjoyed an interest in the property, only one of the owners was required to attend the *fyrd*.[61] Those who remained at home would assist the one who went, presumably with arms, provisions, and salary.

In Lincolnshire, as in Worcestershire and Berkshire, the lords of bookland personally discharged the military service due from their holdings. And this seems to have held true for both large and small landowners. While Chetel and Turuer may have held no more than three-and-a-half carucates between them,[62] Godwine, Siwate's father, possessed more than twenty carucates of land, worth approximately twelve pounds per annum.[63] Furthermore, we know from the claims advanced by their Norman successors, the Bishop of Durham and Eudo fitz Spirewic, that Siwate and his brother held their lands with sake and soke.[64] Apparently, they were men of some standing in the shire.

The *fyrd* service described in the Berkshire and Worcestershire customs is thus best understood as a tenurial obligation arising from book-right. Stenton's attempt to contrast the personal duty of each thegn to serve the king in arms with his responsibility as a landowner to see that the peasants on his estates and those under his jurisdiction fulfilled *their* obligation to serve in the territorial *fyrd*, an obligation that derived from the ancient duty of all free men to defend the nation,[65] involves a

---

[59] *Domesday Book*, i, 375b; Foster and Longley, 212–15. The concluding phrase is puzzling. One might infer from it that Siwate was double obliged to serve the king in arms, since he both held bookland and was personally commended to Edward. On this reading, Siwate's attendance in the *fyrd* acquitted both his duty as a king's man and the obligation he shared equally with his brothers as a landholder. Of the four brothers he was the natural candidate to serve as the *fyrdman*, since he would have been obliged to render such service anyway.
[60] On parage, see Maitland, 145–6; Paul Vinogradoff, *English Society in the Eleventh Century*, Oxford 1908, 245–90, 405.
[61] Maitland, 145. Maitland is undoubtedly correct that one of the parceners would have assumed the role of 'first among equals' and that he would have been charged with representing the holding in respect of the king's demands. Domesday Book thus occasionally refers to one parcener as the 'senior' of the others. See, e.g., *Domesday Book*, i, 145b (Lavendon, Bucks.), and 291 (Winkburn, Notts.). Cf. 375b (Covenham, Lincs.).
[62] The names are too common to determine the extent of their holdings in Lincolnshire. A Chetel and a Turuer only held in common in Covenham.
[63] See *Domesday Book*, i, 340b–341, 342, 359b, 360 (lands held by a man named Godwine who may have been Siwate's father; on which, see Foster and Longley, 218–19).
[64] *Domesday Book*, i, 376.
[65] Stenton, *English Feudalism*, 118–22; *idem*, *Anglo-Saxon England*, 583

strained reading of the relevant texts. And although Hollister's interpretation is on the whole more convincing, he too places insufficient emphasis upon the tenurial aspect of military service. His insistence upon the phrase the 'territorial *fyrd*',[66] while accurately representing the organisation of the host by hundred and shire under local royal agents, underplays the crucial fact that the obligation to serve lay not so much upon the land as upon the landholders, and then only upon those who held by book-right or by royal loan.

Those who held great estates could not acquit their military obligation through personal service alone. The king required that such men should lead to the host a contingent of warriors, the size of which was to be determined by assessments levied upon the landholder's property. Whether one wishes to adopt Hollister's view that the Berkshire five-hide rule 'governed the system of military recruitment throughout most of Anglo-Saxon England outside the carucated region of the Danelaw',[67] or believe with Stenton and most recently Gillingham that it was but one system of assessing service,[68] the evidence of the eleventh-century sources leaves little doubt that military obligation was customarily measured in terms of hides and carucates.[69] But what exactly did 'one soldier from X hides' mean in late Anglo-Saxon England? This brings us to our final topic: the meaning of hidage and its implications for the military organisation of late Anglo-Saxon England.

Long thought to be an artificial assessment 'fixed independently of area or value', hidage was actually based, in large part, upon the value of the rated estate. Prior to 1066 'one pound, one hide' was a general rule subject to local exceptions. Frederic Maitland had surmised this from his intensive study of the Domesday evidence, but could neither prove it nor refute J.H. Round's seemingly cogent statistical arguments for the hide's artificiality.[70] When Round began to add up the individual assessments of the scattered entries belonging to each Cambridgeshire village, he discovered that these sums often came to five hides or a multiple thereof.[71] From this he inferred that hidage had been imposed from above, first upon the shire's hundreds and then distributed on a decimal basis among the vills of the hundred. Even those who doubted Round's ingenious calculations, had difficulty reconciling Maitland's 'one pound, one hide' with the vagaries of Domesday statistics. In every shire one can find lands of equal value bearing wildly disparate hidage assessments, and estates of unequal value rated at the same number of hides. There is no exact mathematical formula that can convert shillings into hides – about this, at least, Round was right.

But the science of statistics has advanced immeasurably from the days of Round and Maitland. What had seemed patently obvious to Round – that hides bore no relationship to area or value – can now be shown through the technique of regression analysis to be statistically improbable. Maitland's impression was sound: overall, the

66 Hollister, 64.
67 Hollister, 40.
68 Stenton, *English Feudalism*, 118; Gillingham, 61–3.
69 The Domesday Book evidence is gathered by Hollister, 38–58. The phrase 'rata expeditione' in a number of late Anglo-Saxon charters is also suggestive. See, e.g., Kemble, nos 1277 (Sawyer, no. 829), 1279 (Sawyer, no. 843), 1292 (Sawyer, no. 887). cf. Robertson, *Charters*, no. 111, pp. 208–9: 'And at the king's summons the holder shall discharge the obligations on these one-and-a-half hides at the rate of one'.
70 Maitland, 464–465.
71 Round, *Feudal England*, 36–69; Cyril Hart, *The Hidation of Cambridgeshire*, Leicester 1974, *passim*.

hidage assessments of individual estates in the south Midlands are closely related to their economic worth.[72]

The hidage assessments of individual estates in the south Midlands generally appear to have been based upon their economic worth.[73] In most cases, these assessments were not the results of private bargains struck by individual landholders with the king and his agents, although 'beneficial hidation' was far from uncommon, especially on the great estates held by the king and his magnates, episcopal and lay.[74] What was true of the south Midlands was equally true of Berkshire, where it would also seem that the recruitment of *fyrd* warriors was grounded firmly in agricultural realities: the more valuable an estate or village, the more warriors it could afford to provision and send on campaign. In fact in every shire in which I have performed a regression analysis of value on hidage, the same conclusion has emerged: hidage was firmly rooted in value. This has significant implications for the military organisation of late Anglo-Saxon England. Whether or not the *fyrd* in 1066 was recruited through a national system based on units of five hides and six carucates, we can be fairly certain that military service was levied on the basis of cadastral units that reflected, by and large, real economic conditions. Once again, one is reminded that William conquered a realm that was far more sophisticated administratively than most of the duchies and kingdoms of western Europe. England's Carolingian-style government was not only capable of taxing its subjects and creating a unified currency, it also was able to exploit the wealth of the kingdom systematically for its defence.

[72] See the discussion and tables on pp. 16–25 in the original article. This should now be read in conjunction with J. McDonald and G.D. Snook, *Domesday Economy: A New Approach to Anglo-Norman History*, Oxford 1986; Richard P. Abels, *Lordship and Military Obligation in Anglo-Saxon England*, Los Angeles 1988, 97–115, 248–55, 187–204.

[73] It is possible, however, that villages rather than individual estates were assessed, as the traditional hypothesis suggests.

[74] On 'beneficial hidation', see Vinogradoff, 176–86; R.S. Hoyt, *The Royal Demesne in English Constitutional History: 1066–1272*, Ithaca, New York 1950, 19–25. The inclusion of royal manors in the linear regression analyses lowers the correlation coefficient, although the results remain significant at the .001 confidence level.

Addendum

The preceding article is largely concerned with the relationship between military obligation and bookland tenure in Late Saxon England. It would be misleading, however, to think of the English armies of this period, and in particular of Harold's at Hastings, as merely a gathering of bookholders and their military representatives. King Harold's army at Hastings, like those of Edmund Ironside a half century before, reflected the three main sources of military obligation at the time: royal lordship, personal lordship and land tenure.[1] Organized territorially by shire and hundred but composed of lords and their personal followings, Harold's army may well have resembled William's as closely in the ties that bound it together as it does in the equipment portrayed in the Bayeux Tapestry.

For a battle as famous as Hastings, it is surprising how little we can ascertain from the sources about the numbers and identities of the English who fought there. No eleventh-or twelfth-century narrative provides reliable figures for troop strengths. Depending on the source, Harold either levied 'vast forces' from 'all regions' (so William of Poitiers)[2] or rushed into battle with too few troops (so William of Malmesbury and John of Worcester).[3] A scholarly consensus seems to have settled on 6,000–8,000 combatants on each side, but this figure is merely a guess based upon the topography of the ridge upon which the English deployed and the manner in which we believe they fought.[4] Since the length of the English line of battle and the depth and density of their formation are matters of conjecture, one ought not to place too great a weight upon these 'textbook' battle strengths. What is well attested is that Harold sacrificed numbers for speed. On 1 October, a week after his hard fought victory at Stamford Bridge, Harold received news of William's invasion and, without

---

[1]   Richard Abels, 'Tactics, Strategy and Military Obligation in the Late Tenth Century', in *The Battle of Maldon A.D. 991*, ed. Donald Scragg, Oxford 1991, 145–47.
[2]   William of Poitiers, *Gesta Guillelmi ducis Normannorum et regis Anglorum*, ed. Raymonde Foreville, Paris 1962, Part 2, sections 14–24, in R. Allen Brown, ed., *The Norman Conquest*, Documents of Medieval History 5, London 1984, 32. William of Poitiers has William the Conqueror declare his own outnumbered forces to be 60,000 strong (Brown, *Norman Conquest*, 30). Cf. William of Jumièges, *Gesta Normannorum Ducum*, ed. J. Marx, Sociétéde l'histoire de Normandie 1914, book vii, ch. 14, in Brown, ed., *Norman Conquest*, 14.
[3]   'Florence' of Worcester, *Chronicon ex chronicis*, ed. B. Thorpe, 2 vols., London 1848–49, i, 227–28, in Brown, *Norman Conquest*, 73; William of Malmesbury, *De Gestis Regum Anglorum*, ed. W. Stubbs, RS, London 1887–89, i, 281–82, in Brown, *Norman Conquest*, 116. E.A. Freeman surveys the testimony of the narrative sources in *The Norman Conquest*, 2nd ed., 6 vols., Oxford 1870–79, iii, 752–54 (Note LL).
[4]   R. Allen Brown, 'The Battle of Hastings', *Anglo-Norman Studies* 3 (1980), 10. If we generalize from the five-hide rule, Harold could call on 14,000 *fyrdmen* from England's 70,000 hides, carucates, and sulungs. From those shires that probably received his summons – East Anglia, Northamptonshire, Hampshire, Berkshire and the 'home counties' – he could raise about 5900 soldiers from some 29,000 hides. In comparison, Henry II a century later could call upon the service of 5300 English and 1200 Norman knights. The Norman arrière-ban, which never seems to have been called upon in the twelfth century, could in theory turn out a force of 2500 knight in 1172. Thomas Keefe, *Fiscal Assessment and the Political Community under Henry II and His Sons*, Berkeley 1983, 73–74, 86. Given these figures, the estimates of 6,000–8,000 might be on the high side. But cf. Bernard Bachrach, 'The Military Administration of the Norman Conquest', *Anglo-Norman Studies* 8 (1986), 2–4, 24–25, which argues strongly for a Norman army of 14,000 men, 10,000 of whom were combatants.

waiting for the forces of Earl Morcar of Northumbria and his brother Earl Edwin of Mercia to recover sufficiently from their battering at Fulford to join him, he force marched his men the 190 miles south to London, arriving on or around 6 October. He delayed in the city for five days gathering local reinforcements, and then, on 11 October, ordered a second forced march to Hastings. If his intention was to catch William napping as he had Hardrada, Harold had, this time, mistaken his man. On the morning of 14 October, some seven miles north of Hastings, it was Harold, not William, who found himself surprised by the sudden appearance of the enemy. The fighting began before the English troops were fully arrayed.[5]

In his typically dramatic style, Edward Freeman declared, 'few indeed . . . are the men whom we know by name as having joined in the great march and fought in the great battle. Still there are a few names which have come down to us, names to be cherished wherever the tongue of England is spoken, names which should sound like the call of the trumpet in the ears of every man of English birth'.[6] Given that 'the flower of the English nobility' supposedly perished in the battle, the names of surprisingly few magnates appear on Freeman's roll of honour: Harold, his brothers, Esgar the Staller, and two prelates, Leofric Abbot of Peterborough, cousin to Earls Morcar and Edwin, and Ælfwig Abbot of the New Minster of Winchester, Harold's paternal uncle.[7] Concerning the last, the late thirteenth-century Hyde Chronicle preserves an odd tradition that twelve monks, all wearing mail beneath their habits, followed the abbot into battle, along with the abbey's quota of twenty 'knights' (which was the New Minster's *servicia debita* in the late twelfth).[8] Abbot Ælfwig and his mail-clad monks, we are told, fell together in the fray. More reliably, the early thirteenth-century Abingdon Chronicle relates that soon after the Conquest Abbot Æthelhelm enfeoffed his kinsmen with tenancies formerly held from the abbey by thegns who had died at Hastings. Among them were a wealthy Berkshire thegn, Thorkell, and the sheriff of Berkshire, Godric.[9] Another monastic tenant who fell at Hastings was Ælfric, whose death in battle cost St Benedict's of Ramsey its Huntingdonshire manors of Yelling and Hemingford.[10] Domesday Book allows us to identify a handful of lesser men who fought and died at Hastings: two who held land *in alodium de rege* in Tytherley, Hampshire; Breme, a 'liber homo' of King Edward, who held one-and-a-half carucates in Suffolk; Eadric the Deacon, a 'liber homo' of Earl Harold, who held property in Cavendish, Suffolk; and a nameless tenant of St Edmunds in Norfolk, who held only 12 acres worth 16p.[11] (The presence of Bury St Edmunds' tenants in the battle may explain an early writ of the Conqueror granting that abbey immunity for the actions of its tenants.[12]) Harold may have been too impatient to have gathered all the forces available to him, but even from the tiny sample group that we have, it would seem that landholders throughout the southeast

---

[5] 'Florence' of Worcester, i, 227–28; *ASC*, s.a. 1066 (D and E). Brown, 'Battle of Hastings', is an excellent overview of the battle.

[6] Freeman, iii, 427, 742–44.

[7] Freeman, iii, 428–29, 744.

[8] Freeman, iii, 744.

[9] *Chronicon Monasterii de Abingdon*, ed. J. Stevenson, 2 vols., RS, London 1858, i, 484; ii, 3–4.

[10] *Domesday Book*, i 207 (Yelling and Hemingford, Hunts.), 208 (claims).

[11] *Domesday Book*, i, 50 (Tytherley, Hants.), ii, 409 (Ward Green, Suffolk), ii, 449 (Cavendish, Suffolk), ii, 275b (Shelfanger, Norfolk).

[12] *Regesta Regum Anglo-Normannorum*, i, ed. H.W.C. Davis, Oxford 1913, no. 40 (p. 119).

of England, from Berkshire and Hampshire to Norfolk and Suffolk, answered his call
to arms.

Many of the English who fought at Hastings did so to acquit the obligation that
arose from their tenures, whether as bookholders or as landed retainers.[13] This was,
undoubtedly, true of those named in Domesday Book and the monastic chronicles.
Others, however, responded to a different obligation, one that arose more immediately from the lordship bond. These were the household men of the great Anglo-
Saxon lords, the earls, bishops, local magnates, and, to be sure, the king. For lordship
played as important a role in the organization and recruitment of *fyrds* in the eleventh
century as did land tenure. Every great English lord, including the king, had a military
household that served as his personal bodyguard and escort in peace and war. King
Harold and his great Saxon nobles undoubtedly rode to Hastings at the head of
personal followings who protected their lords in battle. For William of Malmesbury
stipendiary troops formed the bulk of Harold's forces.[14] We need not go as far. It is
doubtful that even the king's military household numbered more than a few hundred.[15] But given Harold's rush to meet the enemy, his household troops and those of
his brothers may well have assumed an increased importance in this particular battle.
The contemporary sources for the battle are silent as to the composition of the English
army that faced William. The Bayeux Tapestry, however, gives a prominent place to
mailed English warriors wielding fierce two-handed battle axes, the weapon characteristic of the royal housecarls. Did the artist mean us to see these figures as housecarls? We cannot say for certain. But whether William of Malmesbury is correct or
not in downplaying the numbers of *fyrd* warriors in Harold's army, William of
Poitiers leaves little doubt that these axe-wielding English warriors impressed the
Normans with their bravery, skill and ferocity.[16]

Historians have traditionally viewed the royal housecarls as 'a unique, closely-knit
organization of professional warriors who served the kings of England from Cnut to
Harold Godwineson and became the spearhead of the English army'.[17] Much of what
we 'know' about them, however, is based upon late and untrustworthy evidence.[18]
They may well have formed a law-bound guild of disciplined and professional royal
soldiers, as L.M. Larson and Frank Stenton believed, but we cannot be certain. What
we can say is that royal retainers called housecarls were used by Cnut and his
successors in both administrative and military capacities. In 1041, for example, King
Harthacnut used his housecarls to collect taxes, undoubtedly because he knew that
the levy would be unpopular and he expected difficulties in its collection. If so, he

13 For the military obligation arising from dependent tenures in Late Saxon England – and for much
of what follows – see Abels, *Lordship and Military Obligation in Anglo-Saxon England*, 146–75.
14 William of Malmesbury, *De gestis regum Anglorum*, ed. Willam Stubbs, 2 vols., RS, London
1887–89, i, 281–2. William may well have had other mercenaries, such as *lithsmen* and *butsecarls* in
mind.
15 The size of eleventh-century comital households, including administrative as well as military
personnel, might be gauged by the 'more than two hundred household men of Earl Tostig' (*plusquam
cc. viros ex curialibus illius*) slain, according to John of Worcester, by Northumbrian rebels in 1065.
'Florence', i, 223.
16 Brown, *Norman Conquest*, 33.
17 Hollister, 12; F.M. Stenton, *Anglo-Saxon England*, 3rd ed., Oxford 1971, 582–83; L.M. Larson,
The King's Household in England before the Norman Conquest, Madison, Wisconsin, 1904, 153–71.
18 Nicholas Hooper, 'The Housecarls in England in the Eleventh Century', *Anglo-Norman Studies*
7 (1985), 161–76.

was correct; two housecarls were murdered by the townspeople of Worcester when they attempted to collect the tax in the borough. Harthacnut responded by sending his earls and the royal housecarls at the head of a large expeditionary force to burn Worcester and ravage the countryside.[19] In 1054 Edward the Confessor entrusted Earl Siward of Northumbria with a large fleet and a contingent of his housecarls for a full-scale expedition to replace Macbeth as king of the Scots with the exiled prince Malcolm. Siward won a hotly-disputed engagement. Among the dead that the Anglo-Saxon chronicler thought worthy of mention were Siward's son and nephew and the fallen royal and comital housecarls.[20] One might infer from the Chronicle evidence that royal housecarls formed a small military elite, whose participation in a fyrd was not conditional upon the king's presence. In other words, they fought as a tactical unit in addition to serving as the king's personal bodyguard.

In their role as the king's armed household, King Harold's housecarls differed little from the retinues that surrounded earlier Anglo-Saxon kings. Reading Asser's *Life of King Alfred*, one is struck by how much the military households of the last Anglo-Saxon kings (and first Norman rulers) resemble Alfred's.[21] All were paid wages by the king, organized hierarchically, and served their royal lords in war and peace. William of Malmesbury might well have regarded such household warriors as mercenaries and stipendiaries – Florence of Worcester saw no problem in translating *huskarl* as *solidarius* –, but this misses the essence of their obligation. The author of the late twelfth-century *lex castrensis*, looking back upon Cnut's housecarls, explained: 'The king and other leading men who have a household should show their men favour and good will and give them their proper pay. In return men should give their lord loyalty and sevice and be prepared to do all his commands'.[22] Housecarls and other household warriors expected to be maintained according to their deserts. This was to be expected in a world shaped by the ethos of reciprocity. But their obligation to fight did not arise from the cash nexus but from the bond of lordship. If we were to seek the ideal for the housecarls and household thegns who fought and died at Hastings we would find him at Maldon in Earl Byrhtnoth's heroic and loyal thegn Offa rather than in the great mercenary captain Thorkell the Tall.

---

[19] 'Florence' of Worcester, i, 193–94; *ASC* s.a. 1041 (C,D).
[20] *ASC* s.a. 1054 (D).
[21] Simon Keynes and Michael Lapidge, eds. and trans., *Alfred the Great: Asser's Life of King Alfred and other contemporary sources*, Harmondsworth, Middlesex, 1983, 100, 177; cf. Prestwich, 'Military Households'.
[22] Quoted in P.G. Foote and D.M. Wilson, *The Viking Achievement*, London 1970, 104.

8. Marjorie Chibnall, 'Military Service in Normandy before 1066'

Marjorie Chibnall looks at the evidence for military obligation in Normandy before the conquest, and like Abels offers a substantial revision of received wisdom. She focuses on the question of 'feudal military service' – defined and limited military obligations owed to a lord by a warrior (usually a *miles*, or knight) in exchange for the lord granting the warrior a fief. How clearly defined and developed was military obligation in pre-Conquest Normandy? Was there a system of military fiefs with defined incidents of service? In addressing these questions, Chibnall makes clear the importance of non- (or pre-) feudal forces such as household warriors and mercenaries in Norman military organization. Note the irony compared to Abels: he shows that the Anglo-Saxon system was more 'feudal', while Chibnall shows that Normandy was less 'feudal', than is usually thought.

Reprinted from *Anglo-Norman Studies* 5 (1982), 65–77. Copyright © Marjorie Chibnall 1982, 1983.

MILITARY SERVICE IN NORMANDY BEFORE 1066

Marjorie Chibnall

In the half-century that has elapsed since C.H. Haskins published his *Norman Institutions* a number of documents and studies relating to the subject of early Norman military service have appeared. Few scholars who have looked closely at the subject would now accept the clear and persuasive hypothesis Haskins then put forward; indeed he himself, with his keen critical sense and respect for sources, would probably have been one of the first to wish to modify it, had he been writing at the present day. But because his views have crept in an over-simplified form into general histories, to be repeated and exaggerated, the whole question of possible changes after the Normans came to England had tended to become distorted by wrong assumptions about their earlier customs in Normandy.

Haskins looked at the feudal obligations of Norman abbeys and bishoprics in the 1172 returns and, starting from the fact that only the older foundations (though not all the older foundations) owed such service, argued plausibly enough that fixed quotas must have been imposed in ducal Normandy, probably (in spite of the slight anomaly of Saint-Evroult, founded in 1050) at least as early as the reign of Robert the Magnificent.[1] He did not, in fact, explicitly argue that all the later accepted incidents of knight service – forty days a year at the vassal's own expense, castle-guard, reliefs, aids, wardships – existed in their final form at so early a date. But others have certainly assumed that this was so. Henry Naval, for example, saw the obligations of feudal service as fixed and unchangeable over a long period; in discussing the vavassors of Le Mont-Saint-Michel he asserted that the military service owed to the abbey after it acquired certain properties c.1024 must have been imposed in its entirety by the duke at an earlier date, because 'we know how difficult it was for a lord to impose fresh services on a vassal at this period': yet his proof consists of a case occurring in 1157, over a hundred years later.[2] Even Powicke set the seal of approval on the general hypothesis when he wrote: 'Before 1066 the Norman dukes were able to regard their country as divided for the most part into a number of knights' fees . . . The grouping of warriors was symmetrical and was evidently imposed from above'.[3] And as recently as 1979 Eric John alleged, in an article published in the *English Historical Review*, that in pre-Conquest Normandy feudal service was limited to forty days, offering as proof only that 'all the text-books tell us so'.[4] It seems, then, the time has come to look again with care both at the original hypothesis and at

---

[1] C.H. Haskins, *Norman Institutions*. Harvard Historical Studies, xxiv, 1925, 5–30.
[2] H. Navel, 'Les vavassories du Mont-Saint-Michel'. *Bulletin de la Société des Antiquaries de Normandie*, xlv, 1938, 149–51.
[3] F.M. Powicke, *The Loss of Normandy*, 2nd edn 1961, 40.
[4] Eric John, 'Edward the Confessor and the Norman succession', *EHR*, xciv, 1979, 241–67.

the assumptions that have been built upon it. Wrong assumptions, of course, are by no means universal. We have had for over twenty years now, in the edition of Marie Fauroux, a collection of early ducal characters,[5] the need for which was emphasised by Haskins himself. Their evidence has not been overlooked: D.C. Douglas used it to some purpose,[6] and so did Jean Yver. Yver, indeed, was most explicit in his address to the Spoleto conference in 1968: citing Douglas, he suggested that perhaps the Norman feudal and military system was developed only after the conquest of England, in imitation of the more logical order that William had been able to impose in a conquered country. In support of this, he noted that the words *fevium, fevum, feodum, feudum*, do not appear to become widespread in Normandy before the middle of the eleventh century, and that there is scarcely a mention of *feudum militis* or *feudum loricae* except in charters that are suspect or at least tampered with later. In the ensuing discussion A. Marongiu added his complete agreement with what he called 'the important assumption fundamental yet at the same time surprising' that in Normandy before the conquest there were no true fiefs.[7]

To many this may now seem obvious; but it is a point of departure for examining the nature of what might for convenience he called pre-feudal military obligations in early eleventh-century Normandy, and attempting to reinterpret the evidence used by Haskins. For Normandy was full of vassals and mailed knights; the basic fighting unit was in practice the *conroi*, usually of some multiple of ten men; there were castles manned by vavassors and knights, and courts held by some lords for their vassals; from the 1040s sub-vassals even are beginning to be discernible. Yet there is no clear proof of any general system of military quotas imposed from above; or of an accepted norm for feudal services and obligations, legally enforceable on the initiative of either side in a superior ducal court – and this surely is a necessary corollary for any accepted general norm. It is at least arguable that the services owed were either relics of older, Carolingian obligations, or the outcome of individual life contracts between different lords and their vassals, and that their systematisation was the result only of the intense military activity of the period of the conquest, and the very slow development of a common law in the century after it.

In the pre-1066 ducal charters collected by Marie Fauroux the word *feudum* or one of its variants occurs half-a-dozen times: in one charter whose terminology has been characterised as 'suspicious' by Jean Yver;[8] in a notice actually written just after the conquest referring to a grant by bishop John of Avranches to his bishopric of certain lands together with the service of five knights (this is the first reference to the 'honour of Saint-Philbert');[9] and four times in charters from the period 1050–1066, referring to single small 'fees' of land or churches or tithes held by laymen or canons of Norman magnates, not of the duke.[10]

One must, of course be careful not to assume that the *feudum* itself is not there because the language has not yet caught up with it. The concepts familiar to the

---

[5] Marie Fauroux, *Recueil des actes des ducs de Normandie (911–1066)*, 1961.
[6] D.C. Douglas, *William the Conqueror*, London 1964, 96–8.
[7] Jean Yver, 'Les premières institutions du duché de Normandie'. *I Normanni e la loro espansione in Europa nell' alto medioevo*, Settimane di studio del Centro italiano di studi sull'alto medioeve, xvi, Spoleto 1969, 334–7, 591.
[8] Yver, 335 n. 84; Fauroux, no. 208.
[9] Fauroux, no. 229; for Saint-Philbert see below, p. 73.
[10] Fauroux, nos. 120, 165, 183, 213.

writers of charters were the percarial gift, the *beneficium*, and the hereditary tenure, the *alodium*; what is crucial is the date when – in Maitland's words – 'the *beneficium* and *alodium* met in the *feodum*'.[11] Maitland, however, did not attempt to put it before the mid-eleventh century, and Robert Carabie put it decidedly later.[12] Both terms occur here and there in the early charters. Gilbert Crispin (1046–66) conveys to the abbey of Jumièges the *beneficium* of Hauville, which he had obtained from his lord, the duke, by fighting for him.[13] Gifts to Saint-Georges-de-Boscherville include six acres from 'the men who hold Anxtot as a *beneficium*'.[14] Duke William himself, before 1040, grants – or restores – to Fécamp a miscellany of lands and men: 'in the Cotentin one of my knights called Alfred with all his land, and another called Anschetil with his land, Borel and Modol with their whole alod . . . also Godebold the knight and all his brother, with the whole of their alod, but not the *beneficium* which they hold in Le Talou and in the Pays de Caux'.[15] In another early charter (1043–8) Roger I of Montgomery confirms a grant to Jumièges by Geoffrey, one of his vassals, of an alod which Geoffrey held in the village of Fontaines, 'for which he did service to me because that alod was within my sway'; in return for this the abbot and Geoffrey gave Roger of Montgomery a horse worth 30 livres and a hauberk worth 7 livres.[16]

The tenures, then, are loosely defined; the men are clearly visible. There are knights (*milites* and *equites*) and vavassors in plenty in these charter. In 1050–66 Roger of Clères, with the consent of his lord Ralph of Tosny, grants Saint-Ouen various lands with their churches and tithes, reserving only the reliefs of the vavassors and one guard service a year.[17] Ralph the Chamberlain grants Saint-Georges-de-Boscherville everything he holds in Mannerville, in church, lands or meadows, 'without the knights'.[18] Robert Bertram grants Saint-Ouen '40 acres of land, and two peasants, and the tithe of his mares, and two knights, namely Goscelin and Osbern'.[19] Osbern d'Ectot, on becoming a monk at Saint-Ouen, grants 'ten acres of meadow, and fisheries . . . and the churches and tithes of Ectot, and part of the wood, and seven knights at Grainville, and the vineyards of Giverny . . .'[20] Other vavassors and knights are granted, with and without land. At times one is reminded of passages in Domesday Book, where men commend themselves in different ways to their lords, and the land may or may not go with them.

There is no clear pattern; most of the grants are, naturally, to religious houses, in whose archives the records were preserved. Most refer to a single benefice, or perhaps to a group of brothers holding an *alodium*. On the rare occasions when the term *honor* is used it is usually exactly equivalent to *beneficium*.[21] Occasionally a larger

11 F. Pollock and F.W. Maitland, *A History of English Law*, 2nd edn Cambridge, 1968, i, 72.
12 R. Carabie, *La propriété foncière dans le très ancien droit normand*, Bibliothèque d'histoire du droit normand, Caen 1943, 237–8.
13 Fauroux, no. 188.
14 Fauroux, no. 197, p. 383.
15 Fauroux, no. 94.
16 Fauroux, no. 113, 'Is itaque Goisfredus alodum possidebat in villa que dicitur Fontanas, et inde michi serviebat pro eo quod ipse alodus in mea ditione manebat'. Geoffrey had become a monk at Jumièges with Roger's consent.
17 Fauroux, no. 191 (c.1050–1066).
18 Fauroux, no. 197, p. 383.
19 Fauroux, no. 205 (1051–1066).
20 Fauroux, no. 210 (1055–1066).
21 E.g. Fauroux, nos. 122, 197, 234 (a later charter containing details of earlier donations).

unit is just discernible: the grant of Roger of Clères (1050–6) was witnessed by *homines ipsius honoris*.[22] And on the eve of the conquest (1063–6) Odo Stigand made a grant to Saint-Martin d'Ecajeul which the church was to hold 'as freely as his other vassals (*barones*), and as he had received his *honor* from the duke of the Normans'.[23] Both charters are evidence of the existence of large honours where sub-vassals had received grants of land. But they are not evidence of imposed quotas, or of stereo-typed contracts.

The language of the early Norman chroniclers implies the social structure one would expect from the charter. Dudo of Saint-Quentin twice goes into some detail on oaths of fealty. There is the famous agreement between Rollo and Charles the Bald at Saint-Clair-sur-Epte, confirmed by mutual oaths, when Rollo is said to have placed his hands between those of the king, and the king to have granted him the land between Epte and the sea 'in alodo et in fundo' – that is, 'as his patrimony, by hereditary tenure'.[24] Whatever may have taken place in 911, this is likely to have been the relationship between duke and king which would have seemed appropriate in Dudo's day; the fealty implies vassalage on the Carolingian pattern, and it is still too early for any attempt to force it into a pattern of developed feudal homage. Dudo's description of the fealty sworn to young William Longsword belongs to the same world; the Breton count and the magnates of Normandy all swore fealty and vowed to fight for him against neighbouring peoples without further specification.[25] There is no convincing evidence that anything more precise was ever undertaken in the early years of the eleventh century, when Dudo wrote.

The language of William of Poitiers and William of Jumièges, who both wrote a few years after the conquest, is only very slightly more feudal. William of Jumièges calls the county granted to William of Arques a *beneficium*, and uses the same term to describe two or three grants of castles by the duke.[26] Mounted knights (*milites*) are particularly numerous in the long-term garrisons of castles. Neither writer ever calls anyone a vavassor; but William of Poitiers divides the *milites* into those of some standing (*mediae nobilitatis*) and the rank and file (*gregarii*);[27] and William of Ju-mièges distinguishes between the *milites* and the *stipendiarii* in castle garrisons.[28] If both were elements in household troops, which is perfectly possible, the former were probably vassals or the sons of vassals, and the latter fighting men bound by a less formal oath, serving purely for wages. Neither writer ever suggests that military service was owed to the duke by any Norman abbey; and it is worth noting inciden-tally that before 1066 there is no charter or chronicle evidence for the exaction of homage from any Norman abbot for the temporalities which might be granted by investiture.[29]

---

[22] Fauroux, no. 191, 'homines etiam ipsius honoris . . . testes fuerunt'.

[23] Fauroux, no. 222.

[24] Dudo, 168–9. Carabie, 239, stresses that the meaning is most probably tenure with full hereditary right and not, as it has often been interpreted, full possession in contrast to tenure in fee.

[25] Dudo, 182.

[26] Jumièges, 119, 101.

[27] *Gesta Guillelmi*, 232.

[28] Jumièges, 140, 142.

[29] There is one example from the year 1059 of the abbot of Saint-Julien de Tours kissing the duke's knee when he received investiture *cum baculo* of a property near Bavent, which had been granted to him, subject to the duke's permission, by one of the duke's exiled vassals. The complicated transaction is described in Fauroux, no. 142. But this concerns an isolated property, transferred by a vassal to an abbey outside Normandy, and even then the ceremony is slightly archaic.

On the other hand, the charters show that there were a number of knights settled on the lands of some of the older Norman abbeys, and that some kind of unspecified service might be due to those abbeys; moreover a few references in later chronicles give some indication of the forms that service might take. Several monasteries, notably Jumièges, Saint-Wandrille and Fécamp, suffered considerable spoliation of their lands by their hereditary patron and protector, Duke Robert the Magnificent, who was anxious to make provision for his vassals during the years when military needs were pressing and his respect for the Church barely perfunctory.[30] The years immediately after 1028 have been characterised as the years of the great usurpations. His later reconciliation with the Church involved a partial restoration of some of the plundered estates, and this continued during the minority of his son William. One of Robert's charters restoring Argences, Heudebouville, Maromme and other territories to Fécamp states that he had applied them to the uses of his *militia* – his military dependents. Among these dependents was one Haimo, who had been rewarded for his service with a grant of Ticheville, a property of Saint-Wandrille. In this case provision was made for Haimo to be compensated elsewhere when Ticheville was restored to the abbey.[31] Sometimes intruding occupants remained on the land. When Richard restored to Fécamp the lands at Arques, Tourville and Saintigny, which made up a vicomté, he stipulated that the abbot should grant the vicomté to Goscelin son of Heddo, who had a claim to it; and Goscelin subsequently distributed some of the lands to his own men.[32] It was always possible for the duke to retain some rights to the service of his men in his acts of restitution. So there is a possible alternative to Haskins' hypothesis that military quotas must have been imposed early because they affected only the older abbeys. Only the older abbeys had held estates long enough for them to have been secularised and restored with sitting military tenants.

And here the case of Saint-Evroult is particularly valuable. Though much of the evidence comes from the early twelfth century and is recorded in slightly anachronistic language, some facts can be checked against the abbey's re-foundation. A Merovingian monastery had existed on the site, and though no traces of regular life and only ruined buildings remained, the ecclesiastical origins of some of the secularised estates had not been forgotten. Some of those in the Hiémois had been absorbed by the vicomtes of the Hiémois and other lords, of whom Heugon was one. If Orderic's account of the early history of the patrons of his abbey is correct, Giroie, a vassal of William of Bellême, obtained properties in the region of Saint-Evroult by right of his deceased betrothed, a daughter of Heugon, with the consent of Duke Richard, round about 1026.[33] Also, St Peter's church, which was part of the scattered monastic complex of the first abbey, was in the fee of Bocquencé, and at some date before the restoration Baudry the German, who had come to Normandy to serve Duke Richard, was settled on it. The family tree is not entirely clear; but Baudry, one of Duke William's archers, possibly the son of the original Baudry, was settled there in

---

30   See, for example, L. Musset, 'La vie économique de l'abbaye de Fécamp sous l'abbatiat de Jean de Ravenne (1028–1078)', *L'Abbaye bénédictine de Fécamp*, Ouvrage scientifique du xiiie centenaire, Fécamp 1959–60, i, 78.

31   F. Lot, *Études critiques sur l'abbaye de Saint-Wandrille*, Paris 1913, 61–2; the agreement was that the land was to be restored within three years even if Haimo had not been compensated within that time.

32   L. Musset, 'Actes inédits du xie siècle', *Bulletin de la Société des Antiquaires de Normandie*, lii, 1952–4, 32–6.

33   Orderic, i, 11–13; ii, 22–4, 34–6; iii, xv–xviii.

1050 with his brother Viger as a vassal of one of Giroie's grandsons, Arnold of Échauffour, who gave the land to the new abbey. The brothers, according to Orderic, were unwilling to accept the monks as their lords; and when Robert of Grandmesnil succeeded the gentle Thierry of Mathonville as abbot in 1059 he took effective action. He handed them back, apparently with their land, for life to Arnold of Échauffour. Arnold, Orderic relates, piled all kinds of services on them, and forced them and their men to perform guard duties in his castles of Échauffour and Saint-Céneri. As a result they begged the abbot to take them back, and it was arranged that Baudry and his men and the land of Bocquencé should be restored to the monks, who in return gave Arnold a magnificent war-horse they had just received from Engenulf of Laigle. Baudry did homage to Abbot Robert, promised that he and his men would submit to the abbot's justice, and asked that 'his honour should never again be alienated from the lordship of the monks'. If Orderic gave the names correctly, the transfer of homage had not lasted long, for Abbot Robert was driven into exile only two years after taking office. 'To this day', concluded Orderic, writing in the early twelfth century, 'Baudry and his son Robert after him have done military service for the land of Bocquencé to the abbot alone.'[34]

Orderic may occasionally have used technical terms more appropriate to his own day than to the mid-eleventh century; but at least his story of the acquisition of Bocquencé and of Cullei (Rabodanges), the second of the abbey's later military fees, is entirely consistent with the foundation charters, which is more than can be said for some of the charters attributed to Henry I. According to the foundation charter, precisely cited by Orderic, Hugh of Grandmesnil gave Cullei to the monks 'at the request and with the consent of the lords of the vill, who held it as an alod (*quorum alodium erat*)'.[35] This means that they held it by hereditary tenure, and Orderic gives no further information about its later history. But one of the abbey's early charters describes how Samson of Cullei confirmed the gifts of his ancestors to the monks, promising to give himself and all his possessions to the abbey at his death, and received in return a horse from Abbot Roger of Le Sap (1091–1123).[36] Two royal charters of doubtful authenticity carry on the story, progressively converting the tenure of Cullei into a stereotyped knight's fee.

The more reliable of Henry I's charters on the subject confirms the grant of Cullei by the abbot and monks to Nigel of Aubigny, to hold of them in fee and inheritance, on condition that he perform at their summons and on their behalf the service of one knight, which was owed for it.[37] There are already some doubtful features in the wording of this charter, and the alleged confirmation charter of 1128 contains some even more suspicious passages. Haskins judiciously observed that 'there are some difficulties with regard to it'. As it stands in the version printed in *Gallia Christiana* allegedly from a lost original, it runs:

---

[34] Orderic, ii, 80–5.
[35] Orderic, ii, 32, 'Terram uero de Cueleio dedit Hugo petentibus sponte dominis eiusdem uillae, quorum alodium erat'. Cullei is now Rabondanges.
[36] *Orderici Vitalis Ecclesiasticae Historiae libri tredecim*, ed. A. Le Prévost. Société de l'Histoire de France, 1838–55, v, 193–4.
[37] Le Prévost, v, 200–1; *Regesta*, ii, no. 1595. The charter survives in the thirteenth-century cartulary of Saint-Evroult, and there are some suspicious features in the wording, especially in the witness clause beginning, 'Testibus me ipso . . .'. In its present form it may be a later recording of a grant made orally to Nigel. The date is not later than 29 July, 1129.

I grant also to them the whole vill of Cullei . . . by gift of . . . Robert and Hugh of Grandmesnil, which is one knight's fee; and another knight's fee of the gift of William Giroie, which is between Touquettes and the vill of Villers and is called Bocquencé, of the fee of Montreuil; and which my father William (with the consent of Thierry the first abbot . . . and Robert and Hugh of Grandmesnil and William Giroie their uncle, the founders of the abbey) constituted a barony for the service of him and his heirs in all his expeditions throughout Normandy, in such a way that Richard of Cullei and Baudry son of Nicholas, the knights to whom Abbot Thierry gave these two knight's fees in inheritance to hold of him, with the assent of my father William, shall be obliged to perform this service, each one for his fee with horses and arms at his own expense, and his heirs after him, whenever the abbot of Saint-Evroult is summoned by me, and they by the abbot.[38]

If the language of the charter for Nigel of Aubigny is to some extent that of Henry I towards the end of his reign, this is the language of the reign of Henry II. Neither is the language of 1050, though some of the facts recorded are near enough to the truth to have deceived Haskins. Yet the second charter is quite incompatible with what Orderic had to say about the transfer of Baudry's service to Arnold of Échauffour in the time of Abbot Robert. And if we may accept that Orderic's undertaking to write the history of his abbey received impetus from Henry I's visit to Saint-Evroult at Candlemas, 1113, when the monks sought confirmation of their properties and privileges,[39] then his history is likely to contain as true an account of conditions up to that date as he could ascertain from sources then in existence. The cartulary copies of the foundation charters of Saint-Evroult have certainly been tampered with; the election clauses were interpolated at a later date, probably in the 1130s.[40] The process of interpolating Henry I's later charters may have begun at the same time and continued into the reign of his grandson, to bring them into line with what was becoming customary. If the history allegedly recorded in these later, suspicious charter, was true and not interpolated history, why had Orderic nothing to say about it? And why did he say that Baudry of Bocquencé fought only for the abbey? Haskins' interpretation of the more probable truths in these documents is not the only one that fits the few known facts.

In 1050, when Saint-Evroult was founded in a marcher region where war was endemic, knights and vavassors were fairly numerous on lands that came in to the possession of the abbey. The lords of Bocquencé had certainly been military dependants of the duke; the same may have been true of the lords of Cullei, who had come to hold the land alodially under the Grandmesnil. The abbey undoubtedly had its own knights. When William Giroie, old and blind, went to visit his kinsmen in south Italy to collect gifts for the abbey he was accompanied by a dozen of the abbey's knights, who gave him escort. He himself and all but two of the knights died of the fevers of Italy; when one of the two survivors misappropriated the abbey's wealth entrusted to his care he was brought to justice in the abbot's court and condemned to forfeit his land until he made amends.[41] If the abbot did not need knights for castle-guard, he

---

38 Haskins, 11–14; *Gallia Christiana*, xi, instr. 204–10.
39 See Orderic, i, 32.
40 Orderic, i, 66–75.
41 Orderic, ii, 58–65.

needed them for his own protection, and particularly for escort service. Land could be given and service retained; it is possible that the dukes still had a claim to service from one or two of the knights of Saint-Evroult from an earlier period of vassalage. Baudry of Bocquencé had been the duke's archer. We know nothing of Richard of Cullei, but Samson of Cullei may have been a knight who was allowed to hold the property from the abbey for his lifetime, and was equipped to serve the abbot. Though there is no evidence of service being exacted on behalf of the duke when the land was given, ducal claims may have remained dormant and finally been satisfied in the course of the next century by the progressively more feudal arrangements recorded in interpolated royal charters and in the returns for 1172. By that time Saint-Evroult was recognised as a barony, owing the service of two knights; and in the registers of Philip Augustus they were charged against the fees of Cullei and Bocquencé.[42] Whether the arrangements crystallised before the death of William I or – as I think more likely – in the late 1120s or 1130s, they cannot have existed with anything like their final precision before the Norman conquest.

Military service, though variable at all levels, weighed more heavily on lay vassals and even on bishops than on any of the abbeys. These men, in any case, kept up substantial military households for their own protection; and though Duke William aimed at keeping as many of the castles of the duchy as possible in his own demesne under castellans appointed by him, a number of castles – especially in the marcher regions – fell into private hands and remained there.[43] I have already mentioned that Arnold of Échauffour held castles at Échauffour and Saint-Céneri; and there were others in this region at Pont-Échanfray and Moulins-la-Marche, where the duke attempted to assert his authority with only partial success. Some vassals were certainly forced into service in these castles, though hired knights provided some of the garrisons, together with a good stiffening of the châtelain's own brothers and sons.[44] Any evidence that the duke exacted a minimum period of service is sadly lacking; service was governed by need, and household troops and more casual mercenaries were both prominent. Much has been made of Orderic's statement that Guy, count of Ponthieu, was only released from prison after his capture at Mortemer in 1054 on condition that he did homage and promised to give the duke military service every year at his command, with a hundred knights.[45] But even if the figure is correct, the transaction reads more like a treaty of peace and alliance with a neighbouring lord than a record of the normal relations of the duke with his Norman vassals.

That knights would tend to become organised in groups of five or ten was, in the long run, inevitable; it was a fact of military tactics. Chroniclers' accounts of battles in this period were vitiated because they used a language that had been perfected to describe infantry engagements, and was not really adapted to cavalry warfare. They write of lines, columns, squadrons, wedges and so forth with a fine variety of phrase; but not until the vernacular became the language of narrative does the *conroi* clearly

---

[42] *The Red Book of the Exchequer*, ed. Hubert Hall, RS 1896, ii, 626; Haskins, *Norman Institutions*, 12.
[43] See J. Yver, 'Les châteaux forts en Normandie', *Bulletin de la Société des Antiquaires de Normandie*, liii, 1955–6, 42–63 for a discussion of castles in the reign of William the Conqueror.
[44] See, for example, *Gesta Guillelmi*, 54; the case of Arnold of Échauffour, above, p. 85; Fauroux, no. 117.
[45] Orderic, iv, 88–9.

emerge from the classical verbiage.[46] Mounted knights were trained as far as possible in small groups of five or ten, combined in larger units under their *magistri militum*.[47] A number of explanations might be offered for Orderic's statement that, when William fitzOsbern (as regent of Normandy) was summoned to accompany King Philip of France in the disastrous expedition of 1071 against Robert the Frisian, he rode off gaily with only ten knights as though he were going to a tournament.[48] It may mean that ten was the fixed quota obligation owed by the duke of Normandy to the king of France; but alternatively it may mean that ten was the minimum team that a knight of substance would put into the field for a tournament. Charles the Good, count of Flanders, who could have mustered many vassals with their contingents, was said by Galbert of Bruges to keep his knights in training by engaging in tournaments in Normandy or France, with 200 knights.[49]

On the eve of the conquest, or just after, we find the first charter reference to a fief on which five knights were settled, so that the tenurial corresponded with the tactical unit. The place is a charter of Duke William for the church of Avranches, recording a complicated family transaction by which John, bishop of Avranches, arranged for the transfer to his bishopric after his death of part of his own personal inheritance.[50] The Norman episcopate (with the solitary exception of the see of Rouen) was filled at this date with members of the highest Norman aristocracy, who were prepared to use their family lands to provide for the needs of their sees, and whose reconstruction of their bishoprics – as the history of Geoffrey of Coutances and Odo of Bayeux abundantly illustrates – was as military as it was pastoral.[51] John of Avranches had made a gift of half his territory of Vièvre (now Saint-Philbert); his nephew Robert contested this, and was finally bought off by the payment of ten pounds; the commendation of five knights to the bishop was allowed, with the stipulation that after the death of Bishop John the knights should hold their land as a fee of the bishop of Avranches. In 1172 the bishop of Avranches owed the duke of Normandy the service of five knights from the honour of Saint-Philbert; and it is very likely that a promise of service may have been made c.1066 when the gift was confirmed and recorded. At this date military needs were particularly pressing; it was necessary for the duke to know the military resources available both for his expedition and for the defence of the duchy he was leaving behind. The commendation of knights settled on the lands of laymen to a prince of the church would be more acceptable if their swords would remain available for the needs of the duke no less than those of the bishop. I would suggest that it is only at this date, in the thick of the preparations for the great expedition to England, that the widespread obligations of vassalage began to be more clearly systematised as obligations to provide at least a minimum contingent for the

[46] See Orderic, i, 104; J.F. Verbruggen, *The Art of Warfare in Western Europe during the Middle Ages*, trans. Sumner Willard and S.C.M. Southern, Amsterdam, 1977, 16–17.

[47] J.F. Verbruggen, 'La tactique des armées de chevaliers', *Revue du Nord*, xxix, 1947, 163–4, cites examples of groups of 30 or 40 combattants, though the size of the *conroi* might vary.

[48] Orderic, ii, 282.

[49] Galbert of Bruges, *The Murder of Charles the Good*, trans. James Bruce Ross, New York/Evanston/London 1967, ch. 4.

[50] Fauroux, no. 229.

[51] See D.C. Douglas, 'The Norman episcopate before the Norman Conquest', *Cambridge Historical Journal*, xiii, 101–15; J. Le Patourel, 'Geoffrey of Montbray, bishop of Coutances 1049–1093', *EHR*, lcx, 1944, 129–61; David R. Bates, 'The character and career of Odo, bishop of Bayeux (1049/50–1097)', *Speculum*, 1, 1975, 1–20.

ducal armies in Normandy. If the lands of knights had passed into the possession of the Church the men might still be held to a duty of serving the duke, and the responsibility for producing them could be put upon their lord.

The relation of these commended knights to their land is a very complex one. A great deal of the land of Normandy was held by hereditary tenure, and was regarded as an inalienable patrimony; but may of the holders were vassals, and benefices were for life.[52] This apparent contradiction can be explained by the facts that benefices were granted for past service; that a feudal vassal might occasionally be moved from one benefice to another; and that any inheritance, whilst passing by customary family law (a law that was slowly crystallising into *parage*), would not necessarily give the best share to the man most capable of bearing arms.[53] Once lordship and feudal service became so important that the lord's influence on the choice of an heir among the kindred became greater than the influence of the kindred, the benefice and alod could be said to have met in the fief. There is a twilight period when the process of determining the heir, and the nature of his claim to any particular fief, were matters of custom, not of right. In early ducal Normandy the kindred of a minor sometimes acted as guardian; only gradually did the lord assume this function.[54] Henry I, winning the support of his vassals of Norman birth by his coronation charter, would scarcely have agreed that the children of widows should be in the guardianship of their mother or another relative unless this had still been customary in Normandy no less than in England as late as 1100.[55] But his practice of taking money from the chosen guardian shows that the lord's right was making headway.[56] Hereditary right was rooted in the patrimony, and in time this combined with military needs to produce feudal customs. And it was only when feudal custom became feudal law that the lawful incidents could be defined with precision.

There is no clear evidence of the amount of feudal service that would have been regarded as reasonable in early ducal Normandy; if any theories had existed they would have been tempered by the harsh necessities of a struggle for survival and the lure of the spoils of war. Orderic had a story of how, during King William's difficult campaigns in Yorkshire and the West Midlands in the winter of 1069–70, the men of Anjou, Brittany and Maine complained and wished to go home. The king made no concessions; and when the army was disbanded at Salisbury and the men had re-

[52] The complexities of the situation are well illustrated in the *Vita Herluini* of Gilbert Crispin, which describes how, after Herluin had withdrawn from Count Gilbert's service and forfeited what he held of the count, he still had twenty knights among his own men. See J. Armitage Robinson, *Gilbert Crispin, Abbot of Westminster*, Cambridge 1911, 87–90, and the discussion by Christopher Harper-Bill, 'Herluin, abbot of Bec, and his biographer', *Studies in Church History*, ed. Derek Baker, xv, 1978, 15–16.

[53] See R. Génestal, *Le parage normand*, Caen 1911; John Le Patourel, *The Norman Empire*, Oxford 1976, 264. J. Yver, *Égalité entre héritiers et exclusion des enfants dotés*, Paris 1966, 106ff. has described the rapid crystallisation of custom in Normandy before the end of the eleventh century, even though rules of law were not formulated until the twelfth.

[54] R. Génestal, *La tutelle*, Caen 1930, however, considers that in Norman custom the lord had rights of wardship earlier than in French custom, and that in any case the rights of the duke were more extensive than those of another feudal lord.

[55] William Stubbs, *Select Charters*, 9th edn, Oxford 1912, 118, 'Et terrae et liberorum custos erit sive uxor sive alius propinquorum qui justius esse debebit'.

[56] Henry I's dealing with the four orphan children of Walter of Auffay shows how the rights of lord and kindred were kept in balance; he entrusted the wardship to the boys' uncle, who paid for the privilege. Orderic, iii, 258–61.

ceived their rewards he kept back those who had wished to desert, and made them serve an extra forty days as a punishment.[57] If Orderic took all his facts from William of Poitiers, this would be a nearly contemporary tradition; but although the passage has some statements in common with the *Liber Eliensis* which also used the lost text of William of Poitiers for these campaigns, the figure of forty days is peculiar to Orderic; and he wrote in the middle of Henry I's reign, when forty days service was an accepted norm for many vassals.[58] In any case, the men were malcontents from outside the duchy, not Normans. The implication seems to be that those who served under the ducal banner might expect to serve as long as they were needed, or take the consequences. For loyal service the rewards might be great.

As for the other obligations, they seem to have depended on individual contracts and to have been variable, both before the conquest and for some time afterwards; some indeed were never standardised. Baudry of Bocquencé had to meet different demands for castle guard from his two lords. The first aid 'pour fille marier' taken by a Norman king in England was Henry I's aid for his daughter Matilda's marriage in 1109, and it was assessed on the hide, not the fee; there no evidence that it was collected in Normandy.[59] As late as 1133 the Bayeux Inquest produced a statement on the obligations of the bishop's knights.[60] The bishop was entitled to receive from the fief of each knight a relief consisting of a hauberk and stirrup, or fifteen livres; each knight in addition owed an aid of 20s. if the bishop had to go to Rome on the business of his church, and an aid of an unspecified amount for rebuilding the cathedral church if necessary, or rebuilding the houses of the city if they were burnt. These obligations were clearly tailor-made for the bishopric, and were different from those appropriate for a lay lord with daughters to marry or sons to knight. They may very well have been fixed during the period when Odo was most active in building up the wealth and strength of his bishopric some time in the later part of the reign of William I. The duty of support if he went to Rome on the business of his church does not seem realistic before the 1070s at the earliest: although any Norman might undertake a south Italian adventure under guise of pilgrimage in the early eleventh century, constant recourse to Rome on ecclesiastical business was not a characteristic of the Norman church until considerably later, when reform began to bite. When Odo was arrested in 1082 he was accused of trying to take knights to Rome to further his own ambitions, but that was hardly the business of the see.[61] On the other hand some of the obligations might have been found in other lordships; the relief of fifteen livres

---

57 Orderic, ii, 237–7.
58 As late as 1172, however, there are indications that the length of service was not entirely uniform; see *The Red Book of the Exchequer*, ii, 643, 'De honore comitis Mortonii per Ricardum Silvanum, xxix milites et dimidium et octavam partem; ad servitium Regis, per manus Comitis, ad marchiam per xl dies ad custum corum, deinceps ad custum Regis vel Comitis. Et Comiti serviebant prout debebant'.
59 Huntingdon, 237, 'Rex cepit ab unaquaque hida Angliae iii solidos': *ASC* E, *sub anno* 1110, 'This was a very severe year in this country because of taxes that the king took for the marriage of his daughter'. Various churchmen, including the bishops of Lincoln and Norwich, the abbots of Battle and Abingdon and the prior of Spalding, secured writs stating that this aid was not to impair the exemptions granted to some of their lands, or introduce new customs (*Regesta*, ii, nos. 942, 946, 959, 963, 964, 968).
60 *Antiquus cartularius ecclesiae Baiocensis*, ed. V. Bourienne, Société de l'Histoire normande, 1902–3, 19.
61 *De gestis regum*, ii, 334; Orderic, iv, 40; *Liber monasterii de Hyda*, ed. E. Edwards, R S 1866, 296.

in silver, which ultimately became standard in Normandy and remained so for a considerable period, may already have been customary in many honours.[62]

Whatever the terms of individual contracts, feudal obligations were enforceable in honorial courts. There seems little doubt that such courts existed in ducal Normandy before 1066, though it is not easy to separate formal judicial proceedings from general business. The court was a place for the meeting of lords and vassals for various activities, including knightly sports and the discussion of matters of common interest. Witness lists of charters indicate that grants were sometimes made in such assemblies.[63] Chroniclers writing in the first generation after the conquest certainly believed that pleas were heard and judgements enforced in them. Gilbert Crispin's *Vita Herluini* describes a debate on whether Herluin should have been deprived of his lands for failure to carry out a mission on behalf of his lord, Count Gilbert of Brionne, and implies that it took place in the lord's court.[64] Somewhat later, Orderic recorded proceedings in the court of Saint-Evroult, allegedly in the time of the first two abbots. The knight Anquetil of Noyer, who had misappropriated the treasures he was supposed to carry back from Italy, was summoned to judgement in the court of Saint-Evroult and condemned to lose what Orderic, in the language of 1120, calls 'the whole fief he held from Saint-Evroult', but which appears to have included a third of the bourg of Saint-Evroult which he held as his inheritance form his father.[65] Orderic may be less than clear on the precise legal condition of Anquetil's land, and like Gilbert Crispin he may have read back into the earlier period the more formal procedures of his own day. But it is difficult to doubt the existence and competence of the courts whose proceedings both chroniclers described.

Much is obscure in the history of honorial courts in the eleventh century; and the difficulties of interpreting the evidence continue well into the twelfth. Charters no less than chronicles used anachronistic language, and were themselves liable to later interpolation. The cartulary copy of Henry I's charter to Saint-Evroult, confirming the grant to Nigel of Aubigny of Cullei to hold in fee of the abbey, contains detailed arrangements about jurisdiction in these words: 'In order to secure the relief of the land and the royal services or dues granted to the abbey of Saint-Evroult by me or my heirs, the abbot and monks shall have the right of exercising jurisdiction in that vill as often as they find necessary; and if Nigel or his heirs attempt to impose any customs on the knights or other men of the vill beyond those which of right are owed to the abbot and monks of Saint-Evroult, and if the men bring any plea arising out of this, the abbot and monks shall bring him to justice in that vill until suitable penalties have been exacted; similarly for all forfeitures and other penalties which Nigel may incur against the monks.' I have shown that there are suspicious features in the wording of this charter, parts of which may even have been interpolated after the reign of Henry I.[66] But, taking it together with Orderic's narrative, we may safely conclude that the monks of Saint-Evroult were exercising jurisdiction as a matter of course over their vassals in the third decade of the twelfth century, and that they had

---

[62] H. Navel, 'L'enquête de 1133 sur les fiefs de l'évêché de Bayeux', *Bulletin de la Société des Antiquaires de Normandie*, xlii, 1935, 57.

[63] Fauroux, no. 191.

[64] Armitage Robinson, 90.

[65] Orderic, ii, 62–5.

[66] Le Prévost, v, 200–1; and see above, p. 85 n. 37.

held a court of some kind to deal with failure to perform service even before 1066, in the lifetime of the first abbot.

Moreover, anachronistic language shows the way in which feudal law was developing, and may indicate the realities that had underlain earlier customs. The development was slow. But as the duke came to have a defined interest in the military obligations of his sub-vassals, the workings of the honorial courts became a matter of direct concern to him. To a certain extent it is true, as Professor Milsom has clearly demonstrated, that the feudal courts were a law unto themselves; there was at first no regular procedure of appeal from them to a higher court.[67] Nevertheless the ducal power was held in reserve, and might, in the course of time, intervene and guarantee the smooth workings of the honorial courts. By the end of Henry I's reign feudal service, with all its incidents, was becoming precisely defined, and custom was hardening into law. As a consequence of this, the residual power of the ducal court soon became a reality for enforcing customary law. But this is a far cry from the tangle of incipient feudal customs, partly built up from below, that had existed in Normandy during the period before William the Bastard became William the Conqueror of England.

---

[67]	F.M. Stenton, *The First Century of English Feudalism*, 2nd edn ch. 2; S.F.C. Milsom, *The Legal Framework of English Feudalism*, Cambridge 1976, especially 183–6.

B. The Campaign

Many of the questions historians have about the campaign of Hastings revolve
not around what happened but why. Were the choices that William and Harold
made at key points in the campaign forced on them by conditions and
circumstances, or at least constrained within certain limits? If so, how? In
investigating such problems, historians have attempted to establish the ranges
of physical possibility and probability in a number of ways. The next three
articles demonstrate three different approaches to this problem.

9. John Gillingham, 'William the Bastard at War'

In this article, John Gillingham sets the 1066 campaign in the context both of Duke William's military career up to that point and of normal patterns of warfare in the mid-eleventh century. One of his main points of emphasis is that logistics – the need to keep the men and animals of an army supplied with food – shaped medieval warfare in pervasive ways. Indeed, Gillingham shows that the patterns of medieval warfare were also those of ancient and early modern warfare, because the same logistical factors (and technological limits) were at work. Understanding the logistical limits within which armies operated and generals made their decisions is thus crucial to understanding the strategies used by both sides in 1066. His other key point is to show how unusual set-piece battles like Hastings were, even for a leader such as William who was always at war.

Reprinted from *Studies in Medieval History Presented to R. Allen Brown*, ed. Christopher Harper-Bill et al. (Woodbridge, 1989), 141–58. Copyright © John Gillingham 1989.

WILLIAM THE BASTARD AT WAR

John Gillingham

As Allen Brown observed at the end of his paper on his battle at his conference, almost the only thing about the Norman Conquest that isn't controversial is the fact that the Normans won the Battle of Hastings. How and why they won remain matters of opinion. In Allen's view – and, characteristically, he described himself as being 'at least as unbiassed as William of Poitiers' – they owed their victory to their 'superior military techniques' and to William's 'superior generalship'.[1] Now much has been written about military techniques and organisation, both Norman and Anglo-Saxon, but almost nothing has been written about William's generalship. Although what he did – and what Harold did – in 1066 itself has been endlessly discussed, no real attempt has been made to put that decisive campaign into the context of William's whole career as a war leader. Even William's military experience in the years prior to 1066 – the experience on which he presumably drew as he contemplated the greatest enterprise of his life – has been often mentioned but hardly analysed.[2] This omission is all the more curious in view of the fact that the materials for such a study are ready to hand. One of the conqueror's own chaplains wrote an account of his master's life in which he consciously chose to portray him as a model of generalship. Time and again William of Poitiers compares William with the great generals of antiquity, and time and again he concludes that William was the greater soldier. His account of the campaign of 1066 culminates in a sustained comparison between the Norman invasion of England and the Roman invasion of Britain, demonstrating – at least to the author's own satisfaction – that William had faced greater difficulties than Julius Caesar and yet had achieved a much more impressive degree of success.[3] Since the chaplain was writing in the 1070s, and writing a work clearly destined for his master's ears, this was presumably a demonstration very much to William's taste. Throughout his work indeed it is evident that WP was saying what he felt his lord would like to hear. He was producing a justification of William the Conqueror and, at times, a nauseatingly sycophantic one. One of his earliest known readers, Orderic Vitalis, son of an English mother and a Norman father, was clearly shocked by WP's account of the harrying of the North and was moved to comment: 'When I think of the helpless children, the young people in the prime of life, and those whose hair was now grey with age, all alike condemned to die of hunger, then I am so stirred to pity that I would simply lament what was done, rather than vainly attempt, with empty adulation, to flatter the perpetrator of such infamy'.[4] It is also

---

1   R. Allen Brown, 'The Battle of Hastings', *Battle* iii, 21.
2   Except in the excellent but brief chapter entitled 'Military Society and the Art of War', in F. Barlow, *William I and the Norman Conquest*, 1965.
3   *Gesta Guillelmi*, 68, 156, 162, 168, 232–4, 246–54; probably also Orderic ii, 234.
4   Orderic ii, 232

evident that WP was, as R.H.C. Davis has put it, 'intent on producing a work of great literature', a self-conscious stylist, insistently parading his easy mastery of a wide range of classical Latin literature, 'flattering himself' as well as the Conqueror.[5] Reading him indeed I am irresistibly reminded of the opening words of Geoffrey Parker's chapter on warfare in the thematic companion volume to the *New Cambridge Modern History*: 'Part of the charm of Renaissance writers is their firm conviction that . . . the heroes of antiquity would have been miserable failures as Renaissance men, even as Renaissance soldiers'.[6] By these criteria William of Poitiers was a Renaissance writer and William the Bastard a Renaissance soldier. And so indeed they were.

But there is no need to dismiss the work on this account.[7] On the contrary. These features are so obvious that they are relatively easy to make allowances for. Moreover from the point of view of the student of war, the history of WP has two great advantages. First, it was written by someone close to the court, a member, as it were, of the duke's headquarters staff. Second, it was written by an author who had himself been a soldier. In Orderic's words, 'before he entered the church he had himself been keenly involved in the business of war. He had borne arms in the service of his prince and, having himself lived through the dire perils of war, was all the better placed to give an accurate description of the conflicts he had seen'.[8] His account of William's career may be a biassed one, but it is the bias of a man who, on the subject of war at least, knew exactly what he was talking about. Since I have had the good fortune never to have been more than an armchair soldier, I shall follow very closely in the footsteps of William of Poitiers.

My intention then is twofold. Firstly to take Duke William's military career as a model of eleventh-century generalship.[9] Secondly to put the 1066 campaign into the context of mid-eleventh century warfare. This means that in this paper I shall have relatively little to say about the last period of William's career, the years after 1075 when he no longer enjoyed the fortunate constellation of political circumstances which had characterised the 1060s and early 1070s and when, in consequence, his generalship faltered.[10] In Orderic's words, 'In the last thirteen years of his life he never once succeeded in putting an army to flight or capturing by military skill any fortress to which he laid siege.'[11] WP's task as panegyrist was made distinctly easier

---

[5] R.H.C. Davis, 'William of Poitiers and his History of William the Conqueror', in R.H.C. Davis and J.M. Wallace-Hadrill, eds, *The Writing of History in the Middle Ages. Essays presented to R.W. Southern*, Oxford 1981, 71–100, esp. 72.

[6] G. Parker, 'Warfare', in *The New Cambridge Modern History* xiii, Companion Volume, ed. P. Burke, Cambridge 1979, 201.

[7] Any more than it would be right, on similar grounds, to dismiss Richer of Rheims as a source for late tenth-century warfare. See the comments, valuable on this and on all aspects of war in this period, of John France, 'La Guerre dans la France féodale à la fin du IXe et au Xe siècle', *Revue Belge d'Histoire Militaire* xxiii, 1979, 177–198, esp. 179, 192–3.

[8] Orderic ii, 258.

[9] In this respect an exercise very similar to J. Gillingham, 'Richard I and the science of war in the Middle Ages', J. Gillingham and J.C. Holt, eds, *War and Government in the Middle Ages. Essays in honour of J.O. Prestwich*, Woodbridge 1984, 78–91.

[10] The high drama of 1066 rather obscures the fact William's military career falls quite naturally into three parts: the period up to 1060 when he was generally on the defensive against both internal and external enemies; the years of expansion between 1060 and 1075; and finally the period between 1076 and 1087 when he was once again on the defensive.

[11] Orderic ii, 350. In view of the defeats and setbacks which William suffered at Dol in 1076, Gerberoi

by the fact that he happened to be writing at a time when William's military reputation was at its peak.[12] Bearing in mind the defeats and setbacks of William's later career it is doubtless easier for me to be a little more detached.

I begin with an example of the panegyrist at work: WP's treatment of the battle of Val-ès-Dunes (1047), the first military incident to be reported in the surviving portion of his text. Here WP gives the impression that Duke William was in overall command of the 'loyalist' troops, with King Henry I of France merely lending useful assistance.[13] But since in 1047 the king was the greater man in rank, in age and in experience of war, common sense alone suggests that WP was being misleading, probably deliberately so.[14] And in this case common sense is confirmed by the language of William of Jumièges' account of the battle, written half a dozen years earlier than WP's.[15]

If, in fact, it was King Henry who was the army commander at Val-ès-Dunes, then it becomes possible to draw a rather striking conclusion. In 1066, as Frank Barlow pointed out, William had no previous experience of command in a set battle.[16] Whether or not it is quite right to go on to say, as Barlow does, that until he faced Harold, William had never deployed his own army in the face of a large enemy force, probably depends on what is meant by 'in the face of', but it is undoubtedly true that although there were earlier occasions when William offered battle, and may have done so seriously, in fact no battle actually took place.[17] In passing it should also be noted that, so far as we can tell, in the summer of 1066 Harold too was without experience of command in a set battle.[18] What makes this point all the more striking

in 1079, La Flèche in 1081 and St Suzanne in 1084–5, Orderic's judgement seems better grounded than Barlow's 'once he had caught the wind he never got becalmed', Barlow, xvi.

12 Some idea of his reputation in the mid-1070s can be gathered from the rumour that he was planning to attack Aachen and seize the empire reported by Lampert of Hersfeld under the year 1074. Lampert of Hersfeld, *Annales*, ed. O. Holder-Egger, Scriptores Rerum Germanicarum in usum scholarum, Hanover 1894, 195.

13 *Gesta Guillelmi*, 16–18.

14 The king, in WP's words, was *vir strenuus et nominatus in rebus bellicis*, a competent and cautious advisor to the young soldier, *Gesta Guillelmi*, 24, 82.

15 'rex cum duce', Jumièges, 123. Despite this most historians, e.g. Michel de Boüard, *Guillaume le Conquérant*, Paris 1984, 205, or R. Allen Brown, *The Normans*, Woodbridge 1984, 44–5, or David Bates, *Normandy before 1066*, 1982, 73, continue to follow WP in implying that William was in charge at Val-ès-Dunes. More in line with WJ's emphasis is D.C. Douglas, *William the Conqueror*, London 1964, 49. I would like to emphasise that impressed as I am by WP's qualities as a historian of war, I am almost equally impressed by WJ, monk though he may have been. Perhaps indeed in a society where no monastery was immune from the consequences of war – usually destructive, but sometimes in the more acceptable form of gifts from the contrite warrior – it was natural for observant monks to be well informed about war. On WJ see E.M.C. Van Houts, *Gesta Normannorum Ducum*, Groningen 1983, and on the relationship between WJ and WP, Davis, 'William of Poitiers', 76–80.

16 Barlow, 33. One implication of this is that the engagement in 1057 which is conventionally referred to as the 'battle of Varaville' was in fact not a battle. Here I entirely agree with Barlow, 33 and de Boüard, 205, that it was not. See below p. 107. Of course if we eliminate Val-ès-Dunes and Varaville from the roll of William's battle honours then it becomes a little harder to see him as the general who, when he rode into the field of Hastings 'had never fought a battle which he had not won', Brown, *The Normans*, 45. Cf. R. Allen Brown, *The Normans and the Norman Conquest*, 1969, 49.

17 On William offering battle see below pp. 104–5.

18 Though it should be noted that we know a great deal less about Harold's military career than we do about William's. It might, however, be argued that it generally was the case that when battles occurred it was between commanders who had little or no experience of battle. On the battle of Lewes,

is the observation that at Hastings 'the core of the army was a force of fighting men seasoned in the many wars Duke William had fought'.[19] It follows that there were many wars but very few battles.[20] In that case three questions at once arise. The first, why were battles so rare? The second, just what was William's normal style of warfare? The third, why in 1066 did he depart from his familiar methods and try something of which he had no experience?

To start with the first question. Hastings, as every schoolgirl knows, was a decisive victory. And this is how it was understood in the eleventh century.[21] Moreover the battle of Val-ès-Dunes also seems to have been regarded as being decisive. It is true that the defeated Guy of Brionne was able to remain in revolt for a long time after-wards – for three years according to Orderic – nonetheless it does look as though as a result of the battle the military initiative passed into William's hands.[22] But if one of the more dramatic events in William's early career had indeed been his participa-tion in a decisive victory in battle, then this only sharpens the question.[23] Why, if he had learned that battles could bring important advantages to the victor, did he sub-sequently and for so long avoid battle?[24] For there can, I think, be no doubt that he did avoid battle, i.e. the absence of battles in the years 1048 to 1065 is not simply because other generals were afraid of William and ran away whenever he ap-proached. This is undeniably one of the impressions which WP tries to create.[25] Unfortunately he significantly weakens his case in a passage in which he comments generally on William's defence of Normandy from the time of his youth up until his forty-fifth year. He remarks that whenever King Henry attacked, William went out of his way to avoid battle.[26]

---

for example, David Carpenter has observed that 'not a single person on either side in 1264 had ever been in one', D. Carpenter, *The Battles of Lewes and Evesham 1264/5*, Keele 1987, 17.

[19] M. Chibnall, *Anglo-Norman England 1066–1166*, Oxford 1986, 9–10.

[20] Exactly how many wars it is hard to know, but a likely minimum is that he went to war in at least thirteen of the years between 1047 and 1065. Very probably he went to war more often that this but given the gaps in the sources, – none of them by authors who were setting out to compile detailed annals – and given the well-known chronological problems which they present (see Davis, 'William of Poitiers', 75–77 and Bates, Appendix A) we are unlikely to get much further than this minimum estimate. But we must always bear Chibnall's warning in mind. 'In dealing with a period where the evidence is so exiguous and warfare was almost continuous, it is important not to imagine that the few engagements of which we have some knowledge, even if accurately reported, were the only things that happened', Orderic ii, 365.

[21] *Gesta Guillelmi*, 208, 248.

[22] Jumièges, 123; *Gesta Guillelmi*, 18–20; Orderic vi, 210.

[23] Since the first section of WP's History is missing, we have to rely upon WJ for William's earliest military experiences. Whether or not the undated recapture of Falaise (Jumièges, 118) actually was his first experience of war – WJ could well have discreetly passed over less happy experiences, particularly in the previous months when King Henry had invaded Normandy, burned down the ducal town of Argentan, and returned home laden with plunder (Jumièges, 117–18) – the episode nicely illustrates the generalisation, important as it is well-known, that 'the military strategy of the period was based almost entirely on the castle or town', Barlow, 30. See also the chapter on 'The castle in war', in R.A. Brown, *English Castles*, 2nd edn, 1976.

[24] In De Boüard's view William disliked battle so intensely that he fought only two (Val-ès-Dunes and Hastings) in his whole career, and even these two were forced upon him by his adversaries, De Boüard, 205. By my reckoning William the general fought two or three battles, Hastings, probably York 1069 (in both of these it was William who took the initiative) and Gerberoi 1079; and William the soldier fought in a fourth (Val-ès-Dunes).

[25] E.g. *Gesta Guillelmi*, 40, 78, 110.

[26] *Gesta Guillelmi*, 28. True he ascribes this to William's laudable concern for the royal dignity and

Why then did William avoid battle when it could be decisive? The answer surely is, precisely because it could be decisive. Decisive for the loser as well as for the victor and no general could ever be absolutely certain of victory. So far as we can see Hastings was a very close run thing, and Val-ès-Dunes may have been as well.[27] Indeed it is unlikely that any given battle would take place unless both commanders felt they had a reasonable chance of victory. In a fairly evenly balanced situation a few minutes of confusion or panic and the patient work of months or even years might be undone. Moreover although battle might tip the strategic balance one way or the other, it does not follow that all battles did. The advantage won by William's victory over the northern rebels at York in 1069 was to be very short-lived. Later that same year the North was up in arms again, the Danes landed, Edgar Atheling returned to the fray and an army 'marching in high spirits' re-captured York.[28] More directly relevant to the subject of William's generalship prior to 1066 is the battle of Morte-mer in 1054. Here Count Robert of Eu won the victory which effectively put an end to King Henry's invasion in that year, but it neither altered the balance of power in northern France nor led to the break-up of the Capetian-Angevin alliance against William. Thus in 1057 the allies were to invade Normandy again, and it is just possible that they did so in 1058 as well.[29] What was really decisive was neither Mortemer nor William's own victory in the engagement at Varaville in 1057, but the fact that both Henry I and Geoffrey Martel happened to die in 1060.[30] Even victory in battle might, in other words, bring only limited rewards, whereas there was always the possibility that defeat might be disastrous. Seeking battle was a high-risk strategy.

Moreover if the imminent prospect of battle brought to all men the terrible fear of injury, or death, or shame, then to none more so than the commander himself.[31] This is because it was always clear that the surest way to win a battle was to kill or capture the opposing commander. Thus the critical importance of the moment at Hastings when William calmed the fears of his men by showing them that he was still alive

to his memory of their former friendship, but royal dignity may have meant more to William after 1066 (when WP was writing) than it had before. Moreover, as WP himself notes, other Normans were less troubled by such scruples.

27 WP emphasises the strength of the opposition at Val-ès-Dunes – 'the greater part of Normandy' (*Gesta Guillelmi*, 16) and this, together with WJ's statement that 'the king and the duke were undaunted by their enemies' fierce attacks' (Jumièges, 123), might be thought to imply that they had been dangerous attacks. The stories told by Wace in the *Roman de Rou*, composed in the 1160s and 1170s, might be taken to reinforce the impression that the issue hung long in the balance, but it is surely rash to attempt to reconstruct the course of the battle – as do De Boüard, 127–31 and Douglas, 50–1, – from tales told and songs sung for a hundred years before they reached the ears of the man who wrote them down. We only have to listen to a modern guide at a historical monument to realise that topographical precision is not the slightest guarantee of historical accuracy. See also Matthew Bennett, 'Poetry as history? The "Roman de Rou" of Wace as a source for the Norman Conquest', *Battle* v, 21–39. All we really know about Val-ès-Dunes is that Henry and William won it.

28 *ASC* 'D' *ad annum* 1069.

29 O. Guillot, *Le comte d'Anjou et son entourage au XIe siècle*, Paris 1972, 81, citing the *Cart. de Notre Dame du Ronceray*, no. 80, 'Anno . . . MLVIII quando profectus est comes in Normanniam cum exercitu cum rege Francie Henrico super comitem Guillelmum'.

30 As WP implicitly recognised when, immediately after reporting their deaths, he announced his intention of turning to the subject of William's conquests, *Gesta Guillelmi*, 84–6.

31 See, e.g., Orderic's account of a confrontation between William and Fulk le Réchin, probably in 1081: 'Dum utraeque acies ad ambiguum certamen pararentur, horribilesque pro morte et miseriis quae mortem reproborum sequuntur, timores mentibus multorum ingererentur' (Orderic ii, 308–10).

and well.[32] It was not only that Harold – and his brothers – died at Hastings. Harold Hardrada and Tostig were killed at Stamford Bridge. Conan of Brittany had been killed at the Battle of Conquereuil in 992. William fitzOsbern was to be killed at Cassel in 1070.[33] Since we know that, as things turned out, William managed to survive his battles, it is easy to forget the very great risks he was taking. At Gerberoi his horse was killed under him, and 'he who brought up another for him, Toki of Wallingford, was immediately killed by a bolt from a crossbow'.[34] William escaped with an injury to his hand. It sounds minor but just such an injury was to cost William Clito his life in 1128.[35] Hastings was clearly no exception. If WP is right in saying that William had three horses killed under him then it may have been merely a matter of luck as to whether it was he or Harold who was killed first.[36] Even if he escaped death or injury a prince had reason to worry about the political consequences of being taken prisoner.[37] To judge from WP's account of the capture of William of Aquitaine in 1033 and of Theobald of Blois in 1058, it looks as though William's advisers were well aware of this danger.[38]

In the light of all these considerations it would be reasonable to imagine that an eleventh-century prince might be a little nervous about battle. Thanks to the remarkable *Fragmentum Historiae Andegavensis* written by Count Fulk le Réchin, we can show that at least one such prince certainly was. The climax of Fulk's brief history of the counts of Anjou (written in 1096) comes when he describes the war of succession between him and his brother Geoffrey (1060–68):

> Time and again we made war (*guerram*) one upon the other. With interludes for truces this tribulation went on for eight years altogether. Then, on the instructions of Pope Alexander, I released my brother from the chains in which I held him, but still he attacked me yet again, laying siege to my fortress (*castrum*) of Brissac. There I rode against him with those princes whom God, in his clemency, permitted to join me, and I fought with him a pitched battle in which, by God's grace, I overcame him; and he was captured and handed over to me, and a thousand of his men with him.[39]

---

[32] *Gesta Guillelmi*, 190; *BT*, ed. D.M. Wilson, pl. 68. By the early twelfth century it was believed that King Henry had had a close shave at Val-ès-Dunes, *De gestis regum* ii, 287.

[33] Orderic ii, 282.

[34] *ASC* 'D' *ad annum* 1079.

[35] Symeon ii, 282–3. This Durham author was exceptionally well-informed, perhaps reflecting the diplomatic interests of Bishop Flambard.

[36] *Gesta Guillelmi*, 198. I am not convinced that WJ ever really said that Harold was killed at the beginning of the battle, *in primo militum congressu* (Jumièges, 135). The train of thought indicated by the sentences before and after the sentence containing this phrase, in particular the words at the beginning of the next sentence, 'Comperientes itaque Angli regem suum mortem oppetiisse . . . iam nocte imminente' suggests to me that what WJ actually wrote was *in postremo militum congressu; postremo* then being misread by a copyist who overlooked the *post* abbreviation. WJ's autograph does not survive, so all extant MSS may derive from an early copy already containing this scribal error. See the stemma in Van Houts, 67.

[37] William of Malmesbury was to have some sympathetic words for the plight of politically valuable prisoners, *De gestis regum* ii, 288.

[38] *Gesta Guillelmi*, 32–4. Slightly later examples that come readily to mind are Robert Curthose at Tinchebrai and King Stephen at Lincoln.

[39] L. Halphen and R. Poupardin, ed., *Chroniques des comtes d'Anjou et des seigneurs d'Amboise*, Paris 1913, 237. This time Geoffrey stayed in prison. Fulk Rechin was one of the enemies who were

Only on one other occasion does Fulk refer to God's grace, and that is in his reference to Fulk Nerra's victory, *Dei gratia*, over Count Odo of Blois in the battle of Pontlevoy.[40] Battle was a desperate business; the risks terrible; the outcome uncertain. As Fulk Rechin's language shows, it was at this perilous moment that events were felt to move out of human control and into the hands of God. Since then the rewards might be limited while the risks were always terrible, it is not surprising that prudent commanders should prefer to look for other methods, methods which 'did relatively little harm if things turned out badly, and yet brought great gains when they turned out well'.[41] This, after all, would be the professional approach to war and, as Allen Brown has so often emphasised, these were men whose approach was professional through and through.[42] This, moreover, was the advice they received from Vegetius, author of that late Roman handbook on war which, throughout the middle ages and beyond, was to remain 'the soldier's Bible'.[43] For Vegetius was emphatic. Battle should be the last resort. Everything else should be tried first.[44]

What then were these other methods? What was William's normal style of warfare in the years between 1047 and 1066? I begin with an analysis of William on the attack.[45] By far his greatest success before 1066 was his conquest of Maine and WP is very clear as to how this was achieved. His principal target was Le Mans itself, *validissima urbs, caput atque munimentum terrae.* But rather than an immediate and direct assault on the city itself, William preferred a different way. 'This then was his chosen method of conquest. He sowed terror in the land by his frequent and lengthy invasions; he devastated vineyards, fields and estates; he seized neighbouring strong-points and where advisable put garrisons in them; in short he incessantly inflicted innumerable calamities upon the land.'[46] In these succinct phrases we have an excellent outline of the basic strategy of attack: the intention is to seize fortresses and the standard preliminary is to ravage the surrounding countryside.[47] In 1073, when William had to recover Maine, he adopted the same methods. In the words of the

to give William such a hard time in the later years of his life. I entirely agree with Jim Bradbury's re-assessment of this prince elsewhere in *Studies in Medieval History Presented to R. Allen Brown*, ed. Christopher Harper-Bill et al. (Woodbridge, 1989), 27–41.

40 Halphen and Poupardin, 234.

41 'Quae si male cesserint, minus noceant, si bene, plurmum prosint', Vegetius, *Epitoma rei militaris*, ed. C. Lang, Leipzig 1885, 91–2.

42 Here the appropriate footnote is surely Brown, *passim*.

43 On Vegetius see W. Goffart, 'The date and purpose of Vegetius' *De Re Militari*', *Traditio* xxxiii, 1977. I have not seen B.S. Bachrach, 'The practical use of Vegetius' *De Re Militari* during the early middle ages', *The Historian* xlvii, 1985. But wide of the mark is D.J.A. Ross's notion (in 'The Prince Answers Back: "Les Enseignemens de Theodore Paliologue" ', C. Harper-Bill and R. Harvey eds, *The Ideals and Practice of Medieval Knighthood*, Woodbridge 1986, 165) that even when he wrote Vegetius was 'hopelessly out of date'. Eternal common-sense principles – R.C. Smail's apt description of Vegetius' strategic maxims – do not date.

44 'Ideo omnia ante cogitanda sunt, ante temptanda, ante facienda sunt, quam ad ultimum veniatur abruptim.' Vegetius, 86.

45 A narrative of William's wars would take up more space than I have here and would, in any case, be superfluous. For a recent excellent chronological summary of his campaigns in their political and military context see Bates, 73–83.

46 *Gesta Guillelmi*, 90. Characteristically WP explains that this was because William wished to avoid unnecessary bloodshed.

47 As, in the next century, Jordan Fantosme was to put it; 'Let him . . . lay waste their country . . . then besiege their castles' (R.C. Johnstone, ed., *Jordan Fantosme's Chronicle*, Oxford 1981, ll. 439–50). See Gillingham, 83–4.

ASC, 'In this year king William led an English and French host oversea and conquered the province of Maine, and the English laid it completely waste; they destroyed the vineyards, burnt down the towns, and completely devastated the countryside, and brought it all into subjection to William.'[48] Similarly William's enemies were expected to operate in the same way. When Henry I invaded Normandy in 1054, he came, according to William of Poitiers, with the intention of 'destroying *oppida*, burning villages, here putting to the sword, there seizing plunder, and so in the end reducing the whole land to a miserable desert'.[49] Since no system of magazines and supply lines was capable of sustaining an army embarked on operations in enemy territory it followed that armies were forced to forage to stay alive.[50] Of course foraging and ravaging are not quite identical activities, but the fact remains that in most circumstances one man's foraging is another man's ravaging. Thus 'the usual method, indeed the very aim of warfare was to live at the enemy's expense' and by doing so compel him to give in to your demands.[51] Ravaging, and foraging while ravaging, was the principal strategy of attack. All this was strictly the Gospel according to Vegetius. 'The main and principal point in war is to secure plenty of provisions for oneself and to destroy the enemy by famine.'[52] The point about ravaging, and foraging while ravaging, was that it was directed simultaneously to both these ends. At one and the same time moreover it suited both the overall campaign strategy of the commander and the individual interest of the ordinary soldier who was fighting for private profit, for plunder. A method which worked on all these levels at once was clearly a supremely efficient one.

WP's account of the 1063 conquest of Maine is, of course, phrased in very general terms. None the less it is precisely these strategic generalisations which enable us to make sense of his much more detailed account of the earliest episodes in the history of Norman military pressure on the county of Maine, pressure which dated back to the early 1050s. It all began with a counter-attack, William's reaction to a threatening advance made by the most formidable warrior of the day, Count Geoffrey Martel of Anjou.[53] At an unknown date, but probably c.1051 when he acquired a firm grip on Maine, Geoffrey Martel took control of Alençon and Domfront, 'the former within, the latter adjoining the borders of Normandy'.[54] According to WJ, having placed troops in the fortress of Domfront, Geoffrey began to ravage Normandy. Indeed according to WP, it was precisely the licence to plunder which Geoffrey gave them which made his lordship so attractive to the men of Domfront and Alençon.[55] William responded by launching an attack on Domfront. The strength of this fortress's site

[48] *ASC* 'E' *ad annum* 1073.

[49] *Gesta Guillelmi*, 70; cf. 'ad Calcivum subvertendum territorium . . . ad demoliendum comitatum Embroicensem' (Jumièges, 129).

[50] M. Van Creveld, *Supplying War. Logistics from Wallenstein to Patton*, Cambridge 1977, 7–10. Van Creveld's analysis, based on seventeenth century conditions, applies *a fortiori* to the eleventh.

[51] Van Creveld, 23, 27, 32.

[52] 'In omni expeditione unum est et maximum telum, ut tibi sufficiat victus, hostes frangat inopia' (Vegetius, 69). Thus, as Matthew Bennett has pointed out in 'The Status of the Squire: the Northern Evidence', *Ideals and Practice* (as n. 43), 4, even in the *chansons de geste* ravaging is portrayed as an entirely commonplace activity.

[53] For his great reputation as a soldier see *Gesta Guillelmi*, 32, 42; Orderic ii 104; Halphen and Poupardin, 235.

[54] *Gesta Guillelmi*, 42. On the date see Bates, 255–7.

[55] Jumièges, 124; *Gesta Guillelmi*, 38.

meant that it could not be taken by assault so, after an initial attempt to take it by surprise had failed owing to treachery within his won ranks, William settled down to build four siege castles in an attempt to starve it into submission.[56] He adopted, in other words, a strategy of blockade and attrition. But a phrase like 'settling down' to besiege should not be taken to mean that William had adopted an inactive 'wait and see' style of warfare. On the contrary. In WP's words, 'he went out riding by day and night, or lay hidden under cover, to see whether attacks could be launched against those who were attempting to bring in supplies, or carrying messages, or trying to ambush his foragers'.[57] The struggle for Domfront very quickly resolved into a struggle for supplies, a typical example of Vegetian warfare. Precisely this, in the seventeenth and eighteenth centuries, was still the cardinal problem in war: how to capture a town before the resources of the surrounding country gave out.[58]

When he heard that Geoffrey was bringing an army to the relief of Domfront, William, leaving troops behind to maintain the siege, rapidly advanced to meet him. But no battle occurred. Geoffrey, according to WP, was suddenly overcome by fear and fled before he even caught sight of the Norman army.[59] To historians who assumed that most medieval generals were keen to fight battles, this apparently timid behaviour on the part of so formidable a warrior cried out for explanation. Thus Halphen believed that it must have taken a diversionary attack on Anjou to make him turn back, and so he dated these events to 1049 when there is evidence for a campaign waged by Henry I in the Loire valley.[60] It is likely, however, that Geoffrey's withdrawal was both sensible and normal, calling for no special explanation. According to WP, after his adversary's ignominious retreat, William was free to lay waste his rich lands, but, understanding the wisdom of restraint in victory, he decided not to do so.[61] What this most probably means is that Geoffrey's army, though it presumably retreated, had none the less remained close enough to inhibit William's ravaging.[62] In that case William was now in a fix. With his army stationary before Domfront he faced very great logistical problems.[63] It may be that at this stage of the campaign Geoffrey Martel had reason to believe that he had obtained the upper hand. But William, acting with startling speed and ferocity, turned the tables. He turned suddenly against Alençon and took it with scarcely a blow being struck.[64] The additional information provided by WJ allows us to glimpse the reality behind WP's vague and bland words. A fort across the river from Alençon was seized, fired and some of the defenders brutally punished. William's ferocity persuaded the citizens of Alençon that, if they wished to retain their feet and hands, they had better surrender at once.

---

56 *Gesta Guillelmi*, 36. That William initially hoped to take Domfront by surprise seems a very plausible interpretation of WP's words. See De Boüard, 199.

57 *Gesta Guillelmi*, 38.

58 Van Creveld, 28.

59 *Gesta Guillelmi*, 38–40.

60 L. Halphen, *Le comtè d'Anjou au XIe siècle*, Paris 1906, 72–4; followed by Guillot, 72 n. 320. De Boüard (200–1), while dating the Domfront campaign to 1051, none the less retained Halphen's explanation; so also Barlow, 19. At least Douglas (59–60) inserted the word 'perhaps' when writing that Geoffrey left Maine 'owing to a threat to Anjou by King Henry'.

61 *Gesta Guillelmi*, 40–2.

62 This, it may be, is the manoeuvre that Harold had failed to carry out when he was taken by surprise by William's rapid advance.

63 Van Creveld, 25. And for William's insistence on keeping moving in 1066 see below, p. 157.

64 *Gesta Guillelmi*, 42

Equally impressed the garrison of Domfront also decided to yield.[65] The notoriety of the atrocity at Alençon – as Barlow pointed out, WP's silence is good evidence that it was regarded as barbarous – has, quite naturally, tended to overshadow the other details in WJ's account.[66] But these too are very valuable. We are told that William turned on Alençon because his scouts had informed him that the town was in a poor state of readiness; that he then rode through the night and attacked at dawn; finally, having taken and garrisoned Alençon he returned to Domfront 'in great haste'.[67] Unquestionably the Domfront campaign is an extremely illuminating one. It illustrates some very characteristic features of William the Bastard at war. Within a closely-supervised strategy of attrition he succeeded because he ensured that he was kept well-informed – frequently riding out on patrol himself – because he moved rapidly and because he was prepared to be brutal.

The next stage in the Norman Conquest of Maine came in 1055. William ordered the construction of a *castrum* at Ambrières (in the lordship of Geoffrey of Mayenne, a vassal of Martel), and, reports William of Poitiers, the lord of Mayenne knew only too well what this portended: once they had completed Ambrières the Normans would have a free hand to raid, ravage and lay waste his lands.[68] Geoffrey Martel swore to protect his vassal and approached Ambrières, where William, with his army, eagerly awaited his arrival. Geoffrey, however, proved a disappointment, preferring to keep his distance. Despite this apparent timidity on Geoffrey's part, it is evident that his strategy did in fact achieve a degree of success. William withdrew from Ambrières. According to WP he did so because both princes and ordinary soldiers were complaining about food shortages.[69] In other words Geoffrey had successfully undermined William's capacity to supply his troops, presumably by making it unsafe for them to go out foraging. Geoffrey was now in a position to launch an assault on the Norman garrison of Ambrières unimpeded by the presence of William's army. As it turned out, however, his assault failed and William was sufficiently determined to muster fresh troops and return to the scene of the action. Now it would have been Geoffrey's turn, as commander of the army laying siege to Ambrières, to suffer the logistical consequences of immobility and so it is hardly surprising to find him retreating in the face of the Norman advance. Thus William was able to consolidate his hold on Ambrières. Soon afterwards Geoffrey de Mayenne drew the appropriate conclusion and submitted.[70]

Two years earlier the revolt of William of Arques had precipitated a series of events

[65] Jumièges, 126–7.

[66] Barlow, 20. For the nature of the insult see E.M.C. Van Houts, 'The origins of Herleva, mother of William the Conqueror', *EHR* ci, 1986, 399–404. For additional evidence that William came to have the reputation of being an unusually ruthless soldier see J.F. Benton, ed., *Self and Society in Medieval France. The Memoirs of Abbot Guibert of Nogent*, New York 1970, 69.

[67] In WJ's account of William's earliest known campaign we find a similar emphasis on the speed of the young duke's movements (Jumièges, 118, 126–7). Once again one of Vegetius' maxims is to the point: 'courage is worth more than numbers, and speed is worth more than courage', cited by P. Contamine, *War in the Middle Ages* (trans. M. Jones), 1984, 252.

[68] Thus if ravaging was a preliminary to seizing fortresses, so also seizing fortresses was a preliminary to ravaging. In 1074, for example, 'Philip the king of France sent a letter to him (Edgar Atheling), ... he would give him the castle of Montreuil so that thereafter he could daily work mischief upon his enemies' (*ASC* D).

[69] *Gesta Guillelmi*, 76. If William's decision to offer battle before Ambrières meant that his army remained immobile for a while then this would have materially added to his logistical problems.

[70] *Gesta Guillelmi*, 76–80.

which were more characteristic of the defensive warfare of the first period of the duke's military career and which, at any rate as described by WP, were dominated throughout by the question of supplies. First on the scene were the duke's *principes militiae* based at Rouen. They at once did their best to prevent foodstuffs and other supplies being carried to Arques in preparation for the expected siege. But the waggons were too well guarded. By the time William arrived – so great, we are told, was the haste with which he had ridden from the Cotentin that all his horses but six had fallen exhausted by the wayside – there was nothing for it but to build a siege-castle and lay a blockade. Some time later while William, who could not afford to be immobilised for long by the siege of a single castle, was away on other business, King Henry I marched to the relief of Arques. Not all went as he would have wished. He suffered heavy casualties when a section of his army was ambushed by the blockading force, and he was unable to dislodge them from their siege-castle. None the less before returning to France he managed to get both supplies and reinforcements into Arques. In the end, however, hunger forced the garrison of Arques to surrender, and the image of starving men gave WP the opportunity for a few literary flourishes, including, of course, an allusion to Vegetius: *famis acrimonia saevius et arctius quam armis.*[71]

In this period what strategy did William employ when he was confronted by an invading army, as in 1053, 1054 and 1057? As we know already, thanks to WP, he preferred to avoid battle (see above p. 99). But just what did this involve? Did it, for example, mean that he decided to take refuge in his castles and hope for the best?[72] The clearest statement of the defensive strategy he in fact adopted comes in William of Malmesbury's description of how the duke handled the great invasion of 1054. In this year King Henry launched a two-pronged attack on Normandy, one army under his brother's command, entering northeast Normandy, and the other, which he commanded, invading the Evreçin. Faced by this threat William, according to William of Malmesbury, manoeuvred 'so that he neither came to a close engagement nor yet allowed his land to be devastated'.[73] This of course is a twelfth century, not an eleventh-century version, but the point is that WM had read what both WJ and WP wrote about 1054 and, in the light of his understanding of the practice of his own day, he was drawing out and laying bare the strategic principles, principles which are, in any event, implicit in their accounts. Thus WJ wrote that 'with some of his men he shadowed the king and inflicted punishment on any member of the royal army whom he was able to catch'.[74] As this passage makes plain the point of having a force in the field and bringing it fairly close to – 'shadowing' – the invading army was to deter the invaders from detaching small units from their main force, in other words, as WM realised, to prevent them ravaging and foraging. Obviously any defender who could catch an invader while some of his troops were dispersed ravaging was in a strong position. Thus Oderic describes how, in 1069, the Danes landed a great army at Ipswich but were then, *in praedam diffusi*, caught by local levies and defeated, losing

---

71 *Gesta Guillelmi*, 54–62. Cf. Vegetius, 69.
72 The method suggested by J. Beeler, *Warfare in Feudal Europe*, 1971, 57.
73 'ut nec cominus pugnandi copiam faceret, nec provinciam coram se vastari sineret' (*De gestis regum* ii, 290).
74 Jumièges, 129–30.

thirty men. A little later the same invaders met a similar fate when they landed at Norwich and once again went plundering.[75]

In the great invasion of 1054 it was an incident of this sort which was to prove decisive. In the words of William of Jumièges, the duke 'forthwith picked a force of soldiers and sent them with all speed to check the pillagers of the Pays de Caux . . . they came up with the French at Mortemer, finding them engaged in arson and the shameful sports of women. They attacked immediately at day-break'.[76] Commenting on this passage, Beeler noted, evidently with some surprise, that Robert of Eu (the victorious commander) 'seems to have been aware of the value of surprise'.[77] The tone here is very characteristic of some modern historians' approach to medieval warfare – though not, needless to say, of RAB's. The defeat of his brother's army at Mortemer persuaded Henry to call off his invasion. It is clear that William's commanders adopted the same defensive strategy in both 1053 (see below p. 108) and 1057. In 1057 Henry and Geoffrey were defeated at the crossing of the River Dives when the tide came in at Varaville cutting off the rear of their army and exposing it to attack. William came up rapidly and cut it to pieces.[78] William of Poitiers offers the additional information that William attacked *cum exigua manu virorum* and this reinforces the impression that he was once again shadowing the invader, not looking for a pitched battle but ready to exploit any opportunity that presented itself.[79]

Of course it would be different if the invader chose to seek battle, called in his incendiaries and foraging parties, and advanced with a concentrated force. Assuming the defender wished to avoid battle then there was probably little he could do except retreat – or as WP might say 'flee' – taking care to stay just out of reach of the invading force. On the other hand the invader could not advance far in this fashion. Sooner or later, and probably sooner, he would be forced to send out foraging parties and then the defender's opportunities would come.[80]

In fact, of course, since systematic ravaging was the principal strategy of attack, it followed that a defensive strategy based on shadowing and harassing was an extremely effective one. From the point of view of the invading troops, once they could no longer go plundering then soldiering lost its appeal and they just wanted to go home. Paid troops could still, of course, expect their wages, but even they would presumably regret the loss of the anticipated bonus of loot; and, as for unpaid troops, their enthusiasm for war presumably sank even lower. According to William of Malmesbury, after Stamford Bridge Harold made the mistake of not sharing out the plunder and as result he was to have few with him at Hastings except *stipendiarios et mercenarios milites*.[81]

---

75 Orderic ii, 226.

76 Jumièges, 129–30. In this brief passage note the number of words denoting speed and timing: *protinus, celerrime, illico mane*.

77 Beeler, 45. But the attempt to surprise one's opponent was, of course, normal in medieval warfare, even indeed in so-called chivalrous warfare. For a discussion of this see J. Gillingham, 'War and Chivalry in the History of William the Marshal', in P.R. Coss and S.D. Lloyd, eds, *Thirteenth Century England*: *ii*, Woodbridge, 1988. For the importance of surprise in both the northern and southern campaigns of 1066 see Brown, 'Hastings', 7–9.

78 'alacriter superveniens', Jumièges, 131.

79 *Gesta Guillelmi*, 80–82.

80 Presumably it was being able to foresee this that made William decide not to advance into Maine in 1051 (above p. 150).

81 *De gestis regum* i, 281–2.

A strategy of shadowing and harassing involved rapid movement, often with fairly small forces; it involved sudden attacks and equally swift retreats. It is hard to conceive of a type of warfare more dependent upon good group discipline.[82] Equally it is hard to envisage a type of warfare in which tricks like feigned flights would be more natural and more frequently practised. Thus, for example, the feigned flight by which a section of King Henry's army was trapped and ambushed in 1053.[83] So there would be nothing in the least remarkable about the employment of such tricks in the Battle of Hastings.[84]

Clearly in this sort of warfare reconnaissance was vital; and being vital, was standard practice.[85] Significantly William of Poitiers mentions the normal only in order to contrast it with what was not normal. For William, in his biographer's words, was more solicitous of the army's safety than he was of his own life. Therefore, dissatisfied with the customary practice of relying on other men's reconnaissance, he was in the habit of going out on patrol himself. Immediately after landing in England he went on patrol with an escort of just twenty-five men, including one of his key military advisers, William fitzOsbern.[86] Similarly on his 1068 Exeter campaign he rode ahead of the main army 'to reconnoitre the ground and walls and to discover what preparations the enemy were making'.[87] And the implication of William of Poitiers' account of the Domfront campaign (see above p. 103) is that this was a habit which William had developed early. Naturally advance information was particularly valuable; it was therefore normal practice to employ spies.[88] At the same time, of course, spies only become news when they are caught. Thus we hear about one sent across the Channel by Harold because he happened to be detected and was then employed by William as part of his propaganda war against the 'usurper'.[89]

Equally, of course, enemies tried to keep their intentions and movements secret. There is an interesting contrast between the invasion of 1054 when, says William of Poitiers, the duke knew the disposition of the French forces in advance, and the invasion of 1057 when, says William, for fear of the duke they tried to keep their plans secret.[90] Since in 1057, unlike 1054, they were able to penetrate deep into Normandy and 'burn and ravage the duchy all the way to the sea', it seems that this

---

[82] This point is nicely made in Brown, *The Norman Conquest*, 51, though to call this a 'wait and see' method is perhaps to give an unduly passive label to what was an extremely active form of defence.

[83] Jumièges, 120.

[84] *Gesta Guillelmi*, 194. Yet this is a matter on which despite the entirely justified comments of Brown, 'Hastings', 16, doubts continue to be raised. See J.M. Carter, 'The Feigned Flight at Hastings Re-considered', *The Anglo-Norman Anonymous* vi (January 1988).

[85] The early thirteenth-century History of William the Marshal contains several object lessons on how to organise effective reconnaissance. See Gillingham, 'War and Chivalry'.

[86] *Gesta Guillelmi*, 168. This, in WP's opinion, was another of the ways in which William was a greater man than the generals of antiquity. For another medieval commander who liked to involve himself in reconnaissance work, see J. Gillingham, *Richard the Lionheart*, 1978, 193–4, 272, 284–6.

[87] Orderic ii, 212.

[88] Presumably this is one of the reasons for the common practice of sending envoys into the enemy camp. See, e.g., *Gesta Guillelmi*, 38–40, and, in 1066, 172–9. If the good general went out on patrol himself, then the ideal king acted as his own spy, *De gestis regum* i, 126.

[89] *Gesta Guillelmi*, 154–6.

[90] 'hostem distributum praenovit' (1054) (*Gesta Guillelmi*, 70); 'Famam tamen sui motus, quantum potuere, occultantes' (1057) (*ibid.* 80).

is a panegyrist's way of saying that they had actually succeeded in keeping William in the dark.[91]

In general, of course, William succeeded and he succeeded because his information was good – as in the capture of Alençon (above p. 105). Above all his information was good in 1066. It is possible that the timing of the Norman fleet's move to St Valéry from the mouth of the Dives just four days after the dispersal of Harold's war-fleet was no coincidence but the result of information supplied by William's 'frigates'.[92] What is certain is that William owed his chance of victory at Hastings to the fact that he learned of Harold's movements in time. In time, but if we can trust WP's account of the nervous mood in the Norman camp when they learned that Harold was advancing rapidly and that his fleet had cut off their retreat to Normandy, then only just in time. Fearing a surprise attack, possibly at night, William hurriedly called to arms the men left behind in the camp – for the greater part of the army was out foraging. In his anxiety William even put his hauberk on the wrong way round. According to William of Jumièges, the Normans stood to arms throughout the night, fearing an attack.[93] In fact, of course the attack never came. Perhaps, as RAB suggests, Harold halted at or near the ridge at Battle in order to rest his troops, and this respite enabled William to seize the initiative.[94]

If this is so then it is ironic that Harold's fatal miscalculation may, in part, have been the consequence of information he had obtained himself while on his own involuntary 'reconnaissance patrol' in Normandy in 1064. As an eyewitness of the Breton campaign of that year he had enjoyed a rare opportunity to observe William's military style at close quarters, and what he saw, if we may trust WP, was a cautiously conducted war of attrition. The approach of William's relieving army forced Conan of Brittany to abandon his siege of Dol (a strongpoint whose lord, Ruallon, was at the time William's ally). Aware, however, of the problems of taking a large army into unknown and unproductive territory, *per regiones vastas, famelicas, ignotas*, William decided not to pursue Conan. Indeed soon afterwards supply problems compelled him to return to Normandy. Then, learning that Conan had joined forces with Count Geoffrey of Anjou (Fulk Rechin's brother), he re-entered Brittany but ordered his men to refrain from ravaging, presumably because the enemy army was in the vicinity – though according to WP the order was given purely out of consideration for the interests of the lord of Dol on whose territory he was encamped. In the event there was no battle and once again both sides withdrew, though it is characteristic of WP that he should say that William returned home while his enemies fled.[95]

Perhaps if Harold had witnessed William's sudden strike against Alençon in 1051 he might have been more on his guard in 1066. As it was, however, what he saw was a very typical example of William at War – a campaign in which the duke seems to have been prudently content with a small gain: the preservation of the allegiance of the lord of Dol, just as in 1055 he had been content with the establishment of an

---

91 *Gesta Guillelmi*, 80. Similarly the fact that William had to withdraw in haste from Dol in 1076 makes it plain that on that occasion too his information gathering system had broken down (Orderic ii, 352; *ASC* D and E *ad annum* 1076).

92 As suggested by C.M. Gillmor, 'Naval Logistics of the Cross-Channel Operation, 1066', *Battle* vii, 124.

93 *Gesta Guillelmi*, 180–2; Jumièges, 135.

94 Brown, 'Hastings', 9.

95 *Gesta Guillelmi*, 110–12.

outpost at Ambrières. In 1064 there was no sign of an aggressive, battle-seeking, risk-taking strategy. On the contrary it was a struggle of attrition in which, more than anything else, questions of supply seemed to dominate the course of events, a campaign very much in the style of all the other campaigns of the last fifteen years – a good guide, Harold might have thought in the summer of 1066, to the kind of war he was facing now.

Certainly it is clear that throughout the summer of 1066 the organisation of supplies was crucial. Given the fact that armies normally followed the call of their stomachs and kept on the move in order to stay alive, the month when the Norman troops were based at Dives-sur-Mer obviously caused enormous logistical problems. B.S. Bachrach's calculation of what was involved when an army of 14,000 men, including non-combatants, and 2–3,000 horses, remained immobile for a month makes fascinating reading: the 9,000 cartloads of grain, straw, wine and firewood, the river of 700,000 gallons of urine which the horses would have produced, the mountain of five million pounds of horse-shit which it would have taken 5,000 cartloads to remove (presumably, on sanitary grounds, not the same carts as those that brought in the food and drink).[96] We do not need to accept a single detail of Bachrach's calculation to know that, on the general point, he must be absolutely right. The logistical problems which William faced must have been massive ones; and, as Allen Brown observed, he 'triumphantly overcame' them. By contrast, Brown argues, Harold did not.[97] Throughout the summer the English forces were stationed along the south coast but 'when the festival of the Nativity of St Mary (8 September) came, the men's provisions had run out, and no one could keep them there any longer'.[98] In Allen Brown's words, Harold's failure to solve 'logistical problems which were, if anything on a lesser scale than those which Duke William triumphantly overcame' was 'potentially disastrous' and 'must throw light on the Old English military organization and its efficacy'.[99] But this implied criticism underestimates the additional problems which Harold, as a defender, had to face. He had to wait, probably not knowing just when and where the attack would come. Yet he had to be prepared. Moreover as defender he suffered a second significant disadvantage, and one of which William of Poitiers was well aware, as he shows in a speech he put into the duke's mouth. 'He (i.e. Harold) does not have the courage to promise his men the least part of that which belongs to me. I, on the other hand, shall promise and give away not only my own possessions but also those which, at the moment, are said to belong to him. Victory will go to the man who is prepared to be generous not only with his own property but also with that of his enemy'.[100] In fact, of course, despite these disadvantages, Harold actually held his forces together from May until early September, i.e. for longer than William did. Moreover the fact that Harold was eventually forced to disband his army made no difference in the end – since William did not attack in early or mid-September. Perhaps indeed at this time the winds were against him.[101]

---

[96] B.S. Bachrach, 'Some observations on the military administration of the Norman Conquest', *Battle* viii, esp. 11–15, developing the point made by Gillmor. 'Naval Logistics', 124.

[97] Brown, 'Hastings', 6–7.

[98] *ASC* C.

[99] Brown, 'Hastings', 6–7.

[100] *Gesta Guillelmi*, 158.

[101] Although WP insists that William was waiting for a favourable wind throughout the time he was at Dives, it is only after he had arrived at St Valéry that we hear of prayers for a south wind (*Gesta*

Even after the crushing victory at Hastings the question of supplies continued to matter. William's triumphal progress faltered in Kent when, as a result of eating meat and drinking water – presumably the wine had run out – many died of dysentery and even more, according to William of Poitiers, nearly did so. Luckily for William the political disarray of the English after Hastings meant that there was no one to challenge the Normans at this critical juncture. A little later the duke himself fell seriously ill. Nonetheless, in a striking illustration of the problems faced by an immobile army, he permitted no delay for fear they would run out of supplies.[102] If William's speech to the magnates at Dives-sur-Mer accurately reflects the kind of thinking in the Norman HQ, then it may well be that, aware of the attacker's advantage, they deliberately decided to postpone the invasion, to use delay, in other words, as a calculated manoeuvre in a war of attrition, as well, of course, as a means of avoiding battle in unfavourable circumstances, at sea or when disembarking. This suggestion, first made by Marjorie Chibnall, would fit very well with everything we know about William's military career up to that date.[103]

The gospel according to Vegetius said that only in the most exceptional circumstances should a general risk battle.[104] By the night of 13–14 October 1066 we are clearly in such exceptional circumstances. Harold had brought his army close enough to William's to prevent it ravaging; he had also, according to WP, sent a fleet round to cut off William's retreat.[105] In this situation it was obvious that William had no real choice but to risk battle. But it was also so obvious that William might find himself in this situation that it must surely have been anticipated. Indeed it is hard to see how William could have derived an advantage in any way commensurate with the scale of preparations for this war unless he brought Harold to battle. In that case it may well be that for the first time in his life he adopted a battle-seeking strategy, and that the ravaging of East Sussex was intended partly as a provocation to draw Harold into striking range.[106] William may have offered battle before, but that is one thing; beginning a campaign with the intention of bringing the enemy to battle quite another.[107] In that case the delay and attrition of the summer of 1066 might have been employed as a tactical device within a battle-seeking strategy.

But 1066 was exceptional. Just how exceptional is shown by the style of warfare in England during the next five years. There was probably a battle at York in 1069,

---

Guillelmi, 150, 158–60). It is also worth noting that neither WJ nor the *Carmen de Hastingae Proelio* mention Dives as a port of embarkation. For them prayers and/or favourable winds relate only to St Valéry, Jumièges, 134; *Carmen*, 4–6.

[102] *Gesta Guillelmi*, 212.

[103] 'The delay may have been a deliberate tactic of William' (Chibnall, 11); cf. Brown, 'Hastings', n. 20.

[104] Vegetius, 86–91.

[105] *Gesta Guillelmi*, 180–4.

[106] *Gesta Guillelmi*, 180. I.e. whichever strategy you adopted, ravaging remained an important component.

[107] Of course it takes two to make a battle. It may be that, as I have suggested elsewhere (Gillingham, 'Richard I', 85), Harold was adopting the standard defensive strategy. Or it may be that, encouraged by his success in the Battle of Stamford Bridge, Harold himself wanted to repeat this new and intoxicating experience. Cf. Commynes's comment on the effect of the battle of Montlhéry on the mind of Charles of Burgundy (Philippe de Commynes, *Memoirs*, trans. M. Jones, Harmondsworth 1972, 79). Either way, during the night and early morning of 13–14 October, Harold was tactically outmanoeuvred.

and once again it was one in which William was able to take his opponents by surprise.[108] In essence, however, it was to take another long drawn-out war of attrition before William could feel confident that England was a conquered country. The guerilla warfare waged by the English was the normal medieval defence strategy of shadowing and harassing adapted to local conditions, i.e. in a land of few castles the resistance leaders tended to make their bases not in castles but in the wild country.[109] In this grim struggle the castles built by the Normans played a vital role.[110] They enabled the occupying power to control the main towns and to keep at least a watching brief over the main roads. They also functioned as prisons for hostages meant to guarantee the loyalty of local society.[111] But above all else resistance was overcome by ravaging. Thus the Norman Conquest ended, not with a battle, but with a ravaging, the Harrying of the North, the supreme example of the soldier's brutal art. And this, in Orderic's words, 'I do not dare to praise': *laudare non audeo*.[112]

[108] 'King William came unexpectedly upon them from the south with an overwhelming host, and routed them'. *ASC* D.

[109] S. Reynolds, 'Eadric Silvaticus and the English Resistance', *BIHR* liv, 1981, 102–5.

[110] 'For in the lands of the English there were very few of those fortifications which the French call castles; in consequence the English, for all their martial qualities and valour, were at a disadvantage when it came to resisting their enemies' (Orderic ii, 218). This famous judgement is one which Orderic may well have taken over from the old soldier himself; at this point Orderic is still using the lost part of WP's text.

[111] Turgot, later of Durham and St Andrews, 'unus erat inter alios qui, nuper subjugata Normannis Anglia, obsides pro tota Lindesia in Lindicolino castro custodiebatur' (Symeon ii, 202).

[112] Orderic ii, 232 (above pp. 96–7).

10. Carol Gillmor, 'Naval Logistics of the Cross-Channel Operation, 1066'

In the section of this article presented here, Carol Gillmor considers the problem of the numbers and types of ships in William's invading fleet, bringing a number of techniques to bear on the question. She critically assesses the reliability of the primary sources and of the various techniques historians have for adjusting the numbers in sources to make them more realistic, finding that none of these work very well when applied to fleets. She then uses the evidence of naval archaeology to shed light on the question of ship types, and concludes with an incisive analysis of the question of ship-building. Did William build most of the fleet that took him to England? In answering this question, Gillmor performs what might be called a cliometric analysis of the physics of everyday life. In this case, her discovery of the limits of physical possibility offers a convincingly clear answer to the problem.

Reprinted from *Anglo-Norman Studies* 7 (1984), 105–31. Copyright © Carol Gillmor 1984, 1985.

NAVAL LOGISTICS OF
THE CROSS-CHANNEL OPERATION, 1066

C.M. Gillmor

During the six months from the assembly at Lillebonne until August, William mobilised a fleet that transported the army and non-combatants, their horses, and supplies to England. The numerical strength of the fleet and the navigational conditions from Dives to St Valery and thence across the Channel involve logistical difficulties that have largely been overlooked in the secondary literature. The number of ships participating in this operation rests primarily on the reports of twelfth-century sources and scholarly efforts to scale down the estimates in the narrative works have assumed a standardisation of ship types, especially with regard to the horse transports. The uniformity of horse transports has been largely derived from arguments that have adopted either the Ladby ship or a Mediterranean cargo vessel as a model for the horse transports. Such contentions do not retain validity after an evaluation of the written sources and comparatively recent discoveries in nautical archaeology. In emphasising the diverse origins and therefore the different classes of ships engaged in the crossing, the present investigation will indicate the unreliability of standardisation as a model for lowering the number of ships. Moreover, a combination of information on the forest cover of eleventh-century Normandy and modern comparative data on human work output will demonstrate the improbability of building the minimum total number of ships as reported by Wace.

The number of ships in the fleet was mentioned by several twelfth-century sources that differ widely in their estimates. Closest chronologically to the events of 1066 from information provided by his father, Wace explained that the Norman fleet was comprised of 696 ships, but even contemporaries of the Conqueror disputed the number of ships.[1] The plausibility of Wace's estimate at first might appear to be enhanced by the report of William of Poitiers that the Anglo-Saxon fleet was composed of 700 ships,[2] comparative information that can be adduced to indicate the number of ships which could be mobilised by an eleventh-century power except that Harold's fleet was comprised of warships and did not include horse transports. More important than the estimate of 696 ships by his father, Wace's reference to contemporary disputes about the number of ships strongly suggests that even the approximate number of ships cannot be determined. A more questionable piece of evidence is a document purporting to be a list of magnates and their ship quotas numbering 782 vessels that was issued by William the Conqueror. The total size of the fleet was

---

[1] Wace, 6425, 6430–4. On the reliability of Wace, see M. Bennett, 'Poetry as History? The *Roman de Rou* of Wace as a source for the Norman Conquest', *Anglo-Norman Studies*, v, 1982, 21–39, concluding that the poem contained orally transmitted material.
[2] *Gesta Guillelmi*, 180.

expressly stated as 1,000, a number suggesting the presence of smaller vessels.[3] The 3,000 ship estimate by William of Jumièges would seem to be an exaggeration that can be explained by an untrained eye looking at ships in port.[4] A still higher numerical count of ships is found in Gaimar who reported a total of 11,000 vessels in the fleet.[5] The numbers of knights are even more fantastic. William of Poitiers claimed 50–60,000 knights,[6] while Orderic mentioned 50,000 knights and a force of infantry.[7]

In his work on the art of warfare in the western Middle Ages, Verbruggen explained that the tremendously exaggerated numbers appearing in medieval chronicles were either repeated or increased in subsequent works. The rationale for such inflated numbers was to affirm the power of a ruler and to emphasise the strength of an army based on a guess instead of an actual numerical count.[8] Moreover, Verbruggen summarised several ways to arrive at small numbers. The occurrence of low numbers in a few reliable narrative sources could be accepted and he provided a table with sources and numbers from military operations of the Crusades. Unfortunately, this method cannot be applied successfully to the Norman Conquest, for the only reasonably reliable source to report a low number was Wace. Verbruggen also argued that the size of an army could be computed if the number of the smallest tactical unit was known. Such information cannot be derived from the fullest accounts of the battle of Hastings.[9] Verbruggen was able to obtain important numerical information from the archival sources of the twelfth and thirteenth centuries, but the diplomas of William the Conqueror do not mention any references to the number of ships in the fleet of the crossing, but do contain valuable data on the Norman ports.[10] Of the indirect ways for reducing numbers, Verbruggen elaborated on the use of the length and breadth of a formation on the march as well as the size of the battlefield and the number of men who could fight on it. One application of topography is derived from the known distance and route of an overland·march between two points. Then, based on the assumption that the army advanced in a single column, it could be deduced that the formation never exceeded a certain maximum strength. Topography would determine the number of men and horses capable of marching abreast, while the need to maintain lines of communication would establish the length of the formation by a computation of the time required for the rear to reach the starting point of the vanguard. A celebrated example of refuting exaggerated numbers was the conclusion of Delbrück that the Persian army of Xerxes stretched out approximately 672 km, and when the front lines approached Thermopylae, the rear ranks of the army would still

---

[3] Only one manuscript contains the so-called ship list or magnates list printed as an appendix to the *Brevis Relatio*. This is Ms Oxford Bodleian library E Museo 93 (Battle, middle of the twelfth century). The most recent edition is that of J.A. Giles, *Scriptores Rerum Gestarum Willelmi Conquestoris*, London 1845, 21–2. A new edition is being prepared and will be included in: *Three Latin Chronicles from the Anglo-Norman Realm*, ed. E.M.C. van Houts, E.R. Smits and D.E. Greenway (forthcoming, Oxford Medieval Texts).

[4] Jumièges, 134.

[5] Gaimar, *Lestorie des Engles solum la translacion Maistre Geffrei Gaimar*, ed. Ch. T. Martin in *Chronicles and Memorials of Great Britain and Ireland*, xci, London 1888–89, ii, 5248.

[6] *Gesta Guillelmi*, 150, 170.

[7] Orderic, ii, 169.

[8] J.F. Verbruggen, *The Art of Warfare in Western Europe during the Western Middle Ages*, trans. S. Willard, Amsterdam 1977, 7.

[9] *Gesta Guillelmi*, 185–95. Wace, 7699–8922.

[10] Verbruggen, 8–9.

have been waiting at Susa to begin the march. This aspect of Delbrück's method has not been investigated as to the problem of numbers involved in the Norman Conquest.[11] Topography has been utilised in another way to investigate the problem of numbers. Provided that the size of the battlefield could be established, the number of fighting men could be computed, allowing sufficient space for each fighter to perform his function. Historians of the Norman Conquest have applied this method of reducing numbers, determining the position and disposition of Harold's army at Hastings. This method requires reasonably accurate measurements of the battlefield, followed by an explanation of how to position the forces with due consideration to frontage and depth as well as a determination of manœuvering space for each type of fighting man. The numbers emerging from these calculations range from between 5,000 and 6,000 up to between 7,000 and 10,000 combatants,[12] figures that reflect a lack of scholarly consensus on the size of the battlefield, the positioning of forces, and the space for each warrior. With reference to naval logistics, this method will not serve to scale down the number of ships, for the operational area of the fleet was the open sea of the English Channel which has no spatial limitations for the positioning of seven hundred ships, while size and numbers within each class, as will be shown, cannot be determined. The harbours of Dives, St Valery, and Pevensey offered more circumscribed areas for anchoring ships, but an examination of coastal changes indicates that the medieval dimensions of these ports could have easily accommodated a fleet of seven hundred eleventh-century ships of various sizes. The coastline of lower Normandy between the Orne and the Dive has evened out considerably in comparison with an eighteenth-century map of the area, and therefore must have been even more irregular in the Middle Ages. The mouth of the Dive in the Middle Ages more nearly resembled a maritime estuary and its present swampy condition has resulted from alluvial deposits accumulated by the action of western currents and western winds along the lower Norman coast.[13] Wace observed that the Dive flowed into the sea near Bavent. At present, Bavent is more than two leagues or about 4.8 km from the actual mouth of the Dive. In the ninth century there was a bridge across the Dive which implies that the river did not flow into a wide channel but through a fairly narrow entrance into the harbour.[14] Alluvial deposits over the centuries have

---

11 Verbruggen, 9. H. Delbrück, *Geschichte der Kriegskunst im Rahmen der politischen Geschichte*, Berlin 1923, i, 10: for the Persian expedition. C.J. Turner, 'William the Conqueror's march to London', *EHR* cvi, 1912, 209–25, contained no discussion of numbers in relation to the march.
12 Verbruggen, 9, on this method. Estimates of the men who could fight on the battlefield are at Delbrück, iii, 156; F. Lot, *L'art militaire et les armées au Moyen Age en Europe et dans le Proche Orient*, Paris 1946, i, 284–5; W. Spatz, *Die Schlacht von Hastings*, Berlin 1896, 30, 33–4; F.M. Stenton, *Anglo-Saxon England*, 3rd edn, London 1973, 592–3; D.C. Douglas, *William the Conqueror*, Berkeley 1964, 198–9. F. Baring, 'The battlefield of Hastings', *EHR* lxxvii, 1905, 65–70, and C.H. Lemmon, 'The Campaign of 1066', in *The Norman Conquest*, ed. C.T. Chevallier, New York 1966, 100–1, arrived at figures in the 7,000–10,000 range. By contrast, W.J. Corbett in *Cambridge Medieval History*, Cambridge, v, 498. J.F.C. Fuller, *Decisive Battles of the Western World*, London 1954, 372–4, arrived at estimates numbering 5,000–6,500.
13 R.N. Sauvage, *L'abbaye de Saint-Martin de Troarn*, Caen 1911, 247–9. *Gesta Guillelmi*, 82: the French king, Henry I, could not pursue Duke William across the Dive because high tide barred the mouth of the river with so much water that the river could not be crossed.
14 Sauvage, 247–8, citing from B. Guerard, *Cartulaire de l'abbaye de Saint Pierre de Chartres*, Paris 1840, i, 8, and Wace, 2282.

effected similar changes at Pevensey, where the harbour has been filled in completely, and at Dives, a port still in use but with considerable swampy areas.[15]

The present discussion of numerical strength will be limited to naval considerations. Historians who have written on the question of ship numbers have generally accepted the lowest figure of Wace because of the information provided by his father, and have tried to reduce the number further by assuming a standardisation of ship type, emphasising the horse transports, and then calculating the total number of ships in the fleet. One argument stemming from the uniformity of ship size attempted to reduce the number of ships by the time taken to embark and disembark. The indirect methods of calculating from a standard ship type and the time taken for loading and unloading cannot be used to scale down the number of ships below seven hundred. Nor can computations based on the operational areas of the fleet resolve the question of numerical strength.

The ship numbers as reported by Wace have generally been accepted as the starting point for computations which have then assumed that about half of the fleet served as horse transports. Some basis for this division of the fleet exists in the sources, for Baudry of Bourgueil mentioned horse transports and infantry ships, while Wace referred to horse transports and warships; modern scholars have not cited poets to this point.[16] In discussing the horse transports, their knowledge of discoveries in nautical archaeology has been either outdated or non-existent and too much standardisation of ship size has been taken for granted, some arguing for 8 or 10 horses per ship to arrive at an estimate of 2,500 to 3,000 horses.[17]

Based on the position and disposition of Harold's forces, J.F.C. Fuller arrived at 7,500 men and then attempted to reduce the number of ships from 700 to 450 by standardising the horse transports to the largest possible size, the ten horse ship of the Bayeux Tapestry, and extended his argument by stating that this horse transport was the origin of the constabulary of ten knights.[18] But his calculations were marred by an arithmetical error. In support of the numerical capacity of the horse transports, he cited the reference of William of Malmesbury to Robert, Earl of Gloucester, who in 1142 embarked more than 300, but less than 400, *milites* in fifty-two vessels,[19] without explicit reference to the transport of horses. Taking 350 as a reasonably safe number midway between 300 and 400, there are only 7 horses per ship.

The numerical strength of the fleet is impossible to estimate accurately through an

---

[15] J.A. Williamson, *The English Channel*, Cleveland 1959, map p. 77. Pevensey Bay measured five miles at the widest point with the harbour entrance at two miles. For Dives and St Valery, see C. Vergnot, *Carte de navigation cotière*, nos 526, 1011.

[16] Baudry of Bourgueil, *Les oeuvres poétiques de Baudri de Bourgueil (1046–1130)*, ed. P. Abrahams, Paris 1926, 353–4: 'Has praeter turbae fuerat sua cymba pedestri,/ Altera fert dominos, altera navis equos'. Wace, 6427: 'que nes, que batels, que esqueis'. Also, J. Laporte, 'Les opérations navales en Manche et Mer du Nord pendant l'année 1066', *Annales de Normandie* xvii, 1967, 9–10, and M. Graindor, 'Le débarquement de Guillaume en 1066: un coup de maître de la marine normande', *Archaeologia* xxx, 1969, 42. Fuller, 372.

[17] Fuller, 372. Lemmon, 85, compared the cross-Channel invasion with English overseas expeditions of the thirteenth century, when large ships carried only forty-four men. He appears not to know of the Gokstad ship, and his work was published before the archaeological reports on the Skuldelev ships. P. Banbury, *Man and Sea: from the Ice Age to the Norman Conquest*, London 1975, 223–4, concluded that the fleet was comprised of six hundred transports plus warships, pinnaces, and perhaps towed landing craft or small boats.

[18] Fuller, 372.

[19] Fuller, 372; *De gestis regum*, ii, 594.

analysis of ship capacity and naval logistics. The capacity of these ships cannot be determined because of the various sizes known to have been used. The arguments against standardisation will indicate why such computations are invalid. The Bayeux Tapestry portrays four sizes of horse transports with capacities of three, four, eight, and ten horses,[20] but there is no sound method for indicating the numerical distribution of these vessels. There is indirect evidence to suggest different sizes and design variations within the types mentioned by the poets, for Baudry insisted that shipwrights came from all over Europe,[21] with the implication of applying their own local traditions of ship construction.

In estimating the number of ships in the fleet, the scholarly consensus accepts the seven hundred figure of Wace, disregarding the important qualification that even contemporaries of the Conqueror disagreed on the number of ships. Moreover, there is no general agreement that all of the ships were built. Two sources, William of Poitiers and Orderic, explicitly referred to the construction of ships without the clarification that all of the ships were built.[22] Baudry and Wace, in mentioning the appearance of shipwrights, lumberjacks, and carpenters, and the pictorial representations on the Bayeux Tapestry, indicate that at least some of the ships were built.[23] A number of scholars have extended these texts to have William giving orders for all of the ships to be built of wood cut from stands of timber in Normandy according to certain standard specifications, using either Viking merchant ships or war vessels as the models for construction.[24] Of the historians who argued this position, Laporte explained the rationale for uniform construction. In the interests of logistical planning for the cross-Channel invasion, he argued, there must have been standardisation of ship construction so that William would know approximately the number of men and the amount of war material that could be transported. Moreover, to speed up the building process, the shipwrights easily could have been directing their projects under rules of uniform construction issued by William and his advisers. To achieve speed, there must have been some simplification of the overall design and standards of workmanship cannot have been high.[25] A second group of historians has argued that all seven hundred ships were built but varied in type.[26]

An assessment of the two scholarly viewpoints on ship numbers requires a determination of what kind of ships were potentially available in northern Europe during the eleventh century, followed by a computation of the cost in timber and manpower to construct all seven hundred of both merchant ships and warships, in addition to one of each class of ship. Next, the cost of maintaining a work force will be determined from the statistics on the daily nutritional requirements of an average hardworking man in comparison with the ratio of seed grain to consumable for an

20 *BT*, figs 42–3. Also, N.P. Brooks and H.E. Walker, 'The Authority and Interpretation of the Bayeux Tapestry', *Anglo-Norman Studies*, i, 1978, 1–34.
21 Baudry of Bourgueil, 335: 'Mox faber ex toto lignarius orbe vocatur'. Wace, 6332, did not mention the geographical origins of the workers.
22 *Gesta Guillelmi*, 150; Orderic, ii, 144.
23 Baudry of Bourgueil, 335ff; Wace, 6332ff; *BT*, figs 38–9.
24 Cf. R.A. Brown, 'The Battle of Hastings', *Anglo-Norman Studies*, iii, 1981, 7, and his *The Normans and the Norman Conquest*, London 1969, 150; Laporte, 9; Graindor, 42; Fuller, 372; Lemmon, 85.
25 Laporte, 9.
26 D.C. Douglas, *William the Conqueror*, 189; R. Furneaux, *Invasion, 1066*, Englewood Cliffs, N.J., 1966, 69; E. Tetlow, *Enigma of Hastings*, New York 1974, 77; Banbury, 224; D. Howarth, *1066: the year of the Conquest*, New York 1978, 97–8.

evaluation of whether Normandy possessed the material resources to build all seven hundred ships.

A discussion of potential ship types should begin with an elimination of two theories about the kinds of horse transports, specifically, the Ladby ship and vessels of Mediterranean origin. The ships that comprised the Norman fleet, especially the horse transports, should be based on those available then operating on northern seas, particularly those ships whose remains are nearly intact or can be reconstructed by methods of nautical archaeology. Archaeological evidence can provide helpful guidelines. Looking at the ships portrayed on the Bayeux Tapestry, some scholars have concluded that a Viking war vessel, the Ladby ship, most accurately represented the type of horse transport deployed by William. The Ladby ship was excavated on the island of Funen in Denmark, and most experts on Viking ships have dated it to the ninth century. Discovered as a ghost in the sand, little could be known about the details of her construction, but there are several features indicating that the ship was not suitable for a cross-Channel operation. The Ladby ship was a long, narrow, fast rowing vessel, equipped with a mast; it measured 21.60 metres long, approximately 2.85 metres wide, and the depth amidships was only 0.70 metres. The Ladby ship was ideal for riverine operations or for amphibious landings in sheltered coastal waters. But it was not an ocean-going vessel. Danish sea scouts built a replica of the ship and demonstrated that horses could be embarked and disembarked, but the sea trials were carried out along the coast and not on the open sea such as a voyage across the English Channel would entail.[27] The ship was too narrow and too shallow draughted to transport both horses and rowers. The roll and pitch of the sea undoubtedly would have thrown the horses overboard because of the low freeboard which would reach only to the knees of most horses. The narrow beam of the ship with horses aboard would not permit space for the sweep of the oars. Moreover, William was not interested in a fast rowing vessel, as this activity would tire his fighting men.[28] The controversy as to how William was going to find the necessary rowers is not grounded in any of the sources. Laporte cited William of Poitiers and Orderic in support of the shortage of rowers, but the texts make no reference to rowers. Instead, William of Poitiers refers to the lack of ships, not rowers. Similarly, Orderic expressed the concern of the magnates over the problem of raising a fleet, without mentioning rowers.[29] Evidently, Laporte observed the ships of the Bayeux Tapestry with oar ports and therefore concluded that the vessels required rowers. Upon closer observation, the Bayeux Tapestry portrayed oars on only one Norman ship in contrast to oars on most of the ships in Harold's fleet, indicating that the ships of the Norman fleet were propelled primarily by sail with oars as auxiliary power to move the ships from port to open sea.[30] Moreover, a Channel crossing starting in the area of Dives

---

[27] On the Ladby ship, see Knud Thorvildsen, *The Viking Ship of Ladby*, Copenhagen 1967. Also, on the Ladby ship as the horse transport used in the cross-Channel invasion, see B. Greenhill, *Archaeology of the Boat*, London 1976, 215; O. Crumlin-Pedersen, 'The Vikings and the Hanseatic merchants: 900–1450', in *A History of Seafaring based on Underwater Archaeology*, ed. G. Bass, New York 1972, 184; Tetlow, fig. 6, opp. p. 97.

[28] Howarth, 92.

[29] Laporte, 6 n.11, 9 n.18; *Gesta Guillelmi*, 158, 'Navigo quo sufficiente citius gaudebimus, non praepediemur'; Orderic, ii, 142, 'Pericula maris et difficultatem classis opponebant'. Also, Baudry of Bourgueil, 323–4, 'Non desunt nobis nisi si tantummodo naves;/ Ergo quae desunt quisque parate rates.'

[30] *BT*, fig. 45: the only Norman ship on the Tapestry showing the use of an oar. The other ships, figs

to St Valery would require at least two shifts of oarsmen. To fulfil this requirement, the knights and their supporting personnel with little or no previous sailing experience would have to be trained to row in order to perform this task in a synchronised manner. The Channel crossing was planned on such short notice that there was insufficient time for practice.[31] In the interest of mobilising a fleet which was to function essentially as a convoy, William doubtless would have preferred deeper draughted ships relying on sails as the primary means of propulsion with oars as a source of auxiliary power. This argument also can be applied to discredit the Mediterranean thesis as to the origin of William's horse transports.

Although vessels resembling the Ladby ship or Mediterranean horse transports probably did not sail in 1066, the ships that did make the journey were closely related to the Viking design as indicated by the representations on the Bayeux Tapestry and the Skuldelev finds, a group of ships deliberately sunk in the Roskilde Fjord near Copenhagen to act as an obstacle to maritime raids. The ships of the Bayeux Tapestry probably were not longships, but deeper draughted cargo vessels which nevertheless resembled the longships in their clinker built design and in the presence of a mast. Consequently, such a cargo transport vessel matches those on the Bayeux Tapestry.[32] The Gokstad ship and two of the ships discovered at Roskilde, wrecks 1 and 3, are to date the archaeological finds corresponding most closely in chronology and shape to those used by William in 1066,[33] and could transport horses with the use of a ramp, flooring, and stalls. Moreover, such ships could store the vast quantities of supplies required for the operation.

The Gokstad ship, the best preserved of the Viking ships, was constructed c.850–900, and is now thought to have been the possession of a noble. Designed as an ocean-going vessel, measuring 23.33 metres long and 5.25 metres wide amidships, the weight of the ship at 20.2 metric tons when fully equipped, made propulsion solely by oars difficult, except for rowing in and out of port.[34] Of all the finds thus far, the Gokstad ship, if built in a less ornate version, most nearly matches the ten horse transport of the Bayeux Tapestry,[35] and would reconcile with Wace's reference to the fleet as comprised of warships and horse transports.

Skuldelev 1 was a true sailing vessel with only a small number of oars fore and aft that could be used when the wind dropped. The archaeological remains compare to a limited degree with the one Norman ship on the Bayeux Tapestry with oars which were positioned towards the stern. Skuldelev 1 relied primarily on sail as a means of propulsion and was equipped with a tacking spar. Skuldelev 1 was a broad, deep cargo vessel, built to transport heavy or bulky cargo in deep water; the ship measured approximately 16.1–16.5 metres in length; the width amidships was about 4.4–4.8 metres; the height from the bottom of the keep to the gunwale amidships was 1.8–1.9 metres; the draught can be roughly estimated as about 0.6 metres when unloaded with

42–3, are guided with a side rudder, while the ships of Harold's fleet, figs 5, 6, 7, 30, were propelled by oars. See J. Le Patourel, *The Norman Empire*, Oxford 1976, 177ff, for Note on the Use of Oars.

[31] Howarth, 92. B. Farmer, *Sculling and Rowing*, London 1951, 63–70, explained the stages in the training of a successful oarsman.

[32] Olsen and Crumlin-Pedersen, 'Skuldelev Ships, II', 73–174, and Crumlin-Pedersen, 'The Viking Ships of Roskilde', *National Maritime Museum, Aspects of the History of Wooden Shipbuilding*, Maritime Monographs and Reports, ed. B. Greenhill, i, 1970, 7–31.

[33] Olsen and Crumlin-Pedersen, 96–110 and 118–31 for Skuldelev wrecks 1 and 3 respectively.

[34] Brøgger and Shetelig, 112, for the fully equipped weight of the Gokstad ship.

[35] *BT*, fig. 42.

a maximum of 1.5 metres when fully loaded.[36] Skuldelev 1 was a large cargo vessel for its time, while number 3 of this discovery was a more lightly built trading ship, measuring 13.3 metres long with a beam of 3.3 metres, a depth of 1.4 metres and a draught of one metre.[37] Built with a half deck fore and aft, leaving an open hold amidships, it was also equipped with side rudders, a feature Waley contended was likely to have been introduced by the south Italian and Sicilian Normans.

The Gokstad ship as well and Skuldelev 1 and 3 were the basic types of ships available in the North Sea area in the eleventh century and are likely to have varied in size. Although several other ships discovered in the North Sea resembled these Scandinavian ships, the published data on the Gokstad ship and the Skuldelev discovery provide abundant material so that the ships can be examined in detail.[38] To determine whether all of these ships were built, as some scholars believe, it is necessary to compute the cost in timber and manpower to construct first seven hundred merchant ships using Skuldelev 1 as a model and then seven hundred warships with the Gokstad ship as the basis for calculations. The purpose of this exercise is to present conservatively estimated data intended to show the impossibility of building all seven hundred ships to a standardised design. In mobilising the fleet William of Poitiers deliberately omitted a discussion of ship construction, saying that the process was too long to narrate in detail,[39] so a reconstruction of shipbuilding logistics from indirect evidence is necessary, primarily to see whether all seven hundred of them could have been completed in the five month period between the Council of Lillebonne at the end of February to the beginning of August, allowing one month for the concentration of the fleet at Dives.[40]

The design of Skuldelev 1 provides an approximate indication of how much wood was required for construction. The pine planks were tangentially cut in relation to the annual rings of the log. The pith is not visible in the cross-section of the plank, a feature indicating that each pine log provided sufficient wood for two planks and possibly four in some cases.[41] Skuldelev 1 consisted of twelve strakes overlapping from the keel. Their length varied from 2.2–4.2 metres at the stern to 6.4 metres amidships. Each strake averaged about four lengths of plank,[42] and approximately forty-eight planks formed one side of the ship for a total of ninety-six. If each pine log provided enough wood for two planks, Skuldelev 1 would have required forty-eight pine trees for the planking alone. If another ten oak trees were allowed for the remaining parts of the ship, including the keel and the mast, about 58 trees were needed for one ship or 40,600 for a fleet built to this standard.

---

[36] Olsen and Crumlin-Pedersen, 107–9.

[37] R.W. Unger, *The Ship in the Medieval Economy, 600–1600*, Montreal 1980, 153, for the dimensions of Skuldelev 3.,

[38] Ellmers, 272–94, provided brief descriptions of all the ship and boat finds from England, France, Belgium, and the Netherlands, but none can be dated securely to the eleventh century. Only ten finds have emerged from France, seven from Belgium, and seven from the Netherlands, possibly indicating that underwater archaeology in these areas is still in the beginning stages. England has fared considerably better with ship finds numbering twenty-four.

[39] *Gesta Guillelmi*, 150.

[40] *De gestis regum*, ii, 299, for the Council of Lillebonne; *Gesta Guillelmi*, 150–2, for the one month stay at Dives.

[41] Olsen and Crumlin-Pedersen, 156–7. Brøgger and Shetelig, 213, noted that the use of the axe prevented more than two planks from being obtained from the same tree.

[42] Olsen and Crumlin-Pedersen, 100–1.

To construct seven hundred ships on the Gokstad model in such a short time was much more difficult, primarily because the keel of the ship was a single piece of oak over eighteen metres long, the largest obtainable, so that the woodcutters would have to search the forests for seven hundred of them. The Gokstad ship was comprised of sixteen strakes; at 4 planks per strake, the ships would require 64 planks for one side, totalling 128 planks. If each log provided enough wood for 2 planks, 64 oaks would have been needed for the planking alone. Allowing another 10 oaks for the rest of the ship including the mast, 74 trees would have to be felled to build one ship on the Gokstad model; 51,800 for the entire fleet – rather large numbers for those who believe that all seven hundred ships were built in five months.

From this data on the number of trees needed to build one ship and then the entire fleet with Skuldelev 1 and the Gokstad ship serving as models, it is necessary to determine whether Normandy possessed the natural resources in standing timber to construct a fleet of seven hundred ships. For this number of Skuldelev 1 type ships, the masts and keels would have required 1,400 oaks about twelve metres long and thirty centimetres in diameter. The forest acreage for this number of trees with a chest high diameter of thirty centimetres would have been six per .4047 hectares or a total of 93 hectares, according to tables generated by the forest industry in Wisconsin for a tree farm operation. In the virgin forest of eleventh-century Normandy, the random growth of trees would have increased the acreage, but tall, thin oaks for keels and masts must grow in a limited space so the wood cutters would have to search for groups of oaks growing in this manner.[43] For the remaining 40,600 pine trees with a thirty centimetre diameter 2,540 hectares would be required for a total of about 2,630 hectares of forest. Similar computations for the Gokstad ship would arrive at a significantly higher figure, and it is not necessary for the present line of argument specifically to indicate the unfeasibility of such a project.

Some idea of the forest cover in Normandy can be obtained from information developed by Higounet and Musset on the location of forests in northern France.[44] Precise figures on the hectares of these forests do not exist, but it is possible to compare the approximate extent in hectares of the forests in the Seine basin with the timber requirements of ships to ascertain whether the vessels could have been built from available reserves. Eleventh-century Norman forests along the Seine were dispersed for about 100 kilometres between Gaillon and Aizier with large concentrations of timber in the forests near Jumièges (*saltus Gemmeticus*) and St Wandrille (*silva Arelauna*). If the forests extended approximately 1 kilometre on either bank of the river for 100 kilometres,[45] there would have been a rectangular shaped forest of about 1,536 hectares. The ship list, which adherents to the theory for the construction of all 700 ships largely omit from their discussions, gives the names of three barons along the Seine who were to contribute a total of 160 ships: Nicolas of St Ouen received a quota of 20 ships; Count William of Evreux 80 ships; Count Robert of Eu 60 ships.[46] These three quotas com-

[43] R. Zon and R.D. Garver, *Selective Logging in the Northern Hardwoods of the Lake States*, Oshkoch, Wisc., 1927, 9; *The Building and Trials of the Replica of an Ancient Boat: the Gokstad Faering*, National Maritime Museum, Greenwich 1974, i, 51.

[44] C. Higounet, 'Les forêts de l'Europe occidentale du Ve au XIe siècle', *Settimane di Studio del Centro Italiano di Studi sull' alto medioevo*, Spoleto 1966, xiii, 343–97; L. Musset, 'Les forêts de la basse Seine', *Revue Archéologique* xxxvi, 1950, 84–95.

[45] Musset, 84. For a map of the lower Seine forests, see Higounet, Index, 76–9.

[46] Laporte, 7. Count Robert of Eu possessed forests bordering on the Seine with sea frontage at Tréport.

bined would require a total of 9,280 trees or 624 hectares or slightly less than half (forty-one per cent) of the total forest reserves of the Seine area. The amount of timber required for the shipbuilding enterprise of 1066 would have substantially reduced the Norman forests of the Seine basin well before the massive deforestation of northern Europe in the twelfth century. Although the forest reserves of the Seine could have provided sufficient timber, the Norman barons are unlikely to have allowed half of their favourite hunting grounds to be denuded for this project. To argue this position implies that William was willing to convert Normandy to an economic wasteland.

The cost of procurement for ship construction casts even more doubt on the building of all seven hundred ships, especially in view of the pressure placed by the time limit on human work capabilities. To determine the cost of shipbuilding involves the use of modern comparative data on wood cutting which is expressed in average work days (AWD), what a worker could accomplish in a single day. Woodchoppers, using modern steel axes and bucksaws, are seldom able to put in more than 7.5 hours of effective work per day and frequently it is less.[47] Within this amount of time, an experienced cutter could produce one cord of pine (spruce), and the equivalent number of pine trees with a thirty centimetre diameter would be about five.[48] Modern steel axes have to be sharpened only once a day to retain a cutting edge on pine,[49] while medieval iron axes dulled much faster and probably had to be sharpened several times a day. In contrast with pine, the hardness of oak prevented a cutter from felling more than 3 thirty centimetre diameter trees per day.[50] The cutting of oaks to obtain the 1,400 trees needed for the keels and masts comes to a conservative 470 AWD. For 51,800 pines the cost in AWD would be 10,360 for a single worker and a total of 10,830 AWD for cutting the pine and oak.

Once the timber was cut, it had to be transported overland by ox-cart a variable short distance to the river or tributary where the logs were floated to the construction sites, based on an acceptance of the idea that the magnates were to provide wood from their own forests. Conservative estimates for the later Middle Ages have established that the transport of heavy loads, such as logs, cost approximately one-third of an AWD per 1000 kilograms per 1.6 kilometres.[51] A 12 metre wet oak log at 32 kilo-

[47] N.C. Brown, *Logging – Principles and practices in the United States and Canada*, New York 1934, 99. C. Todes, *Labor and Lumber*, New York 1931, 125, compared the efficiency of the new power saw with two hand fellers in a seven hour period.

[48] Brown, *Logging*, 100, reported that a two-man felling crew in virgin Douglas fir could cut about 4–5 trees per day. A. Koroleff, *Pulpwood Cutting, Efficiency of Technique*, in Canadian Pulp and Paper Assn, Woodlands Section, Montreal 1941, table 4, p. 16, gave a cutting time of eleven minutes for an eight inch diameter spruce. Also, *Manual of Military Field Engineering, U.S. Infantry and Cavalry School, Dept of Engineering*, 3rd edn, Kansas City, Mo., 1897, 32, specified that a man could cut down a hardwood tree one foot in diameter in ten minutes and one softwood of the same size in one-third of the time.

[49] Koroleff, *Pulpwood Cutting*, 23.

[50] J.F. Fino, *Forteresses de la France médiévale*, 3rd edn, Paris 1977, 83, explained that two wood cutters could fell a tree in times ranging from 25 minutes to 2.5 hours for trees with diameters varying from forty centimetres to one metre. Fino based his information on the military manual of E. Legrand-Girard and H. Plessix, *Manuel complet de fortification*, Paris 1909, 198.

[51] L.F. Salzman, *Building in England down to 1540: a documentary history*, Oxford 1952, 119, provided this estimate, but then cited considerable evidence that the costs were greater. For this reference I am grateful to Bernard S. Bachrach who provided me with a copy of his unpublished paper, 'The Cost of Castle Building: the Case of the Tower at Langeais, 992–994', n. 32.

grams per 197 cubic centimetres would weigh 1,200 kilograms,[52] and 1,400 of them would weigh 1,680,000 kilograms. The transportation of this quantity of oak would have cost the equivalent of 5,040 AWD. A 12 metre pine log at 15–18 kilograms per 197 cubic centimetres[53] would weigh 617–727 kilograms; 40,600 logs would weigh at least 25,050,200 kilograms and would cost 8,350 AWD or 13,390 total AWD. But these calculations are based on standards of the fourteenth century. By contrast, in the eleventh century, the technology of overland transportation was less than half as efficient. Upon calculating an average distance of 2 kilometres for the transportation of the materials at a cost of one-third of an AWD per 1.6 kilometres per 500 kilograms, the carrying capacity of an ox-cart c.1000,[54] the result is a very conservative equivalent of 10,080 AWD for oak and 16,700 AWD for pine or 26,780 AWD for the transportation cost of the timber.

Once the timber arrived on the construction site, the lands of the magnates assigned ship quotas as Laporte and other believe, the task of shipbuilding required numerous skilled workers. Brøgger and Shetelig provided valuable information on the organisation of medieval Scandinavian shipbuilding from the Norse sagas and modern boatbuilding in Scandinavian countries. A master shipwright oversaw the construction of the ship, making sure that the workers were cutting and fitting the parts together correctly. The prowwright performed the most vital and difficult task of connecting the lines of the ship fore and aft, particularly the transition from the keel and strakes onto the stem and stern. If the timber were cut and conveyed with other building materials to the site in advance, a large Scandinavian warship could be finished in three months.[55] Modern comparative data on Scandinavian boat construction illuminates gradations in the work force even more. Large boats required four masters, each with an assistant, and a smith, and several menial workers who all laboured together, so that there were about twelve men working on a single vessel.[56] If these figures were applied to ship construction in 1066, the number of men for seven hundred ships would be about 8,400, working in groups of 12 for three months.

The cost to Norman society of maintaining these workers during the three months, a total of ninety days, would have been substantial. In the climate of northern France hard-working men require about 3,500 calories daily or about 2 kilograms of unmilled wheat equivalent.[57] During the tenth and eleventh centuries the estimated average ratio of seed grain to consumable was 2:1,[58] and the average agricultural worker produced a surplus of c.950 kilograms of consumable wheat on 6 hectares (158 kilograms per hectare) of average arable. However, the agricultural workers required for yearly sustenance a caloric equivalent of about 730 kilograms of unmilled wheat equivalent and thus only 220 kilograms of true surplus were produced.[59] To provide for calories needed for the shipwrights and their assistants for

52 *Manual of Military Field Engineering*, 154; *The Gokstad Faering*, i, 51.
53 *Manual of Military Field Engineering*, 154.
54 D.W. Engels, *Alexander the Great and the Logistics of the Macedonian Army*, Berkeley 1978, 14–16.
55 Brøgger and Shetelig, 211.
56 Brøgger and Shetelig, 74.
57 Engels, *Logistics*, 123–4.
58 G. Duby, *Rural economy and country life in the medieval west*, trans. C. Postan, London 1968, 25–7.
59 Concerning the seed grain quantities per hectare, see the data provided in B.H. Slicher Van Bath,

three months, a total of 1,512,000 kilograms of unmilled wheat equivalent was required or about 10,200 hectares of average arable for surplus. Moreover, if each worker produced a surplus of 220 kilograms, 6,900 peasants would have been needed to produce 1,500,000 kilograms of unmilled wheat equivalent. Each worker tilled 4.67 hectares to obtain the 730 kilograms for his own sustenance and the total hectares needed to sustain the workers would have been 44,832; 55,032 hectares for both surplus and maintenance of the agricultural workers, or 550 square kilometres.[60] The construction of such large numbers of ships in the specified time was an impossibility in the eleventh century, so the mobilisation of the fleet has to be explained in other ways.

Elaborating on the mobilisation of the fleet, Wace mentioned William's complaint of insufficient ships for the crossing, and Baudry of Bourgueil also referred to the lack of ships; the scholars previously cited assumed that he did not have *any* ships and then published their views which fell into two categories: the standardisation of construction for all seven hundred ships and the building of all seven hundred ships in various sizes. Another way of interpreting Baudry and Wace would be to conclude that William had *some* ships. With these texts as initial support, the following investigation will search out other possible sources of ships. A number of scholars have accepted the magnate list as a quasi-authentic document to account for the collection of ships.[61] Ship quotas imposed on the magnates and bishops were part of William's plan for the invasion, and can be established by the ship list as well as other eleventh and twelfth-century sources, namely William of Poitiers, Orderic, Wace, and William of Malmesbury.[62] Even so, the assignment of quotas in the ship list does not necessarily mean that they were filled. The contemporary validity of the source has to be investigated indirectly by posing questions as to the appearance of the magnates enumerated on the list in other reliable sources and the connection between these magnates and maritime activities, such as their proximity to known ports. Davis drew up a table of barons in his article on the *Carmen*, and indicated the sources that mentioned the name of a given baron, including the *Carmen*, the Bayeux Tapestry, William of Jumièges, and William of Poitiers.[63] Yet an even more reliable way of verifying the names on the ship list is the person index to the diplomas of the Norman dukes edited by Fauroux which contains references to all of the magnates on the ship list so that their historical existence cannot be questioned.[64]

Inaccuracies in the quotas exist in the printed editions of the text and disagreements are to be found in comparison with Wace. A printing error emerges from a five ship discrepancy between Giles and a much earlier text edition by Lyttleton. Giles listed Remi as contributing 15 ships and 100 *milites*, whereas the text of Lyttleton

The agrarian history of western Europe, A.D. 500–1850, trans. O. Ordish, London 1963, 137, and Duby, 24, 128.
[60] Eleventh-century Normandy measured about 26,500 square kilometres. The land for forest, grain, and pasture for the crossing totalled 1,950 square kilometres.
[61] Laport, 7–8; Douglas, *William the Conqueror*, 189; Howarth, 97–8; Brown, *The Normans and the Norman Conquest*, 149.
[62] *Gesta Guillelmi*, 150; Orderic, ii, 144; *De gestis regum*, ii, 299; Wace, 6160; *Brevis Relatio*, ed. Giles, 22.
[63] Davis, 252.
[64] Giles, 22. I am grateful to Dr Elisabeth van Houts who informed me of a printing error that appears in the text of the ship list by Giles. The correct name for Roger of Mortain is Robert.

ascribed 20 ships and 100 *milites* to Remi.[65] A comparison of the magnate list with Wace reveals several disparities in ship quotas. According to the magnate list, Odo of Bayeux contributed 120 ships, while Wace assigned 40 ships.[66] Wace also attributed a quota of 30 ships to the bishop of Le Mans who did not appear on the Bodleian manuscript of the ship list. Wace definitely incorporated material from the *Brevis Relatio*, but the difference in the quota of Odo of Bayeux and the addition of the bishop of Le Mans indicate that he did not have access to the ship list as known from the Bodleian manuscript.[67] The number of ships in each of these quotas cannot be established with certainty.

Laporte believed that the magnates who were assigned ship quotas also built them from the forests of their lands.[68] Wace however explicitly stated that ships were constructed at the various ports in Normandy.[69] Although the magnates may not have been directly involved with the sea and the rivers, they could have had access to harbour facilities because a number of ports known in eleventh-century Normandy were located on their lands. Only three magnates on the list held lands with ready access to the Seine, yet the diplomas of the Norman dukes indicate that there were six ports along the Seine in the eleventh century: Les Dans, Elbeuf, Le Goulet, Saint Aubin-sur-Quillebeuf, Vieux Port, and Rouen.[70] Of these, only Elbeuf and Rouen fell within the lands of these magnates. A greater number of magnates on the list held lands with sea frontage which correlated with known ports in the eleventh century: Tréport in the hands of Count Robert of Eu; Dieppe under Walter Giffard; Hugh of Avranches had access to the ports of the Cotentin;[71] and no doubt we should add Odo of Bayeux. Of the seaports, Berneval, Harfleur, and Lexartum were not situated on the lands of magnates named on the list.[72] The maritime activities of some magnates on the list must have been practically non-existent, if we are to believe William of Poitiers who recorded the reluctance of the magnates to go on an overseas expedition for fear of the sea, and according to Wace the magnates were concerned as to how they were going to obtain the necessary ships. The inland magnates could have reached the sea by the existing rivers: Hugh de Montfort, William fitz Osbern, and Roger de Beaumont via the Risle; Roger de Montgomery via the Dives and the Orne. Moving newly constructed ships along these rivers would have entailed the difficulties of manoeuvering along meandering streams some 200–400 kilometres to reach the coastline, especially with oars as the auxiliary power source. Even with the advantage of rowing with the riverine current, teams of oxen may have been required to pull them along. As a result of these logistical difficulties, the construction of ships

65 Giles, 22; G.L. Lyttleton, *History of King Henry II*, London 1769, i, 463. S. Körner, *The Battle of Hastings, England, and Europe, 1035–1066*, Lund 1964, 251 and n. 74, thought that the discrepancy originated in the manuscripts instead of the printed texts and then concluded that a five ship error existed in the total number, either 776 or 782. See above, n. 3.

66 Wace, 6163–4.

67 Wace, 6165–7,

68 Laporte, 7–8.

69 Wace, 6333–4, 'Donc veissiez a grant esforz / par Normandie a toz les porz/'.

70 Fauroux, 32, Les Dans; 32, Elbeuf; 19, Le Goulet; 36, St Aubin-sur-Quillebeuf; 36, Vieux Port. On Rouen, see S. Deck, 'Les marchands de Rouen sous les Ducs', *Annales de Normandie* vi, 1956, 245–54. Also, L. Musset, 'La Seine Normande et le commerce maritime du IIIe au XIe siècle', *Revue des Sociétés Savantes de Haute Normandie, Lettres et Sciences Humaines*, liii, 1969, 8.

71 Fauroux, 220, Tréport; 61, Dieppe; 58, ports of the Cotentin.

72 Fauroux, 3, Berneval; 90, Harfleur; 71, Lexartum.

by the inland magnates was not a realistic way of fulfilling their quotas; nor would have been an attempt to float logs downstream to the ports. Against the idea of building ships in these remote areas, the lands of these magnates were not known to have contained any ports. Their lands possessed abundant forests for stockpiling ship timber, but there is no evidence of shipbuilding facilities, which may explain their lack of familiarity with maritime affairs. The apprehension of undertaking a sea voyage may have been centred in this group, for it was William fitz Osbern who spoke to William on their behalf, posing the question of where they were going to get the necessary ships. The problem remains of how William arrived at the assignment of ship quotas, especially in regard to the inland magnates. Instead of assigning ship quotas to magnates on the basis of their wealth, a more reasonable procedure logistically would have been to take an inventory of the various ports and then set quotas on the magnates based on the ships already available and the stocks of ship timber, keeping in mind that the sources which agreed on the principle of ship quotas also asked the barons to provide the ships without specifying that they had to be built.[73] The quotas then would have been assigned to the magnates best able to supply ships. The inland magnates could have financed their ship quotas far easier than building and then transporting the ships along the rivers by reimbursing the ports outside those in the lands of the other magnates on the list.

The authenticity of ship quotas in the magnate list remains doubtful. At best it was not an official list because the Bodleian manuscript did not originate from the time of William the Conqueror and the discrepancies that emerged from a comparison of the manuscript with Wace. Moreover, the correlation of maritime activities with magnates on the ship list, except for the four inland magnates, is strong enough to conclude that William assigned the quotas on those magnates who could provide ships and port facilities instead of the wealthiest magnates.

In addition to the contributions of the magnates, William possibly obtained ships by hiring naval mercenaries from Flanders and by deploying the fleet of a small pre-1066 Norman navy. The narrative and archival sources for its existence are sketchy. William of Jumièges reported that a Norman fleet existed as early as the time of Duke Robert I, who in c.1033–34 attempted to reinstate the aethlings Edward and Alfred in England and assembled a fleet for that purpose, but this mobilisation was undertaken for a single mission and there is no other reference to a fleet between c.1030 and 1066. In 1035 a diploma of Robert I mentioned the port of Harfleur as a 'sedes navium', but the phrase is too vague to describe a naval base.[74]

Apart from requisitioning ships from Norman ports and relying on a Norman navy, William would have had the financial resources[75] to purchase the use of ships from Flanders. Of the twelfth-century sources, only Simon of St Bertin (c.1140) explicitly referred to Flemish contributions of ships and infantry.[76] Indirect evidence for hiring mercenaries is indicated by a grant of William the Conqueror in 1066 of the first *fief-rente* to Baldwin V, count of Flanders. William of Malmesbury mentioned that

---

[73] The requisitioning of ships in Anglo-Saxon England during Edward the Confessor's reign was frequent enough to serve as a precedent for the Norman mobilisation. *ASC*, 108, C and D: 1045; 124, E.

[74] Jumièges, 110 (cf. Fauroux, 76); Fauroux, 90.

[75] Musset, 'A-t-il existe en Normandie au XI siècle une aristocratie d'argent?' *Annales de Normandie* ix, 1959, 285–94.

[76] Körner, 229.

the money fief was given in exchange for the homage, counsel, and military aid of the count for the invasion of England; the exact nature of this military aid was left unspecified,[77] but the prominent position of Flanders in supplying mercenaries both on land and sea[78] suggests that ships and their crews as well as infantry forces could have been the objective of the grant. The Flemings were previously engaged as naval mercenaries, for the fleet of Tostig which raided the English coast earlier in the year was comprised chiefly of Flemings.[79]

Even with the ships that could be obtained from these various sources, some ships still had to be built. The Bayeux Tapestry shows woodchoppers hard at work felling trees for ship construction, and the pictorial evidence is supplemented by the accounts of Wace and Baudry of Bourgueil.[80] Resorting to green timber surely indicates a shortage of seasoned timber which must have been stockpiled in port facilities, where it was readily accessible for ship construction and involved no transportation costs. Still, the shipwrights were compelled to build some vessels from green timber which decomposes much faster than seasoned wood.[81] Considerable attention was placed on the preservation of the fleet. The existence of a fleet constructed exclusively or dominantly from green timber would have undermined this effort. William of Poitiers mentioned that upon disembarkation, William ordered the construction of temporary fortifications at Pevensey and then at Hastings to serve as a defence both for themselves and their ships, clearly indicated that the fleet was mobilised for more than just a one-way operation.[82]

The building of ships was undertaken only as a last resort, after the requisitioning of all seaworthy ships in the Norman ports and the hiring of mercenaries. The felling of trees clearly would have taken place after the stores of seasoned timber in the ports had been exhausted. The sources which place in first priority the cutting of green timber for ship construction to the exclusion of other logistically more feasible alternatives must have had a purpose. The emphasis on manual labour engaged in a massive construction project had the political objective of demonstrating the involvement of the total Norman population in preparations for the crossing.[83] Because the Bayeux Tapestry indicates the various sizes of ships known to have been used in the crossing, the numerical strength of the army is impossible to estimate through an analysis of ship capacity. Since the ships were obtained from several sources, it is not unreasonable to conclude that the cross-Channel operation consisted of ships varying in size – vessels of motley composition resembling the fleet involved in the evacuation of Dunkerque.

77 *De gestis regum*, ii, 478. B. Lyon, *From Fief to Indenture*, Cambridge, Mass., 1957, 33, noted that this grant was the first concession of a *fief-rente* by an English ruler.

78 F.L. Ganshof, 'La Flandre', in *Histoire des Institutions françaises au Moyen Age*, i: *Institutions seigneuriales*, ed. F. Lot and R. Fawtier, Paris 1957, 419: the counts of Flanders regularly requisitioned their ships and crews to serve as mercenaries, but the evidence is mostly from the thirteenth and fourteenth centuries. J. Boussard, 'Les mercenaires au xiie siècle: Henri II Plantagenet et les origines de l'armée de métier, *Bibliothèque de l'Ecole des Chartes* cvi, 1945–46, 190 n. 1, noted that the presence of mercenaries in William the Conqueror's army needed further investigation.

79 *ASC*, C, 138 for 1065, contact with the Flemings; E, 140, for the sixty ships.

80 *BT*, figs 38–9; Wace, 6332–42; Baudry, 331–52.

81 *Gokstad Faering*, i, 42–3: Viking shipbuilders generally built their vessels from wood that was seasoned through immersion in seawater, although shipbuilding from green timber was sometimes done, as for example, the *Long Serpent*.

82 But cf. *Gesta Guillelmi*, 168.

83 *Gesta Guillelmi*, 150: 'totius Normanniae studia ferverent'.

11. Christine and Gerald Grainge, 'The Pevensey Expedition: Brilliantly Executed Plan or Near Disaster?'

Christine and Gerald Grainge bring their own experience as sailors to bear on the problems associated with William's crossing. Their analysis illuminates a number of points, above all the question of the timing of the invasion. Did William delay on purpose, waiting for the Anglo-Saxon army and fleet to disperse before sailing, as a number of scholars have suggested, including both Gillingham and Gillmor? Or was he forced to delay by unfavorable winds? In combining sailing wisdom with a close reading of the sources and a reconstruction of tidal data, the authors are also able to weigh in on the question of the reliability of the *Carmen* as a source.

The contrast between the conclusions in this article and those in Gillingham's on the timing of the invasion are instructive in showing that not even the best reconstructions can be completely decisive. The considerations raised by one sort of evidence (logistical demands, for example), may conflict with those raised by another sort of evidence (meteorological pressures and sailing requirements). One can then only weigh such considerations against each other and against the primary sources, deciding which makes the best sense of the limited information we posess.

Reprinted from *The Mariner's Mirror* 79 (1993), 261–73. Reproduced by permission of the Editor of *The Mariner's Mirror*.

THE PEVENSEY EXPEDITION:
BRILLIANTLY EXECUTED PLAN OR NEAR DISASTER?

Christine Grainge and Gerald Grainge

It is well documented that the Norman invasion fleet, which brought Duke William's army to Pevensey in the autumn of 1066, set out from the Dives Estuary and neighbouring ports, made its way along the Norman coast and anchored in the estuary of St Valéry sur Somme, before crossing the Channel to land at Pevensey, a few days after Harold Godwineson had dismissed his *scyp fyrd* from its station in the Isle of Wight. Was this the execution of a carefully thought out plan? Did William time his departure from St Valéry to coincide with Harold's disbanding of his *scyp fyrd*? Did Harold's action matter?

Or was William's passage plan largely dictated in preparation by nautical and navigational constraints and modified in execution by stress of weather? Did in fact St Valéry represent near disaster?

To address these questions we shall first consider the conditions with which the medieval navigator had to contend. Next we shall examine the contemporary records. Then we shall refer to a relevant study by C.M. Gillmor, before putting forward our own reconstruction.

Nautical and Navigational Conditions and Constraints

The overriding concern, not to say obsession, of the medieval mariner must have been with the lee shore. Even in modern times the lee shore is never far from the thoughts of the professional navigator on his high tech bridge or the amateur yachtsman in his high performance yacht capable of clawing to windward in heavy weather. For the lee shore is the ship breaker.

A lee shore is any coastline towards which the wind is blowing, whether at right angles or diagonally. When that wind is blowing strongly across the open sea, perhaps at gale force, heavy waves will build up against the coastline to add to the effect of the wind. In such conditions engine failure will drive a modern ship ashore, should she be unable to anchor, and a modern yacht, capable in calm water of beating to windward, may find herself unable to power her way through the waves which will tend to stop her as she slams into them. Once ashore, the pounding of the waves, lifting the vessel and dropping her, will break her up, whether on rock or on sand.

Such conditions would be lethal for the type of medieval ship available to William (Fig. 1). Such ships, of Viking origin, were essentially double ended open boats, with a long shallow keel and a single mast carrying a square sail. The square sail would

Acknowledgements: We wish to acknowledge the encouragement and helpful comments offered when we presented an early draft of this paper to the Early Medieval Seminar at the Institute of Historical Research, London, on 16 October 1991. We also wish to thank Dr Michael Duffy for his helpful advice offered when we were preparing this paper for publication.

limit the ability of such a vessel to sail to windward, particularly in heavy weather, whilst the long shallow keel would be considerably less effective than modern keels in preventing leeway.[1]

The meteorological feature which exerts the major influence on the weather and, in particular on the winds, in the English Channel is the Atlantic low. Typically these weather systems consist of a low pressure area round which the winds blow in an anti-clockwise direction; forming in the Atlantic, the lows follow each other east-wards across north-west Europe. The central low pressure area almost invariably passes well to the north of the Channel, with the result that, with the passage of each low, the wind in the Channel veers typically from south-westerly through westerly to north-westerly, backing to south-west again with the approach of the next low.

From time to time this pattern of lows is interrupted by a high pressure system, characterised by fine settled weather and winds from other directions, including the south and the east.

Any coastline then can become a lee shore. But where, given the meteorological conditions prevalent in the English Channel, are the lee shores which might threaten an invasion fleet leaving the Norman coast in the area of the Dives estuary? A glance at the chart (Fig. 2) shows them to be: first, the east bank of the Seine estuary and the coast line from Cap de la Hève to Cap d'Antifer (cliff lined, this coast would endanger a fleet leaving the area of the Dives estuary in a westerly and even more in a north-westerly); second, the stretch of coast from Cap d'Antifer to the estuary of the Somme (here the coast bears away to the north-east and would present less risk in a westerly blow, but would become dangerous as soon as the wind veered north-west); last, the shore from the Somme estuary to Cap Gris Nez (the coast here again runs north/south and consisting now mainly of sand dunes, with off lying shallows, becomes dangerous in any winds from the westerly quadrant).

In this context it is not irrelevant to note that in medieval times the men of St Valéry had the right of *lagan*, holding or asking ransom for ships, chattels or persons driven onto its shores (Fig. 3).[2] The fact of its location on this potential lee shore no doubt enhanced the profit which accrued from this privilege, particularly if it were supplemented by a little judicious wrecking, even if the *Carmen de Hastingae Proelio* tries to claim otherwise.

The medieval navigator would be concerned not simply to avoid potential lee shores, but also to remain as far to windward of his intended destination as possible; if he did so, windshifts would be less likely to put him to leeward of his objective. Given the windshift pattern already described, typically south-west through west to north-west, for a voyage south/north across the eastern Channel, keeping to windward of the objective means staying as far west as possible.

Navigation by sail is affected not only by wind, but also by tide. Tide has three effects: first, the direction and speed of the tide will mean that the ship's speed and course over the ground will differ from her speed and course through the water;

---

[1] The performance of modern replicas is recorded by A.J. Binns, *The Viking Voyagers* (Heinemann, London, 1980), 165 and 168 and more recently in *Les bateaux des Vikings* (ISBN 2-902093-20-9), (the catalogue of the 1992 exhibition mounted in Rouen in association with the Viking Ship Museum, Roskilde, Denmark), 24.

[2] Guy Bishop of Amiens, *Carmen de Hastingae Proelio*, edited by Catherine Morton and Hope Muntz (Clarendon Press, Oxford, 1972), 4–5. It seems to have been by exercise of the same right that Harold Godwineson was held by Count Guy when he came ashore in a Channel gale at Ponthieu. See R. Allen Brown, *The Norman Conquest* (Edward Arnold, London, 1984), 13 and 23.

Fig. 1. Bayeux Tapestry: William's ship on passage to Pevensey.

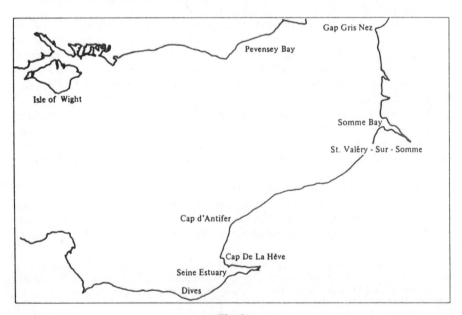

Fig. 2.

Fig. 3. Bayeux Tapestry: Harold is seized by Count Guy when he is driven onto the lee shore of Ponthieu.

second, the height of the tide will determine at any particular time whether a ship can leave or enter a shallow or drying harbour; third, if the wind blows in a different direction from the tidal set, the sea will be rougher than when the tide is running in the same direction as the wind.

How do these considerations affect a passage such as that facing the invasion fleet? In the eastern Channel the tidal streams flow up and down Channel, reversing direction just over every six hours. The distance from the Norman to the English coast (60 to 90 sea miles) might be covered in two tides, which would cancel each other out; although the ships might cover a greater distance over the ground, the distance through the water would not be affected. If, however, the fleet travelled along the coast, say from Dives to St Valéry, its progress would be hastened or retarded, according to the set of the tide. Moreover, if the fleet was running before the wind and against the tide, it would experience the uncomfortable wind over tide conditions. Finally, the fleet might be expected to leave port at or around high water, both to ensure that there is enough water to clear the harbour and to take advantage of the seaward flowing ebb to give it a good start on its journey.

A feature of the events of 1066 difficult to explain in nautical terms is the decision of Harold Godwineson to deploy his housecarls and his fleet on the Isle of Wight for the summer and part of the autumn, until their enforced departure on the feast of the Nativity of St Mary on 8 September.[3]

Was Harold expecting an invasion to take place via the Island en route to Winches-

---

[3]   *The Anglo-Saxon Chronicle*, trans. by G.N. Garmonsway (Dent, Everyman's Library, London, 1972), 194–7.

ter? Certainly the Island and the mainland across the Solent afford a number of outstanding natural harbours, opening on to an expanse of sheltered water, features which make it a world class yachting area today. A fleet making its way from Brittany in the prevailing westerlies might just make the Isle of Wight. A fleet sailing from Normandy could not; to reach the Island it would need a wind in a southerly or easterly quadrant. In any event, since the harbours further east along the English south coast, later designated as the Cinque Ports, had not yet been silted up, there would appear to be no particular navigational reason for invading via the Isle of Wight and in the event William did not do so.

Was the Isle of Wight a good look out position? On a day with perfect visibility, from the highest point on the Island (780 ft), Harold would be able to see the sea horizon at a distance of 32 sea miles. Dives is 90 sea miles away, St Valéry even further and summer days in the English Channel rarely have perfect visibility. Moreover, the evidence of the sources, in particular of the *Carmen*, was of an unusually wet summer, when the visibility would have been far from perfect.

Just as the master of the medieval sailing ship would seek to remain upwind of his destination, so too would the commander of a medieval naval force seek to remain upwind of an enemy fleet; what C.S. Forrester called gaining 'the weather gauge'.[4] It is possible that Harold was there to be upwind of any fleet in the Channel, but the effectiveness of this would depend entirely on the quality of his intelligence; if he did not sight the invasion fleet from his hill, it is difficult to see how he could have learnt of its departure before it arrived.[5] The effective purpose of the fleet would therefore have been limited to bringing his troops to the scene of an invasion, once it had happened, by sea rather than by land.

As we show later, we conclude that Harold's presence in the Isle of Wight is not to be explained in navigational or nautical terms.

Contemporary Records

The contemporary records relevant to our study are the *Bayeux Tapestry*, believed to have been commissioned by Odo, Bishop of Bayeux; *Gesta Normannorum Ducum* written by the monk William of Jumièges around 1070; *Gesta Guillelmi ducis Normannorum et regis Anglorum*, written between 1071 and 1077 by William of Poitiers, who served Duke William as a knight and later as chaplain; *Carmen de Hastingae Proelio*, thought by some to be by Guy, Bishop of Amiens; and the *Anglo-Saxon Chronicle*.

Let us compare the two fullest accounts of the crossing to England, those of William of Poitiers and of the *Carmen*. They are in essence very similar. They both say that the fleet was delayed by contrary winds and did not sail initially from St Valéry. William of Poitiers says that it left from Dives and the neighbouring harbours, after being delayed there for a month; although it does not specify the original port of departure, the *Carmen* says that it left, turning back, because of rough seas and easterly winds, then deciding to leave anyway and sailing to St Valéry. William of Poitiers indicates that William left Dives, having long awaited a southerly wind, and

---

4 Compare, for example, Drake and Howard's tactic of bringing their fleet of 'race bred galleons' to windward of the Armada before engaging it off Plymouth. See Ryther's plan in *Armada* by Peter Padfield, (Gollancz, London, 1988), 105.
5 *The Anglo-Saxon Chronicle*, 178, records the inability of the fleet lying in wait at Sandwich to prevent the return of Earl Godwine from Bruges.

was blown by westerlies towards St Valéry. He also says that some men were drowned.

The *Carmen* is on the defensive about the reputation of St Valéry as a port with wrecking rights and suggests that St Valéry was known to be hospitable towards seafarers! It does, however, speak of 'a sea treacherous to voyagers (and) a shore fraught with punishing rocks', surely a classic description of a lee shore. We think that both sources imply that had he not sailed from the area of the Dives estuary when he did almost irrespective of the weather, more of his men would have deserted. In any event autumn was setting in and the likelihood of favourable weather must have seemed to be decreasing with every passing day.

In fact the *Carmen* makes significant comments about the weather conditions: first, it speaks of the 'threatening approach of winter'; second, it speaks of the 'foul weather and ceaseless rain' at Dives and of 'the sky hidden by clouds and rain' at St Valéry, fair descriptions of the sort of weather which would arise from a series of deep Atlantic lows proceeding across north-west Europe; only the reference to the easterly wind at Dives is inconsistent with this picture, but the word used (*eurus*) is unusual and Virgil uses it to mean wind in general; third, when the weather changed, the *Carmen* records:

> He (God) drove the clouds from the sky and the winds from the sea, dispelled the cold and rid the heavens of rain. The earth grew warm, pervaded by great heat, and the sun shone with unwonted brilliance.

Anyone surely will recognise a classic Indian summer, a period of fine settled weather associated with an area of high pressure.

Both William of Poitiers and the *Carmen* imply that the fleet left St Valéry, when the south wind finally blew. The *Carmen* says that this was after a delay of a fortnight, and shortly before the feast of St Michael (29 September). Chronicle D of the *Anglo-Saxon Chronicle* confirms this by recording that the fleet sailed from Normandy to Pevensey on the eve of Michaelmas, whilst Chronicle E records that William landed at Hastings on St Michael's day. The *Carmen* states that he left St Valéry towards nightfall and this is not inconsistent with William's statement that the fleet anchored for part of the night as soon as it reached the open sea. They must have left at high water; nowadays the whole of the estuary of the Somme dries out at low water up to 3 miles seaward from Le Hourdel.[6] Although the configuration of the estuary was undoubtedly different in medieval times, it would still have been shallow and probably dried out to a significant extent.

There is a discrepancy between the evidence of William of Poitiers and the *Carmen* about what actually happened next. William of Poitiers writes that the ships were ordered to anchor close to William's ship as soon as they were out on the high sea, to wait for part of the night until, at the sign of a lantern and the sound of a trumpet, they should set course for England, for it was not intended that they should reach the coast of England until daybreak. The *Carmen* records that the fleet stood out to sea in ordered formation, but that it anchored later during the night in the middle of the open sea, which is unlikely without quite extraordinary lengths of anchor warp. It does, however, record that all ships carried lanterns at their mastheads and that they reached Pevensey at about 9 a.m. The *Carmen* also records that 'the hidden moon

---

6 *MacMillan and Silk Cut Nautical Almanac, 1986,* 681.

denied you her service', which given the cloudless conditions prevailing can only mean that the moon had set.

Both William of Poitiers and the *Carmen* have significant comments to make about Duke William's state of mind during the wait at St Valéry. William of Poitiers speaks of the Duke's utter confidence; his unbroken spirit, of his meeting adversities with prudence: he says that Duke William concealed the loss of those who drowned by burying them in secret and increased the rations to mitigate their scarcity. Like William of Poitiers, the *Carmen* mentions Duke William's prayers, but otherwise presents a rather different, but not inconsistent picture: one of anguish and worry; whilst recognising his determination and fearlessness, it tells of his lamentations and tears alternating with joy, as unfavourable weather alternated with favourable.

C. M. Gillmor's Study

We wish to mention C.M. Gillmor's 'Naval Logistics of the Cross-Channel Operation, 1066' in *Anglo-Norman Studies VII*, because, although we disagree with much of her interpretation, we acknowledge that her work has acted as a stimulus to our own reconstruction of the invasion passage. Her paper includes a detailed analysis of the passage, first to St Valéry, then to Pevensey. This is supported by much data about the weather, the tides and astronomical phenomena. We have made our own assessment of this data, including our own calculation of the astronomical data,[7] and in the main we believe it to be valid. We believe, however, that her interpretation is flawed by a lack of understanding of what the data and the sources mean in nautical terms.

Gillmor's principal conclusion is that Duke William took a planned decision to move the fleet to St Valéry before setting out on the final invasion passage to Pevensey. She argues that 'his mariners must have advised William to move up the coast where the chance of a south wind would be greater'.[8] She also proposes that William timed his departure from Dives on 12 September to follow the disbanding on 8 September of the *scyp fyrd*, which 'had been waiting for William to emerge from Dives so that the warships could pounce on the unescorted Norman convoy'.[9]

We have indicated the dangers St Valéry offers as a lee shore and we consider that William would have needed powerful reasons to move the fleet there. If the likelihood of favourable winds was greater further east, then, with the prevalent westerlies, he could no doubt have moved his fleet to St Valéry on a number of times during the previous month. He certainly had no need to wait until 12 September and, because of the impossibility of effective action by the *fyrd* from its base 90 miles away, we do not consider that the fact that it was still on duty would have inhibited William from moving to St Valéry earlier.

However, given the time of year, with every day that passed the probability was that the weather would worsen and we cannot see William deliberately risking his fleet in the dangerous St Valéry area. Let the last word on this be with the contemporary records. Neither the *Carmen* nor William of Poitiers sound as if they are describing a planned passage to St Valéry: the *Carmen* says 'leaving your own shores

---

7   Using a Casio FX–730P pocket computer and mathematical formulae drawn from *Practical Astronomy with your Calculator* by Peter Duffet-Smith (Cambridge University Press, 1988).

8   C.M. Gillmor, 'Naval Logistics, 1066', 124.

9   C.M. Gillmor, 'Naval Logistics, 1066', 124.

willy-nilly (*velis nolis*), you directed your fleet to the coast of another'; William of Poitiers says that the fleet 'was blown by westerlies in to the roadstead of St Valéry'.

Our Proposal for the Reconstruction of the Invasion Passage

In formulating our proposal for the reconstruction of the passage of the invasion fleet, we have taken as our starting point the contemporary records, particularly the *Carmen de Hastingae Proelio*, William of Poitiers and the *Bayeux Tapestry*. We have attempted to understand what they say in terms of the best assessment we can make of the performance of the ships available at the time and of our experience of sailing in inshore and offshore waters.

We consider that Duke William's passage plan was to sail direct from Dives to England when a favourable southerly blew. That is confirmed by William of Poitiers and the *Carmen*.[10] The distance is some 90–95 sea miles and, judging by the timing of the eventual crossing from St Valéry, we may assume that William wished to arrive in daylight, perhaps to avoid the dangers of a night landing on an unlit shore, perhaps to allow enough time in daylight to consolidate his position on shore before nightfall. Depending on the speed which the fleet could achieve, which itself would depend on the wind strength, the time needed for the passage might be twelve hours (8 knots) to sixteen hours (6 knots). Of course the passage might be much shorter if the wind blew really strongly and vice versa, if the wind were light; but all the indications are that a night passage was planned.

With a passage straight across the Channel the effect of the tide would be minimal, but we may expect that William would leave at high water, as the tide was about to ebb. Therefore the likelihood is that he planned to leave with an afternoon or evening high tide.

During August and the first half of September the weather was characterised by a succession of Atlantic lows bringing rain and westerly winds. By the middle of September Duke William must have been getting desperate. The season was getting late and holding his invasion army together would have been getting increasingly difficult. He made his move and brought his fleet out of harbour.

There is no information as to the wind direction at the time. Perhaps it was south-westerly, arising from an approaching low, and Duke William hoped to take it as a quartering breeze to England; perhaps it was still blowing from the west and Duke William hoped to claw his way close hauled to England. Either way it was soon blowing from the west and so strongly that the fleet could no longer continue close hauled to make its way north and was forced to turn downwind, finding shelter in what perhaps was the only harbour open to it, the Somme estuary.

There are likely to have been losses during the passage to St Valéry. The only direct evidence is the statement of William of Poitiers that Duke William 'concealed the loss of those who were drowned by burying them in secret'.[11] We may assume that the need to conceal the loss of these men implies that their numbers were considerable, and the description of William's state of mind in the *Carmen* shows him in a state of distress, arising no doubt from his worries about the weather and the lateness

---

10 R. Allen Brown, *The Norman Conquest*, 28: William of Poitiers states that the fleet 'had long lain in the mouth of the Dives and the neighbouring harbours awaiting a south wind to take them to England'. The *Carmen* (1.40), speaking of Duke William being prevented by the weather from leading the fleet across the Channel, must also imply an original intention to cross straight to England.
11 R. Allen Brown, *The Norman Conquest*, 28.

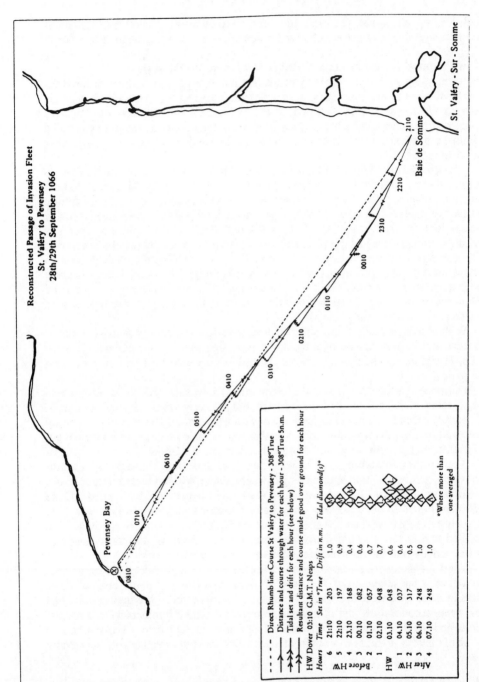

Reconstructed Passage of Invasion Fleet
St. Valéry to Pevensey
28th/29th September 1066

St. Valéry - Sur - Somme

Baie de Somme

Pevensey Bay

- - - - Direct Rhumb line Course St Valéry to Pevensey - 308°True
↗ Distance and course through water for each hour - 308°True 5n.m.
↗ Tidal set and drift for each hour (see below)
↗ Resultant distance and course made good over ground for each hour

HW Dover 03:10 G.M.T. Neaps

Hours	Time	Set in °True	Drift in n.m.	Tidal diamond(s)*
6	21:10	203	1.0	
5	22:10	197	0.9	
4	23:10	168	0.4	
3	00.10	082	0.6	
2	01.10	057	0.7	
1	02.10	048	0.7	
HW	03.10	048	0.6	
1	04.10	037	0.6	
2	05.10	317	0.5	
3	06.10	248	1.0	
4	07.10	248	1.0	

Before HW / HW / After HW

*Where more than one averaged

Fig. 4.

of the season, but also entirely consistent with the loss of a significant part of his invasion force. We may assume too that the loss of a significant number of men by drowning implies the loss of ships, although there is no specific reference to shipwreck.

We have already referred to the dangers of the lee shore along the east bank of the Seine estuary and between Cap de la Hève and Cap d'Antifer, and further east around the coast line running north from the Somme estuary. The conditions prevailing at the time may have made this area even more difficult. Our analysis is based on the supposition that William left Dives on 13 September (although the exact date is not crucial) with the afternoon high water, hoping to arrive in England the next morning.

High water at Dives would have been around 13:00 and the next high water at St Valéry would have been around 03:30 the next morning. As the fleet left Dives, the tide in the Channel would be on the point of setting westward. As the wind strengthened, the fleet, therefore, would experience increasingly uncomfortable wind against tide conditions exacerbated by the shallow banks in the Baie de la Seine.[12] As the fleet proceeded eastwards along the coast, wind against tide conditions would have continued until well into the evening, perhaps around 21:00.[13] Running before a westerly gale, the fleet would be making fast progress, in spite of the contrary tidal stream: it would have arrived in the dark and quite possibly several hours before high water (fourteen hours after high water at Dives), when there was little water in the estuary. That would have been a recipe for chaos and conceivably many ships were lost.

The weather continued unfavourable for a further two weeks, until 28 September, when a high pressure system brought a change in the weather with warm sunshine, clear skies and a southerly wind. In both the *Carmen* and William of Poitiers you can almost feel the relief. Our assessment of high water at St Valéry that day is 15:14 GMT. The sun set at 17:24 GMT and rose the next day at 06:01 GMT. The moon, which was six days old, set at 22:17 GMT.

Duke William and the invasion force hurried to embark and sailed with the afternoon tide, with the intention of arriving in England after daybreak the next day. Because St Valéry is a drying harbour there would be no choice but to sail with the tide. Both the *Carmen* and William of Poitiers speak of the fleet anchoring, William more plausibly recording that this happened as soon as they reached deep water. We believe that this was to allow the fleet to establish the ordered formation mentioned in the *Carmen*, which certainly could not otherwise have been achieved by the fleet straggling out of the estuary. We also accept William of Poitiers' explanation that this was to ensure that the fleet did not arrive before daybreak. If they left harbour between 15:00 and 16:00 and travelled at 5 knots, a speed which might be more realistic in these conditions than in those prevailing during the passage to St Valéry, they would arrive two or three hours before sunrise. Fig. 4 shows our reconstruction of the invasion passage.[14]

It would be important to maintain formation. With a following wind this would

---

[12] *MacMillan and Silk Cut Nautical Almanac, 1986*, 662, states: 'The Seine estuary . . . is encumbered by shallow and shifting banks which extend seawards to Banc de la Seine, 15M W of le Havre. With wind against tide there is a heavy sea on this bank.'

[13] *Tidal Stream Atlas: The English and Bristol Channels* (Hydrographic Department, Taunton, 1973, NP250).

[14] Tidal data drawn from *Admiralty Chart 5052* (Hydrographer of the Navy, Taunton, 1976).

have been line abreast and no doubt in the moonless night each ship carried a lantern as the *Carmen* records. However, two pieces of evidence indicate that the fleet was not entirely successful in holding formation. William of Poitiers records that the Invader's ship lost contact during the night with the remainder of the fleet. He also records that some of William's men had come to Romney by mistake as a result, it would seem, of losing contact with the fleet during the crossing.[15]

Did Harold have a defensive strategy? The Anglo-Saxon Chronicle shows that he was aware of the Norman threat and that he raised land and naval forces to counter it. Chronicle E merely records that he 'sailed out against William with a naval force', while Chronicle C reports that he lay in the Isle of Wight 'the whole summer and autumn, and the levies were stationed everywhere along the coast, although in the end it was all to no purpose'. Gillmor surmises that 'the Anglo-Saxon fleet had been waiting for William to emerge from Dives so that the warships could pounce on the unescorted Norman convoy';[16] the only way that this could have been a realistic possibility would have been for the Anglo-Saxon fleet to lie in wait off the Norman coast, as later navies did, for example during the blockades of the Napoleonic Wars. What, in the more weather-proof ships of later navies, was a hard and onerous duty, would in the open ships of the eleventh century have been an unendurable and impossible task and we suspect Duke William would have known it. He would, therefore, not have expected to meet opposition until he approached the English coast. Whether that opposition would have been from a naval force while still at sea, we believe is open to doubt; although there is some evidence of actions fought at sea during the reign of Alfred, the military function of ships during the reigns of Edward the Confessor and Harold appears to have been limited to the transport of raiding or invading forces and to providing a means of flight after defeat.[17] Moreover, unless the invasion fleet landed close to a concentration of Anglo-Saxon ships, it simply would not have been possible to deploy the Anglo-Saxon fleet fast enough to make a naval engagement possible; William would have relied on this and rated the chances of interception at sea as negligible.

We suspect that Harold's decision to station himself on the Isle of Wight was based on the calculation that it defended the route to Winchester, some of his own estates,[18] but above all his power base *vis-à-vis* Stigand as Bishop of Winchester. Stigand, who retained the See of Winchester with its estates after his irregular elevation to Canterbury, held the strategically situated Pagham coastal estate[19] and key land near the south coast between the Solent and the Thames estuary. Stigand had been the confidant of the formerly powerful Emma of Normandy, widow of King Æthelred, widow of King Cnut, mother of Edward the Confessor: Emma, through whom William claimed the throne of England. Harold would also be acutely aware that the Isle of Wight had displayed its allegiance to his hostile brother Tostig in April 1066, and that the Norman Fitz Osbern family held lands in the area.

Harold's defensive strategy seemed to be no more subtle than to move his troops

---

15 R. Allen Brown, *The Norman Conquest*, 29 and 36.

16 C.M. Gillmor, 'Naval Logistics, 1066', 124.

17 J. Haywood, *Dark Age Naval Power* (Routledge, 1991), 4.

18 Ann Williams, 'Land and power in the eleventh century: the estates of Harold Godwinson' in the *Proceedings of the Battle Conference* 1980.

19 N. Brooks, *The Early History of the Church of Canterbury* (Leicester University Press, 1984), 312.

by forced marches to wherever danger threatened and engage in immediate pitched battle. Though admired in later times, this strategy did not confirm with military precepts of the age[20] and resulted in disaster, which might have been avoided by a longer term strategy and which, by his death and that of his brothers, deprived the Anglo-Saxons of leaders who might have inspired them to effective long term resistance to the Normans.

From William's point of view, we suspect that none of this had any bearing on the timing of the departure of the invasion fleet. He would certainly have expected to have to fight, but it is likely that he discounted the possibility of a naval engagement. He may have been aware that the Anglo-Saxon levies could be expected to disband in mid-September, but given the likelihood of worsening weather, not to say worsening morale and increasing supply difficulties, we do not believe that he would have deliberately delayed sailing until he knew that they had disbanded. We believe that he would have sailed as soon as the wind blew fair, and this is what both William of Poitiers and the *Carmen* imply.

Clearly we cannot claim certainty in the detail of our interpretation. We do, however, think that, interpreted in the light of the prevailing meteorological conditions and with a proper understanding of nautical and navigational issues, the contemporary records suggest that the invasion fleet sailed from Dives in the middle of September in marginal conditions, with the intention of reaching England, but was forced to run downwind to the Somme estuary. The fleet suffered losses which were probably significant. Only Duke William's strength of character and the change in the weather by the end of September saved the invasion plans; had the change in weather not happened, the fleet would have been disbanded for the winter, like Hitler's operation 'Sealion', and, like 'Sealion', it could not have been reconstituted the following year. St Valéry did indeed represent near disaster. Duke William held on in spite of all and by the time he reached Pevensey, the battle for England was all but over.

Final Thoughts

As we have worked on this study, we have become increasingly convinced of the status of the *Carmen* as a source.

The value of the *Carmen* is that its evidence is more independently based than either of the two main Norman contemporary sources, but that is not to say that it is without bias. Guy of Amiens was not under the jurisdiction of the Norman Church. His uncle, Guy of Ponthieu, held his land outside Normandy. He had a freedom to say what he liked. The *Carmen* was a wonderful opportunity for him to denigrate the rapidly expanding Church of the Ducal house of Normandy, which was becoming so well thought of by the Pope, for it showed William and the Normans to be so like their pagan Viking ancestors. Significantly, and perhaps because of its poetic form, it also reflects the thoughts and feelings of William, his worries about the weather, his fear of losing ships and men by drowning or desertion.

It is all too easy to discount the *Carmen* as a poetical extravagance and to regard the events and human emotions it describes as being hopelessly distorted by panegyric hyperbole. But when stripped of the poetic language, it rings true. The author

---

[20] J. Gillingham, 'William the Bastard at War', in *Studies in Medieval History presented to R. Allen Brown*, edited by C. Harper-Bill (The Boydell Press, 1989), 148, quotes Vegetius: 'Battle should be the last resort. Everything else should be tried first'.

of the *Carmen* understood the importance of wind force and direction to people whose main way of travel was by water, and the sailor's obsession with this if he is going out to sea.

Above all, the *Carmen* is not only consistent with other contemporary accounts of the crossing, it also is consistent with the weather conditions which may be expected to have prevailed that summer and gives an insight into Duke William's mind at a time of considerable stress. Only the *Carmen* recognises the dangers of a lee shore; only the *Carmen* describes a weather pattern which would be consistent with a period of unfavourable winds, followed by a weather system which would have brought the required southerly wind; only the *Carmen* records the moonless night of the crossing. Finally, while both William of Poitiers and the *Carmen* give an insight into the Duke's mind during that crucial wait following the near disaster of St Valéry, only the *Carmen* recognises the depth of despair which he must have felt.

C. The Battle

The Battle of Hastings was fought once on the field. It has been refought countless times since in words. Each retelling, from William of Jumièges and his contemporaries on, puts the Duke of Normandy and the King of England in charge of contrary historical forces; the Duke's army must always win the battle, but the King's forces sometimes win the war. The following selection of articles narrate the battle (or aspects of it) from a variety of perspectives. Whether the Normans or the Anglo-Saxons are the heroes varies with the view of the field and the combatants on it.

12. David Hume, *The History of England*

The dawn of the 'modern science of history' is usually dated to the nineteenth century. This first selection therefore comes from the pre-dawn glow of the eighteenth century Enlightenment. The Scottish philosopher David Hume wrote a seven volume history of England; this account of Hastings comes from volume 1. It is notable for its balance and caution in interpretation, its reliance on a range of sources still considered reliable, and its commendable brevity – Hume does not make more of the battle than his sources allow him to – while a fine literary style speaks to the 'pre-scientific' nature of the narrative. Hume is uncritical about the numbers reported in his sources, accepting Orderic's figure of 60,000 for the size of William's army and 15,000 for the Norman casualties; even the latter figure is greater than the total number of combatants on both sides as reckoned by today's scholars. But this is otherwise a clear account, perhaps because the field is not yet overcluttered with academic combatants.

Reprinted from David Hume, *The History of England from the Invasion of Julius Caesar to the Revolution in 1688*, vol. I, 192–5.

14th October

The English and Normans now prepared themselves for this important decision; but the aspect of things, on the night before the battle, was very different in the two camps. The English spent the time in riot, and jollity, and disorder; the Normans in silence, and in prayer, and in the other functions of their religion.[1] On the morning, the duke called together the most considerable of his commanders, and made them a speech suitable to the occasion. He represented to them, that the event, which they and he had long wished for, was approaching; the whole fortune of the war now depended on their swords, and would be decided in a single action: That never army had great motives for exerting a vigorous courage, whether they considered the prize which would attend their victory, or the inevitable destruction which must ensue upon their discomfiture: That if their martial and veteran bands could once break those raw soldiers, who had rashly dared to approach them they conquered a kingdom at one blow, and were justly entitled to all its possessions as the reward of their prosperous valour: That, on the contrary, if they remitted in the least their wonted prowess, an enraged enemy hung upon their rear, the sea met them in their retreat, and an ignominious death was the certain punishment of their imprudent cowardice: That, by collecting so numerous and brave a host, he had ensured every human means of conquest; and the commander of the enemy, by his criminal conduct, had given him just cause to hope for the favour of the Almighty, in whose hands alone lay the event of wars and battles: And that a perjured usurper, anathematized by the sovereign pontiff, and conscious of his own breach of faith, would be struck with terror on their appearance, and would prognosticate to himself that fate which his multiplied crimes had so justly merited.[2] The duke next divided his army into three lines: The first led by Montgomery, consisted of archers and light-armed infantry: The second, commanded by Martel, was composed of his bravest battalions, heavy-armed, and ranged in close order: His cavalry, at whose head he placed himself, formed the third line; and were so disposed, that they stretched beyond the infantry, and flanked each wing of the army.[3] He ordered the signal of battle to be given; and the whole army, moving at once, and singing the hymn or song of Roland, the famous peer of Charlemagne,[4] advanced in order and with alacrity towards the enemy.

Harold had seized the advantage of a rising ground, and having likewise drawn some trenches to secure his flanks, he resolved to stand upon the defensive, and to avoid all action with the cavalry, in which he was inferior. The Kentish men were placed in the van; a post which they had always claimed as their due: The Londoners guarded the standard: And the king himself, accompanied by his two valiant brothers, Gurth and Leofwin, dismounting, placed himself at the head of his infantry, and expressed his resolution to conquer, or to perish in the action. The first attack of the Normans was desperate, but was received with equal valour by the English; and after a furious combat, which remained long undecided, the former, overcome by the difficulty of the ground, and hard pressed by the enemy, began first to relax their vigour, then to retreat; and confusion was spreading among the ranks, when William, who found himself on the brink of destruction, hastened with a select band to the

1   W. Malm. p. 201. De Gest, Angl. p. 332.
2   H. Hunt. p. 368. Brompton, p. 959. Gul. Pict. p. 201.
3   Gul. Pict. 201. Order. Vital. p. 501.
4   W. Malm. p. 101. Higden, p. 286. Matth. West. p. 223. Du Cange's Glossary in verbo *Cantilena Rolandi*.

relief of his dismayed forces. His presence restored the action; the English were obliged to retire with loss; and the duke, ordering his second line to advance, renewed the attack with fresh forces, and with redoubled courage. Finding that the enemy, aided by the advantage of ground, and animated by the example of their prince, still made a vigorous resistance, he tried a stratagem, which was very delicate in its management, but which seemed advisable in its desperate situation, where, if he gained not a decisive victory, he was totally undone: He commanded his troops to make a hasty retreat, and to allure the enemy from their ground by the appearance of flight. The artifice succeeded against those unexperienced soldiers, who, heated by the action, and sanguine in their hopes, precipitately followed the Normans into the plain. William gave orders, that at once the infantry should face about upon their pursuers, and the cavalry make an assault upon their wings, and both of them pursue the advantage, which the surprise and terror of the enemy must give them in that critical and decisive moment. The English were repulsed with great slaughter, and driven back to the hill; where, being rallied by the bravery of Harold, they were able, notwithstanding their loss, to maintain the post, and continue the combat. The duke tried the same stratagem a second time with the same success; but even after this double advantage, he still found a great body of the English, who, maintaining themselves in firm array, seemed determined to dispute the victory to the last extremity. He ordered his heavy-armed infantry to make an assault upon them; while his archers, placed behind, should gall the enemy, who were exposed by the situation of the ground, and who were intent in defending themselves against the swords and spears of the assailants. By this disposition he at last prevailed: Harold was slain by an arrow, while he was combating with great bravery at the head of his men: His two brothers shared the same fate: And the English, discouraged by the fall of those princes, gave ground on all sides, and were pursued with great slaughter by the victorious Normans. A few troops, however, of the vanquished had still the courage to turn upon their pursuers; and attacking them in deep and miry ground, obtained some revenge for the slaughter and dishonour of the day. But the appearance of the duke obliged them to seek their safety by flight; and darkness saved them from any farther pursuit by the enemy.

Thus was gained by William, duke of Normandy, the great and decisive victory of Hastings, after a battle which was fought from morning till sunset, and which seemed worthy, by the heroic valour displayed by both armies, and by both commanders, to decide the fate of a mighty kingdom. William had three horses killed under him; and there fell near fifteen thousand men on the side of the Normans: The loss was still more considerable on that of the vanquished; besides the death of the king and his two brothers. The dead body of Harold was brought to William, and was generously restored without ransom to his mother. The Norman army left not the field of battle without giving thanks to Heaven in the most solemn manner for their victory: And the prince, having refreshed his troops, prepared to push to the utmost his advantage against the divided, dismayed, and discomfited, English.

13. E.A. Freeman, *The Norman Conquest*

Edward Augustus Freeman was the first 'modern' historian of the Norman Conquest, if current bibliographies are to be trusted. His account of the battle comes from the third volume of his *Norman Conquest*, and in contrast to the balance of Hume's account Freeman's sympathies are clearly with the 'English' (Anglo-Saxon) warriors. A Whig historian who saw the origins of his own nineteenth century English democracy in the supposed Germanic tribal democracy of the Anglo-Saxon kingdoms, Freeman brings to his analysis of Hastings the full panoply of nineteenth century *mentalité*: intense nationalism; the essentialization of race in characterizing peoples; and faith in Progress and the eventual triumph of Right. Whether this represents an advance over Hume is doubtful. Freeman also relies heavily on Wace's *Roman de Rou*, now largely discredited as a reliable source for the events of 1066. For both his politics and his methodology Freeman ran afoul of the great champion of the Normans in nineteenth century historiography, John Horace Round. The battle between Freeman and Round still resonates in the historiography of the Conquest.

Reprinted from E.A. Freeman, *The History of the Norman Conquest of England, its Causes and Results* (Oxford, 1873), III.301–37.

The Battle. October 14, 1066.

And now the night came on, the night of Friday the thirteenth of October, the night which was to usher in the ever-memorable morn of Saint Calixtus. Very different, according to our Norman informants, was the way in which that night was spent by the two armies. The English spent the night in drinking and singing,[1] the Normans in prayer and confession of their sins.[2] Among the crowds of clergy in William's host were two prelates of all but the highest rank in the Norman Church.[3] One was Geoffrey, Bishop of Coutances, who in his temporal character was soon to have so large a share of the spoils of England.[4] The other was the Duke's own half-brother, the famous Odo, who, to his Bishop's seat at Bayeux, was soon to add the temporal cares of the Kentish Earldom.[5] Under the pious care of the two Bishops and of the other clergy, the Norman host seems to have been wrought up to a sort of paroxysm of devotion. Odo extracted from every man a special vow, that those who survived the struggle of the coming Saturday would never again eat flesh on any Saturday that was to come.[6] Tales like these are the standing accusations which the victors always bring against the vanquished. The reproach which is cast on the English host on the night before the fight of Senlac is also cast on the French host on the night before the fight of Azincourt.[7] And yet there may well be some groundwork of truth in these

1 Will. Malms. iii. 241. 'Angli, ut accepimus, totam noctem incomnem cantibus potibusque ducentes.' So Wace, 12465, who gives us some curious bits of English:

> Quant la bataille dut joster,
> La nuit avant, ço oï conter,
> Furent Engleiz forment haitiez,
> Mult riant è mult enveisiez;
> Tote nuit mangierent è burent
> Unkes la nuit et lit ne jurent.
> Mult les véissiez demener,
> Treper, è saillir è chanter;
> *Bublie* crient è *weissel*
> E *laticome* è *drincheheil*,
> *Drinc Hindrewart* è *Drintome*,
> *Drinc Helf* è *drinc Tome*.

2 Will. Malms. iii. 242. 'Contra Normanni, nocte totâ confessioni peccatorum vacantes, mane Dominico Corpore communicârunt.'
3 Will. Pict. 131. 'Aderant comitati e Normanniâ duo Pontifices, Odo Baiocensis et Goisfiedus Constantinus; una multus clerus et monachi nonnulli. Id collegium *precibus pugnare* disponitur.' So Ord. Vit. 501A. Of Odo at least the Tapestry tells another story. Compare the English Prelates at Assandun, vol. i. p. 264.
4 On Geoffrey of Mowbray (Bishop 1048–1093) and his vast possessions in England, see Ellis, i. 400.
5 Chron. Petrib. 1087. 'He wæs swiðe rice bisceop on Normandige: on Baius wæs his bisceopstol ... and he hæfde eorldom on Englelande.' Cf. 1088.
6 Wace (12478–12522) is very full on the ministrations of the two Bishops, and on the devotions of the army, both during the night and on the morning before the battle. The vow is thus described (12485–12490):

> Por ço ke samedi esteit,
> Ke la bataille estre debveit,
> Unt Normanz pramis è voé,
> Si com li cler l'orent loé,
> Ke à cet jor mez s'il veskeient,
> Char ne saunc ne maingereint.

7 The piety of the English on the night before Azincourt is insisted on in some of our accounts. Take Elmham for instance (479):

stories. The English were not, like the Normans, fighting under the influence of that strange spiritual excitement which had persuaded men that an unprovoked aggression on an unoffending nation was in truth a war of religion, a Crusade for the good of the souls of Normans and English alike. It may therefore well be that there was more of ceremonial devotion in the camp of William than in the camp of Harold. And yet even a Norman legend gives us a picture of the English King bending before the body of his Lord,[8] and Englishmen may deem that the prayers and blessings of Ælfwig and Leofric were at least as holy and as acceptable as the prayers and blessings of Geoffrey and Odo. And we must not forget that the devotions of William and his followers are recorded by William's own chaplain and flatterer, while no narrative of that night's doings survives from the pen of any canon of Waltham or any monk of the New Minster. And we shall hardly deem the worse of our countrymen, if that evening's supper by the camp-fires was enlivened by the spirit-stirring strains of old Teutonic minstrelsy. Never again were those ancient songs to be uttered by the mouth of English warriors in the air of a free and pure Teutonic England. They sang, we well may deem, the song of Brunanburh and the song of Maldon; they sang how Æthelstan conquered and how Brihtnoth fell; and they sang, it well may be, in still louder notes, the new song which the last English gleeman had put into their mouths,

> How the wise King
> Made fast his realm
> To a high-born man,
> Harold himself,
> The noble Earl.[9]

And thoughts and words like these may have been as good a preparation for the day of battle as all the pious oratory with which the warlike Prelate of Bayeux could hound on the spoilers on their prey.

And now the fight began. It was one of the sacred hours of the Church, it was at the hour of prime, three hours before noon-day,[10] that the first blows were exchanged between the invaders and the defenders of England. The Normans had crossed the

Nox pluvialis ibi plebem sine pane madebat:
Ad Dominum vigiles quique dedere preces.

So Walsingham, ii. 310, ed. Riley; Monstrelet, vol. i. c. 146, p. 227b. What the French are chiefly charged with is playing at dice for English ransoms. see Redman, p. 45, ed. Cole. This is the point chiefly brought out by Shakespeare, Henry V, Act iv. Chorus. Compare also the accounts of the night before Lewes, the piety of the patriots and the foul excesses of the royalists. Rishanger, Chron. p. 25; Chron. Lanercost, 75; Political Songs (Camden Soc.), p. 80.

[8] See the legend in Appendix II in E.A. Freeman, *The History of the Norman Conquest of England, its Causes and Results* (Oxford, 1873).

[9] See E.A. Freeman, *The History of the Norman Conquest of England*, p. 12.

[10] Flor. Wig. 1066. 'Ab horâ diei tertiâ.' So Roman de Rou, 13265:

Dez ke tierce del jor entra,
Ke la bataille comença,
De si ke none trespassa
Fust si de si, fust si de là,
Ke nus ne sout lequel veincreit,
Ne ki la terre cunquerreit.

But I cannot help noticing the tendency to make the hours of battles and of other great events coincide with the hours of the Church.

English fosse,[11] and were now at the foot of the hill, with the palisades and the axes right before them. The trumpet sounded, and a flight of arrows from the archers in all the three divisions[12] of William's army was the prelude to the onslaught of the heavy-armed foot. But, before the two armies met hand to hand, a juggler or minstrel, known as *Taillefer*, the Cleaver of Iron,[13] rode forth from the Norman ranks as if to defy the whole force of England in his single person. He craved and obtained the Duke's leave to strike the first blow; he rode forth, singing songs of Roland and of Charlemagne[14] – so soon had the name and exploits of the great German become the spoil of the enemy. He threw his sword into the air and caught it again;[15] but he presently showed that he could use warlike weapons for other purposes than for jugglers' tricks of this kind; he pierced one Englishman with his lance, he struck down another with his sword, and then himself fell beneath the blows of their comrades. A bravado of this kind might serve as an omen, it might stir up the spirits of men on either side; but it could in no other way affect the fate of the battle. William was too wary a general to trust much to such knight-errantry as this. After the first discharge of arrows, the heavier foot followed to the attack, and the real struggle now began. The French infantry had to toil up the hill, and to break down the palisade, while a shower of stones and javelins disordered their approach,[16] and while club, sword, and axe greeted all who came within the reach of hand-strokes. The native

---

11 Roman de Rou, 13215:

> En la champaigne out un fossé;
> Normanz l'aveient adossé;
> En belliant l'orent passé,
> Ne l'aveient mie esgardé.

12 Od. ix. 156:

> Αὐτίκα καμπύλα τόξα καὶ αἰγανέασ δολιχαύλουσ
> εἱλόμεθ᾽ ἐκ νηῶν διὰ δὲ τρίχα κοσμηθέντεσ
> βάλλομεν

13 Wace (13149 et seqq.) introduces him as 'Taillefer ki mult bien cantout.' Guy of Amiens first calls him (391)

> Histrio, cor audax nimium quem nobilitabat;

and afterwards (399)

> Incisor-ferri mimus cognomine dictus.

14 Roman de Rou, 13151:

> Devant li Dus alout cantant
> De Karlemaine è de Rollant,
> E d'Oliver è des vassals
> Ki morurent en Renchevals.

Will. Malms. iii. 242. 'Tunc cantilenâ Rollandi inchoatâ, ut martium viri exemplum pugnaturos accenderet.' So in the Ludwigslied:

> Sang was gesungen,
> Wig was bigunnen.

After the profanation of the name of the great Emperor, it is refreshing to turn to a word or two of his own speech.

15 I should hardly have ventured to accept this juggling trick on the sole authority of Henry of Huntington (M.H.B. 763B), but we find it also in Guy, 393:

> Hortatur Gallos verbis, et territat Anglos;
> Alte projiciens ludit et ense suo.

16 Will. Pict. 133. 'Iis [the English missiles, see above, p. 316], veluti mole letiferâ, statim nostros obrui putares.'

Normans had to do this in the face of the fiercest resistance, in the teeth of the heaviest axes, wielded by the hands of men with whom to fight had ever been to vanquish, the kinsmen and Thegns and Housecarls of King Harold. Their own missiles, hurled from below, could do comparatively little damage. Both sides fought with unyielding valour; the war-cries rose loud on either side;[17] the Normans shouted 'God help us'; the English, from behind their barricades, mocked with cries of 'Out, out' every foe who entered or strove to enter.[18] But our fathers also mingled piety with valour; they too called on holy names to help them in that day's struggle.[19] They raised their national war-cry of 'God Almighty',[20] and in remembrance of the relic which their King so well loved to honour, they called on the 'Holy Cross', the Holy Cross of Waltham, little knowing perhaps of the awful warning which that venerated rood had given to their King and to his people.[21] The Norman infantry had now done its best, but that best had been in vain. The choicest chivalry of Europe now pressed on to the attack.[22] The knights of Normandy, and of all the lands from which men had flocked to William's standard, now pressed on, striving to make what impression they could with the whole strength of themselves and their horses on the impenetrable fortress of timber, shields, and living warriors. But the advantage of ground enjoyed by the English, their greater physical strength and stature,[23] the terrible weapons which they

[17] Ib. 'Altissimus clamor, hinc Normannicus, illinc barbaricus, armorum sonitu et gemitu morientium superatur.'

[18] Roman de Rou, 13193:

> Normanz escrient; dex aïe;
> La gent englesche, *Ut* s'escrie.

Compare the dying words of Lewis the Pious in the Astronomer's Life (64, Pertz, ii. 648); 'Bis dixit, *Hutz, butz*, quod significat *foras*. Unde patet quia malignum spiritum vidit,' &c. The English had to drive out less ghostly foes.

[19] As we have two ensigns, a national and a personal one, so we evidently have a national and a personal war-cry. As, besides the Standard, Harold's own Standard, we have the national Dragon, so we have the cry of 'Holy Cross,' which cannot fail to be an invocation of Harold's own Holy Cross of Waltham, and we have also another cry of 'God Almighty,' which we must infer to be more strictly a national cry. We may fancy that the irregular levies shouted 'God Almighty,' while the King's Thegns and Housecarls shouted 'Holy Cross.'

[20] Compare the description of a widely different warfare:

> And one enormous shout of 'Allah!' rose
> In the same moment, loud as even the roar
> Of war's most mortal engines, to their foes
> Hurling defiance: city, stream, and shore
> Resounded 'Allah!' and the clouds which close
> With thickening canopy the conflict o'er,
> Vibrate to the Eternal name. Hark through
> All sounds it pierceth, 'Allah! Allah! Hu!'   Don Juan, viii. 8.

[21] We here get some more of Wace's English. Roman de Rou, 13119:

> *Olicrosse* sovent crioent,
> E *Godemite* reclamoent;
> *Olicrosse* est en engleiz
> Ke *Sainte croix* est en franceiz,
> Et *Godemite* altretant
> Com en frenceiz *Dex tot poissant*.

[22] Will. Pict. 133. 'Subveniunt equites, et qui posteriores fuere fiunt primi. Pudet eminus pugnare; gladiis rem gerere audent.'

[23] Ib. 'Angli nimium adjuvantur superioris loci opportunitate, quem sine procursu tenent, et maxime conferti; atque ingenti quoque numerositate suá atque validissimâ corpulentiâ; præterea pugnæ

wielded, all joined to baffle every effort of Breton, Picard, Norman, and of the mighty Duke himself. Javelin and arrow had been tried in vain; every Norman missile had found an English missile to answer it.[24] The lifted lances had been found wanting; the broad sword had clashed in vain against the two-handed axe;[25] the maces of the Duke and of the Bishop had done their best. But few who came within the unerring sweep of an English axe ever lived to strike another blow. Rank after rank of the best chivalry of France and Normandy pressed on to the unavailing task. All was in vain; the old Teutonic tactics, carried on that day to perfection by the master-skill of Harold, proved too strong for the arts and the valour of Gaul and Roman. Not a man had swerved; not an inch of ground was lost; the shield-wall was still unbroken, and the Dragon of Wessex still soared unconquered over the hill of Senlac.

The English had thus far stood their ground well and wisely. The tactics of Harold had thus far completely answered. Not only had every attack failed, but the great mass of the French army altogether lost heart. The Bretons and the other auxiliaries on the left were the first to give way. Horse and foot alike, they turned and fled. A body of English troops was now rash enough, in direct defiance of the King's orders, to leave its post and pursue. These were of course some of the defenders of the English right. They may have been, as is perhaps suggested by a later turn of the battle, the detachment which guarded the small outlying hill. Or they may have been the men posted at the point just behind the outlying hill, where the slope is easiest, and where the main Breton attack would most likely be made. They had succeeded in beating back their assailants, and the temptation to chase the flying enemy must have been almost irresistible. And it may even be that old differences of race added keenness to the encounter, and that Englishmen felt a special delight in cutting down *Bret-Wealas* even from beyond sea. At any rate, the whole of William's left wing was thrown into utter confusion. The central division could hardly have seen the cause of that confusion; the press of the fugitives disordered their ranks, and soon the whole of the assailing host was falling back; even the Normans themselves, as their historian is driven unwillingly to confess, were at last carried away by the contagion.[26]

instrumentis, quæ facile per scuta vel alia tegmina viam inveniunt.' 'Corpulentia' doubtless means height and general bigness. The English in the Tapestry are decidedly taller than the Normans. Compare the same remark on our continental kinsfolk, p. 60.

24 Will. Pict. 133. 'Vulnerant et eos qui eminus in se jacula conjiciunt.' So Wid. Amb. 415:

Anglorum stat fixa solo densissima turba,
Tela dat et telis et gladios gladiis.

25 Will. Pict. u.s. 'Fortissime itaque sustinent vel propellunt ausos in se districtum ensibus impetum facere.' Cf. Il. xv. 708:

οὐδ' ἄρα τοίγε
τόξων ἀϊκὰσ ἀμφὶσ μένον οὐδέ τ' ἀκόντων
ἀλλ' οἵγ' ἐγγύθεν ἱστάμενοι, ἕνα θυμὸν ἔχοντεσ,
ὑξέσι δὴ πελέκεσσι καὶ ὑξίνῃσι μάχοντο,
καὶ ξίφεσιν μεγάλοισι καὶ ἔγχεσιν ἀμφιγύοισι.

26 Will. Pict. 133. 'Ecce igitur hâc sævitiâ perterriti avertuntur pedites pariter atque equites Britanni et quotquot auxiliares erant in sinistro cornu; cedit fere cuncta Ducis acies; quod cum pace dictum sit Normannorum invictissimæ nationis.' So Guy, 444:

Normanni fugiunt, dorsa tegunt clipei.

(On the difference in the order of events between William and Guy see Appendix KK.) Cf. Eadmer (5, 6, copied by Roger of Howden, Bromton, and others): 'De quo prœlio testantur adhuc Franci qui interfuerant, quoniam, licet varius casus hic inde exstiterit, tamen tanta strages ac fuga Normannorum fuit, ut victoria quâ potiti sunt vere et absque dubio solo miraculo Dei adscribenda sit.'

For the moment the day seemed lost; men might well deem that the Bastard had no hope of being changed into the Conqueror, the Duke of the Normans into the King of the English. But the strong heart of William failed him not, and by his single prowess and presence of mind he recalled his flying troops. Like Brihtnoth at Maldon,[27] like Eadmund at Sherstone,[28] he was himself deemed to have fallen or to have fled.[29] He tore his helmet from his head,[30] and with his look and his voice[31] he called back his men to the attack. 'Madmen,' he cried, 'behold me. Why flee ye? Death is behind you, victory is before you. I live, and by God's grace I will conquer.'[32] With a spear, snatched, it may be, from some comrade, he met or pursued the fugitives, driving them back by main force to the work.[33] Yet one version tells us that at this very moment a counsellor of flight was at his side. One Norman poet has sung how Eustace of Boulogne bade William turn his rein, and not rush on upon certain death.[34] If such counsels were ever given, they were cast aside with scorn; the bold words and gestures of the Duke restored the spirits of his men, and his knights once more pressed on, sword in hand,[35] round him. His brother the Bishop meanwhile rode, mace in hand, to another quarter, and called back to their duty another party of fugitives.[36] Encouraged by this turn in the fight, the Breton infantry themselves, chased as they were across the field by the over-daring English, now turned and cut their pursuers in pieces.[37] Order was soon again established throughout the whole

---

[27] See vol. i. p. 184.

[28] Ib. p. 260.

[29] Will. Pict. u.s. 'Credidere Normanni Ducem ac dominum suum cecidisse.'

[30] Will. Pict. 134. 'Nudato insuper capite detractâque galeâ.' So Guy, 448: 'Iratus galeâ nudat et ipse caput.' In the Tapestry, pl. 15, he simply raises his nose-piece. This was perhaps the real action, which it was hard to describe in an heroic fashion.

[31] Wid. Amb. 449. 'Vultum Normannis dat, verba precantia Gallis.'

[32] Will. Pict. u.s. 'Me, inquit, circumspicite. Vivo, et vincam, opitulante Deo. Quæ vobis dementia fugam suadet?' &c. The exact words are of course given differently in different accounts.

[33] Ib. 'Fugientibus occurrit et obstitit, verberans aut minans hastâ.' So Guy, 445:

> Dux ubi perspexit quod gens sua victa recedit,
>   Occurrens illi signa ferendo manu,
> Increpat et cædit, retinet, constringit et hastá.

Yet it is at this moment that the Tapestry (pl. 15, 'Hic est Willelm Dux') shows him in the most marked way with his mace.

[34] On the part taken by Eustace in the battle, see Appendix KK.

[35] In the Tapestry, pl. 15, all William's immediate comrades at this point, except Eustace, are shown with drawn swords.

[36] Roman de Rou, 13243:

> Quant Odes li boen corunez,
> Ki de Baicues ert sacrez,
> Poinst, si lor dist, Estez, estez;
> Séiez en paiz, ne vos movez;
> N'aiez poor de nule rien,
> Kar se Dex plaist nos veincron bien.
> Issi furent asséuré.
> Ne se sunt mie remué
> Odes revint puignant arière
> U la bataille esteit plus fière,
> Forment i a li jor valu.

He is very plainly shown in the Tapestry, pl. 15; 'Hic Odo Episcopus, baculum tenens, confortat pueros.' Odo is most prominent in the two authorities connected with his own church.

[37] Will. Pict. 134. 'Exardentes Normanni, et circumvenientes millia aliquot insequuta se, momento

line of the assailants, and William and Odo, with all their host, pressed on to a second and more terrible attack.

A new act in the awful drama of that day has now begun. The Duke himself, at the head of his own Normans, again pressed towards the Standard. Now came what was perhaps the fiercest exchange of handstrokes in the whole battle. As in the old Roman legend,[38] the main stress of the fight fell on three valiant brethren on either side. William, Odo, and Robert pressed on to the attack, while Harold, Gyrth, and Leofwine stood ready to defend. The Duke himself, his relics round his neck, spurred on right in the teeth of the English King. A few moments more, and the mighty rivals might have met face to face, and the war-club of the Bastard might have clashed against the lifted axe of the Emperor of Britain. That Harold shrank from such an encounter we may not deem for a moment. But a heart, if it might be, even loftier than his own beat high to save him from such a risk. In the same heroic spirit in which he had already offered to lead the host on what seemed a desperate enterprise,[39] the Earl of the East-Angles pressed forward to give, if need be, his own life for his King and brother. Before William could come to hand-strokes with Harold, perhaps before he could even reach the barricade, a spear, hurled by the hand of Gyrth, checked his progress. The weapon so far missed its aim that the Duke was himself unhurt. But his noble Spanish horse, the first of three that died under him that day, fell to the ground.[40] But Duke William could fight on foot as well as on horseback.[41] Indeed on foot he had a certain advantage. He could press closer to the barricade, and could deal a nearer and surer blow. And a near and sure blow he did deal. William rose to his feet; he pressed straight to seek the man who had so nearly slain him. Duke and Earl met face to face, and the English hero fell crushed beneath the stroke of the Duke's mace.[42] The day might seem to be turning against England, when a son of Godwine had fallen, nor did the blow come singly. Gyrth had fallen by a fate worthy of such a

---

deleverunt ea, ut ne quidem unus superesset.' But Guy (463) seems to include other parts of the army also:

> Post illum reliqui feriunt ad cordâ reversi;
> Vires assumunt rejiciendo metum.
> Ut stipulæ flammis percunt spirântibus auris,
> Sic a Francigenis, anglica turba, ruis.

[38] I need hardly refer to the story of the Horatii and Curiatii in Livy (i. 24): 'Forte in duobus tum exercitibus erant trigemini fratres, nec ætate nec viribus dispares.'

[39] See above, p. 290.

[40] Wid. Amb. 471:

> Heraldi frater, non territus ore leonis,
>   Nomine Gernt, Regis traduce progenitus,
> Librando telum celeri volitante lacerto,
>   Eminus emisso cuspide corpus equi
> Vulnerat, atque Ducem peditem bellare coegit;
>   Sed pedes effectus dimicat et melius.

So Will. Pict. 136. 'Equi tres ceciderunt sub eo confossi. Ter ille desiluit intrepidus, nec diu mors vectoris inulta remansit.' So Will. Malms. iii. 244. 'Dum ubique sævit, ubique infrendet, tres equos lectissimos sub se confossos eâ die amisit.' I find no account of the third unhorsing.

[41] Od. ix. 49:

> Ἤπειρον ναίοντεσ, ἐπιστάμενοι μὲν ἀφ' ἵππων
> ἀνδράσι μάρνασθαι, καὶ ὅθι χρὴ πεζὺν ἐόντα

[42] On the different accounts of the death of Gyrth, see Appendix KK.

spirit, a fate than which none could be more glorious; he had died in the noblest of causes and by the hand of the mightiest of enemies. Nor did he fall alone, close at his side, and almost at the same moment, Leofwine, fighting sword in hand, was smitten to the earth by an unnamed assailant, perhaps by the mace of the Prelate of Bayeux or by the lance of the Count of Mortain.[43] A dark cloud indeed seemed to have gathered over the destinies of the great West-Saxon house. Of the valiant band of sons who had surrounded Godwine on the great day of his return, Harold now stood alone. By a fate of special bitterness, he had seen with his own eyes the fall of those nearest and dearest to him. The deed of Metaurus had been, as it were, wrought beneath the eyes of Hannibal;[44] Achilleus had looked on and seen the doom of his Patroklos and his Antilochos. The fate of England now rested on the single heart and the single arm of her King.

But the fortune of the day was still far from being determined. The two Earls had fallen, but the fight at the barricades went on as fiercely as before. The men of the Earldoms of the two fallen chiefs relaxed not because of the loss of their captains. The warriors of Kent and Essex fought manfully to avenge their leader.[45] As for the Duke, we left him on foot, an enemy as dangerous on foot as when mounted on his destrier. But Norman and horse could not long be severed. William called to a knight of Maine to give up his charger to his sovereign. Was it cowardice, was it disloyalty to the usurper of the rights of the old Cenomannian house, which made the knight of Maine refuse to dismount at William's bidding?[46] But a blow from the Duke's hand brought the disobedient rider to the ground,[47] and William, again mounted, was soon again dealing wounds and death among the defenders of England.[48] But the deed and the fate of Gyrth were soon repeated. The spear of another Englishman brought William's second horse to the ground, and he too, like the East-Anglian Earl, paid

---

[43] The death of Leofwine as well as of Gyrth is placed at this point in the Tapestry, pl. 14. On the sword, see Appendix KK.

[44] Liv. xxvii. 49. 'Ibi, ut patre Hamilcare et Hannibale fratre dignum erat, pugnans cecidit.' Compare the reception of the news by Hannibal in c. 51.

[45] Roman de Rou, 13874:

Là ù la presse ert plus espesse,
Là cil de Kent è cil d'Essesse
A merveille se cumbateient,
E li Normanz ruser faiseient,
En sus les faiseient retraire,
Ne lor poeient grant mal faire.

[46] Wid. Amb. 489:

Ille timens cædem negat illi ferre salutem;
    Nam pavitat mortem, ceu lepus ante canem.

But the other motive is just as likely in one 'ex Cenomannorum progenitus genere.'

[47] Ib. 491:

Dux memor, ut miles subito se vertit ad illum,
    Per nasum galeæ concitus accipiens,
Vultum telluri, plantas ad sidera volvit;
    Sic sibi concessum scandere currit equum.

Mark the mention of the *nose-piece*, so conspicuous in the Tapestry.

[48] Wid. Amb. 501:

Postquam factus eques Dux est, mox acrius hostes
    Vulnerat, aggreditur, fulminat, insequitur.

the penalty of his exploit by death at the Duke's own hand.[49] Count Eustace had by this time better learned how to win the favour of his great ally. His horse was freely offered to the Duke; a knight of his own following did him the same good service, and Duke and Count pressed vigorously on against the English lines.[50] The struggle was hard; but the advantage still remained with the English. The second attack had indeed to some extent prevailed. Not only had the English suffered a personal loss than which one loss only could have been greater, but the barricade was now in some places broken down.[51] The French on the right had been specially active and success-ful in this work. And specially distinguished among them was a party under the command of a youthful Norman warrior, Robert the son of the old Roger of Beau-mont.[52] They had perhaps met with a less vigorous resistance, while the main hopes and fears of every Englishman must have gathered round the great personal struggle which was going on beneath the Standard. Still those who were most successful had as yet triumphed only over timber, and not over men. The shield-wall still stood behind the palisade, and every Frenchman who had pressed within the English enclosure had paid for his daring with his life.[53] The English lines were as unyielding as ever; and though the second attack had been less completely unsuccessful than the first, it was still plain that to scale the hill by any direct attack of the Norman horsemen was a hopeless undertaking.

But the generalship of William, his ready eye, his quick thought, his dauntless courage, never failed him. In the Norman character the fox and the lion were mingled in nearly equal proportions;[54] strength and daring had failed, but the object might perhaps still be gained by stratagem.[55] William had marked with pleasure that the late flight of his troops had beguiled a portion of the English to forsake their firm array and their strong position.[56] He had marked with equal pleasure that some

---

[49] Ib. 503–518. The Englishman is described as

> Filius Hellocis, vir celer et facilis.

I wish I knew how to identify him.

[50] Ib. 525:

> Talibus auspiciis Comes et Dux associati,
> Quo magis arma micant, bella simul repetunt.

[51] Will. Pict. 134. 'Patuerunt tamen in eos viæ incisæ per diversas partes fortissimorum militum ferro.'

[52] Ib. 'Tiro quidam Normannus Robertus, Rogerii de Bello-Monte filius ... prœlium illo die primum experiens, egit quod æternandum esset laude, cum legione quam in dextro cornu duxit irruens ac sternens magna cum audaciâ.' Wace (13462) seemingly confounds Robert with his father Roger, who was not there. See Prevost's note, ii. 229, and above, p. 227. Mark how the allies and mercenaries are put under Norman officers.

[53] Roman de Rou, 12941:

> Jà Normant se s'i embastist,
> Ke l'alme à hunte ne perdist,
> Fust par hache, fust par gisarme,
> U par machue u par altre arme.

[54] See E.A. Freeman, *The History of the Norman Conquest of England*, p. 108.

[55] Wid. Amb. 421:

> Nec penetrare valent spissum nemus Angligenarum,
> Ni tribuat vires viribus ingenium.

(The metaphor of the 'nemus' or 'silva' runs throughout Guy's description.) So William of Malmes-bury (ii. 228) speaks of Harold as being 'astutia Willelmi circumventus.'

[56] Will. Pict. 135. 'Meminerunt quam optatæ rei paullo ante fuga dederit occasionem.'

impression had at last been made on the English defences. If by any means any large portion of the English army could be drawn down from the heights, an entrance might be made at the points where the barricade was already weakened. He therefore ventured on a daring stratagem. If his army, or a portion of it, pretended flight, the English would be tempted to pursue; the pretended fugitives would turn upon their pursuers, and meanwhile another division might reach the summit through the gap thus left open. He gave his orders accordingly, and they were faithfully and skilfully obeyed. A portion of the army, seemingly the left wing[57] which had so lately fled in earnest, now again turned in apparent flight.[58] Undismayed by the fate of their comrades who had before broken their lines, the English on the right, mainly, as we have seen, the irregular levies, rushed down and pursued them with shouts of delight.[59] But the men of Britanny, Poitou, and Maine had now better learned their lesson. They turned on the pursuing English; the parts of the combatants were at once reversed, and the pursuers now themselves fled in earnest.[60] Yet, undisciplined and foolhardy as their conduct had been, they must have had some wary leaders among them, for they found the means to take a special revenge for the fraud which had been played off upon them. The importance of the small outlying hill now came into full play. Either its defenders had never left it, or a party of the fugitives contrived to rally and occupy it. At all events it was occupied and gallantly defended by a body of light-armed English.[61] With a shower of darts and stones they overwhelmed a body of French who attacked them; not a man of the party was left. Another party of English, evidently consisting of the levies of the neighbourhood, had the skill to use their knowledge of the country to the best advantage. They made their way to the difficult ground to the west of the hill, to the steep and thickly-wooded banks of the small ravine. Here the light-armed English turned and made a stand; the French horsemen, recklessly pursuing, came tumbling head over heels into the chasm, where

---

[57] The Brevis Relatio however (7) calls them 'cuneus Normannorum fere usque ad mille equites.' But he adds that they were 'ex alterâ parte' from the Duke's own post.

[58] Will. Pict. u.s. 'Animadvertentes Normanni, sociaque turba, non absque nimio sui incommodo hostem tantum simul resistentem superari posse, terga dederunt, fugam ex industria simulantes.'

[59] Guy of Amiens (425) marks clearly what troops they were who broke their order:

Rustica lætatur gens et superâsse putabat,
Post tergum nudis insequitur gladiis

William of Poitiers (135) is here very graphic: 'Barbaris cum spe victoriæ ingens lætitia exorta est. Sese cohortantes exsultante clamore nostros maledictis increpabant, et minabantur cunctos illico ruituros esse.'

[60] Will. Pict. 135. 'Normanni repente regirati equis interceptos et inclusos undique mactaverunt, nullum relinquentes.' Brevis Relatio, 8. 'Normanni, qui erant cautiores bello quam Angli, mox redierunt, atque inter illos et agmen a quo se disjunxerant, se immiserunt.' Wid. Amb. 433;

Quique fugam simulant instantibus ora retorquent,
Constrictos cogunt vertere dorsa neci.
Pars ibi magna perit, pars et densata resisit,
Millia namque decem sunt ibi passa necem.

[61] Will. Malms. iii. 242. 'Ita ingenio circumventi, pulcram mortem pro patriæ ultione meruere: nec tamen ultioni suæ defuere, quin crebro consistentes, de insequentibus insignes cladis acervos facerent; nam, occupato tumulo, Normannos, calore succensos acriter ad superior nitentes, in vallem dejiciunt, levique negotio in subjectos tela torquentes, lapides rotantes, omnes ad unum fundunt.' The scene is vividly shown in the Tapestry, pl. 15, and the defenders of the little hill are all light-armed.

they were slaughtered in such numbers that the ground is said to have been made level by their corpses.[62]

The men who had committed the great error of pursuing the apparent fugitives had thus, as far as they themselves were concerned, retrieved their error skilfully and manfully. But the error was none the less fatal to England. The Duke's great object was now gained; the main end of Harold's skilful tactics had been frustrated by the inconsiderate ardour of the least valuable portion of his troops. Through the rash descent of the light-armed on the right, the whole English army lost its vantage-ground. The pursuing English had left the most easily accessible portion of the hill open to the approach of the enemy.[63] While French and English were scattered over the lower ground, fighting in no certain order and with varied success, the main body of the Normans made their way on to the hill, no doubt by the gentle slope at the point west of the present buildings.[64] The great advantage of the ground was now lost; the Normans were at last on the hill. Instead of having to cut their way up the slope and through the palisades, they could now charge to the east, directly against the defenders of the Standard. Still the battle was far from being over. The site had still some advantages for the English. The hill, narrow and in some places with steep sides, was by no means suited for the evolutions of cavalry, and, though the English palisade was gone, the English shield-wall was still a formidable hindrance in the way of the assailants. In short the position which the keen eye of Harold had chosen stood him in good stead to the last. Our Norman informants still speak with admiration of the firm stand made by the English. It was still the hardest of tasks to surround their bristling lines. It was a strange warfare, where the one side dealt in assaults and movements, while the other, as if fixed in the ground, withstood them. The array of the English was so close that they moved only when they were dead, they stirred not at all while they were alive. The slightly wounded could not escape, but were crushed to death by the thick ranks of their comrades.[65] That is to say, the array of the shield-wall was still kept, though now without the help of the barricades or the full advantage of the ground. The day had now turned decidedly in favour of the invaders;

[62] Will. Malms. iii. 242. 'Item fossatum quoddam præruptum, compendiario et noto sibi transitu evadentes, tot ibi inimicorum conculcavere, ut cumulo cadaverum planitiem campi æquarent.' On this last proverbial saying, see above, pp. 235, 247, and Appendix CC. This scene is most vividly shown in the Tapestry, pl. 15: 'Hic ceciderunt simul Angli et Franci in prœlio.' It must not be confounded with the similar event later in the day on the other side of the hill. See Appendix KK.

[63] Wid. Amb. 427:

Amotis sanis labuntur dilacerati,
Silvaque spissa prius rarior efficitur.

[64] This was evidently the case, and this is, I suppose, what Guy of Amiens means in his somewhat difficult lines (429):

Conspicit ut campum cornu tenuare sinistrum,
Intrandi dextrum quod via larga patet.

'Dextrum' would thus mean the *English* right.

[65] Will. Pict. 135. 'Fit deinde insoliti generis pugna, quam altera pars incursibus et diversis motibus agit, altera, velut humo adfixa, tolerat ... Mortui plus dum cadunt, quam vivi moveri videntur. Leviter sauciator non permittit evadere, sed comprimendo necat, sociorum deusitas.' He had before said (134), 'Ob nimiam densitatem eorum labi vix potuerunt interempti.' So Guy, 417:

Spiritibus nequeunt frustrata cadavera sterni,
Nec cedunt vivis corpora militibus:
Omne cadaver enim, vitâ licet evacuatum,
Stat celut illæsum, possidet atque locum.

but the fight was still far from being over. It was by no means clear that some new chance of warfare might not again turn the balance in favour of England.[66]

All bear witness to the enduring valour displayed on both sides, and to the fearful execution which was wrought by the national English weapon. But at last the effects of this sort of warfare began to tell on the English ranks. There could have been no greater trial than thus to bear up, hour after hour, in a struggle which was purely defensive. The strain, and the consequent weariness, must have been incomparably greater on their side than on that of their assailants. It may well have been in sheer relief from physical exhaustion that we read, now that there was no artificial defence between them and their enemies, of Englishmen rushing forward from their ranks, bounding like a stag, and thus finding opportunity for the personal encounters which I have been describing.[67] Gradually, after so many brave warriors had fallen, resistance grew fainter;[68] but still even now the fate of the battle seemed doubtful. Many of the best and bravest of England had died, but not a man had fled; the Standard still waved as proudly as ever; the King still fought beneath it.[69] While Harold lived, while the horse and his rider still fell beneath his axe, the heart of England failed not, the hope of England had not wholly passed away. Around the two-fold ensigns the war was still fiercely raging, and to that point every eye and every arm in the Norman host was directed. The battle had raged ever since nine in the morning, and evening was now drawing in.[70] New efforts, new devices, were needed to overcome the resistance of the English, diminished as were their numbers, and wearied as they were with the livelong toil of that awful day. The Duke ordered his archers to shoot

[66] Will. Pict. u.s. 'Reliquos majori cum alacritate aggressi sunt, aciem adhuc horrendam et quam difficillimum erat circumvenire.'

[67] Roman de Rou, 13395:

En la bataille el primer front,
La ù Normanz plus espez sont,
En vint saillant plus tost ke cers.

This encounter (described by Wace, 13387–13423) is worth notice on several grounds. I have quoted some lines in the last page. The Englishman is at last killed by Roger of Montgomery, who exclaims, 'Ferez, Franceiz.' M. Pluquet (ii. 227) here comments on the Norman Roger calling his men 'French'. The name of 'Franci' (see above, p. 280) would take in all William's followers, but Roger of Montgomery was (see above, p. 307) in the immediate command of the distinctly French contingent.

[68] Will. Pict. 135. 'Languent Angli, et quasi reatum ipso defectu confitentes vindictam patiuntur'. So Guy, 527:

Amborum gladiis campus rarescit ab Anglis,
    Defluit et numerus, nutat et atteritur
Corruit appositâ ceu silva minuta securi,
    Sic nemus Angligenûm ducitur ad nihilum.

[69] Wid. Amb. 533:

. . . Dux prospexit Regem super ardua montis
Acriter instantes dilacerare suos.

Will. Malms. iii. 242. 'Valuit hæc vicissitudo, modo illis modo istis vincentibus, quantum Haroldi vita moram fecit.'

[70] Flor. Wig. 1066. 'Ab horâ diei tertiâ usque noctis crepusculum suis adversariis restitit fortissime, et seipsum pugnando tam fortiter defendit et tam strenue ut vix ab hostili interimi posset agmine.' Od. ix. 56:

ὄφρα μὲν ἠὼσ ἦν καὶ ἀέξετο ἱερὸν ἦμαρ,
τόφρα δ' ἀλεξάμενοι μένομεν πλέονάσ περ ἐύντασ
ἦμοσ δ' ἠέλιοσ μετενίσσετο βουλυτόνδε,
καὶ τότε δὴ Κίκονεσ κλῖναν δαμάσαντεσ Ἀχαιούσ

up in the air, that their arrows might, as it were, fall straight from heaven.[71] The effect was immediate and fearful. No other device of the wily Duke that day did such frightful execution. Helmets were pierced; eyes were put out; men strove to guard their heads with their shields,[72] and, in so doing, they were of course less able to wield their axes. And now the supreme moment drew near. There was one point of the hill at which the Norman bowmen were bidden specially to aim with their truest skill. As twilight was coming on, a mighty shower of arrows[73] was launched on its deadly errand against the defenders of the Standard. There Harold still fought;[74] his shield bristled with Norman shafts; but he was still unwounded and unwearied. At last another arrow, more charged with destiny than its fellows, went still more truly to its mark. Falling like a bolt from heaven, it pierced the King's right eye; he clutched convulsively at the weapon, he broke off the shaft, his axe dropped from his hand, and he sank in agony at the foot of the Standard.[75] The King was thus disabled, and

---

71 See the full account in the Roman de Rou, 13275–13296. So Henry of Huntingdon (M.H.B. 763): 'Docuit igitur Dux Willielmus viros sagittarios ut non in hostem directe sed in aëra sursum sagittas emitterent, cuncum hostilem sagittis cæcarent, quod Anglis magno fuit detrimento.' Henry is copied by Ralph of Diss, X Scriptt. 480, and Bromton, 960.

72 Roman de Rou, 13287:

> Quant li saetes reveneient,
> De sor les testes lor chaeient,
> Chiés è viaires lor perçoent,
> Et à plusors les oilz crevoent;
> Ne n'osoent les oilz ovrir,
> Ne lor viaires descovrir.

73 Ib. 13293:

> Saetes plus espessement
> Voloent ke pluie par vent.

So Henry of Huntingdon (u.s.) who is again followed by Ralph and Bromton: 'Interea totus imber sagittariorum cecidit circa Regem Haraldum, et ipse in oculo percussus corruit.'

74 Wid. Amb. 543:

> Per nimias cædes nam bellica jura tenentes
>   Heraldus cogit pergere carnis iter.

75 Roman de Rou, 13297:

> Issi avint k'une saete
> Ki de verz li ciel ert chaete,
> Féri Heraut de sus l'oil dreit,
> Ki l'un des oilz li a toleit;
> E Heraut l'a par aïr traite,
> Getée a les mains, si l'a fraite.
> Por li chief ki l'a dolu
> S'est apuié sor son escu.

This scene, the turning-point of all English history, is vividly shown in the Tapestry, pl. 16. Wace places it too early in the battle. William of Poitiers and the English writers do not mention the manner of the King's death. All that Florence can utter is 'heu, ipsemet cecidit crepusculi tempore.' William of Malmesbury (iii. 242) says, 'Jactu sagittæ violato cerebro procubuit,' and in the next chapter, after describing Harold's exploits (see above, p. 474), how every Norman who came near him was cut down, adds the remarkable expression, '*quapropter*, ut dixi, eminus letali arundine ictus mortem implevit.' Compare – if any comparison be not sacrilege – the death of Richard, son of Richard King of the Romans, at the siege of Berwick in 1296 (Walt. Hem. ii. 98): 'Ibi corruit frater Comitis Cornubiæ, miles strenuissimus [Harold's own epithet], qui quum ad hostes caput in altum erigeret, in ipsum oculari aperturâ galeæ percussus telo, confestim cecidit et expiravit.' Between 1066 and 1296 the nose-piece had been exchanged for the vizor.

the fate of the day was no longer doubtful. Twenty knights now bound themselves to lower or to bear off the ensigns which still rose as proudly as ever while Harold lay dying beneath them. But his comrades still fought; most of the twenty paid for their venture with their lives, but the survivors succeeded in their attempt. Harold's own Standard of the Fighting Man was beaten to the earth; the golden Dragon, the ensign of Cuthred and Ælfred, was carried off in triumph.[76] But Harold, though disabled, still breathed; four knights rushed upon him and despatched him with various wounds.[77] The Latin poet of the battle describes this inglorious exploit with great glee. One of the four was Eustace; in such a cowardly deed of butchery he might deem that he was repeating his old exploit at Dover. Nor are we amazed to find the son of Guy of Ponthieu foremost in doing despite to the man who had once been his father's prisoner. But one blushes to see men bearing the lofty names of Giffard and Montfort, names soon to be as familiar to English as to Norman ears, taking a share in such low-minded vengeance on a fallen foe.[78] The deeds of the four are enumerated, but we know not how to apportion them among the actors. One thrust pierced through the shield of the dying King and stabbed him in the breast; another assailant finished the work by striking off his head with his sword. But even this vengeance was not enough. A third pierced the dead body and scattered about the entrails;[79] the fourth, coming, it would seem, too late for any more efficient share in the deed, cut off the King's leg as he lay dead.[80] Such was the measure which the boasted chivalry of Normandy meted out to a prince who had never dealt harshly or cruelly by either a domestic or a foreign foe. But we must add, in justice to the Conqueror, that he pronounced the last and most brutal insult to be a base and cowardly act, and he expelled the perpetrator from his army.[81]

---

[76] Hen. Hunt. M.H.B. 763C. 'Viginti autem equites strenuissimi fidem suam dederunt invicem quod Anglorum catervam perrumpentes signum regium quod vocatur Standard arriperent. Quod dum facerent, plures eorum occisi sunt; pars autem eorum, viâ gladiis factâ, Standard asportavit.' But it would seem from Wace that it was rather the Dragon which was carried off (13956):

> L'estendart unt à terre mis,
> Et li Reis Heraut unt occis
> E li meillor de ses amis;
> Li gonfanon à or unt pris.

So directly after (13965): 'E l'estendart out abatu'. And so again, 14013.

[77] Hen. Hunt. M.H.B. 763C. 'Irrumpens autem multitudo equitum Regem vulneratum interfecit.'

[78] Guy of Amiens (537) gives their names. Eustace has been already mentioned:

> Alter ut Hectorides, Pontivi nobilis hæres;
>   Hos comitatur Hugo promptus in officio;
> Quartus Gilfardus patris a cognomine dictus;
>   Regis ad exitium quattuor arma ferunt.

[79] Compare the four murderers of Saint Thomas, who however needed a fifth, and that a clerical hand, to imitate this particular act of brutality. Will. Fil. Steph. 303. 'Quidam Hugo de Horsea, cognomento Malus Clericus, sancti martyris procumbentis collum pede comprimens, a concavitate coronæ amputatæ, cum mucrone cruorem et cerebrum extrahebat.' Cf. Edw. Grim. 77; Reg. Pont. 168.

Guy leaves out all mention of the wound from the arrow.

[80] Wid. Amb. 549:

> Abscidit coxam quartus procul egit ademptam;
>   Taliter occisum terra cadaver habet.

This action is very clearly shown in the Tapestry, pl. 16. So Wace, 13942.

[81] Will. Malms. iii. 243. 'Jacentis femur unus militum gladio proscidit; unde a Willelmo ignominiæ notatus, quod rem ignavam et pudendam fecisset, militiâ pulsus est.' But I certainly cannot identify

The blow had gone truly to its mark; but still all was not over. Harold had fallen, as his valiant brothers had fallen before him. The event too truly showed that England had fallen with the sons of Godwine; that, as ever in this age, everything turned on the life of one man, and that the one man who could have guarded and saved England was taken from her.

Such being the case, it is from the memorable day of Saint Calixtus that we may fairly date the overthrow, what we know to have been only the imperfect and temporary overthrow, of our ancient and free Teutonic England. In the eyes of men of the next generation that day was the fatal day of England, the day of the sad overthrow of our dear country, the day of her handing over to foreign lords.[82] From that day forward the Normans began to work the will of God upon the folk of England, till there were left in England no chiefs of the land of English blood, till all were brought down to bondage and to sorrow, till it was a shame to be called an Englishman,[83] and the men of England were no more a people.[84]

the one among the four mentioned by Guy who was punsihed in this way by William.
	The death of Harold reminds one of the death of Patroklos (Il. xvi. 818):

"Εκτωρ δ', ὡσ εἶδεν Πατροκλῆα μεγάθυμον
ἄψ ἀναχαζύμενον, βεβλημένον ὀζέϊ χαλκῷ,
ἀγχίμολόν ῥά οἱ ἦλθε κατὰ στίχασ, οὖτα δὲ δουρὶ
νείατον ἐσ κενεῶνα διὰ πρὸ δὲ χαλκὸν ἔλασσε

82 Will. Malms. iii. 245. 'Illa fuit dies fatalis Angliæ, funestum excidium dulcus patriæ, pro novorum dominorum commutatione.'
83 Hen. Hunt. lib. vi.; Scriptt. p. Bed. 212. 'Quum jam Domini justam voluntatem super Anglorum gentem Normanni complessent, nec jam vix aliquis princeps de progenie Anglorum esset in Angliâ, sed omnes ad servitutem et ad mœrorem redacti essent; ita etiam ut Anglicum vocari esset opprobrio.'
84 Ib. lib. vii.; Scriptt. p. Bed. 213. 'Declaratum constat quomodo Dominus salutem et honorem genti Anglorum pro meritis abstulerit et jam populum non esse jusserit.'

14. J.F.C. Fuller, 'The Battle of Hastings, 1066'

By the mid-twentieth century, the historiography of Hastings had almost
settled into a scholarly consensus in which the views of J.H. Round had
definitely eclipsed those of Freeman. The Normans were considered the
superior army, William the superior general. Major General J.F.C. Fuller's
detailed reconstruction of the battle represents a cautious synthesis of this state
of affairs. Fuller brought his own military experience to bear in his history,
though it is the military perspective which focuses on the 'art of war' – on
strategic and tactical eternal truths rather than on logistical realities – and on
decisive battles: the selection here is from Fuller's *Military History of the
Western World*, which alternates chapters of sweeping narrative with close
examinations of the 'decisive battles' which marked the path of western
history. His focus on topography and his appeals to military necessity attempt
to take the account beyond the bare bones of the sources to the more detailed
reality behind them.

Reprinted, by permission, from J.F.C. Fuller, *A Military History of the Western World* (Minerva
Press, 1954), I.374–82.

On October 11, Harold set out from London to cover the sixty miles to Hastings, and on the night of October 13–14 he arrived at the site of the present town of Battle, and encamped his men on or near a rise in the downs marked by a 'hoary apple-tree'.[1] William of Poitiers says, 'they [the English] took up their position on . . . a hill abutting the forest [of Anderid] through which they had come. There, at once dismounting from their horses . . .'[2] And William of Jumièges writes: 'after riding all night, he [Harold] appeared on the field of battle early in the morning.'[3] If surprise was Harold's aim, then, in all probability he encamped in the forest, and only occupied the 'hoary apple-tree' position early on the following day.

According to Malmesbury and Wace, Harold's men passed the night of October 13–14 in drinking and singing and the Normans in confessing their sins and receiving the sacrament.[4] Though, no doubt, after a forced march the English were thirsty, and before an impending battle many Normans offered up fervent prayers, common sense dictates that Harold's men – certainly his foot – slept like logs, and that, as William had learnt through his scouts of his enemy's approach,[5] his men spent most of the night in preparing for battle.

What was Harold's plan? Was it to surprise William, as has already been mentioned, or was it to assume a passive defensive – that is, to block the London Road and await attack? That Harold did fight a purely defensive battle is true, but he may have been compelled to do so because he had not reached the Battle position as early as he had hoped. To have pushed on the remaining seven miles to Hastings after dark, and then to have attempted a night attack, unpreceded by a daylight reconnaissance, would have been madness. In the circumstances, the only chance to surprise William was to attack him at dawn, which would have demanded an advance soon after midnight. Even if considered, the weariness of Harold's men must have prohibited this. That surprise based on speed was in his mind is supported by his previous generalship. In his Welsh campaign of 1063[6] and in his Stamfordbridge campaign he had moved like lightning in order to surprise; therefore, probably Mr Round is right in surmising that this was also his intention in the present campaign.[7] Simply to hold the 'hoary apple-tree' position was not sufficient to rid England of her invaders, because it did not prevent William from re-embarking his army under the cover of his archers and moving it to some other spot along the coast. Therefore, its occupation did not pin William down, nor did it compel him to attack Harold. Yet, as we shall see, William did attack, and he moved so rapidly against his enemy that it was Harold and not he who was surprised. This is supported by the Chronicle, which states that 'William came against him by surprise before his army was drawn up in battle

1   The Anglo-Saxon Chronicle (D) 1066, in English Historical Documents, vol. 2, 1042–1189, ed. D.C. Douglas and G.W. Greeaway (London, 1953) [hereinafter EHD], p. 144.
2   William of Poitiers, The Deeds of William, duke of the Normans and king of the English, in EHD, p. 225.
3   William of Jumièges, The Deeds of the duke of Normandy, in EHD, p. 216.
4   William of Malmesbury, Chronicle of the Kings of England, trans. J.A. Giles (London, 1904), p. 274; Wace, Roman de Rou, ed. Pluquet (Paris, 1827), p. 184.
5   William of Poitiers in EHD, p. 224.
6   Florence of Worcester, Chronicle, trans. T. Forester (London, 1854), p. 164.
7   J.H. Round, 'La bataille de Hastings', Revue Historique 65 (Sept. 1897), pp. 61–77.

array'.[8] In other words, Harold and his men would appear to have overslept themselves.

Harold's position must next be considered.

The high ground (Wealden Hills) north of Battle is connected with a rise or ridge – now in part occupied by the abbey buildings – by a neck or isthmus along which the present High Street of Battle runs. The highest point on this ridge is the site of the Abbey House, and from it the ground falls gently east and west. On its southern side the slope drops about a hundred feet in 400 yards to the head of the Asten brook, now dammed to form a series of fishponds. From the Asten it rolls southward, gradually rising to Telham Hill one and a half miles south-east of the abbey. To the north of the ridge the flanks of the isthmus are sufficiently steep to form serious military obstacles, and, in 1066, the drainage from the high ground had cut them into ravines, which were covered with brushwood. Further, on the northern side of the ridge, and in each case 300 yards from the Abbey House – on the western along a little brook, and on the eastern at the junction of the Hastings and Sedlescombe roads – the ridge drops so sharply that its slope forms an effective obstacle to cavalry.

In all probability, it was on the summit of the ridge that Harold first planted his two standards, the Dragon of Wessex and his personal banner, the Fighting Man, which at the close of the battle fell at a spot seventy yards to the east of the Abbey House, and marked later by the high altar of the Abbey Church. Rightly, Harold drew up his housecarles on their flanks, because – assuming he occupied the crest of the ridge – his centre was more open to cavalry assault than his wings, which must have been composed mainly of fyrd-men. Although we have few details of Harold's formation, the normal Saxon one was that of the shield-wall – a phalanx: 'shield to shield and shoulder to shoulder' as Asser describes it at Ashdown in 871. It was an admirable formation against infantry armed with sword, spear and axe, and an essential one for infantry against cavalry relying on shock.

Tactically, Harold's problem was both to maintain an unbroken front and to prevent the flanks of his shield-wall from being overlapped; therefore, as Mr Baring suggests, it is highly probable that he occupied the 600 yards between the little brook west of the Abbey House and the junction of the Hastings and Sedlescombe roads in order that his flanks might rest on the two steep depressions.[9] If Harold drew up his army in a phalanx of ten ranks deep, allowing two feet frontage for each man in the first rank – the shield-wall – and three feet frontage for those in the nine rear ranks, then, on a 600 yards front, his total strength would be 6,300 men, and, if in twelve ranks – 7,500. These figures tally closely with those suggested by Spatz – 6,000 to 7,000.[10]

Because we are told that the battle of Hastings opened at nine o'clock on the morning of October 14, William must have set out at an early hour. He had nearly six miles to cover before reaching Telham Hill, somewhere north of which he deployed. Therefore, after reckoning the time taken for assembly, march and deployment, he must have started at between 4.30 a.m. and 5 a.m. His order of battle was in three divisions, left, centre, and right. The left consisted mainly of Bretons, under Count

---

8 *Anglo-Saxon Chronicle* (D) 1066 in *EHD*, p. 144.
9 See F.H. Baring, *Domesday Tables for the Counties of Surrey, Berkshire, Middlesex, Hertford, Buckingham and Bedford and for the New Forest* (London, 1909), appendix B, pp. 217–232. There is an excellent plan of the battle in this book showing contours at ten-foot intervals.
10 W. Spatz, *Die Schlacht von Hastings* (Berlin, 1896), p. 33.

Alan of Brittany; the right of William's French and other mercenaries, under Eustace of Boulogne; and the centre of Normans, under his personal command: before him was carried the papal banner. Each division was divided into three *échelons* or lines: the first, archers and crossbow men in front; the next, the more heavily armed infantry; and lastly the mounted knights.[11] Therefore, tactically, the order of battle closely resembled that of the early Roman legion, the *triarii* now being mounted.

At nine o'clock, to the blast of trumpets, the battle opened when the Normans slowly advanced up the rise toward the wall of English shields crowning its crest. The lay of the ground suggests that, when William's central division, which must have advanced on the western side of the Hastings Road, moved directly on Harold's standards, the right and left divisions moved outwardly in order to prolong his front. Further, that the left wing, before mounting the slope on the English right, must have crossed the Asten brook, which runs into a stream coming from the ravines on the western side of the isthmus.

As William's centre closed on Harold's, the Norman archers began to discharge their arrows, but as they had to shoot uphill, most of them must either have struck their enemies' shields or passed over their heads. Following William of Poitiers' description of the battle,[12] the English resisted valiantly and met the assault with showers of 'spears and javelins and weapons of all kinds together with axes and stones fastened to pieces of wood'. Then 'the shouts both of the Normans and of the barbarians were drowned in the clash of arms and by the cries of the dying, and for a long time the battle raged with the utmost fury'.

Harold's men had the advantage of ground, and, as William of Poitiers points out, 'profited by remaining within their position in close order', and maintained an impregnable front. Further, he informs us that the attackers suffered severely because of 'the easy passage' of the defenders' weapons through their shields and armour, which does not speak much for them. The English, he continues, 'bravely withstood and successfully repulsed those who were engaging them at close quarters, and inflicted loss upon the men who were shooting missiles at them from a distance' – namely, the Norman archers. Should this be correct, it points to a failure on the part of the Norman archers and infantry to make any real impression on the shield-wall.

The next recorded event supports this contention, for without further introduction William of Poitiers tells us that 'the foot-soldiers and the Breton knights, panic-stricken by the violence of the assault, broke in flight before the English', and that soon the whole army of the duke was in danger of retreat'. This suggests that when it mounted the slope the Norman left wing got into difficulties, and that the English right, or part of it, suddenly counter-attacked, and swept the Breton archers and infantry down the slope so that they carried away with them in their flight the knights in rear. Next, William's central division found its left flank uncovered and began to fall back, as did his right division.

Now was Harold's chance, and he failed to seize it. He has often been blamed for not having rigidly maintained his shield-wall throughout the battle. Though to have done so might have saved him from defeat, it could not have gained a victory. Had he now seized his chance, he would have ordered a general advance, and pouring down the slope on both sides of the Hastings road would, almost certainly, have annihilated the Norman archers and infantry. True, the Norman cavalry would have

---

11   William of Poitiers in *EHD*, p. 225.
12   William of Poitiers in *EHD*, pp. 226–229.

got away, but bereft of their infantry, in all probability they would not have drawn rein until they had found security behind their stockade at Hastings. The victory would have been Harold's, and it might well have been decisive enough to have compelled William to re-embark and abandon the campaign.

As it happened, as soon as the panic on the Norman left wing began to affect the morale of the centre, a fortuitous event occurred which would have gone far to crown a general counter-attack on Harold's part with success.

During the initial attack William was in the rear and, it seems, when the front of his central division broke back, in the resulting confusion he was unhorsed, and a cry went up that he had fallen. For him, this must have been the most critical moment in the battle; for in classical and medieval warfare the loss of the general-in-chief, which carried with it the loss of the entire command, as often as not led to immediate defeat. It was as if in a modern battle the whole of an army's general staff were suddenly eliminated. In the present case, the danger though critical was momentary, for William mounted another horse, pushed back his helmet so that he might be recognized by all, and stayed the panic in the centre by shouting out: 'Look at me well. I am still alive and by the grace of God I shall yet prove victor.' Meanwhile, on the left, presumably around the Asten brook, the English counter-attackers had got into difficulty, and when the Norman centre turned about a general rally followed, and some of the pursuers were cut off and slaughtered. William of Poitiers mentions 'several thousands', but immediately qualifies this estimate by informing us that, even after this loss, the English 'scarcely seemed diminished in number'.

As soon as the Normans had re-formed their ranks, the attack was renewed, but this time under William's personal leadership, which means that the knights were brought forward and the infantry withdrawn from the immediate front. From now on for several hours the struggle raged along the whole line, individual bodies of knights riding forward at the charge to hurl or thrust their spears at the shield-wall. Nevertheless, all attempts to force a gap proved ineffectual.

Unable to break the shield-wall, William now made use of a *ruse de guerre* common in Byzantine and Oriental warfare. He determined to lure his enemy down from the hoary apple-tree hill by means of a feint retreat.

The most suitable part of the field for this somewhat risky operation, for we may assume that the Normans were not exercised in it, was probably on the right, for there a withdrawal would bring William's men down to the valley and next up to high ground where they could face about as their pursuers moved uphill. Also a withdrawal in this direction would enable his centre to take the pursuers in flank. Clearly this was a purely cavalry operation; therefore we may assume that, while the fighting was in progress, the Norman infantry was withdrawn out of harm's way.

All this is, of course, conjecture, for all William of Poitiers tells us is the following:

> Realizing that they could not without severe loss overcome an army massed so strongly in close formation, the Normans and their allies feigned flight and simulated a retreat, for they recalled that only a short while ago their flight had given them an advantage. The barbarians thinking victory within their grasp shouted with triumph, and heaping insults upon our men, threatened utterly to destroy them. Several thousand of them, as before, gave rapid pursuit to those whom they thought to be in flight; but the Normans suddenly wheeling their horses surrounded them and cut down their pursuers so that not one was left alive. Twice was this ruse employed with the utmost success.

Harold has been blamed for falling into the trap, but probably the discipline of his troops was such that they acted on their own initiative, and wrongly, because the tactical situation was very different from the one which led to the initial counter-attack.[13] Then they were faced by foot, but now by horse, therefore they could not possibly hope to outpace them.

Though, after the second feigned flight and slaughter of the pursuers, William of Poitiers tells us that Harold's army 'was still formidable and very difficult to overwhelm', it is certain that its left wing must have been seriously weakened, and it may have been now, in order to strengthen it morally, that Harold moved his standards from the summit of the hill nearer to his left. Also it may have been at this time that to prepare the way for what was to be the final assault, William instructed his archers to use high-angle fire[14] – that is, to shoot their arrows into the air so that they would pass over the heads of his knights and, falling vertically on the enemy, induce the men of the shield-wall to raise their shields.

Night was closing in when the final phase of the battle opened, and by then we may assume that the English missiles had been spent and that Harold's men were exhausted. What happened is largely conjectural, but the most probable sequence of events would appear to be as follows: When twilight was setting in, Harold was hit in the eye by an arrow,[15] and a moment after was cut down.[16] As his brothers Gyrth and Leofwine had already fallen there was no one to replace him. Next, the weakened English left gave way before Eustace of Boulogne. The whole shield-wall then began to disintegrate, and Harold's men, some on horseback and some on foot, fled the field to the west and north-west to escape from Eustace, who would appear to have led the pursuit. Nevertheless, in spite of the panic, a number of Harold's men – probably housecarles – remained unaffected, fell back on the isthmus, and showed so bold a front that Eustace signalled his men to fall back. A moment later, William came up, counter-ordered the signal and urged his men forward. They scattered the housecarles, and a group, in the twilight, following the fugitives through the undergrowth, fell headlong into a ravine on the west of the isthmus, at a spot to become known as the Malfosse – probably the present Manser's Shaw.[17]

It must have been nearly dark when William returned to the main battlefield, to find Harold's body stripped and so hacked that it was barely recognizable. He had it brought to his camp, and later it was buried by the seashore.

Of William, William of Poitiers writes: 'He dominated this battle, checking his own men in flight, strengthening their spirit, and sharing their dangers. He bade them come with him, more often than he ordered them to go in front of him. Thus it may be understood how he led them by his valour and gave them courage . . . Thrice his horse fell under him.' Unfortunately, no friendly pen has depicted the part played by his valiant antagonist.

Two days after the battle William returned to Hastings, and five days later he

13 With reference to these advances, it should not be overlooked that in all early warfare in which javelins and arrows were the missiles, the normal way of replenishing their stock was to drive the enemy back and gather them from the ground he abandoned.
14 This incident is mentioned by Henry of Huntingdon, see *The Chronicle of Henry of Huntingdon*, trans. Thomas Forester (1853), p. 212.
15 Florence of Worcester (p. 170) says that Harold fell at twilight.
16 For both see the Bayeux Tapestry.
17 See *Domesday Tables, etc.*, p. 229. Mr Baring writes: 'The original name being Malfosset, corruption was easy to Manfussé (?Manfsey), Mansey and finally Manser's.'

occupied Dover. When he had strengthened its castle, he set out for Canterbury. Thence, following Mr Baring's account,[18] he advanced by way of Lenham, Seal, and Westerham to Godstone, where he gained the London-Hastings road. From Godstone he sent a party of horsemen north, who burnt Southwark, while the main body marched on westward through Guildford and Micheldever to Basing. From Alresford he appears to have been reinforced from either Chichester or Portsmouth, where his fleet had moved at some time after the battle. Next, he swept northward by way of Lambourn to Wallingford, where his army crossed the Thames, circled round the Chilterns and came southward to Little Berkhampstead. There William was met by the magnates of London, who tended to him the submission of the city and offered to him the crown.

From the ravagings deduced from Domesday Book, Baring's conclusion is that William's army cannot have been more than from 8,000 to 10,000 strong. 'Nor', he writes, 'can he have had much time for mere devastation; he could hardly have covered some 350 miles between Canterbury and Little Berkhampstead within seven weeks, if he had allowed his troops to be scattered for wide-spread ravage ... Outside the line of march the immediate effect of the conquest on the value of land in the south-east seems to have been very slight.'[19]

[18] Who traces the march by the ravages deduced from Domesday Book. See *ibid.*, appendix A, pp. 208–16.

[19] *Ibid.*, pp. 14 and 16. *Anglo-Saxon Chronicle* (D) 1066, *EHD*, p. 145, says: '. . . and ravaged all the region that he overran until he reached Berkhamsted.'

15. Richard Glover, 'English Warfare in 1066'

At about the same time that Fuller was synthesizing the scholarly consensus of the day, Richard Glover upset it and reopened a number of the debates about Hastings with this article. In it he challenges the received wisdom about the inherent superiority of the Normans and their military technology that had developed since the time of Round and Freeman. Two particular aspects of his project, his attempted rehabilitation of Snorre Sturlason as a source for the battle of Stamford Bridge and the Anglo-Saxon use of cavalry tactics based thereon, have been almost universally rejected by later historians, but this has tended to obscure his general points. He argues for a basic similarity in the level of military technology and training on both sides of the battle in 1066, and argues further that the level of training and discipline was quite low. This leads him to question the sophistication of the tactics on both sides, including a sceptical look at the Norman feigned flights. Glover's conclusions are controversial, but should be taken each on its own merits – the similarity of the forces is a separate question from their level of training, for instance. And certainly Glover's readings of the sources, especially the Tapestry, must be taken account of.

Reprinted from *English Historical Review* 67 (1952), 1–18, by permission of Longman Group Limited.

ENGLISH WARFARE IN 1066

Richard Glover

Half a century ago F.W. Maitland cautiously remarked that in all Saxon history there was 'no matter . . . darker than the constitution of the English army on the eve of its defeat'.[1] His caution has not won universal imitation. Where Maitland was hesitant, other historians have stepped boldly in and the result is, up to a point, a remarkably clear picture of the English army in 1066. It was an unwieldy host of men who had all but forgotten how to use the bow and never learnt to fight on horses; their military science rose to no higher concept than 'the stationary tactics of a phalanx of axe-men';[2] if they had a military virtue it was a readiness to stand and die where their leader stood, something that we might admire as courage but for the haunting suspicion that it was just another manifestation of national stupidity. Evidently this army of 'a decadent nation . . . on the outer fringe of European politics'[3] was such a living fossil as had only to meet an up-to-date eleventh century army to be instantly overthrown: H.W.C. Davis does not hesitate to say as much – 'on any field and in an engagement on any scale nothing short of the most desperate odds could have prevented the superiority of Norman tactics and equipment from producing their natural effect'[4] he wrote in 1905; and Sir Frank Stenton, writing in 1943, does not disagree with him.[5] So the result of the battle of Hastings appears as the inevitable defeat of men who knew only how to fight at close quarters and on foot by a mixed force in which two arms beyond the ken of Englishmen, cavalry and archery, played decisive roles. Such is the picture that has won and long held general acceptance. Yet it is hard to avoid wondering whether the English army of 1066 could possibly have been as bad as it is painted. Longer consideration increases these doubts till there appear to be a number of reasons for dissenting from the accepted opinion of the army that was beaten at Hastings.

In the first place it is clear that the inevitability of Norman victory, which was so obvious to Mr Davis, was far less apparent to Duke William. The Conqueror of England was not a timid soul, and it is therefore curious that so little heed is paid to the extreme caution with which he hugged the coast of Sussex till his battle was won. When he landed at Pevensey, southern England was undefended, the road to London lay wide open and the armed forces of the country were concentrated 250 miles away at York; but even so nothing lured William from his ships while Harold's army was

---

[1] F.W.Maitland, *Domesday Book and Beyond* (Cambridge, 1897), p. 156.
[2] Sir Charles Oman, *Art of War in the Middle Ages* (London, 1924), i. 165.
[3] H.W.C. Davis, *England under the Normans and Angevins* (London, 1905), p. 1.
[4] *Ibid.*, p. 4.
[5] F.M. Stenton, *Anglo-Saxon England* (Oxford, 1943), p. 576, 'In Action, Harold's army could only function as infantry, confined by its nature to a type of warfare which was already obsolete in the greater part of Western Europe'.

in being. This striking caution merits attention. To ignore it is to reject a factor with a direct bearing on the quality of the English army in 1066. To ascribe it to mere ignorance of the weakness of the opposition is to imply that William knew less about the fighting value of an eleventh-century English army than does the modern historian, and that would seem a risky assumption. William, already a tried and experienced commander, had been in England before; he was personally acquainted with his opponent; there are ample indications that he had had his eye on the crown for some time, and occasion to expect that he must fight for it. He had therefore long had every reason to make himself informed about his enemy and cannot have lacked opportunities of doing so. Even at the moment of landing his conduct must have been based on a better knowledge of the English army than is now available, and of course information continued to come in after he had landed. Everyone has read of how Robert Fitz-Wimarch sent word to William warning him that he had no hope of success against Harold's forces and if he did not abandon his expedition he must at least fight behind fortifications.[6] Fitz-Wimarch's message has gained him little credit at the hands of modern critics, but it is to be observed that he at least had every occasion to know what he was talking about. Being 'dives quidam . . . natione Normannus' (in William of Poitiers' phrase[7]) he should have known his continent[8] and as ex-Staller to King Edward he must certainly have known his England. It is hard to see how anyone could have been in a better position to assess the chances of the rivals. Moreover his message, however gloomy, coincided far more closely than is generally conceded with William's own appreciation of the situation, as William's conduct indicates. For all the haughty reply he is supposed to have made, William had begun acting on the lines advised by Fitz-Wimarch before receiving his message and continued to do so after receiving it. His very first act on landing had been to provide himself with the fortifications Fitz-Wimarch was to recommend by repairing the Roman works at Pevensey; but almost immediately he moved to Hastings, in order, says the Bayeux Tapestry, to seize rations.[9] But Hastings provided more than rations; it was one of the Cinque Ports, and as such offered better facilities for a re-embarkation than the anchorage at Pevensey. Once there, William swiftly conscripted all the local labour he could lay hands on to build more fortifications, another purely defensive work,[10] of the slenderest value for mastering a whole hostile kingdom, but invaluable for covering an enforced re-embarkation. It would appear therefore that, however much he wanted the English crown, the importance of securing a safe re-embarkation was a consideration that remained very active in William's mind till he at last moved out to fight *after* his scouts had seen and reported the actual condition of the inadequate force with which his rival hurried prematurely into

---

[6] 'Adversus quem non amplius tuos quam totidem despectabiles canes aestimo valere. . . . Suadeo, inter munitiones mane, manu ad praesens confligere noli' is how William of Poitiers reports Fitz-Wimarch's advice – *Gesta Willelmi Ducis Normannorum in Scriptores Rerum Gestarum Willelmi Conquestoris*, ed. J.A. Giles (London, 1845), p. 128.

[7] *Ibid.*

[8] And so should he also if he were a Breton, as J.H. Round argued, *Feudal England* (London, 1909), p. 331.

[9] E. Maclagan, *The Bayeux Tapestry* (King Penguin Books, London and New York, 1945), pls 47, 48.

[10] William of Poitiers, *op. cit.* p. 127, describes the Conqueror's fortifications at Pevensey and Hastings as works 'quae sibi receptaculo, navibus propugnaculo forent' – language instinct with the defensive spirit.

Sussex; then he immediately becomes eager for prompt battle to seize his moment of opportunity before Harold's weakness is made good;[11] till that moment he clings to the coast and his ships in a manner that indicates a marked respect for the English army as no obsolete force, but a thoroughly formidable opponent. And if William's estimate of his opponent is not accepted, there is no creditable explanation of his otherwise supine loitering from 28 September to 14 October almost on the beach of the undefended country he had invaded.[12] Upholders of the accepted view of the English army can hardly explain his inertia on the grounds that he might have found himself outnumbered by Harold's forces. The 'superiority of tactics and equipment' attributed to the Normans are such, if they existed, as should have left William with no undue fear of numerical odds.

William's caution and Fitz-Wimarch's warning grow more understandable when we seek to find that overwhelming superiority of Norman equipment which Davis takes for granted. The Bayeux Tapestry hardly seems to provide decisive evidence of a Norman superiority of equipment. The weapons and equipment of the armoured men on the two sides are almost precisely the same – the knee-length birnie, the helm with nosepiece, the spear that is occasionally couched under the horseman's arm, but far more often thrown overhand, whether wielded by Norman on horseback or Saxon on foot, the two-edged cutting sword and the long pointed shield are common to both sides.[13] The solitary English archer differs not a whit from three of the four shown on the Norman side.[14] Even the long two-handed axe is no English monopoly for it appears earlier in the Tapestry in the hands of Count Guy as he receives William's

---

11   Maclagan, *Bayeux Tapestry*, p. 53, 'Hic nuntiatum est Willelmo de Harold'; pls 54, 55, 'Hic milites exierunt de Hastinga'; and these scenes of the news arriving and the advance of the Normans from Hastings are divided only by the burning of houses which goaded Harold into action while still well below his maximum strength – cf. Wm of Poitiers, 'accelerabat enim eo magis Rex furibundus quod propinqua castris Normannorum vastari audierat', *op. cit.* p. 131. For the incompleteness of Harold's forces, see Stenton, *Anglo-Saxon England*, p. 584.

12   Stenton has not failed to observe the Conqueror's caution (*Anglo-Saxon England*, p. 583). He remarks that 'it was a matter of elementary prudence for him to remain within a short distance of the sea' – though he has already written (p. 576) that 'Harold's army [was] confined by its nature to a type of warfare which was already obsolete'. But against a foe already obsolete there would be no occasion for such prudence as William showed. William's unenterprising caution must either be justified on the grounds that he was opposing a foe of quality amply good enough to have a fair prospect of beating him; or it must be dismissed as the timidity of a second-rate commander who feared where there was no cause for fear.

13   A few of the English housecarles are represented as carrying the obsolescent round shield and not the pointed shield (Maclagan, *Bayeux Tapestry*, pls 68, 76, 77). This is sometimes regarded as a manifestation of English conservativism and slowness to adopt the latest improvements, but that hardly seems a reasonable conclusion here. None of the light-armed English spearmen shown in pl. 71 carry any but the pointed shield and it would be very strange if heavy-armed professional troops voluntarily carried obsolete equipment when such equipment as the light-armed had was up-to-date. Harold's housecarles, however, had just hurried south after fighting the Norse who still used the round shield (Oman, *Art of War*, i, 129) and it is entirely probable that those shown with the round shield had re-equipped themselves with enemy arms picked up on the field of Stamford Bridge. The Tapestry offers abundant evidence that a man's own shield became, as might be expected, very much the worse for wear during a long day's fighting (e.g. Saxon shields in pl. 76) and the practice of re-equipping oneself with serviceable captured enemy material is common in every war in every generation. The Bayeux Tapestry shows one man collecting nothing but swords (pl. 76), another collecting nothing but shields (pl. 77) and all birnies are gathered up till in pls 78, 79, the dead lie naked.

14   Maclagan, *Bayeux Tapestry*, pls 63, 64, 65, 66.

embassy.[15] The military equipment used on both sides of the Channel was thus interchangeable; and as it is one of the oldest rules of war that weapons dictate tactics[16] (however ground and role may modify their application), it would not be altogether surprising to find that given similar conditions the English would fight on horseback as the Normans fought. It is also normal for a foreign novelty introduced to a backward people to be known by its foreign name, but the Anglo-Saxon chronicler unhesitatingly recognized the mounted Norman soldier as a *cniht*, something he had a word of his own for, and the English name has prevailed.[17] The idea that the Englishman of 1066 attached no value to the bow is intrinsically equally unlikely. The frequency of its pre-Conquest use is obscured by the ambiguity with which the Anglo-Saxon language uses the same word to describe both an arrow and a throwing-spear, but the Song of Maldon still has one clear reference to bows being busy.[18] That they were English bows the poem does not say, but its author, who had a defeat to explain, found no alibi in any inferiority of armament on his side; he turned instead to the repellent explanations of cowardice and treachery. Again, a century after the Conquest, William Fitz-Stephen found archery practice as normal a holiday pastime for the young Londoner as jumping, wrestling or throwing stones,[19] while in the days of Henry I, fatal accidents arising from happy-go-lucky archery practice had been common enough to call for special legal notice.[20] Indeed bows would seem as common as dogs in the England ruled by the Conqueror's son, if Petit Dutaillis is correct in tracing the second clause of the Assizes of Woodstock back to the reign of Henry I.[21] These indications that the bow was indeed familiar to eleventh century England enhance the improbability that a kingdom with so much recent battle experience as Harold's should wantonly neglect a weapon at once so primitive and designed to so vigorous a future as the bow.

Here, then, are general considerations all tending to the view that the English army of 1066 may have been underrated. In the light of them the less apology may be necessary for now reopening discussion of Snorre Sturlason's familiar, but contemned, description in the *Heimskringla* of the battle of Stamford Bridge. There is no need to quote him at length: suffice it to say that in his account English horsemen

---

[15] *Ibid*, pl. 11.

[16] Nowadays, of course, this remark is only a half-truth. Today new weapons are constantly invented to provide new solutions to tactical problems, but the systematic application of deliberate invention to war is a relatively modern novelty. It is in general true that the tactics of any given period have been those made possible by the accepted weapons of the period, subject to two important qualifications – the standard of training permitted by accepted standards of discipline, and the amount of recent battle-experience available. Thanks to Welsh, Irish and Scandinavian invasions, added to highly successful Scottish and Welsh campaigns, the English of 1066 were not without recent battle experience.

[17] In his *English Feudalism, 1066–1166* (Oxford, 1932), pp. 132 *seqq.*, Sir Frank Stenton calls the supersession of the Norman word *chevaler* by the English *cniht* 'a curious anomaly', but the anomaly would disappear if the common opinion of the Anglo-Saxon army turned out to be untenable.

[18] 'bogan wæcron bysige', line 110.

[19] 'In festis tota aestate juvenes ludentes exercentur arcu, cursu, saltu, lucta, jactu lapidum; *Materials for the History of Thos. Becket* (e.d. Robertson, Rolls Ser.), iii. 11. See also *Norman London* (Hist. Association Leaflets, nos 93–4 (1934)), pp. 25–35.

[20] 'Si quis in ludo saggitandi vel alicuius exercicii iacule vel huiusmodi casu aliquem occidat, reddat sum.' Leges Henrici, 88, 6; F. Liebermann, *Die Gesetze der Angelsachsen* (Halle, 1903), i. 603.

[21] 'Quod nullus habeat arcus nec sagittas nec canes . . . in forestis . . .' Petit Dutaillis, *Studies supplementary to Stubbs* (Manchester, 1914), ii. 176.

ride against their enemies with spears, but do so quite ineffectually till the Norse break formation and then 'when they had broken the shield line the English rode upon them from all sides and threw spears and shot at them'. In this melee the Norse King Harald Sigurdsson is killed by an arrow through the windpipe. There follows a lull, and the battle is renewed and sustained by the arrival of Norse reinforcements come hot foot from the fleet. In the heat of the day the Norse threw off their ring-birnies and 'then it was easy for the English to find places to strike them', and heavy fighting with heavy casualties continued till 'it also grew dark in the evening before all the man-slaying was at an end'.[22] The picture of the horsed Englishmen riding against their foes, and of the Norse King being mortally wounded by an arrow, is a vivid one, and would imply a mixed force of horsemen and bowmen, just such a force as might account for the caution of Duke William.

Detailed accounts of the tactics of English armies in this period are so rare that the historian of war might be expected to give due consideration even to Snorre as a possible source of light. Snorre, however, has been treated as an unwelcome intruder into English history. 'The details of the fight', says Oman of Stamford Bridge, 'are absolutely lost – we cannot unfortunately accept one word of the spirited narrative of the *Heimskringla* . . . we cannot trust a saga which says that Morcar was King Harold Godwineson's brother and fell at Fulford; that Earl Waltheof (then a child) took part in the fight, and that the English army was mostly composed of cavalry and archers. The whole tale of the *Heimskringla* reads like a version of the Battle of Hastings transported to Stamford Bridge by some incredible error. The one detail about it recorded in the Anglo-Saxon chronicle, namely, that the fighting included the desperate defence of a bridge against the pursuing English, does *not* appear in the Norse narrative at all. We can only be sure that both sides must have fought on foot in the old fashion of Viking and Englishmen.'[23]

Thus Oman would sweep Snorre out of court, but in R.W. Chambers he has found a vigorous defender.[24] Chambers concedes that 'the Saga is demonstrably inaccurate as to the family relationships of the English leaders', but reasonably observes that 'these are points with regard to which the Norse invaders might well be in error', and, noting that the Anglo-Saxon Chronicle makes similar mistakes about the Norse leaders, insists that such errors do not invalidate any race's documents. Turning, then, to the military field, Chambers finds saga and chronicle in agreement on detail after detail – in particular as to the date of the battle of Fulford and 'as to the capture of York and the events leading up to the battle of Stamford Bridge. The details also of the battle of Stamford Bridge', he continues, 'are confirmed by the *Chronicle*, at any rate in so far as the two accounts emphasize that Harold caught the Northmen unawares, whilst they were awaiting the hostages whose surrender had been promised and were expecting no further resistance in the North'; and to these points on which Chambers finds the Chronicle explicitly in agreement with Snorre, we may add another detail on which his story is substantiated by independent contemporary testimony – namely the statement that the Norse lacked armour at Stamford Bridge, which Freeman, Snorre's original detractor, found confirmed in Marianus Scotus.[25]

---

22 Snorre Sturlason, *Heimskringla or the Lives of the Norse Kings*, edited by Erling Monsen and translated into English by A.H. Smith (Cambridge, 1932), pp. 566–68.
23 Oman, *Art of War*, i. 150–51.
24 *England before the Norman Conquest* (London, 1926), pp. 303–05.
25 Marianus Scotus (Pertz, v. 559), cited by Freeman, *Norman Conquest*, iii (2nd edn), 370, n. 2.

Proceeding from mutual agreements of the Chronicle and Saga, Chambers goes on to show that where statements in either source are not repeated in the other, they are often explained by it and to declare that the scaldic poems, whence Snorre drew his facts, are 'excellent evidence'. He concludes 'that whereas the *Saga* is entirely inaccurate as to English affairs, it gives the traditional account of the battle of Stamford Bridge, such as was taken back to Scandinavia by the surviving Norsemen. This agrees remarkably with the *Chronicle* account, and where it does differ . . . it is the *Chronicle* which is in error.'

Snorre, then, stands as an important and dependable witness to the weapons and tactics of the English army of 1066, yet the dogma that Harold's England had no cavalry and slighted archery was so strong as to cause even Chambers virtually to reject the account of the battle he had just so trenchantly vindicated.[26] The bases of so potent a dogma demand examination. Its general acceptance probably rests on Oman's *Art of War in the Middle Ages*, but its author was Freeman, who deduced it from the battle of Hastings, and, once his theory was made, fortified it with the examples of the battle of Dyrrachium in 1081 and the disastrous Welsh campaign of Earl Ralph of Hereford in 1055.[27] In accepting Freeman's conclusion Oman had no addition to make to the examples on which Freeman based it, but he did buttress it with a quotation described as from the 'Anglo-Saxon Chronicle of 1055', to the effect that Earl Ralph was beaten 'because he attempted to make the English fight on horseback contrary to their custom'.[28] In fact the Chronicle does not quite say this, and even though such a custom might be deduced from Florence of Worcester's language, it can hardly be universally applied. That fighting on horseback was contrary to the custom of the Englishmen of the Welsh marches may be believed, with good reason. Hardly any part of England was more secluded from continental influences than the central counties of the middle west; cavalry, moreover, is only an effective arm in good cavalry country and it would be hard to find in England a worse cavalry country than the steep, broken and timber-clad hillsides of the Welsh border. There at least the custom of fighting on foot was a good one, as the Herefordshire *fyrd* must have learnt from many generations' experience of meeting the Welsh on their own ground. But the moment one seeks to expand the custom of not fighting on horseback from a local Herefordshire custom into a broad national custom one runs into some embarrassing facts. Not very many years after the Conquest Englishmen are found fighting on horseback at the Conqueror's side in continental campaigns.[29] Before the Conquest England produced in Harold himself a man perfectly capable

---

[26] Compare Chambers's description on page 304 of the English as 'mounted infantry' who 'might well have continued to use their horses in rounding up and riding down bodies of half-armed men' with his excerpt from the Saga on page 311 which sketches a protracted struggle in which English mounted assaults were repeatedly turned back by steady Norse spearmen in a solid formation.

[27] Freeman, *Norman Conquest*, ii (2nd edn), 388–89; iii (2nd edn), 732; iv (2nd edn), 626.

[28] *Art of War*, i. 115. But where did Oman get this quotation? The nearest thing to it that I can find is the Abingdon Chronicle's 'But before there was any spear thrown the English people fled because they were on horses'; and Florence of Worcester's 'Radulfus . . . Anglos contra morem in equis pugnare jussit'. These passages are quoted together by Freeman, *Norman Conquest*, ii (2nd edn), 389, n. 1. Oman would seem to be quoting Freeman's footnotes from memory and conflating the passages there cited.

[29] In the fighting between William and Robert at Gerberoi in 1080 William's forces consisted of '*Normanni et Angli regiique auxiliares*' (Ordericus Vitalis, 572 C.D.; cited by Freeman, iv (2nd edn), 643, n. 1). It was one of those 'Angli', Tokig Wiggodsson, who saved William's life by providing him with another mount when he was unhorsed by his own son (Thorpe, B., *Anglo-Saxon Chronicle* (Rolls

of serving with credit in a mounted Norman force.[30] Again, before the Conquest, English troops are apparently capable of serving as cavalry against the Welsh under Earl Tostig in 1063 – but Tostig, it seems agreed, had the wit to confine his operations to the coastal strip of North Wales whose terrain gave cavalry a chance.[31] A decade earlier still all 'the superior tactics and equipment of his Norman allies wholly failed to give Macbeth the victory over Earl Diward of Northumbria in 1054. The Normans, on the contrary, suffered especially disastrous casualties – 'Nortmannis omnibus . . . occisis',[32] says Florence of Worcester who also states explicitly that Siward invaded Scotland 'cum equestri exercitu'.[33] True to form Freeman was sure that this *equester exercitus* dismounted to fight,[34] but, had they really done so, it is hard to see how they could have killed so many Normans. Even in defeat men whose practice was to go into action mounted should have had little difficulty in escaping death at the hands of men who discarded their horses before the fight began. Finally, that some sort of fighting on horseback was within the abilities of native English soldiers, even before Canute had been accepted as king, is at least suggested by the Chronicler's description of Edmund Ironside's pursuit of the Danes in Kent in 1016 when 'the army fled before him with their horses to Sheppey; and the King slew as many of them as he could overtake;[35] and a pre-Conquest artist has left a sketch which may show how the king's men fought on this and other occasions.[36] Even if Snorre's witness were rejected, these examples seem damaging to the immutable 'custom of the English' as cited by Oman from monkish comments on Earl Ralph's fiasco. Nor does the example of Dyrrachium fortify his case. That was a battle of the Sicilian Normans against, not the English, but the Byzantine army; in no state were the distinct functions of the separate arms better understood than in the Byzantine empire, in whose forces Englishmen fought on foot because they were hired to serve as infantry in a formation whose infantry traditions long antedate the Norman conquest and that was mainly recruited from a kindred race with a familiar tongue.[37] Snorre's witness is not to be overridden by such arguments as these.

Series, London, 1861), i. 350). That the particular 'Anglus' who provided William with a new horse was the solitary Englishman who went into action mounted seems unlikely.

[30] Maclagan, *Bayeux Tapestry*, pls 19–25; William of Malmesbury says of this campaign against the Bretons, 'Ibi Haroldus, et ingenio et manu probatus Normannum in sui amorem convertit' (*De Gestis Regum Anglorum* (ed. Wm Stubbs, London, 1887), i. 279.

[31] Stenton, *Anglo-Saxon England*, p. 568, and J.E. Lloyd, *A History of Wales* (London, 1912), ii. 370.

[32] *Florentii Wigorniensis monachi Chronicon ex Chronicis*. Edited by Benjamin Thorpe (London, 1848), i. 212.

[33] *Ibid.*

[34] Freeman, *Norman Conquest*, ii (2nd edn), 643.

[35] Thorpe, *Anglo-Saxon Chronicle*, i. 282–83.

[36] This sketch, from the Harleian MSS. CO3, is reproduced in L.M. Larson, *Life of Canute* (London, 1912), opposite page 88. It shows two horsemen, riding side by side one throwing a spear, the other a two-edged axe. It might be objected that this could depict, not soldiers, but a hunting scene; reasons for rejecting this objection, however, are that, were it a hunting scene, one would expect to see hounds, but none appear; that at least the nearer horseman carries a shield on his bridle arm, and this hardly seems normal hunting equipment; finally, that their formation and equipment – a file of two abreast, with missile weapons – seems to concur with the Tapestry's representation of eleventh-century mounted tactics; on which see notes 2, p. 13, and 3, pp. 14–15 below.

[37] It is also relevant to add that in behaving as they did at Dyrrachium the Varangians were acting under the orders of a commander who, so far from being an Englishman, bore the very Hollenized name of Nampites.

But if Snorre's credit is re-established, his vindication revives the very difficulties that were eliminated by discrediting him. If the English had archers at Stamford Bridge, why could they make so little reply to the hail of Norman arrows at Hastings? If they could offer cavalry assaults in one battle, why are they rooted to the ground as 'a stationary phalanx of axemen' in the other? These are questions that demand answering and answers may emerge if we will look, first, to the broad circumstances of the whole campaign of 1066, instead of treating its two great actions as isolated and unconnected incidents; and, secondly, to the general nature and the conduct of cavalry in 1066.

In considering the archers, it is first to be recalled that Harold Godwinsson took a very large army to Stamford Bridge. Medieval chroniclers are notoriously prone to exaggerate numbers, but Saxon, Norman, Scandinavian and other continental sources are at least strikingly unanimous in the impressive picture they paint of the great size of Harold's forces at Stamford Bridge.[38] 'The whole strength of southern and central England took part in that great campaign',[39] concludes Freeman, who supports his statement with Domesday evidence from counties as far afield as Worcestershire and Essex.[40] Freeman's is a large claim, but it is backed by all the weight of probability. Harold's blow at the Norse invaders had to be a knock-out, for the alternative to a swift decision was the probability of a war on two fronts, and an enemy who came in upwards of 300 ships took some knocking out. It was therefore right to throw everything available into the northern campaign, and to the north apparently everything available went. When William landed, southern England had no defenders capable of putting up even such a fight as the men of Scarborough made against the Northern invaders.

But then came the return march. Here the vital points are that not earlier than the night of 1 October Harold is informed at York of William's landing; that on the night of 14 October his dishonoured carrion lies stripped and mangled on Battle Hill; and that Battle Hill is 250 miles and more from York.[41] This is an immense distance covered in an astonishingly short time. Many have admired the speed of Harold's movements; fewer have paused to consider that a march of 250 miles in a dozen days, which would be hard on well-disciplined and well-serviced modern infantry, was hopelessly beyond the capacity of any eleventh-century infantry. The statement that 'the victorious army of Stamford Bridge was with Harold'[42] on his march south is unbelievable in any literal sense. None but mounted men could possibly have kept up with him; the archer could rarely afford a horse,[43] and must have been left behind.

---

[38] Then came Harold, King of the Angles '*mid ealre his fyrde*', says the Abingdon chronicle (Thorpe, *op. cit.* i, Cott. Tib. Bl., p. 339); or '*mid mycclum here*', as the Laudian MS. puts it (*ibid.*, p. 337); '*numerosissimus ac robustissimus*' is the description of Harold's army that William of Poitiers puts into the mouth of Robert Fitz-Wimarch (*op. cit.* p. 128), 'a mighty host of cavalry and infantry', says Snorre (Smith and Monsen, *Heimskringla*, p. 564); an army amounting to seven separate divisions, says Marianus Scotus (v. 559, cited by Freeman, *Norman Conquest*, iii (2nd edn), 362, n. 4).

[39] Freeman, *Norman Conquest*, iii (2nd edn), 362.

[40] *Ibid.* n. 2 and n. 3.

[41] From York to London is 190 miles; from London to Battle is nearly 60 miles as the crow flies; but even today the roads of Sussex rather conspicuously refrain from travelling as the crow flies.

[42] Oman, *Art of War*, i. 151.

[43] It would seem rare for the archer to be wealthy and well born. One, but only one, of the thirty-two archers shown in the Tapestry can afford defensive armour (pl. 63); only one mounted Norman archer appears in pursuit of the routed English, though Hastings would have been a very unusual battle if

The point that only a fraction of the vast army of Stamford Bridge could have accompanied Harold southwards is duly appreciated by Sir Frank Stenton, who writes that at London Harold 'expanded the force at his command to the dimensions of an army.'[44] But to this point must be added another – namely, that the new army which Harold sought to scrape together for Hastings could only be raised from a country already stripped of the materials of which armies were to be made. It was from London that Harold had started for Stamford Bridge;[45] the area in which he sought to recruit on his return was the one that must have contributed most to the great force whose victorious survivors were now straggling home from York. Add that the number of fighting men an English shire could raise was at best limited[46] and the scarcity of English archers at Hastings will hardly seem surprising. If the majority of those available had gone to Stamford Bridge, it is wholly understandable that Harold could find but few for his second battle.[47] If this be the case, Snorre Sturlason does not on this topic contradict the evidence of the witnesses for the battle of Hastings; rather, he explains it.

The problem of cavalry in 1066 cannot be satisfactorily discussed till three questions have been considered and their implications grasped; first, what are the 'characteristics', the military qualities and uses, of the cavalry arm? Secondly, how far were these characteristics understood by anyone in 1066 and hence, thirdly, what sort of skills and what sort of conduct were required of the cavalryman of 1066? These may be thought needless questions; it is perhaps too readily supposed that we are all familiar with the tactics of the mailed knights who launched irresistible charges with lances couched beneath their strong right arms, and that the use of this heavy cavalry, which was so long to dominate European warfare, was already perfectly understood by the Normans in 1066. Everyone has read Oman's description of the Norman army

by that time there had not been many riderless horses to catch and mount on and near the battlefield. The normal archer appears to be a peasant who can afford neither mail shirt nor helmet and follows his lord to war equipped only with his bow and quiver and clad as simply as he follows the plough in peace – compare the archers in pls vii. 63, 64, 65, the lower borders of pls 72, 73, 74 and 75 with the peasants shown ploughing with a donkey in pls 10 and 11, and again in pl. 80. Since the publication of J.H. Clapham's article on 'The Horsing of the Danes' (*ante*, xxv. 287 *seqq.*) it has been customary to regard the *fyrd* as a highly mobile force of mounted infantry and, so far as the thegns are concerned, this view is doubtless correct; but it seems unlikely that men of a class that had often to be content to plough with asses could go to war with saddle horses. It is perhaps relevant to add here that in the French forces of the second Crusade the archers were those whom 'nature or fortune' had rendered horseless (Odo of Deuil, *De Profectione Ludovici VII in Orientem*, edited V.G. Berry (New York, 1948), pp. 124, 125).

[44] Stenton, *Anglo-Saxon England*, p. 584. Stenton duly notes here that however speedily Harold had summoned the Fyrd, it would be impossible for 'thegns of distant shires . . . to set out with him for Sussex'. But the situation must have been even worse than that, for its diversion to the North would have made the fyrd of even the southern shires equally unavailable at Hastings on 14 October.

[45] Freeman, *Norman Conquest*, iii (2nd edn), 339, 359.

[46] Stenton, *Anglo-Saxon England*, p. 575, and *English Feudalism, 1066–1166* (Oxford, 1932), pp. 116, 117; F.W. Maitland, *Domesday and Beyond* (Cambridge, 1897), pp. 156 *seqq.*

[47] Freeman's statement (*Norman Conquest*, iii (2nd edn), 425) that on his way south Harold received swarms of reinforcements from the earldoms of Waltheof and Gyrth is contradicted on the same page by his own footnote from William of Malmesbury, Bk ii, 228 – 'practer stipendiarios et mercenarios milites, paucos admodum ex provincialibus habuit'; it is also in conflict with Freeman's own conclusion based on Domesday, that 'the whole strength of southern and central England' had already responded to the call to go to Stamford Bridge; it rests merely on Freeman's inability to disbelieve Wace. William of Malmesbury's evidence strongly supports the argument advanced here.

at Hastings as 'the now fully-developed cavalry of feudalism',[48] and Oman's authority seems generally trusted. To the writer, however, it seems that Oman has fallen into
an anachronism here, and that the striking thing about the battle of Hastings is how
little it reveals the Normans as knowing of the true conduct and employment of
cavalry, how slight were the special skills required of the horses soldier of the day.

'*L'union fait la force*' applies to the actions of cavalry as well as to those of every
other arm. Its best effects on the field of battle were only to be gained when men
worked together in regular formations; to work together they must be armed identi-
cally, whether the arm be the jousting lance of later chivalry or the sword that was
the classic *arme blanche* of cavalry from Prince Rupert to mechanization, and they
must be trained in making combined and orderly movements executed on a definite,
given word of command; only so could they exploit to best effect their greatest asset
– the shock of the horse's own splendid power and speed. This was an asset that
demanded to be used offensively; hence the classic cavalry charge of horsemen
riding knee to knee as one thundering, galloping wall of horses, men and steel which
crashed into their opponents as a single, close, unwavering line. Infantry caught
disordered and unready had no hope of surviving such a shock – they were cut down
as they stood or fled, they were knocked over individually and ripped up as they lay.
The only answer to the classic shock action of cavalry was to make the horse 'refuse'
to charge home. This was readily done; it was only necessary for well-disciplined
infantry to stand firm in regular formation and present the oncoming horses with a
steady line of pikes (as at Falkirk) or bayonets (as at Waterloo), on which they would
be impaled if they did not 'refuse'; they would 'refuse' if the infantry were steady
enough.

On mature tactics such as these there is no trace on either side at Hastings. There
is no uniformity of Norman armament – some are shown with spears, some with
swords, some with maces (and if the spear is generally the primary, the sword a
secondary, weapon, a swordsman nevertheless appears in the Norman's opening
charge).[49] Their swords are cutting swords with scant resemblance to the long pointing sword that is the true cavalryman's proper weapon and their light slender spears
have almost less resemblance to the long, bulbous-butted jousting lance of later days.
There is little unity of action or regularity of formation about the Norman charges –
witness the disorderly groups in which the Tapestry shows them riding to attack,[50]
the individual performance of the exhibitionist Taillefer, and the catalogue of

---

[48] 'As the last great example of an endeavour to use the old infantry tactics against the now
fully-developed cavalry of feudalism we have to describe the Battle of Hastings.' *Art of War*, i. 149.
[49] Maclagan, *Bayeux Tapestry*, pl. 67.
[50] As far as the Tapestry leaves any general impression of Norman tactics it is of charges launched
by horsemen who ride at the enemy in a somewhat succession of couples, or, less often twos and
threes (pls 21, 22, 23–4, 64–5, 73–4, 77–8). So far, then, as modern terms are applicable to primitive
conditions the Norman attack would seem to have been an attack in column. Here it may be recalled
that this was also the method of cavalry about the turn of the sixteenth and seventeenth centuries,
when the weight of armour worn, and the impenetrability of solid infantry formations equipped with
the pike, confined horsemen in the first instance to the use of a missile weapon – the pistol; this in
turn dictated a drill of riding up to the enemy in column, firing and wheeling away by files to reload,
return and fire again (G.M. Trevelyan, *England under the Stuarts* (London, 1924), p. 246, and Sir
J.W. Fortescue, *History of the British Army*, i (London, 1910), 102–4). Since the Norman horsemen
likewise (*vide* n. 3, pp. 14–15, below) placed his first reliance in a missile weapon – the throwing
spear – the use of a column in attack would be equally natural to him.

personal combats with which Freeman was able to garnish his account of the battle.[51]
Indeed, the efficient handling of cavalry is not to be expected of armies so primitively
undisciplined as those that met at Hastings. A proper cavalry charge, as remarked, is
a regular drill movement calling for a high standard of training; drill in turn demands
the ability to give, to receive and to carry out definite and clearly understood words
of command; but how is it to be supposed that such words of command could ever
be heard at Hastings over the conflicting yells of '*Dex aie*' and '*Olicrosse*' that rent
the battlefield? It is impossible to give regular commands in forces where all ranks
feel at liberty to make the 'altissimus clamor, hinc Normannicus illinc barbaricus'[52]
described by William of Poitiers.[53]

As the Norman horseman is thus not up to making regular and orderly movements
in close formation, he naturally has little notion of charging home. He does not
despise an opportunity of thrusting a spear into an opponent's bosom when he gets
the chance, but as against Conan's Bretons at Dol, so against Harold's Saxons at
Hastings, his commonest practice is to ride up to throw his spear overhand – after
which there can have been little for him to do but gallop away and then repeat the
performance. So time and again the Normans ride against the English, even to within
slashing distance, but only one scene in the Tapestry shows an Englishman being
ridden down. The Norman horsemen of the Tapestry is thus not yet a specialized
lancer; he is for the most part only a mounted javelineer,[54] and that is a far cry from

---

51 Freeman, *Norman Conquest*, iii. (2nd edn), 492–95).
52 William of Poitiers, *op. cit.* p. 133.
53 For this reason I also think the story of feigned flights is to be regarded with much suspicion. But
there are other reasons, too, namely: (*a*) the extraordinary danger attached to feigning flight; panic is
infectious and a flight simulated in sham by one group would be painfully likely to be mistaken for
the real thing by the others on the same side, whereupon panic could too easily become both genuine
and general. (*b*) The fact that cavalry once repulsed in a charge have no course open but to withdraw
and try again. Ney did this repeatedly on the afternoon of Waterloo, but no one has credited him with
any deep laid stratagem; likewise the Norman horse, too, would have to *reculer our mieux sauter*,
and if the least experienced and worst led men on the other side mistook such withdrawals for flight,
with the happy result of their being slaughtered in large quantities, it is easy to see how readily clerical
reporters rationalizing after the event could declare such withdrawals a smart trick, worthy of a
cunning Norman. (The retreating Normans would of course have no difficulty whatever in turning to
counter-attack; men on horseback, chased by men running on foot and flourishing javelins, would
have only to canter 500 yards to perfect safety and find time to turn and get together to charge their
by now much disorganized and badly blown pursuers.) (*c*) The feigned flight is a point on which the
earliest authorities, William of Poitiers and Guy of Amiens, are in conflict; they cannot tell us which
flights were feinged and which were not; the sham of the one is the genuine article of the other
(Freeman, *Norman Conquest*, iii (2nd edn), 767). (*d*) Round's analogy drawn from the relief of Arques
in 1053 (*Feudal England*, pp. 380–87) is decidedly unimpressive; to lay an ambush before an
engagement is one thing; to improvise it as a happy thought on the open field of a battle already joined
is quite another.
54 In three cases (Maclagan, *Bayeux Tapestry*, pls 65, 68, 71), the Tapestry shows Normans running
their enemies through with spears couched under the arm in such a way as to receive the power with
which they are thrust home from the force of the horse's charge, in the familiar manner of later knights,
or the modern sport of pig sticking. In nearly every other case the spear is shown poised over arm for
a throw or a downward jab, but in only four cases does a downward jab actually seem to be being
delivered (pls 68, 69, 70 and perhaps 66), whereas in seven cases we are fairly clearly shown spears
flying through the air toward the Norman's enemies after being actually thrown – three in pls 23, 24,
two in pl. 66, one in pl. 65 (where another also comes back) and one in pl. 76; and in seven more
cases we are shown spears untouched by anyone's hand and apparently thrown – two sticking in
shields in pl. 66 well in advance of the Norman first charge; one going past a Saxon's shoulder in pl.

the 'fully developed cavalry of feudalism'. It is highly significant that against these infantile Norman mounted tactics the English neither know how, nor have need, to present the classic line of levelled spears to make the horses refuse to charge home; it is enough for them to throw spears in reply or to brain with an axe the horse which comes in alone unsupported by others close on either hand. The adjective 'infantile' which we have used of the Normans' mounted tactics, is equally appropriate to the defensive Saxon infantry tactics. The swinging axe would never have halted a proper knee-to-knee charge of mounted lancers or swordsmen; some horses might be brought down but the majority would escape disabling wounds and by their own impetus would be swept on, crashing into, through and over the wretched infantry most of whom would be knocked flat.[55] The only way to stop the charge of cavalry who knew their job was to make the horses stop themselves, and that required pike or bayonet levelled at the horse's breast and offering the certainty of injury if he did not stop. Yet infantile as the English anti-cavalry tactics were,[56] they sufficed to repel each and every mounted assault that the Normans made. The mere success of the English in turning back Norman charges with their javelins and battle axes shows how little the Normans were capable of acting as true cavalry. On the contrary the Norman horseman's weapons, the cutting sword and throwing spear, are the same as the weapons of the English foot soldier at Maldon and Hastings and he uses them as nearly as possible in the same way (except, of course, the axe, which is wielded with both hands and the swinging weight of the whole body,[57] a feat impossible on horse-back). The Norman moreover is so far from being a specialized cavalryman that he will cheerfully leap to the ground, let his horse trot free, and mix it with the English

68; another going past a Saxon's ear as he 'axes' a horse in pl. 77; also in pl. 77 a spear flies shoulder high between two Saxons and another sticks into a Saxon shield at an angle and distance from the Normans that is suggestive of throwing; and in pl. 69 an apparently thrown spear is sinking into the breast of a Saxon who clutches it as he falls. Throwing the spear overhand was thus the rule, while thrusting was the exception, if the Tapestry is acceptable evidence of how men handled weapons in 1066. Overarm is, of course, the only way to throw a spear, and much the most forceful method of thrusting it with one hand when on foot (e.g. it is the method used by the native East African lion-hunter, who, like the soldiers at Hastings, carries a shield as well as a throwing and thrusting spear); but for cavalrymen the overarm method squanders that most potent asset – the force of 'the resolute charge done with the might of their horses' (to use the fine sixteenth-century phrase recovered by C.H. Firth, *Cromwell's Army* (London 1902), p. 120). This is best harnessed by couching the spear under the arm, a point nearly all the Normans in the Tapestry fail to appreciate, and their failure here should by itself suffice to stamp them as the most embryonic of cavalrymen; they still think as infantrymen – not very unnaturally either, since their weapons do not differ from infantry weapons.

[55] A horse's brain is a small and difficult target, occupying surprisingly little of his head; a glancing blow on neck or shoulder would rarely stop a galloping horse in his tracks, however ghastly a flesh wound it might inflict, and in a proper, close, knee-to-knee charge of horsemen in line a wounded horse has little room or time to swerve away.

[56] It is most interesting that, ignorant as the English are of the infantryman's classic anti-cavalry tactics of later days, yet Snorre makes Harald Sigurdsson employ them at Stamford Bridge. However, Oman (*Art of War*, i. 376) traces the origin of the pikemen in western Europe to the Netherlands 'as early as 1100' and Flemings formed a large part of Tostig's forces. Snorre's story need not, therefore, be dismissed as an anachronism.

[57] At any rate it is normally used with two hands (Maclagan, *Bayeux Tapestry*, pls 68, 69, 70, 75, 77), but in two cases (pls 69, 74) Saxons hold axes with one hand only. The axe, however, is a much overstressed weapon in English hands at Hastings. The Tapestry indicates that a man does not begin to use his axe till he has thrown all his spears – of which he carries sheaves (pl. 66). The only axe shown in the first scene of the Saxon army (pls 56, 66) is a small throwing axe (whose cutting edge is held away from the direction in which it is to be thrown).

on foot – as the Tapestry shows him doing in scenes whose significance seems unappreciated.[58] The armoured horseman of 1066, it thus appears, is interchangeable with the heavy infantryman; he uses the same weapons in the same manner and is quite ready to discard his horse.

That being the case, Harold's natural horsed soldiers were his heavy-armed house-carles; and a distinction that seems to merit more attention than it gets lies in the fact that the housecarles, a relative novelty introduced into England by Canute, were not the *fyrd*. Over and above the national militia they were a body of permanent, special-ized professional soldiers – with an immense reputation at home and abroad.[59] No more than that of any other professional force is their capacity for war to be measured by that of a militia, of the Herefordshire *fyrd* whose refusal to fight on horseback in 1055 has been accepted as conclusive evidence of the Old English soldier remaining to the last an unteachable infantryman;[60] still less is their tactical development to be gauged by the conduct of Byrthnoth's followers three generations earlier in 991, in the very darkest years of England's military decadence. They were the companions in arms of the king, and, as noted earlier, their king was a man able to give a respectable account of himself in a continental campaign with a mounted Norman army; it is anything but likely that his companions in arms were content to be his inferiors in skill-at-arms. On the contrary, having the same equipment as the Nor-mans, they should have been perfectly well able to act at Stamford Bridge, where the ground is ideal for cavalry,[61] in the same way as the Normans are depicted on the Tapestry as having acted at Hastings. And that, be it noted, is precisely what Snorre describes them as doing; when the shieldline was broken, he says 'the Englishmen rode upon them from all sides and *threw spears*'; he does not make them charge home with lances at rest, like thirteenth-century chivalry, so Freeman's conjecture that Snorre's 'whole conception of the English army was clearly taken from an English army of (his) own age'[62] is falsified; it is on the contrary a strong tribute to Snorre's fidelity to the story as he received it that, though he writes in the thirteenth century, he still describes the true eleventh-century battle-drill of the mounted javelineer. The fact that he is accurate on so particular a military detail of a bygone age offers the best possible reason for accepting his story that the English army was indeed strong in cavalry at Stamford Bridge.

But Hastings was for Harold a very different affair from Stamford Bridge. At the earlier battle every advantage had been his. He had with him 'the whole strength of southern and central England'; he caught the Norse divided, surprised, and weakened by the casualties of Fulford. These advantages enabled him to adopt, on ideal ground,

---

[58] Maclagan, *Bayeux Tapestry* (pl. 75), shows two spurred Normans on foot hacking down English-men; in one case the discarded horse still trots close beside his late rider. In pl. 69 another horseless Norman slashes at an Englishman from behind; in this case one cannot see his legs, but the horse is conspicuously absent.

[59] The English 'warriors who were called the thingmen troop were so bold that one of them was better than two of Harald's best men', said the Norse who opposed their king's support of Tostig (Smith and Monsen, *Heimskringla*, p. 558).

[60] It is curious that this conclusion drawn from Earl Ralph's fiasco of 1055 is allowed to stand beside the accepted facts that the *fyrd* was not, but the housecarles were, a body of specialized professional soldiers.

[61] 'The ground on each side of the Derwent forms at this point a nearly flat plain' (Freeman, *Norman Conquest*, iii (2nd edn), 357).

[62] *Norman Conquest*, iii (2nd edn), 732.

the offensive role which has always been the golden opportunity of cavalry. At Hastings the boot was on the other foot. There the Normans, who had fought no battles and made no great marches, were at full strength, while Harold's force was too largely composed of the scrapings of shires whose best had been expended in the North, of wretchedly armed men whose weapons were the mere 'lignis imposita saxa' described by William of Poitiers[63] and figured in the Tapestry.[64] In these circumstances Harold had no choice but act on the defensive, as the weaker commander constantly must, whether he likes it or no. But in the defensive, cavalry has no role except to stand by in idleness awaiting a propitious moment for counter attack, or to be put unhorsed into the line, like the British cavalry in the winters of 1914–15 and subsequent war years; and Harold could not possibly let his housecarles stand by in idleness. His ill-armed, scratch force needed all the stiffening he could give it. Once he was forced to act on the defensive, his housecarles had therefore to be deployed and committed as infantry to slash and hew it out to the finish on the crest of Senlac Hill; the moment they dismounted Harold ceased to have any cavalry. Yet in spite of every disadvantage under which the English laboured and all the supposed superiority of his Norman army, William won his victory only after a most prolonged and bitter struggle; a truly obsolete foe should surely have given him less trouble.

If the arguments detailed above be sound, they point to the conclusion that Harold's loss of life and throne, with such consequences for England, were not due to his country's 'decadence' or his army's obsolescence. Rather these events spring from his own impetuosity, from the superb over-confidence engendered by his splendid triumph at Stamford Bridge, from the impatience with which, as former earl of Wessex, he heard of violence done to his own people at Pevensey and Hastings. This may not be a popular conclusion – no one likes ascribing momentous developments to mere chance – but neither is it an original conclusion. The Anglo-Saxon Chronicle, Florence of Worcester and William of Malmesbury all point to it, and it gains some support from Williams of Poitiers too.[65] It is a conclusion that may also have the merit of eliminating a number of difficulties from eleventh-century English history. The supersession of the Norman word *chevaler* by the English *cniht* as the name for a horsed soldier ceases to be an anomaly. So do the instances we have quoted of individual Englishmen fighting on horseback, or numbers of them forming *equestres exercitus* which, in defiance of an accepted historical canon, are able to destroy whole contingents of reputedly superior Normans. The generalship of the Conqueror after his landing at Pevensey must surely appear in a much more creditable light, a light more worthy of the man. His use of the *fyrd*, which is rather surprising if it could offer nothing better than the unarmoured spearmen whose last moments are depicted in the Tapestry,[66] becomes readily understandable if it could normally provide a respectable body of archers. The art of war in England is placed upon the road where one

---

[63] Wm of Poitiers, *op. cit.* p. 133.

[64] Maclagan, *Bayeux Tapestry*, pl. 65. Stenton holds that men thus armed are not the *fyrd* but outraged peasants seeking revenge on the invader for the harrying of their farms and burning of their homes (*Anglo-Saxon England*, p. 575).

[65] Thorpe, *A.S. chron.* i. 337 (Laud. MS.). Florence of Worcester, *op. cit.* i. 227. William of Malmesbury, *De Gestis Regum Anglorum*, i. 282. And William of Poitiers, though, when he comes to the actual battle, he rather naturally makes the most of the force his hero overcame, has already borne witness to the causes of Harold's weakness, his haste and impetuosity, in a passage quoted above (p. 3, n. 3).

[66] Maclagan, *Bayeux Tapestry*, pl. 71.

would expect to find it, a road closely parallel with the progress of the art of war upon the continent (a development equally indicated in another branch of warfare by the building of Harold's pre-Conquest castle at Hereford). Last, but not necessarily least, an undeserved aspersion upon the historical reputation of Snorre Sturlason is removed.

16. Bernard Bachrach, 'The Feigned Retreat at Hastings'

In this brief article, Bernard Bachrach examines the question of the feigned retreats, placing the tactic in the wider context of early medieval cavalry warfare and critically examining other historians' rejections of the tactic. While not a direct reply to Glover, Bachrach's article does point out that modern assumptions about training and group movements in combat cannot always be applied to medieval warfare, and that the military traditions of one area do not exist in isolation from those in other areas.

Reprinted from *Mediaeval Studies* 33 (1971), 344–47, by permission of the publisher. Copyright © 1971 by the Pontifical Institute of Mediaeval Studies, Toronto.

THE FEIGNED RETREAT AT HASTINGS

Bernard S. Bachrach

Concerning a key episode at the Battle of Hastings in 1066 William of Poitiers writes:

> The Normans and their allies, observing that they could not overcome an enemy which was so numerous and so solidly drawn up, without severe losses, retreated, simulating flight as a trick . . . among the barbarians there was great joy . . . some thousands of them . . . threw themselves in pursuit of those whom they believed to be in flight. Suddenly the Normans reined in their horses, intercepted and surrounded [the enemy] and killed them to the last man.[1]

William of Malmesbury gives largely the same account of this episode:

> The English . . . formed an impenetrable body, which would have kept them safe that day, if the Normans had not tricked them into opening their ranks by a feigned flight.[2]

For well over half a century medievalists have generally accepted accounts of the feigned retreat as true.[3] In the spate of works which have appeared more or less in conjunction with the nine-hundredth anniversary of the Battle of Hastings, however, there has been a tendency to reject the feigned retreat as a hoax perpetrated by Norman chroniclers who 'dared not record that the Norman cavalry ran away.'[4]

Colonel Charles H. Lemmon has presented the most influential criticism of the

---

[1] *Gesta Guillemi Ducis Normannorum et Regis Anglorum*, II. 20, ed. Raymonde Foreville (Paris, 1952).

[2] *De Gestis Regum Anglorum*, bk III, 242, ed. William Stubbs (R.S.) (London, 1889). For other accounts of the feigned retreat see *Maistre Wace's Roman de Rou et des Ducs de Normandie*, lines 8200 ff. ed. Hugo Andresen (London, 1879) and *Chronicon Monasterii de Bello*, 1066, ed. J.S. Brewer (London, 1846).

[3] F.M. Stenton, *Anglo-Saxon England* (2nd edn Oxford, 1947), 587, and David C. Douglas, *William the Conqueror* (Berkeley, 1964), 203–04 are the two most notable examples. Among military historians Charles Oman, *A History of the Art of War in the Middle Ages* (London, 1924), I, 162; B.H. Liddell-Hart, *Strategy* (New York, 1954), 76; and J.F.C. Fuller, *Decisive Battles of the Western World* (London, 1954), I, 380 also accept the feigned retreat.

[4]. See Charles H. Lemmon, *The Field of Hastings* (St Leonards-on-Sea, 1956), 44 for the quotation. There have been earlier rejections. Hans Delbrück, *Geschichte der Kriegskunst im Rahmen des Politische Geschichte* (Berlin, 1907), III, 162 rejected the feigned retreat. Alfred H. Burne, *The Battlefield of England* (London, 1950), 31, 42, 43 also rejected it. The list of recent rejections is quite extensive: R.J. Adam, *A Conquest of England* (London, 1965), 127; Timothy Baker, *The Normans* (London, 1966), 112; Denis Butler, 1066 *The Story of a Year* (London, 1966), 246; C.N. Barclay, *Battle 1066* (London, 1966), 81; D.J.A. Mathew, *The Norman Conquest* (London, 1966), 84: and especially John Beeler, *Warfare in England 1066–1189* (Ithaca, New York, 1966), 21–22. This list is not in any way comprehensive. George Slocumbe, *William the Conqueror* (London, 1959), 153–54 accepts the feigned retreat as do Alan Lloyd, *The Making of a King* (New York) 1966), 214 and R.

190

feigned retreat. He asserts that such a tactic 'would demand that every man taking part in it had to know when to retreat, how far to retreat and when to turn around and fight back; and, moreover, that these movements had to be carefully synchronized, or disaster would result.' He contends that it would have been impossible to arrange such a manoeuvre in the heat of battle and rejects equally the possibility that feudal cavalry of the eleventh century could carry out such a tactic even with extensive training. Lemmon tries to support this latter contention by asserting that well-drilled and well-disciplined modern troops, even in small numbers, have difficulty carrying out similar actions in military tournaments. Moreover, he implies that any talk about feigned retreats is nonsense since they violate a 'military maxim, evolved after long years of experience in warfare, that "troops once committed to the attack cannot be made to change direction." '[5]

Lemmon does not demonstrate that William the Conqueror adhered to or even knew about the maxim of irreversible troop commitment. In fact Colonel Lemmon does not present any evidence that the above-mentioned maxim was current among medieval military commanders. C.N. Barclay finds Lemmon's characterization of the difficulties involved in carrying out a feigned retreat to be exaggerated. In contrast to Lemmon he argues that it was 'quite practicable' to employ the feigned retreat tactic at Hastings.[6] But, reliance upon the assertions and counter-assertions of modern military officers for the solving of problems in medieval history is a dubious historical method. Argument from military maxims is hardly any better, especially when there is more reliable evidence to be examined.

Arrian, one of the first Roman generals to fight against steppe horsemen, wrote a tactical plan for dealing with the Alans. A part of this work, *Tactic and Formation against the Alans*, still survives, and in one section of it Arrian makes special note of precautions which are to be taken by his troops to avoid being trapped by a feigned retreat. Arrian notes that only a part of his cavalry are to pursue the retreating enemy rapidly while another part of the cavalry advances behind them in tight order. The infantry must not break ranks, but must remain in good order.[7]

In the 560's, the Byzantine historian Agathias tells his readers that the feigned retreat was a well known barbarian trick used especially by the Huns. In the tenth century both Regino of Prüm and Liutprand of Cremona discuss the Magyars' use of the feigned retreat tactic. These authors reinforce the impression that it was a traditional steppe tactic.[8]

People who had contact with steppe cavalry also adopted this tactic. The Visigoths apparently learned it during their sojourn in southern Russia and on one occasion, at

---

Allen Brown, *The Normans and the Norman Conquest* (New York, 1968), 51, 171–72. Rupert Furneaux, *Conquest 1066* (London, 1966), 165 presents a selection of evidence and invites the reader to decide.

[5] Lemmon's ideas originally set forth in *Field of Hastings*, are reiterated in 'The Campaign of 1066,' *The Norman Conquest* (London, 1966), 109–10. The former has reached a 3rd edition, St Leonards, Sussex 1965.

[6] *Battle 1066*, 81.

[7] *Scriptura Minora*, ed. R. Hercher (Leipzig, 1885), 84–5.

[8] *Agathias Myrinaei Historiarum Libri Quinque*, II, 6, ed. R. Keydell (Berlin, 1967); Regino of Prüm, *Chronicon*, an 889 (ed. F. Kurze; *MGH: SS. in us. schol.*, [Hannover, 1890]); and Liutprand of Cremona, *Antapodosis*, II, 3, 4 (ed. J.B. Becker; *MGH: SS. in us. schol.*, [Hannover, 1915]). On these steppe tactics see Oman, *Art of War*, I, 118 and Karl Leyser, 'The Battle of Lech,' *History*, 50 (1960), 20.

least, used it successfully against the Franks. The Byzantine commander Narses adopted the feigned retreat tactic and used it successfully against a force of Franks which was positioned much as was Harold's force at Hastings. The Franks reacted in a manner similar to that attributed to the English when faced with the enemies' retreat, including the alleged joy at seeing the attackers flee and the pursuit of them. The Byzantines acted much as the Normans at Hastings are said to have acted, wheeling their horses after the enemy had broken its line and slaughtering the scattered infantry. The Byzantine Emperor, Leo the Wise, was so favourably impressed by the feigned retreat tactic that he strongly advocated its use in his work on military tactics.[9]

Even this brief elaboration of the evidence demonstrates that the feigned retreat tactic was widely accepted in the years before the Battle of Hastings. But the steppe peoples practically lived in their saddles, and the Byzantines were among the best trained troops in the middle ages; could William's followers do what the Byzantines, the Alans, the Huns, the Magyars, and the Visigoths did? Lemmon and his supporters think not, but Stenton and Douglas disagree. The latter argues that William's followers had a consciousness of unity and a cohesiveness which comes from fighting together for many years. William's vassals had long fought together and these men had knights of their own who were accustomed to fighting as a unit.[10]

Yet assertions of knightly togetherness are of as little value for proving the use of the feigned retreat as invocations of modern military maxims are in disproving its use. In short, is there any real reason to believe the chroniclers who tell of the feigned retreat? Is there any reason to conclude that William or his followers knew of the feigned retreat tactic and could be expected to execute it? Though the steppes of southern Russia are far indeed from the west of France, even Lemmon admits that Norman horsemen used the feigned retreat tactic on at least two occasions previous to the Battle of Hastings. Normans apparently executed a feigned retreat at Arques (Normandy) in 1053 and at Messina in 1060. The commander at Arques, Walter Giffard, served at Hastings as did a number of knights who had fought in the Sicilian campaigns.[11]

It may be argued that two such examples of the feigned retreat in less than a decade (three in thirteen years if Hastings is counted) were lies to cover up real retreats or aberrant actions with little or no relation to events at Hastings.[12] Such arguments,

9   Gregory of Tours, *Historiarum libri X*, ix, 31 (eds B. Krusch and W. Levision; *MGH: Scr. rer. merov.*, I, 1 [2nd edn Hannover, 1937–51]) and Agathias II, 6. A detailed discussion of Byzantine tactics is given by Oman, *Art of War*, I, 205 ff. He gives special attention to Leo's advocacy of the feigned retreat tactic. Lemmon, 'Campaign of 1066,' 109, rejects the feigned retreat as a 'recognized tactical operation in ancient warfare . . .' He does this partly 'In view of the disbelief with which a "retreat according to plan" in an enemy communiqué during the last wars was received . . .' and he concludes, 'would it not be more correct to say that a "feigned retreat" was the recognized method by which chroniclers concealed the fact that troops on their own side ran away?' Such presentism is worse than dubious historical method, it is absurd. Gregory of Tours, *op. cit.*, hated the Visigoths whom he describes as using the feigned retreat effectively. Both Regino and Liutprand (*op. cit.*) describe enemy forces using the feigned retreat successfully, and Leo the Wise advocates its use as a military tactic for his own forces. R.C. Smail, *Crusading Warfare 1097–1193* (Cambridge, 1956), 78–80 notes the use of the feigned retreat by both crusaders and their enemies.
10   Stenton, *Anglo-Saxon England*, 587 and Douglas, *William the Conqueror*, 203–04.
11   Lemmon, 'Campaign of 1066,' 109; cf. D.P. Waley, 'Combined Operations in Sicily A.D. 1060–1078,' *Papers of the British School of Rome*, 22 (1954), 123–24.
12   Lemmon, 'Campaign of 1066,' 109.

however, ignore the fact that steppe influences permeated the military tactics of western France. The Alans, mentioned above, were a nomad people of the steppes, and a group of them had been settled by the Romans in Armorica. Alan influence on Armorican cavalry tactics dated from the fifth century and can be traced right up through the twelfth century. In the tenth century, for example, Regino of Prüm, in describing the cavalry tactics of the Magyars, who used the feigned retreat extensively, notes their great similarity to the tactics of the Bretons.[13] Count Alan of Brittany served under William at Hastings and in fact commanded the left wing of the Conqueror's forces.

In conclusion, the feigned retreat can be considered a well established part of the tactical repertoire in western France. It was part of the Alan heritage in Armorica before the Norman settlement in the tenth century, and the Normans with their usual hospitality to effective military innovations learned the tactic and used it at least three times, including Hastings, in little more than a decade. I find it impossible to reject the evidence of contemporary and near contemporary chroniclers who record the use of this tactic in the second retreat at Hastings and indeed I am inclined to speculate that the first retreat at Hastings, that by the Bretons which is usually considered to have been real, was also a feigned retreat.[14]

[13] For a detailed discussion of Alan influences in Armorica see my articles 'The Alans in Gaul,' *Traditio*, 23 (1967), 480–82, 484–89 and 'The Origin of Armorican Chivalry,' *Technology and Culture*, 10 (1969), 166–171. Armorica is used here in its early medieval sense *e.g.* the area between Orleans in the south and *Baie de la Seine* in the north and extending west through Brittany. For the similarity of Magyar and Breton tactics see Regino, an. 889.

[14] Geffrei Gaimar, *L'Estoire des Engleis*, ed. Alexander Bell (Oxford, 1960), lines 5309 ff., dwells upon the effective role played by Count Alan of Brittany at the Battle of Hastings. The first retreat was put to very good use by William, and by interpreting it as feigned, William of Poitiers' remark (II, 21): 'Twice the same trick was used . . .' is made more understandable.

17. R. Allen Brown, 'The Battle of Hastings'

Unlike Hume's brief account, Allen Brown's detailed retelling of the battle
pauses frequently to survey the historiographical as well as the historical
combatants who by now litter the field – Brown knows all the primary and
secondary sources. But he has a definite perspective: Brown stands in direct
line of descent from William of Poitiers and J.H. Round as a champion of the
Normans and particularly of the Norman heavy cavalry. He therefore answers
Glover's challenge to the orthodox position directly, reasserting the superiority
of Norman military techniques over those of Anglo-Saxon England, defending
the professionalism of the Norman knights, and polishing the heroic image of
Duke William to a high gloss. In its views on the battle, the Normans, heavy
cavalry, and feudalism, this article is a summation of Brown's career.

Reprinted from *Proceedings of the Battle Conference on Anglo-Norman Studies* 3 (1980),
1–21. Copyright © R. Allen Brown 1980, 1981.

THE BATTLE OF HASTINGS

R. Allen Brown

I had thought of beginning with an explanation of my temerity in presenting to this assembly a paper in which there is little new beyond what I wrote in my book some years ago,[1] but, finding myself, like the Normans in the generally accepted version of the battle, in grave difficulties in the Malfosse at the end thereof, I now know there is no time for any lengthy *apologia*. Suffice to say, therefore, that I thought we should have an account of Hastings on our agenda and in our *Proceedings*, for others to alter later if they wish or can, and that I was selfish enough to want to write it myself.[2]

There must be, however, an introduction which places the Battle of Hastings in a treble context. The broadest is the context of medieval military history, more specifically its neglect and, worse than neglect, the travesty which is generally made of it. Of course there are honourable exceptions,[3] but, neglected for the most part by serious historians, the subject tends to fall into the hands of antiquarians, amateurs and, not least, retired military gentlemen with whom an admittedly valuable military experience is no substitute for historical knowledge and scholarship. Such neglect is amazing, for war is one of the fundamentals of history and as such is far too important to be left to military historians as I have unhappily defined them. Michael Howard, on the first page of his *Franco-Prussian War*,[4] observed of the French defeat at Sedan in 1870 that it was 'the result not simply of a faulty command but of a faulty military system; and the military system of a nation is not an independent section of the social system but an aspect of it in its totality'. Yet while we are told often enough that feudal

---

[1] R. Allen Brown, *The Normans and the Norman Conquest*, London 1969.
[2] The principal modern accounts and discussions of the Battle of Hastings are those of E.A. Freeman, *The Norman Conquest*, iii, Oxford 1869, Chapter xv, 377–507 (Cf. J.H. Round, 'Mr Freeman and the Battle of Hastings', *Feudal England*, London 1909, 332–98); W. Spatz, *Die Schlacht von Hastings*, Berlin 1896; F.H. Baring, *Domesday Tables . . .*, London 1909, Appendix B, 217–32; H. Delbrück, *Geschichte der Kriegskunst im Rahmen des Politische Geschichte*, iii, Berlin 1923, 150ff; Sir Charles Oman, *A History of the Art of War in the Middle Ages*, 2nd edn, London 1924, 151–66; F. Lot, *L'art militaire et les armées au moyen âge en Europe et dans le proche Orient*, Paris 1946, i, 282–5; F.M. Stenton, *Anglo-Saxon England*, 2nd edn, Oxford 1947, 583–8; A.H. Burne, *The Battlefields of England*, London 1950, 19ff; Richard Glover, 'English Warfare in 1066', *EHR* lxvii, 1952; G.H. White, 'The Battle of Hastings and the Death of Harold', *Complete Peerage*, xii, London 1953, Pt. i, Appendix L; J.F.C. Fuller, *The decisive Battles of the Western World*, London 1954, i, 360ff; D.C. Douglas, *William the Conqueror*, London 1964, 194–204; C.H. Lemmon, 'The Campaign of 1066', in *The Norman Conquest, its setting and impact*, ed. D. Whitelock and others, London 1966; John Beeler, *Warfare in England 1066–1189*, Cornell U.P. 1966, 11–33; Brown, *Normans*, 158–76.
[3] One thinks especially, in this country, of the work of R.C. Smail, notably *Crusading Warfare*, Cambridge 1956; and, on the continent, of J.F. Verbruggen, especially his brilliant summary article, 'La tactique militaire des armées de chevaliers', *Revue du nord* xxix, 1947. Examples could and should be multiplied if this were a full bibliographical note.
[4] London 1960; Fontana paperback 1967.

society is society organized for war, there is no Michael Howard for the so-called Middle Ages. In his absence, what we know in London as the myth of medieval warfare, or more specifically of the feudal period, has become established and appears ineradicable. It is represented in English historical literature by Sir Charles Oman's *A History of the Art of War in the Middle Ages*,[5] which was first written as an undergraduate prize essay in 1884 and thereafter, expanded but only slightly ameliorated, went on to become the standard work which it has ever since remained. Moreover, the first, and worst, edition was quite recently reissued by the Cornell University Press,[6] without a word of warning (quite the reverse) to the student for whom it is intended. In that edition the young Oman wrote, amongst many other outrageous travesties of the truth, that while 'arrogance and stupidity combined to give a certain definite colour to the proceedings of the average feudal host', nevertheless 'a feudal force presented an assemblage of unsoldierlike qualities such as have seldom been known to coexist'.[7] I will not go on, but here is the myth of feudal warfare as disorganized and amateur chaos in all its unbelievable absurdity. Further it is not, of course, confined either to this country or to Oman, for the erudite works of Spatz[8] and Delbrück,[9] invariably cited in footnotes as authorities for Hastings, are little or no better in their conviction that contemporary warfare was, above all, lacking in discipline – a point to which we shall assuredly return.

The second context, with some apology, is feudalism and the origin of feudalism in this country. It is a sharp indication of the fundamental importance of military history properly understood and properly studied, that the 'military' question of whether Old English armies in the eleventh century used cavalry or not – which even Maitland thought only a matter of tactics as opposed to anything fundamental[10] – is basic to the larger question of the presence or absence of feudalism in England on the eve of the Norman Conquest. No cavalry, no knights, we may say; and no knights, no feudalism. Yet in the virtual absence of any serious study of military matters by serious historians, the old arguments seem never to be ended, and it is well-known that one of the few recent studies of 'English Warfare in 1066', by Richard Glover,[11] argues for the use of cavalry by Old English armies, though not at Hastings itself – and without, unless I am mistaken, ever seeing the profound social implications of what he was saying. To this we shall obviously have to return, albeit as briefly as possible. And, lastly, all this brings me to my third context of this or any study of the Battle of Hastings, for which I do not so much apologise as express my profound regret. I refer, of course, to that controversy, leading to or even based on prejudice, which still does vitiate the study of almost every aspect of the Norman Conquest of England, and not least, of course, any study of that most famous of victories on Saturday, 14 October 1066. Pots call kettles black and the disinterested pursuit of truth is lost in the fog of war and forgotten in the heat of battle. Freeman himself, for whom the defeat of clean-limbed Liberal Englishmen on that occasion was an agony to be explained away only by the foreign use of Dirty Tricks like horses and archery,

---

5 2nd edn, London 1924.
6 Ed. John H. Beeler, Ithaca, New York, 1953.
7 Ed. Beeler, 58.
8 *Die Schlacht von Hastings*.
9 *Geschichte der Kriegskunst*.
10 F.W. Maitland, *Domesday Book and Beyond*, Fontana paperback 1960, 363.
11 *EHR* lxvii, 1952.

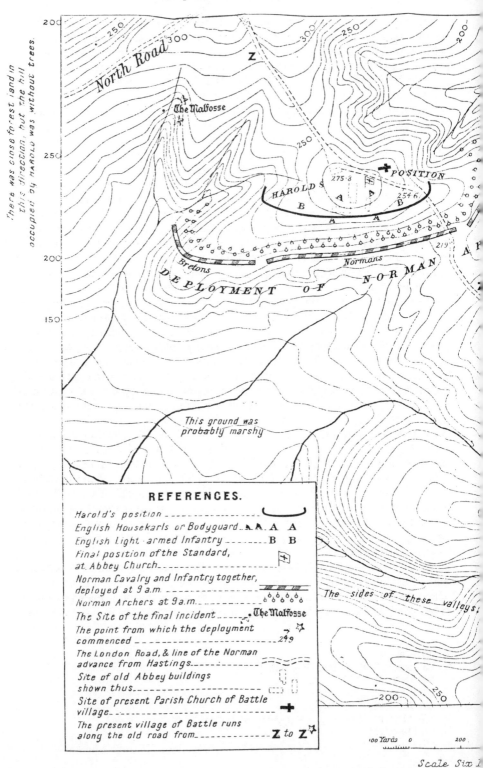

Map 1. Map of the Battle of Hastings by General E. Renouard James, from F. H. Baring, D

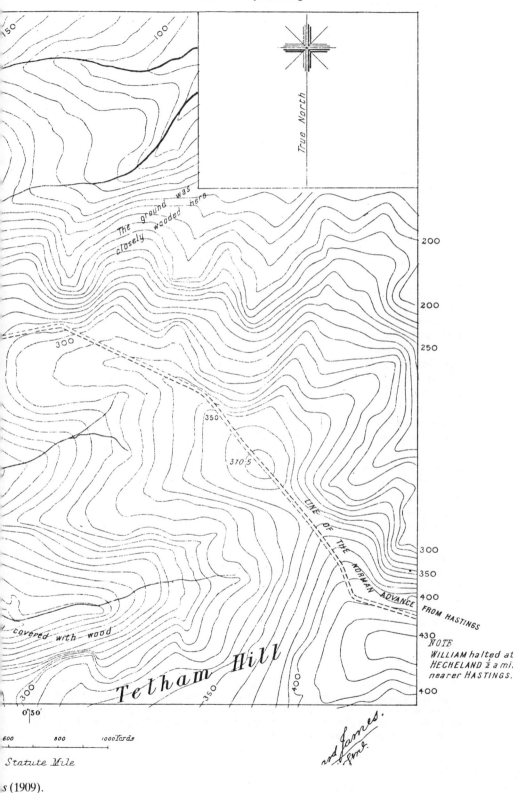

True North

150   100

The ground was closely wooded here

200

200

250

300

350

310·5

LINE OF THE NORMAN ADVANCE FROM HASTINGS

300

350

400

430

400

400

350

400

NOTE
WILLIAM halted at
HECHELAND ½ a mi.
nearer HASTINGS.

covered with wood

Telham Hill

300

150

0'|30'

600   800   1000 Yards

Statute Mile

would have stood in admiration at that latest study of the battle which comes as close as it is possible to get to making Hastings an English victory and attributes what little credit there is for the real victors to participants called the French and not the Normans.[12]

The context thus delineated, let us approach our actual subject with the observation that we probably have more information and potential knowledge about Hastings than any other medieval battle – appropriately, and fortunately, enough, since it is also one of the most decisive battles in Western history. This observation remains true, I hasten to add (lest I be thought out of date), even if R.H.C. Davis has successfully dismissed the *Song of the Battle of Hastings* from the canon of early or contemporary and acceptable texts for the study of the Norman Conquest[13] – as I am inclined to think that he has, though we shall in some respects miss it – and even if Eleanor Searle has dismissed the Conqueror's vow before the battle, to found an abbey on the site of his victory if God granted it, to the realm of monastic myth – as, again, I am much afraid she has.[14] For we are left with the long and detailed account of William of Poitiers, who had every qualification to write it save that of an eye-witness, including that of having first been a knight in the service of the duke before he became his chaplain. We have also the near-miraculous survival of the Bayeux Tapestry, more than one quarter of whose length is explicitly devoted to the battle and whose patron, it is now generally agreed, was Odo bishop of Bayeux, the Conqueror's half-brother and certainly present on the field.[15] To these two outstanding sources we add, of course, the briefer testimony of other contemporary and near-contemporary accounts in William of Jumièges, the Anglo-Saxon Chronicle and Florence of Worcester; and to these we add in turn, though with increasing scholarly caution, the accounts and traditions recorded in such later sources as William of Malmesbury, Henry of Huntingdon and even Wace (who may give us the correct number of ships in the Norman fleet[16]) – and here I would add also those local traditions which survive to be enshrined, for example, in the *Chronicle of Battle Abbey*, and indeed survive, alive and well, even today. Further, the mention of local tradition brings me to that other type of evidence, topographical, even archaeological, which we are so fortunate as to possess for the Battle of Hastings. We know the site of the engagement (Fig. 1): we know with an unusual degree of precision where it was fought, and thus, with the aid of the generous literary and artistic evidence, we have a good chance of knowing *how* it was fought also. The Normans like others in this period were adept at putting great buildings on difficult sites, as witness Mont St Michel, but such dramatic undertakings require a good reason, usually religious or military. If the Conqueror's vow before the battle to found his penitential abbey on the battlefield is now discredited, there remains no reason at all to disbelieve the tradition preserved at Battle of his eventual determination to build his church with

---

12 *Carmen*, especially Appendix B.

13 *EHR* xviii, 1978. Cf. *Proceedings of the Battle Conference on Anglo-Norman Studies* ii, 1979, 1–20.

14 *The Chronicle of Battle Abbey*, Oxford Medieval Texts, Oxford 1980, 17–23; *Proceedings of the Battle Conference* ii, 1979, 155–6.

15 I wish in this note to do public penance and make amends to bishop Odo. I do not believe he *fought* at Hastings, any more than did Geoffrey, bishop of Coutances. In the famous pl. 68 of the *BT* the mace he carries is not an offensive weapon but evidently the eleventh-century equivalent of the field marshal's baton (cf. pls 21, 55–6), and the garment he is wearing is not a hauberk (cf. pl. 21).

16 Wace, ll.6423–5. The number given is 696.

its high altar on the spot where Harold fell, and only this can satisfactorily explain its awkward architectural position, on a hill requiring artificial levelling, and without water. The first monks from Marmoutier and the lush valleys of the Loire were appalled when they initially surveyed the site, and promptly chose a better one, north-west of the present abbey, which was still marked in the 1180s. The king when he heard of this was exceeding wrath, and sweeping aside all difficulties 'ordered them to lay the foundations of the church speedily and on the very spot where his enemy had fallen and the victory been won ... And so at length, the foundations were laid of what was in those days thought an outstanding building, and they prudently erected the high altar as the king had commanded, on the very place where Harold's emblem, which they call a "standard" [*sic*], was seen to have fallen'.[17] (Which spot, incidentally, according to the chronicle, had been carefully marked at the end of the battle.[18])

All save the very narrowest military historian of the old school would accept that military history must deal with something more than battles, and that at least the preparations leading up to them and the campaigns of which they form a part must be included. Certainly we must spend some time on the process of bringing our contenders together on the battlefield and the preliminaries of the battle, for several important matters arise therefrom. I must unfortunately pass over briefly the impressive preparations in Normandy, many of which are graphically portrayed upon the Bayeux Tapestry and all of which illuminate Norman military might and the quality of the Conqueror's leadership.[19] They began at once on the speedy receipt of the news of Edward's death and Harold's coronation, and included a series of great councils, the building of a fleet and the assembly of an army including many volunteers from overseas (if we now exclude the *Carmen* from the canon we must also exclude Normans from southern Italy, who always were unlikely), the maintenance of that great force in good order through more than six weeks of weary waiting, first at Dives-sur-Mer and then at St Valery-sur-Somme.[20] They also included a veritable diplomatic offensive, to which for whatever reason Harold made no answer, and which obtained the support both of the Papacy and, so to speak, of the public opinion of most of Latin Christendom for the Norman cause. When at last the Conqueror got the wind we are told he prayed for, the rapid and ordered embarkation of the Norman army must also be admired, and so, of course, must be the transportation of the horses across the Channel. There is also one other point that I would add. Because, owing to the nature of our sources, events may often seem to happen in the so-called Middle Ages out of the blue without explanation, it is silly to suppose that they did so in reality; and so here it really will not do to suppose that on the evening tide of 27 September 1066 the Conqueror set sail in the general direction of England without knowing where exactly he was going. Hypothesis is as dangerous as it is unavoidable in any account of the whole business of the Norman Conquest, but it is surely reasonable to suppose that duke William, after such careful preparations on such a scale as this, made his landfall at Pevensey the next morning also according to plan.

---

[17] *Battle Chronicle*, 44, 45.

[18] *Battle Chronicle*, 40.

[19] For the sources and some commentary upon what follows, see Brown, *Normans*, 145ff.

[20] In a private discussion after this paper had been read, Dr Marjorie Chibnall suggested to the writer that the long delay of the invasion force may even have been at least in part a deliberate feint by William to confuse his adversary.

And in this connection I would call attention to a searching paper given by A.J. Taylor at the Château-Gaillard Conference at Battle in 1966, suggesting that both Pevensey, which the Normans first occupied, and Hastings, to which they soon afterwards repaired as a better base, were Old English boroughs in 1066.[21] At both places, of course, they raised castles – but we have quite enough to discuss in this paper without involving ourselves in that other quasi-military controversy, *viz* the origin of castles in England, equally significant though it is for the nature of society.

On the English side of the Channel there are three points concerning Harold's preparations that seem to me to require emphasis, and also further investigation. First, that the logistical problems, if anything on a lesser scale than those which duke William triumphantly overcame, proved too much for him. Harold had first mobilized his forces in May against the renegade Tostig, and thereafter kept them in the south-east against the expected invasion from Normandy throughout the summer, the fleet with the king himself off the Isle of Wight and the fyrd 'everywhere along by the sea'. But, says the 'C' version of the Chronicle, 'in the end it was no use. When it was the Feast of the Nativity of St Mary (8 September), the provisions of the people were gone, and nobody could keep them there any longer'.[22] In short, the army had to be dismissed and the ships sent back to London (with losses on the way). The potentially disastrous incident calls out for explanation from Anglo-Saxon military historians, and must throw light on the Old English military organization and its efficacy in the situation it had to face in 1066. My second point to call for emphasis and investigation is the striking ease with which Old English leaders, not only the king, are able to raise fleets in this period, whether it be, for example, Tostig in 1066 or the Godwinsons in 1052. On the broadest interpretation, I should like to think this reflects the essentially Anglo-Scandinavian nature of our Old English society, but, if so, it throws into sharper contrast the situation in Normandy, the land after all of the Norsemen, where a fleet – or at least a suitable fleet – had to be constructed for the invasion. Perhaps in feudal society, with its emphasis upon horses, knight service and chivalry, navies were taken less seriously. Third and last, it has always seemed to me amazing that Harold should have had no foreknowledge or expectation of Harold Hardrada's impending invasion from Norway; yet all military preparations of his own that we hear of are in the south-east against Normandy, and the 'C' version says specifically that 'Harold, king of Norway, came *by surprise* north into the Tyne', the English king being informed at the very moment of disembarking at London from his fleet returned from the Isle of Wight.[23]

Harold's dramatic reaction to the news of the Norwegian landing, compounded as it soon was by the defeat of the northern earls Edwin and Morcar at Gate Fulford on 20 September, is well known – his assembly of an army, his great and impressively rapid march north, his muster of his forces at Tadcaster on 24 September. Then on the morning of the 25th he 'went right on through York' to take Harold Hardrada, now with his ally Tostig, 'by surprise' at Stamford Bridge and win a great victory.[24] One would ideally like to know how these things were done precisely, in terms of the raising of troops, and of what kind, and of their movement; but again there are three

---

[21] 'Evidence for a pre-Conquest origin for the chapels in Hastings and Pevensey castles', *Château-Gaillard, European Castle Studies* iii, 1966, London 1969, 144–51.
[22] *ASC*, 142.
[23] *ASC*, 142, 143.
[24] *ASC*, 'C', 143–4; Brown, *Normans*, 156–7.

points for us of particular relevance to the subsequent engagement at Hastings. The first is Richard Glover's recent resurrection of the credibility of Snorri Sturluson, whose *Heimskringla* contains the only detailed account of the battle, as evidence for the Old English use of cavalry at it.[25] Glover, of course, does not seek to argue for the use of cavalry by Harold at Hastings, which in the light of the abundant evidence to the contrary would be impossible; but in a somewhat unnecessary defence of Old English armies against their detractors who are nowadays few if any, he seeks to show that they could use cavalry when they wished but did not so wish at Hastings because it was for them a defensive action. The latter proposition is merely a misguided hypothesis, and the former, dependent exclusively upon Snorri Sturluson's thirteenth-century account of Stamford Bridge of demonstrable unreliability, is simply unacceptable. There is more than sufficient contemporary evidence to show that Old English armies habitually fought on foot, and so did their time-honoured opponents, the Danes and the Norse.[26] In this at least Freeman was right, and Stamford Bridge was the last major battle fought on English soil in the ancient manner, hand to hand and axe to axe.[27] Our next point must be that of course the engagements of Gate Fulford and Stamford Bridge, fought within a week of each other (20 and 25 September) must have seriously affected Harold's strength at Hastings three weeks later. And the third point is that Harold's brilliant success at Stamford Bridge and the manner of it – the rapidity of movement, the thundering march north (190 miles from London to York) and the taking of the Norwegians by surprise – surely determined his conduct of his next and immediate campaign against the Normans. Of that I wrote in my book of 'reckless and impulsive haste'[28] and I think I still stand by it, though the qualification should be added that the ravaging by duke William of Sussex, the very patrimony of the house of Godwin, would, according to contemporary notions of honour, demand immediate retaliation to demonstrate and defend one's lordship. Nevertheless, in terms of military appreciation, we are also surely right to see in Harold's movements before Hastings the intention to repeat the strategy and tactics which had given him such success at Stamford Bridge. Within two weeks or thirteen days at most from his receipt of the news of William's landing (on or soon after 1 October and traditionally at York) he had repeated his great march, this time in the reverse direction from York to London, delayed in the later city for what was clearly the minimum time to make his final preparations and raise more troops, and made another forced march over the fifty-seven miles from London to Battle to engage his enemy.[29] William of Jumièges and William of Poitiers followed by Orderic Vitalis all state that Harold's intention was to take William by surprise, the last two adding even the possibility of a night attack.[30]

In the event it was not to be, but before we proceed to duke William's counter measures it may surely be urged that all this precipitate speed was as unwise as it was unsuccessful. For time, like the homeland, was on Harold's side and ran against the

---

[25] Glover, *EHR* lxvii.

[26] R. Allen Brown, *The Origins of English Feudalism*, London 1973, 34–43; *Normans*, 94–8.

[27] Freeman, *Norman Conquest*, ii, 2nd edn, London 1870, 126–7. 'Shield-wall to shield-wall, sword to sword or axe to axe, had men waged the long warfare which had ranged from the fight of Reading to the fight of Assandun.'

[28] *Normans*, 158.

[29] *Normans*, 158–60.

[30] Jumièges, 134; *Gesta Guillelmi*, 180; Orderic, ii, 172.

Norman duke, at the end of a long and hazardous line of communications across the Channel (Poitiers followed by Orderic – and the *Carmen* for what it is worth – say that Harold sent a fleet to cut off the Normans[31]), in an alien country, and not even knowing at first who his opponent would be, Harold or Harold Hardrada. And certainly Harold's haste brought material disadvantages: fatigue must have been amongst them, though I know of no contemporary source to say so, and lack of numbers on the scale he might have had is another. For that, the 'E' version of the Chronicle explicitly states that the king fought William 'before all the army had come',[32] and Florence of Worcester is both more emphatic and more detailed. Commenting on Harold's haste, he writes 'and although he knew very well that some of the bravest men in all England had fallen in the two battles [i.e. Fulford and Stamford Bridge], and that half his army was not yet assembled, yet he did not hesitate to meet his enemy in Sussex as quickly as he could, and nine miles from Hastings he gave them battle, before a third of his army was drawn up'.[33] On the second of those two seemingly cumulative statements by Florence we shall have occasion to comment again in a moment, but meanwhile there seems a case here for bad generalship for anyone who wants to take it up.

Although according to the Oman myth of medieval warfare reconnaissance was seldom if ever practised by commanders in the feudal period, it is clear that duke William at Hastings, unlike Harold Hardrada at Stamford Bridge, learnt of Harold's approach in ample time to prepare his counter measures and put them into practice. Further, while the night before the battle is not explicitly mentioned by William of Poitiers, it is quite clear from his account supplemented by William of Jumièges that the news was received the day before the battle, i.e. on Friday, 13 October. In Poitiers the mounted patrols return to report Harold's rapid advance while the greater part of the Norman army is out foraging,[34] while in Jumièges the duke orders his army to stand to arms from dusk to dawn in case of a night attack, and at day-break moves off in the known direction of the enemy.[35] From Hedgland on Telham Hill, according to the local tradition in the Battle Chronicle,[36] the scouts of the advancing Norman army first saw the English on the Battle ridge two miles away, and the battle itself began at 'the third hour' or 9 a.m. according to Poitiers, Jumièges and Florence of Worcester.[37] From Hastings to Battle there are some seven miles to be covered by foot as well as horse. The decisive speed of all this is impressive enough as it is: clearly we cannot envisage the report of the English approach being received that morning as well, as has sometimes been maintained,[38] and to the accumulated evidence and argument we may cautiously add the later traditions (most memorably written up, of course, by Wace) of how the two armies passed the night before the battle, the Normans in prayer and the English in whooping it up.[39] No contemporary

---

31 *Gesta Guillelmi*, 180; Orderic, ii, 172; *Carmen*, ll.319–20.
32 *ASC*, 141.
33 Worcester, i, 227.
34 *Gesta Guillelmi*, 180.
35 Jumièges, 135.
36 Ed. Eleanor Searle, 15, 36; Baring, *Domesday Tables*, 225–6.
37 *Gesta Guillelmi*, 186–8, 208; Jumièges, 135; Worcester, i, 227. One should perhaps add Freeman's comment here (*Norman Conquest*, ii, 1969, 477 n.2), 'I cannot help noticing the tendency to make the hours of the battles and of other great events coincide with the hours of the Church'.
38 E.g. Morton and Munz in *Carmen*, 74, 76–7.
39 E.g. *De Gestis regum* ii 302; Wace, ll.7323 *et seq.*

source in fact gives us any details of how Harold spent the night before his last engagement, but though William of Jumièges has him marching through the night to appear on the battlefield in the morning,[40] he must surely have rested his troops, presumably not far from the modern Battle and its ridge, from which he evidently first saw the Norman host advancing[41] and upon which he then arrayed his troops. If this reconstruction of events be accepted, two points follow. The first is that far from succumbing to a surprise attack, William (by good reconnaissance) turned the tables upon Harold, seized the initiative, and took his opponent by surprise; and the second is that Harold cannot possibly have selected the place of battle well in advance, as Freeman insisted and others have since suggested.[42] The one version of the Anglo-Saxon Chronicle which is contemporary explicitly states that 'William came against him [Harold] by surprise before his army was drawn up in battle array',[43] and Florence, as we have seen, has Harold engage the Normans 'before a third of his army was drawn up'.[44] If, as thus seems certain, Harold lost the initiative and was constrained to fight at that place and time by William's advance from Hastings, then all the more credit to him for selecting on the spur of the moment a site so admirably suited to the defensive tactics which alone he could offer – but yet it was not perfect. There was no way of withdrawal save the narrow isthmus which is now Battle High Street and along which he had come, while the space on the ridge was so confined that according to Florence many deserted before the action began.[45] Finally, in view of what has been written one should at least suggest that, far from 'supine loitering' on the Sussex coast (the phrase is Richard Glover's[46]) the Norman duke, since his landing at Pevensey, had achieved one of the most difficult strategic intentions, of drawing his opponent to give him the decisive action which he wanted, and that as soon as possible and without leaving his beach-head and his fleet. In this the ravaging of the countryside about Pevensey and Hastings, which William of Poitiers cites as one reason for Harold's haste,[47] may well have been a deliberate and calculated provocation – as may indeed have been the landing in Sussex in the first place.[48]

If the *Carmen de Hastingae Proelio* is to be dismissed, then we are confined for detailed contemporary information about the Battle of Hastings itself to William of

[40] Jumièges, 134.

[41] *BT*, pl. 58.

[42] Freeman, iii, 1869, 438ff; C.H. Lemmon, 'The Campaign of 1066' in *The Norman Conquest . . .*, 79–122; Morton and Munz, *Carmen*, 76 n. 3.

[43] *ASC*, 'D', 143.

[44] Worcester, i, 227.

[45] Worcester, i, 227. For desertions see also *De gestis regum*, i, 281–2, ii, 300; Brown, *Normans*, 161; and *ASC*, 'D', 143 ('the king nevertheless fought hard . . . with the men who were willing to support him').

[46] *EHR* lxvii, 2–4.

[47] *Gesta Guillelmi*, 180.

[48] Cf. Freeman, iii, 411–12; D.C. Douglas, *William the Conqueror*, 197. Intentional provocation was accepted by Spatz (*Hastings*, 23, 25) but rejected by Delbrück (*Kriegskunst*, iii, 160). The concentration of Harold's patrimony, *i.e.* the lands of the house of Godwin, in Sussex, however, as shown by Dr Williams (Ann Williams, 'Land and Power in the eleventh century: the estates of Harold Godwinson', *Proceedings of the Battle Conference* 3 (1980), pp. 176–7, 185–6), gives a new dimension to this hypothesis of the Conqueror's strategy, for what was at issue in contemporary terms was very much more than the modern and anachronistic concept of the defence of subjects by the king. One wonders, indeed, if William's first intention was to cross from Dives-sur-Mer to Bosham, the eventual crossing from St Valéry to Pevensey (where there were also Godwinson lands) being later substituted.

Poitiers and the Bayeux Tapestry. Generous as both sources are, hypothesis is inevitable, but it must be informed by a knowledge of the warfare of the period. Later sources must be used with discretion since tradition and even myth soon gather about so famous and even elegiac an occasion. Something of a modern consensus puts the numbers of each army at some 7000 men.[49] On the English side one assumes this number to have been made up of the quasi-professional housecarls[50] of the king and of the households of his brothers and other great lords, well-armed thegns (if the distinction be allowed) who had ridden with Harold from London or even from York or come in since, together with less well-armed levies from neighbouring shires. The élite of housecarls is not mentioned specifically, *eo nomine*, in any contemporary source, though the two-handed battle-axe, their weapon *par excellence*, is much in evidence in the account (it is *hache norresche* in Wace and *haches danesches* in Benoit de Sainte-More[51]). William of Malmesbury seems to vouch for their predominance when he states[52] that Harold had with him mostly stipendiary troops (*stipendiarios et mercenarios milites*) and comparatively few from the provinces (*ex provincialibus*) i.e. the local levies, *vulgariter dicitur* 'fyrd', and it seems to me that in this connection more attention than is usual should be paid to William of Poitiers' unique remark that abundant help (*copiosa auxilia*) had been sent to the English from their kith and kin in Denmark.[53] The king planted his standard and took up his own position thereby on the highest point of the ridge, where the high altar of the abbey church was later to be placed.[54] According to William of Malmesbury his two brothers were with him there,[55] but since Gyrth and Leofwine were killed early in the battle[56] and long before Harold they were presumably in a different part of the line, and presumably with their own contingents – which in turn may be further reason to suppose that the housecarls were disposed along the entire English front and not massed in the centre as some commentators have argued.[57] The English position comprised the whole crest of the ridge facing south towards the Normans and extending for some 600–800 yards, i.e. 400 yards to the west or right of the king and standard, where the ground falls steeply away, and 200–400 yards to the east or left, where it ended roughly opposite the present 'Chequers' inn or somewhere between the junction of the Hastings and Sedlescombe roads and the school on the latter.[58] (Fig. 1) The entire English host, from the king downward, were dismounted to fight on foot. Of this there is not a shadow of doubt and all sources, contemporary and later, are agreed[59] – though one may and should add that this fact only makes it

---

49   Brown, *Normans*, 150 n. 47.
50   I shall continue to use the term until such time as Mr Nicholas Hooper of King's College, London, currently working on pre-Conquest English warfare, tells us what we should mean by it.
51   Wace, l.8257; *Chroniques Anglo-Normandes*, ed. F. Michel, i, Rouen 1836, 201.
52   *De gestis regum*, i, 282.
53   *Gesta Guillelmi*, 186. Cf. Sten Körner, *The Battle of Hastings, England, and Europe 1035–1066*, Bibliotheca Historica Lundensii xiv, Lund 1964, 220.
54   Above, p. 200.
55   *De gestis regum*, ii, 302. 'Rex ipse pedes juxta vexillum stabat cum fratribus, ut, in commune periculo aequato, nemo de fuga cogitaret.'
56   *BT*, pls 64–5.
57   Thus Freeman, iii, 472–6; Spatz, 40–1; Fuller, *Decisive Battles*, 376. For Freeman's dispositions, cf., of course, J.H. Round, *Feudal England*, especially 359ff.
58   See Brown, *Normans*, 167 n. 127, and especially Baring, *Domesday Tables*, 217–20.
59   Thus William of Poitiers, *Gesta Guillelmi*, 186 – 'Protinus equorum ope relicta, cuncti pedites

extremely improbable that Old English armies ever fought in any other manner. To a complete absence of cavalry, it seems there has to be added a more surprising deficiency of archers[60] – because, one can only surmise, Harold's rapidity of movement eliminated most of those who had to march on foot. We do not know how many ranks composed the line, but we do know that they stood in very close order, so close, wrote William of Poitiers, that the dead could scarcely fall and the wounded could not remove themselves from the action.[61] This, then, was the famous formation of the 'shield-wall', the 'war-hedge' of the Song of Maldon,[62] though an element of poetic licence must be allowed it, for clearly the shields must part for the weapons to be wielded and the great two-handed battle-axe especially required space on either side (it also, as Wace pointed out, left the warrior raising it dangerously off his guard.[63] Doubtless we must assume experience, training and team-work, all of which are as necessary for the effective use of ancient hand weapons as they are for modern military technology).

Against this seemingly impregnable position, at the foot of the steep slope of the ridge, the Norman duke deployed his forces in three lines, archers and, less certainly, crossbow-men in front,[64] heavy infantry, some at least with mail coats, next, and the heavy cavalry of knights and esquires not, as is sometimes said, in reserve but in the rear, to deliver the hoped for *coup de grâce* of their irresistible shock charge.[65] Such are the dispositions listed by William of Poitiers.[66] In the absence of the *Carmen* we have to be less confident than heretofore on the three lateral divisions (i.e. each in the above formation) of Bretons on the left (west), Normans in the centre and French on the right (east), though Poitiers later refers to the Bretons being on the left, and has duke William in the centre of the knights – and thus we may assume with Norman contingents – where he could direct operations by voice and gesture.[67] The presence

constitere densus conglobati'. In the later sources the note of contempt by cavalry for flat-footed infantry already comes echoing across the ages – thus the *Carmen*, ll.369–70:

> Nescia gens belli solamina spernit equorum,
> Viribus et fidens, heret humo pedibus

and Wace, ll.8623–6

> 'Engleis ne saveient ioster,
> Ne a cheval armes porter,
> Haches e gisarmes teneient,
> Od tels armes se combateient

[60] Only one English archer is shown on the Tapestry (pl. 63), though it should be noted that in the song of Maldon 'bows were busy' (trans. in *EHD* i, 295).

[61] *Gesta Guillelmi*, 192, 194.

[62] *EHD* i, 294.

[63] Wace, ll.8627–30.

[64] The least ambiguous references to crossbows unfortunately occur in the *Carmen* (ll.337–8, 381–2, 411 and see Appendix C, 112–15). Cf. *Gesta Guillelmi*, 184 – 'Pedites in fronte locavit, sagittis armatos et balistis.' No crossbow is shown on the Tapestry.

[65] Cf. Burne, 28–9, 30–1; Fuller, 378–9; Lemmon, 106, 108.

[66] *Gesta Guillelmi*, 184.

[67] *Gesta Guillelmi*, 184 ('ipse [Guillelmus] fuit in medio [equitum] cum firmissimo robore, unde in omnem partem consuleret manu et voce'), 190 ('Britanni, et quot-quot auxiliares erant in sinistro cornu'). There were, however, also Normans on the right with the French, e.g. Robert de Beaumont and his contingent (192). Those modern commentators who place William in some rear 'headquarters' or 'command post' are obviously ignorant of the facts as well as of the spirit of the age and the man (Spatz, 67; Burne, 34; Fuller, 378–9; Lemmon, 104, 106).

of large numbers of well-armed infantry, who were given an important rôle to play, in the Norman army should remind us that Hastings was a battle of cavalry against infantry only in the sense that the English had no cavalry, not that the Normans had no infantry. It should also dispel another lingering Oman myth that infantry was despised by the commanders of the feudal period.[68] Nevertheless, the tactics of their enemy at Hastings were a source of some wonder to the hard-riding Norman and Frankish cavalry and their writers. 'It was,' wrote William of Poitiers, 'a strange kind of battle, one side attacking with all mobility, the other withstanding, as though rooted to the soil.'[69]

At Hastings, however, the battle having opened with a terrible sound of trumpets on both sides, the Norman infantry went in first until, having achieved no marked success, they were followed by the knights, spurring their horses up the hill. And thus, writes William of Poitiers, the last became first. Again, there was no success, which failure Poitiers carefully explains by the superiority of the English position on the hill-top, their dense ranks and close order, and the effectiveness of their arms (presumably their axes), which could easily cleave both shield and armour (presumably hauberk).[70] At this point in his narrative Poitiers proceeds to the first and real retreat of the Norman forces and the first climax of the battle.

But at this point we must pause to consider the true use and tactics of the Norman heavy cavalry of knights at Hastings – or indeed of Frankish chivalry anywhere else in this age – in the light of Richard Glover's tendentious remarks.[71] Seeking, as we have noted, to upgrade the Old English military capacity, and thus seeking to show that they could use cavalry when they wished, he turns, in the most unforgivable section of his monograph, to denigrate the Norman, so to achieve, by levelling up on the one hand and levelling down on the other, a kind of double equality. In any case, runs his argument, there was nothing to the Norman use of cavalry in this period, anyone could do it; and he goes on to speak of 'infantile' Norman cavalry tactics, and of Norman knights at Hastings as mere 'mounted javelineers' while citing yet others without horses as 'happily mixing it in on foot'. All this is said to be based on the evidence of the Bayeux Tapestry, but, to dismiss the last allegation first, I can find only one or two [*sic*] candidates for dismounted knights on the Tapestry[72] and they and any others there may have been in a similar predicament are likely to have had their horses killed under them (and to have been thus anything but happy) – as duke William had three horses killed under him that day according to William of Poitiers.[73] As for the infantile cavalry tactics, one must read above all D.J.A. Ross on these matters.[74] While we have the unimpeachable testimony of Ordericus Vitalis for the throwing of spears from the saddle as a knightly skill to be practised,[75] it was obviously not very effective in battle and it is accordingly very difficult indeed to find certain instances of it in the Bayeux

---

68 Oman, ed. Beeler, 63–4.
69 *Gesta Guillelmi*, 194.
70 *Gesta Guillelmi*, 186–8.
71 'English Warfare in 1066', *EHR* lxvii, 1952.
72 *BT*, pls 70–1.
73 *Gesta Guillelmi*, 198.
74 'L'originalité de "Turoldus": le maniement de lance', *Cahiers de civilisation médiévale* vi, 1963.
75 Orderic, ii, 30. Cf., perhaps, 132.

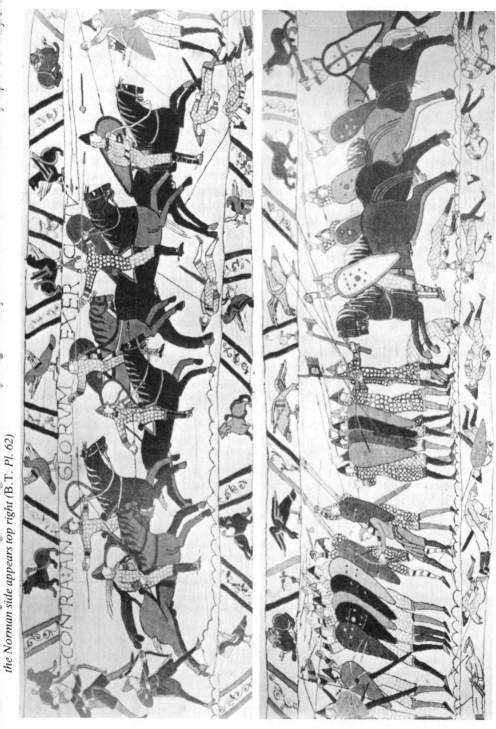

the Norman side appears top right (B.T. Pl. 62)

Plate 2 Norman knights at Hastings: the lance used overarm (B.T. Pl. 63)

Tapestry's depiction of Hastings.[76] Those many knights on the Tapestry apparently brandishing their lances above their heads, and whom Mr Glover assumes to be about to throw them, are in fact about to strike over-arm in the manner most likely against infantry,[77] the two methods of using the lance on horseback inherited from antiquity being the overarm and underarm[78] thrust (Pl. 1, 2). Already at this date, however, what is to be the classic medieval usage of the couched lance was being developed, whereby with a heavier lance, no longer a spear, locked under the rider's arm, the whole momentum of horse and armoured horseman is concentrated in the point, to make possible the shock tactic of the charge. This is what Anna Comnena had in mind when she wrote of the Frankish chivalry of the time of the First Crusade that the charging knight would pierce the walls of Babylon.[79] Some of the Norman knights depicted on the Tapestry are quite clearly couching their lances,[80] (Pl. 3) and the fact is all the more remarkable in that the new tactic was developed on the Continent for the unhorsing of horsed opponents of whom there were none at Hastings. All the relevant evidence of the Tapestry, properly understood, points in the same direction, *viz* of the Norman chivalry in the van of the new developments: the heavier lances in some cases clearly shown,[81] the gonfanons on lances which are obviously not meant therefore to be thrown away,[82] the built-up saddle-bows to hold the rider in his seat at the shock of contact, and the very long stirrup leathers to afford the same security.[83] In the literary sources, including William of Poitiers, it is true that the *arme blanche* of the sword is more prominent than the lance, but this is presumably because the latter was liable to break at the first contact (thereafter to be renewed), and it is significant that in Poitiers' account of Hastings William the Conqueror is found at the end of the battle with the stump of a broken lance in his hand.[84]

To revert to the progress of the battle as recounted in the narrative of William of Poitiers,[85] after the failure of the initial hard-pressed assaults to make any significant impression on the English line, the Bretons and other auxiliaries on the Norman left, both horse and foot, began to fall back. The movement spread as such movements will, fanned by an ugly rumour that the duke was dead – though this alone, Poitiers assures us, could have caused the Normans themselves to yield. Some of the English forces, with or without orders,[86] began to advance down the hill in pursuit – and we reach one of the two best known incidents in the battle, dramatically depicted on the Tapestry,[87] as the duke himself stops the rot. Galloping in front of his retreating

---

[76] The only certain instance I can find, i.e. of a lance or spear detached from any (Norman) hand and going in the right direction, occurs in Pl. 62. Cf. perhaps, 64. The circumstance of the attack on the castle of Dinan (pl. 25) is, of course, different.

[77] E.g. pl. 63, 64, 65.

[78] E.g. pl. 62.

[79] *The Alexiad of Anna Comnena*, ed. and trans. E.R.A. Sewter, Harmondsworth 1969, 416.

[80] E.g. pls 62, 65, 67.

[81] E.g. pl. 55.

[82] E.g. pls 55, 59, 60, 61.

[83] Pls 12, 53 and *passim*.

[84] *Gesta Guillelmi*, 202.

[85] *Gesta Guillelmi*, 188–90.

[86] It is generally assumed that they broke orders in advancing, though it is only Wace who makes Harold specifically order his forces to stand firm no matter what (ll.7757 *et seq*).

[87] Pl. 68.

*Plate 3 Norman knights at Hastings: the lance couched and the overarm thrust (*B.T. Pl. 65)

Plate 4 Pl. 67 from the Bayeux Tapestry, *with the caption 'Hic ceciderunt simul Angli et Franci in prelio'*

troops, 'shouting and brandishing his lance', he lifted his helmet to reveal himself and harangued the faint-hearted, 'Look at me. I am alive, and, by God's help, I shall win. What madness puts you to flight . . .' etc. On the Tapestry count Eustace of Boulogne on the right points to the living, gesticulating duke (who in this scene bears a mace) while on the left bishop Odo, also with a mace '*comfortat pueros*', i.e. turns back the young men, the *tirones*, the esquires, who are about to ride off the field.[88] The duke himself, sword in hand, then led a counter attack and the Normans, en-flamed, surrounded and cut down those who had pursued them down the hill.

After this crisis the general assault upon the English position was renewed by the knights especially, any breaches made being followed up by the men of Maine and Aquitaine, the French and the Bretons, 'but above all by the Normans with a courage beyond compare'. Thus William of Poitiers,[89] who goes on to praise the exploits in particular of the young lordling or *tiro*, Robert, the son of Roger de Beaumont, who in this his first battle particularly distinguished himself at the head of his contingent over on the right wing. But, Poitiers continues, 'the Normans and their allies, realiz-ing that they could not overcome an enemy so numerous and standing so firm without great loss to themselves, retreated, deliberately feigning flight' – *terga dederunt, fugam ex industria simulantes* – remembering what success had attended their counter-attack upon the pursuing English after the recent real retreat.[90] And so we reach the second of the best-known incidents of the battle, the feigned flight, accord-ing to William of Poitiers twice repeated, and very well attested by all the principal sources for Hastings, contemporary and later, save only, perhaps, the Bayeux Tapestry, whose medium scarcely lent itself to its depiction.[91] Further, the attested manoeuvre was triumphantly successful, so much so that William of Malmesbury, the historian, in his *Gesta Regum* (*c*.1125) presented it in his account as the turning point of the battle and the chief reason for the eventual Norman victory.[92] Each time numbers of English were tempted to break ranks and drawn down from the ridge in pursuit, to be cut down as the knights wheeled their horses (*regiratis equis*[93]). Yet most modern commentators and *soi-disant* military historians have doubted the feigned flight to the point of its rejection.[94] For this they have no reason whatever save the persistent and persisting myth of Oman and others to which I have so often, and necessarily, referred. The feigned flight, so the argument runs, cannot have happened because it could not have happened; and it could not have happened because it would have required to a high degree discipline and training which feudal armies, and most especially the exhibitionist knights who formed them, notoriously did not possess. The truth is, of course, that our Frankish knights and Norman knights were as professional as the age could make them, born and bred to war and trained from early youth, in the household which is the contingent of a lord, in the art and science of horsemanship and arms. Not only do we have entirely acceptable, one might almost say overwhelming, evidence for the tactic of the feigned flight em-

---

88 Cf. n. 15 above.
89 *Gesta Guillelmi*, 192.
90 *Gesta Guillelmi*, 194.
91 For the possibility that *BT* pls 66–7 represent this incident, see p. 217 below.
92 *De gestis regum*, ii, 302, 303.
93 *Gesta Guillelmi*, 194.
94 Thus Spatz, 55ff, 61–2, 67; cf. Delbrück, 165; Burne, 31, 42–3; Lemmon, 108–10; Beeler, 21–2. Fuller (380) is an honourable exception in this company.

ployed at Hastings, but we also have further evidence of its practice on other occasions by other knights of this generation – by the Normans at St Aubin-le-Cauf near Arques in 1052–53 and near Messina in 1060, and by Robert le Frison of Flanders at Cassel in 1071.[95] If this is not enough, then we can find much earlier references to the manoeuvre, which was thus evidently a well-known *ruse de guerre*, in e.g. Nithard under the year 842, over two-hundred years before Hastings, and in Dudo of St Quentin writing in the first decades of the eleventh century.[96] Clearly of all the arguments which surround the Norman Conquest and Hastings, this one at least must stop. If some military writers, blind in the arrogance of their ignorance, still demur, the key to understanding the feigned flight in practice is the *conroi*,[97] the comparatively small unit of the feudal host, presumably to be identified with the contingents and military households of individual lords, each marked out by the *gonfanon* of its leader. Such units, trained together over long, arduous years, and bound by the companionship of expertise, had ample discipline and the capacity not only to work and fight together but also to combine with other similar units. One need not, if one does not wish to, envisage the entire Norman cavalry at Hastings, or even very large sections of it, executing the feigned flight *en masse* – though personally I would not put it past them.

Still those many of the English who were left stood firm, 'still a formidable force and extremely difficult to surround'. Thus William of Poitiers,[98] and the last words are significant as presumably indicating that no part of the ridge had yet been taken. There follows, as the English at last seem to begin to weaken, what in the event becomes the final Norman all-out assault with horse and foot. Poitiers' prose rises to the occasion as in his poetic onomatopoeia one can almost hear the shock and thud of battle – *sagittant, feriunt, perfodiunt Normanni. Sagittant* is perhaps important here as a possible source for the later tradition of arrows shot on a high trajectory at this stage in the battle. It is not otherwise mentioned by Poitiers and appears first in Henry of Huntingdon to be worked up by Wace, which means its credentials are not very good.[99] And so we approach the final scenes of the battle, admittedly blurred, as the fog of war descends and the autumnal daylight wanes, as king Harold is slain and the English at length give way. It seems appropriate to quote William of Poitiers,[100] in the absence of the *Carmen* the nearest of our sources to the events he describes. Again he achieves a poetic and this time elegiac note in a paragraph admirably beginning *Jam inclinato die* . . . 'Now as the day declined the English

---

[95] Jumièges, 120; D.P. Waley, 'Combined operations in Sicily, AD 1060–1078'. *Papers of the British School at Rome* xxii, 123; A. Fliche, *Le règne de Philippe I, roi de France* Paris 1912, 258–9.

[96] *Histoire des fils de Louis le Pieux*, ed. P. Laver, Classiques de l'Histoire de France au Moyen Age, Paris 1964, 110–12; *De moribus et actis primorum Normanniae ducum*, ed. J. Lair. Soc. des Antiquaires de Normandie, Caen 1865, 143. In Nithard the two sides at a kind of review or tattoo before Charles the Bald and Louis the German are evidently on foot in spite of current published translations. I owe the first reference to my son G.P.A Brown and the second to Professor Eleanor Searle. One suspects that others could be found if looked for.

[97] Here, therefore, cf. Delbrück, 165 and Stenton, p. 587. In general, see J.F. Verbruggen, 'La tactique militaire des armées de chevaliers', *Revue du Nord* xxix, 1947.

[98] *Gesta Guillelmi*, 194.

[99] Huntingdon, 203; Wace, ll.8139 *et seq.* It should perhaps be mentioned that some of the archers in the lower border of the Tapestry hereabouts (pls 70–1) are apparently shooting high. This is very slender evidence but might conceivably be the source of a legend.

[100] *Gesta Guillelmi*, 200–2.

army realized beyond doubt that they could no longer stand against the Normans. They knew that they were reduced by heavy losses; that the king himself, with his brothers and many magnates of the realm had fallen; that those who still stood were almost drained of strength; that they could expect no help. They saw the Normans not much diminished by casualties, threatening them more keenly than in the beginning, as if they had found new strength in the fight; they saw that fury of the duke who spared no one who resisted him; they saw that courage which could only find rest in victory. They therefore turned to flight . . . some on looted horses, many on foot; some along the roads, many across country.'

For the victorious Normans only the matter of the Malfosse remained, but for us there are two matters and the first is the death of the king. It is notable that no details at all of the manner of Harold's death are given by William of Poitiers, and the same is true of William of Jumièges who makes, indeed, a rare mistake in having him slain by lethal wounds at the beginning instead of the end of the battle – in which he was to be followed by Ordericus Vitalis.[101] It is perhaps strange, too, that there is no tradition of the matter in the Chronicle of Battle Abbey (where Harold is slain by a chance blow[102]), though it was certainly not the business of the monks there to contribute to any cult of the dead king and usurper. The Bayeux Tapestry, however, as our second detailed and contemporary source after William of Poitiers, has its famous scene, labelled '*Hic Harold rex interfectus est*', where *Harold* is written above the figure with an arrow in the eye and *interfectus est* above the falling figure being cut down by a mounted knight whose sword is against its thigh.[103] In recent years it has been fashionable to say that contemporary artistic convention prevents both figures from being Harold, that only the second one is (interfectus *est*) but the first is not, and that therefore the tradition of Harold's being slain by an arrow in the eye is false, derived probably from a misunderstanding of the Tapestry. In 1978, however, Dr N.P. Brooks in a paper given at the first Battle Conference and entitled 'The authority and interpretation of the Bayeux Tapestry'[104] re-examined the whole question and showed beyond reasonable doubt that the Tapestry *did* intend both figures to represent the stricken king. The tradition therefore – perhaps one of the best known facts in all English history after the date 1066 itself – is thus restored to something more than respectability as derived from no less an authority than the Tapestry, before taking off via Baudri de Bourgueil, William of Malmesbury, Henry of Huntingdon and, inevitably, Wace.[105] Perhaps matters should be left there, but the lack of detail in William of Poitiers especially remains curious and may prompt two further comments. The first is that William of Malmesbury's account, though close to the Tapestry, may yet provide some explanation. There, Harold is first lethally struck by a chance arrow which pierced his brain and then slashed on the thigh by the sword of a knight as he lay prostrate – for which cowardly and shameful act the unfortunate knight was subsequently stripped of his knighthood by William (*militia pulsus est*). Here then are no feats of arms to be celebrated by the victorious duke's biographer. But what cannot be accepted is the version of the death of Harold given

---

[101] Jumièges, 135; Orderic, ii, 177 (and in his edition of Jumièges).

[102] *Battle Chronicle*, 38.

[103] *BT*, pls 71–2.

[104] *Proceedings of the Battle Conference* i, 23ff.

[105] *Les Oeuvres Poétiques de Baudri de Bourgueil*, ed. P. Abrahams, Paris 1926, 209, ll.461–4; *De gestis regum*, ii, 303; Huntingdon, 203; Wace, ll.8161 *et seq*.

by the *Carmen* and its interpretation by its recent editors, wherein there is no arrow but the king is slain by four knights led by duke William himself.[106] Had William, duke of the Normans, with only three companions, attacked the heavily defended headquarters of the English army – which is what the alleged exploit amounts to – to kill the king and thereby take the crown, far from being hushed up as Morton and Munz will have it, the feat of arms would have been bruited abroad in every court and *chanson* in Latin Christendom and beyond. Meanwhile, as it seems to me, the whole improbable incident recorded by the *Carmen* goes far to condemn that source itself.

And so we come finally to the Malfosse incident, by which of course I mean what we all think we mean, the well-known incident at the end of the battle – more precisely, *after* the end of the battle – in which the Norman knights, hotly pursuing the fleeing English, ride pell-mell in the gathering gloom and broken countryside into a deep fosse or ravine with heavy and tragic losses. The dilemma is, however, that for this incident there is very little if any contemporary evidence; most modern commentators, with no excuse at all after Marx's edition of 1914, having confused Ordericus Vitalis' interpolations in William of Jumièges with William of Jumièges himself.[107] The story (and perhaps we must use such a word) clearly has its origins in William of Poitiers, yet in his version there is no Malfosse in the generally accepted sense of the Normans riding into it.[108] Some of the fleeing English are encouraged to make a stand by 'a broken rampart or entrenchment [the word used is *vallum* with its suggestion of a man-made obstacle] and a labyrinth of ditches'. Duke William comes galloping up, armed only with the stump of a broken lance, intent on attacking even though he assumes they are English reinforcements. He meets, already there, count Eustace of Boulogne with a contingent of fifty knights, all of whom are withdrawing. Eustace advises the duke also to withdraw, and even as he speaks is severely wounded between the shoulder blades by a missile and has to be helped away. The duke, nothing daunted, equating caution with defeat, presses on and tramples his enemies underfoot [*sic*]. We are given no military details of the brief action save the statement that a number of Normans lost their lives because their prowess was inhibited by the difficult country. For anything else and more familiar we have to wait until Ordericus Vitalis' Interpolations in William of Jumièges, dating from before 1109 to after 1113.[109] There[110] we are told that 'when the Normans saw the English fleeing from the battlefield they pursued them relentlessly through the whole night until Sunday [evidently one may detect elements of exaggeration in this] but to their own harm. For by chance long grasses concealed an ancient rampart (*antiquuum aggerem*) and as the Normans came galloping up they fell, one on top of the other, in a struggling mass of horses and arms'. There then follow some sentences on casualties (15000) and God's judgement on both sides, which must surely relate to the whole battle. Here, then, is a recognizable Malfosse incident, but we do not get, so

---

[106] *Carmen*, 34–6 and Appendix D.
[107] Thus e.g. W.H. Stevenson, 'Senlac and the Malfosse', *EHR* xxviii, 1913, 292–303; also the most recent discussion of the Malfosse and its location by C.T. Chevalier, 'Where was the Malfosse? The End of the Battle of Hastings', *Sussex Archaeological Collections* ci, 1963, 1–13.
[108] *Gesta Guillelmi*, 202–4.
[109] Elizabeth M.C. Van Houts, 'Quelques remarques sur les interpolations attribuées à Orderic Vital dans les *Gesta Normannorum Ducum* de Guillaume de Jumièges', *Revue d'Histoire des Textes* viii, 1978, 213–22.
[110] Jumièges, 197.

to speak, the full version until Ordericus Vitalis' *Ecclesiastical History* where, in his Book III finished in the early 1120s,[111] in his account of the battle which in general follows William of Poitiers very closely, he awkwardly combines William's passage on the post-battle affair with his own seemingly independent version from the Interpolations.[112] Both are given more or less verbatim but cut into each other, to produce a combined version which seems to me to have given Orderic much trouble. The result of all this is that pursuing Normans ride into an *antiquum aggerem*, as in the Interpolations. The English, encouraged by this, and also by the *praeruptum uallum* and labyrinth of ditches as in William of Poitiers, make a stand and inflict severe losses. Next we have the passage from the Interpolations on casualties on both sides, wherein Engenulf castellan of Laigle is named amongst the Normans[113] and which is now much more ambiguous than before as to whether it relates to the Malfosse incident or the whole battle. Finally we have the advent of duke William, his meeting with count Eustace and his dealing with the situation, as in William of Poitiers.

After Orderic there is nothing, so far as I can see, until the Battle Abbey Chronicle of the late twelfth century, where, at the end of the battle, 'a final disaster was revealed to the eyes of all'.[114] A little ambiguously we are told that 'just where the fighting was going on, and stretching for a considerable distance, an immense ditch yawned'. Hidden by brambles and thistles it engulfed great numbers, especially of pursuing Normans – 'For, when, all unknowing, they came galloping on, their terrific impetus carried them headlong down into it, and they died tragically, pounded to pieces'. The author goes on to say that the place of the disaster (which now becomes a 'deep pit') is known in his day as the *Malfosse*. He does not, unfortunately, identify it on the ground – and nor am I going to try to do so, partly because, as I think you will have anticipated, in my essentially literary approach there is more, and worse, to come. Meanwhile it is rather alarmingly clear that the literary credentials of the well-known *Malfosse* incident *after* the Battle of Hastings – which henceforward we had best call Version A – are not very good. This Version A may well begin in William of Poitiers, *i.e.* one of our two best and contemporary sources; but he says nothing of its best-known feature of knights riding into a ditch – he says nothing, in short, of the *Malfosse*. For that we have to wait until Ordericus Vitalis (who may have had his own source, which may have been the family of Engenulf castellan of Laigle[115]), and after him there is nothing until the local Battle Chronicle of *c*.1180 – where and when, incidentally, we meet for the first time the word, the name, *Malfosse*. The situation is equally alarming in negative terms; that is to say, these are the only sources to relate Version A, which does not appear in any others. The negative side of the dilemma is best emphasized by stressing that Version A does not even appear in Wace who, though not in my view a source altogether to be despised for the Norman Conquest, is certainly not a man every knowingly to omit a good story.

Let us therefore turn to what I will call Version B, wherein a Malfosse incident occurs not at the end but in the middle of the Battle of Hastings. For this, too, it appears we can begin with one of our two best, contemporary sources, this time the Bayeux Tapestry, and I refer back again to that enigmatic scene – artistically mag-

---

[111] Orderic, ii, xv.
[112] Orderic, ii, 176–8.
[113] For Engenulf see Dr Chibnall's note 4 to Orderic, ii, 177.
[114] Ed. Searle, 38. See also 8, 15–16.
[115] See above.

nificent – labelled *Hic ceciderunt simul Angli et Franci in prelio*[116] (Pl. 4). It occurs in the middle of the battle, and, more specifically, immediately between the scene representing the death of Harold's brothers Gyrth and Leofwine and that representing the real retreat of the Norman forces, i.e. the scene of bishop Odo's turning back the retreating young men or esquires and of duke William's bearing of his head to show he is alive. I have previously suggested that this possibly may be the Tapestry's representation of the feigned flight[117] (which, in that case, would precede and not follow the real retreat), but what matters to us now is what is actually shown, namely a group of Stenton's 'half-armed peasants'[118] making a stand upon a hillock, at the foot of which, and in a marsh or bog,[119] Norman cavalry are in grave difficulties. If one has studied all the sources for the Battle of Hastings one cannot but be reminded by this scene of the Malfosse incident and, more important, William of Malmesbury in his *Gesta Regum* of *c*.1125 thus interpreted it. Evidently knowing his Tapestry, and following it closely here as he does for the death of Harold,[120] having told us how, unable to force an issue any other way, duke William ordered the feigned flight with devastating effect, he goes on to say that the English nevertheless took their toll by frequently making stands. Thus for example, 'getting possession of a hillock (*occupato tumulo*), they drove down the Normans . . . into the valley beneath where, easily hurling their javelins and rolling down stones upon them, they destroyed them to a man'. Then he adds, 'Besides, by a short passage, with which they were acquainted, avoiding a deep ditch (*fossatum quoddam praeruptum*, wherein we may have an echo of William of Poitiers, whose account of the battle William of Malmesbury also uses), they trod under foot such a multitude of their enemies in that place that they made the hollow level with the plain by the heaps of carcasses'. Here, then, is certainly a Malfosse incident in the middle of the battle. Henry of Huntingdon, writing at much the same date (*c*.1125–30?), also has a Malfosse incident in the midst of the battle, and as part of the feigned flight,[121] in which the Normans ride into a great but concealed ditch (*quandam foveam magnam dolose protectam*). So also does the ebullient Wace, though in his account the disaster occurs in the course of the real retreat of the Norman forces (which, as in the *Carmen* and perhaps the Bayeux Tapestry, follows the feigned flight) and the fosse (*sic*) is that which Harold had caused to be dug before the battle began.[122] Wace's rival, Benoit de Ste-Maure[123] has no Malfosse incident of any kind, either during or after the battle, and nor do the *Carmen*, Gaimar,[124] the *Brevis Relatio*[125] or Baudri de Bourgueil whose early date would have made his testimony especially valuable.[126]

And there, I am afraid, we must leave it. There are thus two versions of the

[116] *BT*, pls 66–7.

[117] Above, p. 210.

[118] *Anglo-Saxon England*, 584.

[119] The Tapestry's depiction of the terrain on the right of pl. 66 is very similar to that of the bay of Mont St Michel in pls 21–2, with the addition of tufts of marsh grass or other vegetation.

[120] *De gestis regum* 303 and cf. p. 215 above.

[121] Huntingdon, 203.

[122] Wace, ll.6969–72, 7847–8, 8079 *et seq.*

[123] Ed. F. Michel, *Chroniques Anglo-Normandes*, i, Rouen 1836, 197ff.

[124] *Chroniques Anglo-Normandes*, i, 6ff.

[125] Ed. J.A. Giles, *Scriptores Rerum Gestarum Willelmi Conquestoris*, London 1845, 7–8. See Searle, *Chronicle of Battle Abbey*, 19–20.

[126] Ed. Phyllis Abrahams, cxcvi, 207–9, 232. The date is 1099–1102.

Malfosse incident, A and B, both, it must be confessed, making a somewhat shaky start in one or other of the two most detailed and certainly early accounts of the Battle of Hastings, and I can find no way of choosing between them.[127] Two maddening points remain. One is (and the feeling of frustration will be familiar to many of you) that, as it turns out, J.H. Round said all that I have said, and more, in his diatribes against E.A. Freeman some eighty years ago.[128] The other is that the Malfosse incident, whether or not it took place, whenever it took place, and wherever it took place, quite simply does not matter – that is to say, that as a disaster which overtook the Normans it demonstrably did not affect the issue of the battle. And that, I think, gives me my cue to end this paper, and to do so by returning to the safe ground of what is known and certain. It may conceivably surprise our very welcome French participants at this Conference that almost everything about the Norman Conquest is controversial amongst English-speaking historians, but one thing I do insist upon, which is that the Normans won at Hastings. They won, this paper would suggest, amongst other means by superior military techniques and by superior generalship – and they also gained, I would further suggest, one of the most decisive victories of Western history. But because, though I thus perceive the truth and cling to it, I am at least as unbiased as William of Poitiers, let me finally end by quoting that splendid epitaph of William of Malmesbury upon the English – 'they were few in number but brave in the extreme'.[129]

---

127 Freeman, perhaps characteristically, took both (iii, 490–1, 502–3).
128 See *Feudal England*, 'Mr Freeman and the Battle of Hastings', 332ff, especially 372ff.
129 *De gestis regum*, i, 282.

18. Stephen Morillo, 'Hastings, An Unusual Battle'

This last article, like Glover's, challenges some of the common views of the battle, but not in the same way that Glover's did. It argues that the Normans and the Anglo-Saxons armies were of very similar quality (and in doing so questions the role of technology in influencing the battle), but unlike Glover sees that quality as relatively high on both sides. This leads to conclusions stressing the subsequent synthesis of Anglo-Saxon and Norman elements in Anglo-Norman military history. But even more, the article stresses the ways in which Hastings was an atypical battle from which it is dangerous to draw too many inferences without reference to a broad range of comparative material. This emphasis not only leads to conclusions about the role of leadership (beyond just 'generalship') in shaping the course of the battle, but is a reminder that the closest study of Hastings should not stand in isolation from the larger history of which it is a part.

Reprinted from *The Haskins Society Journal* 2 (1990), 95–104. Copyright © Stephen Morillo 1990.

See S. Morillo, *Warfare under the Anglo-Norman Kings, 1066–1135* (Woodbridge, 1994), for a detailed elaboration of the points in this article and the context of the battle.

HASTINGS: AN UNUSUAL BATTLE

Stephen Morillo

Historians have refought the battle of Hastings regularly since the days of Freeman and Round, and its importance justifies the attention paid it. Part of the reason academic warriors have covered the ground so often is that the battle is by no means easy to understand. It was unusual in a number of ways; so unusual, that the battle demands special care in interpretation. Hastings must be placed in a broader context of medieval military history than it sometimes has been. Only thus can we see the unusual features of the battle clearly and understand better what the battle 'means'.[1]

Hastings was unusual. It was unlike the vast majority of medieval battles (and, in fact, most ancient and early modern battles) in three major ways. First, it was unusually long. We are told that the fighting lasted from 'the third hour of the day until dusk,' at least nine hours.[2] It is difficult to find more than a handful of ancient and medieval battles that lasted more than an hour or two. Tinchebrai, the other great

---

[1] I would like to thank James Alexander, Robert Patterson and Thomas Campbell for numerous helpful comments on earlier drafts of this paper, Thomas Keefe for his encouragement, and J.F.A. Mason for guiding the original research behind this paper. The main sources for the battle are William of Poitiers, *Histoire de Guillaume le Conquerant*, ed. R. Foreville (Paris, 1952); and the Bayeux Tapestry: *The Bayeux Tapestry: A Comprehensive Survey*, ed. Sir Frank Stenton, 2nd edn (London, 1965). *The Carmen de Hastingae Proelio of Bishop Guy of Amiens*, ed. C. Morton and H. Muntz (Oxford, 1972) also offers a full account, but R.H.C. Davis, 'The *Carmen de Hastingae Proelio*', *EHR* 93 (1978): 241–61, casts doubt on the *Carmen* as an independent source for the battle. If approached cautiously, however, it can at least offer some useful information about common battle tactics. Brief narratives which provide a few extra details are found in *The Anglo-Saxon Chronicle*, trans. Dorothy Whitelock, et al. (London, 1961); Guillaume de Jumièges, *Gesta Normannorum Ducum*, ed. Jean Marx (Rouen, 1914); and Florence of Worcester, *Chronicon ex Chronicis*, ed. B. Thorpe, 2 vols (London, 1848–49). William of Malmesbury, Orderic Vitalis, and Henry of Huntingdon add even less and are more distant from the event. The secondary accounts tend to place the battle into one of two contexts: the conquest of England by the Normans, in which case the battle is taken as evidence about the two societies involved; or the history of 'the art of war', especially battle tactics. The latter approach is far too narrow from the point of view of medieval military practice, in which the battle played a secondary role (on this point, see, for example, John Gillingham, 'Richard I and the Science of War in the Middle Ages', in *War and Government in the Middle Ages: Essays in Honour of J.O. Prestwich*, ed. John Gillingham and J.C. Holt [New Jersey, 1984], 81–82). A broader approach to medieval military history could profitably be incorporated into the context of the Norman conquest. No modern account of the battle is fully satisfactory, but most are useful to some extent. These accounts include David C. Douglas, *William the Conqueror* (London, 1964), 196–204; John Beeler, *Warfare in England, 1066–1189* (Ithaca, N.Y., 1966), 15–24; R. Allen Brown, *The Normans and the Norman Conquest* (London, 1969), 158–74; F.M. Stenton, *Anglo-Saxon England* (Oxford, 1943), 585–88; J.F.C. Fuller, *Decisive Battles of the Western World* (London, 1954), 1: 360–85; C.H. Lemmon, 'The Campaign of 1066', in D. Whitelock, et al., *The Norman Conquest* (London, 1966); A.H. Burne, *The Battlefields of England* (London, 1950); and, least usefully, Charles W. Oman, *A History of the Art of War in the Middle Ages*, 2nd edn (New York, 1924), 149–66.
[2] William of Jumièges, 135; Florence of Worcester, 1:227.

battle in Anglo-Norman history, was decided fairly quickly, for example: in about an hour, according to one source.[3] In fact, it is hard to find a longer battle until well into the age of gunpowder.

The length of the battle reflects its second unusual feature: how hard and evenly matched the fighting was. Two phases of the battle stand out in this respect.[4] First, both armies came close to breaking fairly early in the day. The Normans, believing William dead, fell into a general panic after the failure of their first attacks. William, baring his head, rallied them and led a counterattack on those Saxons who had pursued.[5] Now it was the Saxons' turn to hold steady despite this setback. Thus passed the moment when most battles would have been won – one side panics and flees, or one side panics, rallies, and the other side breaks. At Hastings neither side broke, for even the Saxons' final collapse was not sudden and panic-stricken but grudgingly slow and stubborn.[6]

The second phase followed this crisis and was strange to those who saw it. 'There followed an unknown sort of battle,' says William of Poitiers, 'in which one side launched attacks and numerous manoeuvres, the other stood like rocks fixed to the ground.'[7] It was this sort of strange fighting which then lasted the rest of the day, indicating that neither side had a decisive advantage.

The third unusual aspect of Hastings is that it was in the end so completely and far-reachingly decisive.[8] There were, of course, many battles in which one side beat the living daylights out of the other. But few of these transferred rule of a major kingdom from one people to another, with little subsequent opposition after the battle, and few transfers have had such fundamental consequences for the kingdom involved. Much of this is the result of a context for the battle that goes far beyond the scope of this essay. However our understanding of the events on the field of Hastings must account for this decisiveness.

[3] H.W.C. Davis and R.L. Poole, 'A Contemporary Account of the Battle of Tinchebrai', *EHR* 25 (1910): 295–96 (letter of Priest of Fécamp).

[4] Briefly, the major stages of the battle were as follows: An initial Norman attack commenced about 9 a.m. involving archers and heavy infantry as well as cavalry (William of Poitiers, 186–88; William of Jumièges, 135; *Bayeux Tapestry*, pls 60–63). This was repulsed, and the Norman army began to retreat in growing disorder, with indications of a Saxon pursuit (William of Poitiers, 188–90; *Bayeux Tapestry*, pls 66–68; and see infra, 99). William rallied his army, halted the Saxon advance, and led another unsuccessful attack (William of Poitiers, 190–92). The rest of the day saw a series of Norman attacks and feigned flights which, though they failed to break the Saxon line, depleted it to some extent, especially on the wings. Finally, with darkness falling and Harold dead, the Saxon line gave way (William of Poitiers, 196–204; *Bayeux Tapestry*, pls 70–73). See also the secondary accounts, supra, n. 1.

[5] William of Poitiers, 190–92; *Bayeux Tapestry*, pl. 68. See infra, 100 for a further discussion of the Saxon pursuit and William's counterattack.

[6] William of Poitiers, 202–4.

[7] Ibid., 194.

[8] By this I do not mean to imply that William was effectively king on October 15. There remained the campaign aimed at London and even after his coronation several years of consolidation. But Hastings seems to have brought organized Saxon resistance to an end. The move to crown the child Edgar as king and rally military forces around Edwin and Morcar was abortive: as the Anglo-Saxon Chronicle put it, 'always the more it ought to have been forward the more it got behind, and the worse it grew from day to day, exactly as everything came to be at the end.' *ASC* (D), a. 1066. Indeed, the most severe threat to the result at Hastings was William's bout with dysentery at Dover: William of Poitiers, 212. On the decisiveness of Hastings, cf. R.H.C. Davis, *The Normans and Their Myth* (London, 1976), 103.

One way to account for the decisiveness of the Norman victory is by reference to the supposed superiority of Norman cavalry over Saxon infantry. This is in fact a standard view of Hastings, proposed most forcibly by R. Allen Brown and echoed by many others. In this view Hastings was the inevitable victory of stirruped cavalry over helpless infantry,[9] infantry which was 'already obsolete in the greater part of western Europe'[10] and which had 'failed to keep abreast with the latest developments in military science.'[11] I see a number of problems with this explanation.

On a level of analysis specific to Hastings, such a view seems in conflict with the unusual length and difficulty of the battle noted above. One would not expect inevitable victories to take so long, to be so hard, or to be almost lost. And the dominant tactics of the day were in fact evenly matched. The English defensive formation was just the sort that would turn back charging cavalry – densely massed infantry[12] – while the hand-to-hand combat along the line matched Norman swords and lances against Saxon battle axes which 'easily found their way through shields or other armor,'[13] as William of Poitiers says, with no advantage either way. Furthermore, this view necessarily ignores the large body of infantry, exclusive of archers, which Duke William deployed on the battlefield. While these troops play little or no explicit role

---

9 Brown, *Normans and the Norman Conquest*, 95–99, 166. The notion of an 'Age of Cavalry' goes back to Oman, *Art of War*, for whom the battle of Adrianople in 378 ushered in a period when heavy cavalry 'had become the arbiter of war, the lineal ancester of all the knights of the Middle Ages, the inaugurator of that ascendancy of the horsemen which was to endure for a thousand years.' (p. 14) But Oman describes more than he explains. The fountainhead of the 'stirrup theory' of cavalry dominance is Lynn White, Jr, *Medieval Technology and Social Change* (Oxford, 1962), chap. 1, 'The Stirrup, Mounted Shock Combat, Feudalism and Chivalry'. For White, the fusion of horse and rider, which the stirrup allowed, created an irresistable fighting machine against which no infantry stood a chance. Bernard S. Bachrach, 'Charles Martel, Shock Combat, the Stirrup and Feudalism'. *Studies in Medieval and Renaissance History* 7 (1970): 47–75, offers some telling criticisms of many details of White's analysis, but the theory in broad outline seems to have passed into the realm of accepted textbook canon. J.F. Verbruggen, *The Art of Warfare in Western Europe during the Middle Ages*, trans. Sumner Willard and S.C.M. Southern (Amsterdam, 1977), 5, places the stirrup at the heart of knightly dominance; Philippe Contamine, *War in the Middle Ages*, trans. Michael Jones (Oxford, 1984), 179–84, notes some of the problems associated with dating the introduction of the stirrup, but accepts its eventual impact. John P. McKay, Bennett D. Hill, and John Buckler, *A History of Western Societies*, 2nd edn (Boston, 1988), 1:335, is but one example of the theory's spread to introductory textbooks, while Michael Howard, *War in European History* (Oxford, 1976), chap. 1, 'The Wars of the Knights', represents the acceptance of the theory into a scholarly synthesis of European military history. Martin van Creveld, in his survey, *Technology and War from 2000 B.C. to the Present* (New York, 1989), 18, sums up the case: 'Modern authors, however much they may differ in detail, are united in their opinion that, sometime between 500 and 1000 A.D., the stirrup and the high saddle . . . spread to Europe. Add the horseshoe, the origin of which is simply unknown, and the ascent of cavalry over ancient infantry becomes at least understandable.' It is the contention of this paper that while the stirrup may indeed have appeared in Europe sometime between 500 and 1000, it does not explain the ascent of cavalry and more particularly cannot explain the details of Hastings.

10 Stenton, *Anglo-Saxon England*, 576.

11 *English Historical Documents*, 2: *1042–1189*, ed. David C. Douglas and G.W. Greenaway (London, 1953), 20 (editor's introduction).

12 'pedites densius conglobati': William of Poitiers, 186, describing the Saxon shield wall at the start of the battle; again, 192, William's attack after checking the Norman rout was turned back by the density of the Saxon line. The *Carmen* makes much of the density of the Saxon formation: lines 368, 415, 417–22. *Bayeux Tapestry*, pls 62–63 show a massed shield wall about as well as the format allows, while pls 66–67 (esp. pl. XII, detail from 66 – one of the finest pieces of draughtsmanship in the whole tapestry) show the disastrous results a cavalry charge against such a formation could have.

13 William of Poitiers, 188. See also Lemmon, 'The Campaign of 1066', 92.

in the details our sources give of the battle, it seems illogical to assume that they were mere spectators to the action.

It is possible to argue that it was not in hand-to-hand combat, but in larger operations on the battlefield that the presence of cavalry on the Norman side was decisive. Briefly, it is alleged that the Norman cavalry, by its superior mobility, forced the Saxon army to remain on the defensive. Thus the Saxons might hold out, but they could not win.[14]

I will note first that this should not be the argument of those who see the stirrup as central to the dominance of cavalry. To the extent that this argument is true, it could be true of any cavalry. But if we grant this advantage to William's cavalry, the question becomes, did the presence of cavalry on the Norman side force Harold into a defensive battle he could not win? This is essentially a question of Harold's generalship.

Could Harold have considered an attack? He knew his enemy from his stay in Normandy.[15] His army was capable of attacking, as Harold Hardraada learned at Stamford Bridge.[16] Finally, that Harold thought he could attack William is implied by his actions in the campaign up to that point: his offensive strategy is otherwise incomprehensible.[17]

Was Harold mistaken? When William's army retreated after its first unsuccessful attack, at least part of the Saxon army pursued. The duke's knights were able to rally and cut down a number of the Saxons who had left the solid defensive position.[18] The success of the Normans' counterattack against their Saxon pursuers would seem to suggest that Harold was mistaken; but I believe the episode may be read in another way. The knights were able to cut down those pursuers who scattered in the advance, but those who maintained their formation in the advance were able to defend themselves.[19] Had the entire Saxon army advanced in close order, *densatim progredi-*

---

[14] This is the implication of Brown's argument that 'indeed, only a strong element of surprise could crown with success an offensive action by an infantry force against an enemy strong in cavalry.' Brown, *Normans and the Norman Conquest*, 160.

[15] *Bayeux Tapestry*, pls 17–29.

[16] *ASC*, a. 1066. The army at Hastings was not exactly the same one as at Stamford Bridge, but the core of housecarls was the same and the rest of the troops would have been similar in type and training, if not all the same soldiers.

[17] William of Poitiers, 154, describes Harold as 'eager for battle'. For Harold's offensive intentions, see also Fuller, *Decisive Battles*, 373, 375; Douglas, *William the Conqueror*, 197; Brown, *Normans and the Norman Conquest*, 159; Lemmon, 'Campaign of Hastings', 95, 107; but cf. Morton and Muntz, *Carmen*, 73–83, who argue that Harold's strategy was to trap William on the Hastings peninsula by establishing a strong defensive position on Battle Hill (and see maps in *Carmen*, 110–11). This does not necessarily imply a defensive approach to the battle itself; in fact, Morton and Muntz (following William of Poitiers and the *Carmen*) say that 'the king was preparing to blockade him [Duke William] by sea and surprise him in great strength on land', (76) and suggest that the story of the fleet (for which there is no sure evidence) was 'calculated to bring the duke to battle forthwith'. (77–78, n. 5) In fact, a real strategy of blockade and delay seems problematical: Harold was as likely as William to have run into supply problems from sitting still in the immediate vicinity, and unless there really were a Saxon fleet able to contain and defeat William's fleet, William would not, in fact, be trapped. It should be noted that if William did land first at Pevensey (William of Poitiers, 164 and n. 3), then the move to Hastings would have involved use of the fleet as well as marching (see map in *Carmen*, 110.).

[18] William of Poitiers, 190.

[19] *Carmen*, 11, 429–35, 'pars ibi magna perit – pars et densata resistit'.

entes,[20] as it had in taking up its battle position, no opening for the cavalry would have existed. The duke's army, demoralized, disordered, and thinking him dead,[21] was ready to be swept from the field by a general counterattack. Why was it not?

David Douglas concluded that Harold failed to order an advance and so missed the opportunity, and was furthermore unable to impose discipline and hold back those of his troops who did advance.[22] But the matter is not clear. Failure to attack does not seem consistent with Harold's record as a general up to that point, including his probable intentions regarding William's invasion. In addition, there are indications that a general advance was ordered: William saw 'a great part of the enemy leave their positions, and pursue his troops.'[23] The question then becomes, if Harold did order a general advance, what happened to it?

Perhaps the answer lies in the deaths of Earls Gyrth and Leofwine, Harold's brothers and main subordinates. No conclusive moment in the battle has been found for their deaths, for the sources are not specific on this point. If Harold had ordered them to lead the counterattack, which is not unlikely, and they were killed in front of the Saxon army just as the advance was getting under way, the whole effort may have collapsed from this sudden loss of leadership. The placement of their deaths in the Bayeux Tapestry is consistent with such an interpretation, coming just after the first Norman attack, before William rallies his army, and well before the climactic battle scenes and Harold's death;[24] and the fact that their deaths were noticed by the sources may indicate that they died prominently.[25] If, moreover, they were near the center of the Saxon line to lead the attack, which is also not unlikely, this would account for the disordered advances taking place on the wings of the Saxon army, which might not have seen their leaders' fate and thus been halted.[26]

In any case the Saxon attack was halted and William was given time to rally his army. The crisis of the battle had passed, and neither side had won. The Saxons were given no more opportunities for a general attack and perhaps by now lacked enough

---

20   Ibid., 1. 367.

21   William of Poitiers, 190; *Bayeux Tapestry*, pl. 68.

22   Douglas, *William the Conqueror*, 200.

23   William of Poitiers, 213. Cf. Orderic, 2:174, who follows William word for word on this point. Interestingly the *Carmen* has the Saxons pressing their attack against a feigned flight, turning it into a real rout: 11. 439–44. The problem, of course, is telling an abortive general advance from an undisciplined pursuit.

24   *Baueux Tapestry*, pls 62–68. The Normans charge (pl. 62), and are repulsed by the shield wall (pl. 63). Then Leofwine and Gyrth are killed (pls 64–65), apparently out in the open, away from the dense mass of the shield wall depicted in the preceeding scene. Why would they be separated at this stage except to lead an attack? Following their deaths, we see French and English killing each other (pl. 66) and what appear to be less well-armed English troops isolated on a hillock (pl. 67). Finally, William bares his head and rallies his army for further attacks (pl. 68). The *Carmen*, 1, 478, also may support this view, as Gyrth is named as a victim of William himself (which we need not accept at face value) as the duke led the counterattack on the Saxon pursuit.

25   In addition to their portrayal in the Tapestry, Gyrth and Leofwine are mentioned as killed along with Harold in *ASC* (D, E), a. 1066, and Florence of Worcester, 1:227, but not (unsurprisingly) by William of Jumièges. William of Poitiers notes their deaths having taken place (p. 200), but does not name them or place their deaths in the sequence of events.

26   William of Poitiers, 206, states that their bodies were found near Harold's. Paradoxically, the loss of leadership may have inspired the Saxon army to fight even harder in defense, as the Saxon tradition, at least in literature, emphasized rallying around a fallen lord. See, for example, the reactions of the followers of Ealdorman Byrhtnoth in *The Battle of Maldon: Anglo-Saxon Poetry*, trans. R.K. Gordon, rev. edn (London, 1970), 332–33.

leaders to pull one off. Their resulting immobility gave the Normans the security to carry out their famous feigned flights on the wings, the existence of which I see no reason to doubt.[27] Yet the issue was still not settled; the Saxons were not doomed. The strategic situations meant that the Saxons could afford a draw, while the Normans could not. Had the Saxons held together for an hour more, or through one more Norman attack, they might have won the war without winning the battle.[28]

So the theory of cavalry dominance does not account convincingly for the details of the action at Hastings. On a more general level, the theory of cavalry dominance based on the stirrup is, I believe, untenable. A full analysis of this issue is beyond the scope of this paper; I shall present my arguments on this subject elsewhere. To state the outlines of my argument briefly, Hastings took place in a period of decreased military effectiveness brought about by the reduced effectiveness of central authority. Medieval armies were closer to armed mobs than were classical or early modern armies.[29] This reduction generally affected infantry more than

[27] William of Poitiers, 194, where he notes that the feigned flights were modelled on the real flight earlier in the day. Richard Glover, 'English Warfare in 1066', *EHR* 67 (1952): 1–18 argues that the Norman cavalry did not have the training to execute such manoeuvres (p. 12) and Lemmon, 'The Campaign of 1066', 108–10, also doubts the tactic; but for horsemen operating against slower moving foes, infantry or more heavily armored cavalry, the tactic is natural and not difficult. R.C. Smail, *Crusading Warfare, 1097–1193* (Cambridge, 1956), 78–79, discusses feigned flights as a normal tactic of the part-time, non-professional Turkish armies and notes the use of feigned flights by Syrian Frankish armies as well. Norman knights had used the tactic in Sicily in 1060: D.P. Waley, 'Combined Operations in Sicily, A.D. 1060–1078', *Papers of the British School at Rome* 23, p. 123. See also Brown, *Normans and the Norman Conquest*, 171–72, n. 147, and Douglas, *William the Conqueror*, 201, n. 2. In general, see also Verbruggen, *Art of Warfare*, 89–90.

[28] William's army was not going to get any bigger; Harold probably fought with only a part of his military forces gathered: *ASC* (E), a. 1066; Florence of Worcester, 1:227. William, in a hostile country, without a firm base of operations, and probably having to contend with the Saxon fleet (William of Poitiers, 180), was also more likely to run into supply problems than was Harold. Finally, Harold was the sitting king, and a boxing analogy is here apt: the challenger has to win; the champion only has to not lose.

[29] By this I do not mean to place myself on the side of what Allen Brown called the 'heresy' that 'medieval warfare was chaos, incompetently waged by individualistic exhibitionists' (*Normans and the Norman Conquest*, 164, n. 115). I believe medieval commanders were as intelligent and skillful, as a group, as commanders from any other period of history and that usually medieval fighting men were not only brave, but skilled in their individual tasks. What I do mean is that medieval commanders did not have comparable social, economic, and institutional resources with which to mold their warriors as effectively into coherent large groups, so that medieval fighters were apt to be better warriors than soldiers. Simply stated, medieval commanders did not have the luxury of standing armies. Cf. John Keegan, *The Face of Battle* (London, 1976), 175–77. As R.C. Smail, *Crusading Warfare*, 203, points out about Bohemond of Antioch on the First Crusade, 'he had not the well-drilled regiments of the old East Roman army, but a motley host of pilgrims which included many non-combatants. Among the knights were adventurers and individualists, unused to military discipline and not inclined to accept it.' To some extent (usually excluding the non-combatants), this was true of most medieval commanders. Thus, medieval armies could be molded together, especially by long mutual experience, but the process was less complete than it can be in standing armies with extensive peacetime drill. *All* armies are prone to become armed mobs under too much stress (Keegan refers to the 'crowd' inside every army: *Face of Battle*, 175). The stronger the glue of group training and discipline that holds them together, the more stress they may withstand before panicking and becoming a mob. Medieval armies generally could withstand less stress than Augustan legions or Louis XIV's regiments, for example. On this topic, see also Keegan, *Face of Battle*, chap. 2; Verbruggen, *Art of Warfare*, 39–52, 76–82; Contamine, *War in the Middle Ages*, 15–16, 30–32, 162–72, 250–60; J.R. Hale, *War and Society in Renaissance Europe, 1450–1620* (Baltimore, 1985), 46–74.

cavalry.[30] In other words, it takes strong government to produce strong infantry; in the Middle Ages, cavalry did not get better, infantry got worse. Saxon and then Norman England, with their relatively strong governments, were affected less than elsewhere, accounting for the good showing of the Saxon infantry at Hastings, for the discipline both sides showed that day, and for the continuity of the Anglo-Norman infantry tradition after Hastings.[31]

Another way of saying this is that the Saxon and Norman armies on the field of Hastings were the products of two societies which were not all that different in their organization, their values, and their ways of governing.[32] The Saxons perhaps had the edge in sophistication; the Normans, in vigor. Given the broad similarites of the two societies, should we really expect one side's forces to be radically superior to the other's? Probably not. Hastings as a victory of advanced cavalry over backward infantry is thus a problematical construct.[33]

How then are we to understand the unusual features of this difficult battle? Leadership is crucial to how any army performs. Armies which were somewhat less than disciplined machines magnified the effects of leadership. Leadership, I believe, can account for the unusual features of the battle of Hastings.

First, the length of the battle is a credit mostly to the resolve of the two commanders. William, by personal example and sheer force of his personality, held his army together when by all odds it should have broken. On the other side, as long as Harold stood under his banner, both in the sense of remaining alive and in the sense of refusing to run, the Saxon army stood with him. Their respective armies were disciplined enough to follow their lead, and certainly the length and difficulty of the

---

30 This is because infantry depends more for its effectiveness on group cohesion than cavalry does, though it is important to both, and because infantry needs somewhat larger numbers than cavalry to be effective; and medieval armies were generally small. On infantry, see Keegan, *Face of Battle*, 95–96, 156; Howard, *War in European History*, 14. On numbers, see Verbruggen, *Art of Warfare*, 6–11.

31 Infantry was of necessity almost always present in medieval armies: Gillingham, 'Richard I', 91. Anglo-Norman armies not only contained infantry per se (as did William's army at Hastings: William of Poitiers, 184), but emphasized infantry tactics in battle to the extent that most or all of the knights regularly dismounted, a development first conspicuous at Tinchebrai in 1106: Orderic, 6:88–90; the Priest of Fécamp's letter, 296; Henry of Huntingdon, *Historia Anglorum*, ed. T. Arnold, R.S. (London, 1879), 235; Eadmer, *Historia Novorum*, ed. M. Rule, R.S. (London, 1884), 184. A full consideration of this topic is once again beyond the scope of this essay.

32 The core of both armies was made up of semi-professional household warriors: the *familia*, or household knights of the Normans and the housecarls of the Saxons; and both included stipendiary troops. In broader terms, much of both sides' forces were recruited and held together by systems of hierarchical lordship in which soldiers served a superior out of personal loyalty and obligation, the obligation sometimes being tied to grants of land tenure in some form. The differences, such as the presence or absence of fiefs per se and of feudal tenure, though significant from many perspectives, are from the point of view of raising field armies matters of detail. On terms of service in late Saxon armies, see Richard Abels, *Lordship and Military Obligation in Anglo-Saxon England* (Berkeley, 1988), 146–84; and C. Warren Hollister, *Anglo-Saxon Military Institutions on the Eve of the Norman Conquest* (Oxford, 1962). On Normandy, see David Bates, *Normandy before 1066* (London, 1982); Charles Homer Haskins, *Norman Institutions* (Cambridge, MA., 1925). And see especially J. O. Prestwich, 'The Military Household of the Norman Kings', *EHR* 96 (1981): 1–37.

33 By concentrating on the question of stirruped cavalry, I have necessarily slighted the role of the Norman archers in the battle. It is a commonplace that combined arms tactics are more effective than reliance on one arm only, and the archers certainly played a role in the Norman victory. I would argue, however, that the advantage of having archers was largely independent of the role of Norman cavalry. Norman *infantry* with archers would have had an advantage over Saxon infantry without archers.

fighting argues for the relatively high quality of the armies raised on both sides of the conflict. It was the examples of William and Harold (and their subordinates) which prevented either side from giving in. The flight of Robert of Bellême from Tinchebrai provides an instructive counterexample here.[34]

Second, I have argued that the peculiar tactical standoff which characterised much of the day's fighting was the result, not of the Saxons' inability to attack, but of a critical loss of leadership. The unusual difficulty of the battle for both sides, contributing also to its length, stemmed not from the Saxons' lack of options imposed by the presence of enemy cavalry, but from a loss of options imposed by a loss of its own leaders.

Finally, the role of leadership in the decisiveness of the battle is clear. The battle William won decided the war because Harold died. Indeed not just Harold, but a large proportion of the entire Saxon leadership class perished, including any possible effective heirs to Harold's position. In this the decisiveness of the battle was partly accidental. It is possible to imagine Harold beaten at the end of the day, yet escaping into the darkness to raise new forces. William's road to the throne would at that point have become much longer and harder. Yet the decimation of the Saxon leadership was also partly a result of Harold's decision to stand firm and of William's relentless determination. It seems that both leaders in the end decided to risk all on one throw of the dice; William rolled the sevens.

What can we as historians learn from Hastings? For one, the length and difficulty of the battle supports the conclusion that this was a hard-fought battle between armies essentially equal in strength,[35] with high levels of leadership, discipline, and morale obtaining on both sides of the conflict. The Saxon and the Norman military establishments both produced good warriors. If it is true that Hastings was a battle between an army that included some of the best cavalry in Europe and an army that included the best infantry in Europe, it is equally true that the battle was not decided by the inevitable superiority of one arm over the other. Given essentially equal armies, William simply outgeneraled Harold and had a bit more luck.

Hastings should rather be seen as confirmation of the effectiveness of both military establishments. The combined Anglo-Norman military organization under firm royal control not only continued to produce good warriors, it continued to produce soldiers capable of effective infantry tactics and effective cavalry tactics. From the dismounted knights and English infantry at Tinchebrai through the Assize of Arms to the levies who took up the longbow and fought beside dismounted knights in Scotland and France, this tradition would persist throughout English medieval history.

---

[34] The Priest of Fécamp's letter, 296.
[35] D.J.A. Matthew, *The Norman Conquest* (London, 1966), 84; Lemmon, 'The Campaign of 1066', 114.

FURTHER READING

The selections in this book are only the tip of the scholarly iceberg of works on Hastings and the historical topics related to the battle. The footnotes in the secondary articles provide one entryway into the wider world of Anglo-Norman, Anglo-Saxon and medieval military scholarship. This guide is another. It is not intended as an exhaustive bibliography, so I particularly emphasize recent works that provide extensive bibliographies of their own, as well as some classics in the field. The list should help readers whose interest has been piqued by this collection to find out more about Hastings and the rich history and historiography that surrounds the battle.

On **Anglo-Norman warfare**, Stephen Morillo, *Warfare under the Anglo-Norman Kings, 1066–1135* (Boydell, 1994) presents a complete study of warfare from its various contexts and the administration of the military system to the practices of armies in the field. *Anglo-Norman Warfare*, ed. Matthew Strickland (Boydell, 1992), is an excellent collection of articles with an introduction by the editor and a very useful bibliography. And R. Allen Brown's *The Normans and the Norman Conquest* (London, 1969) is a foundational work in Anglo-Norman military and political history. On **Anglo-Norman history** generally, Marjorie Chibnall, *Anglo-Norman England, 1066–1166* (Oxford, 1986) and Frank Barlow, *The Feudal Kingdom of England, 1042–1216* (4th edn, London, 1988) are the best surveys, while *Anglo-Norman Studies* (the proceedings of the annual Battle Conference) and its American sister publication *The Haskins Society Journal* are the journals of record in the field. Finally, David C. Douglas, *William the Conqueror* (London, 1964) and David Bates, *William the Conqueror* (London, 1989) are both valuable biographies of the dominant figure at Hastings and in the settlement that followed.

There are excellent works on **Normandy and England before 1066**. Two books should be read together on Normandy before the conquest: David Bates' *Normandy before 1066* (London, 1982) and Eleanor Searle's *Predatory Kinship and the Creation of Norman Power, 840–1066* (Berkeley, 1988). The two debate the fascinating question of Roman and Carolingian continuity (or lack thereof) into eleventh century Normandy, and in the process say most of what there is to say about the duchy before the conquest. On the other side of the Channel, the Anglo-Saxon military system is given definitive treatment in Richard Abels' *Lordship and Military Obligation in Anglo-Saxon England* (Berkeley, 1988). The best general introductions to Anglo-Saxon history are the lavishly illustrated *The Anglo-Saxons* edited by James Campbell, Eric John and Patrick Wormold (Oxford, 1982), and Sir Frank Stenton's classic and still valuable *Anglo-Saxon England* (3rd edn, Oxford, 1971). A good introduction to the third set of players in the drama of 1066 is Gwyn Jones, *A History of the Vikings* (Oxford, 1968).

For more about the **primary sources** for Anglo-Norman history, an interesting introduction to the narrative sources is Antonia Gransden's *Historical Writing in England, c.550–c.1307* (London, 1974). And Marjorie Chibnall's *The World of Orderic Vitalis* (Oxford, 1984) is a wonderful book that says much about how our sources came to know what they tell us. Her edition of Orderic's own work, *The*

Ecclesiastical History (6 vols, Oxford, 1969–78) is a most valuable source; she is also bringing out a new edition of William of Poitiers, unfortunately too late to be taken into account by this book, that in addition to making a new text and translation available should have interesting things to say about the author. Further sources are collected in *English Historical Documents*, vol. 2, 1042–1189, ed. D.C. Douglas and G.W. Greenaway (2nd edn, Oxford, 1981).

The best general introductions to **medieval miliary history** are Philippe Contamine, *War in the Middle Ages*, trans. M. Jones (Blackwell, 1984), which has an extensive bibliography, and J.F. Verbruggen, *The Art of Warfare in Western Europe during the Middle Ages* (a partial edition), trans. S. Willard and S. Southern (Oxford, 1977). This is soon to appear as a full edition in the present *Warfare in History* series. Much older but still useful if used carefully is Charles Oman, *A History of the Art of War in the Middle Ages* (2 vols, 2nd edn, London, 1924). Of more specialized works, the model monograph and perhaps the most influential book in modern medieval military historiography is R.C. Smail, *Crusading Warfare, 1097–1193* (Cambridge, 1956). Its only rival would be John Keegan's *The Face of Battle* (London, 1976), both for its chapter on Agincourt and for its discussion of the historiography of the 'decisive battle' paradigm. Useful starting points for other facets of medieval military history include Jim Bradbury's *The Medieval Siege* (Boydell, 1992) for siege warfare and Norman Pounds, *The Medieval Castle in England and Wales* (Cambridge, 1990) on castles; Kelly DeVries' survey, *Medieval Military Technology* (Lewiston, NY, 1992) – which also has a good bibliography; and David Nicolle, *Arms and Armour of the Crusading Era, 1050–1350* (2 vols, White Plains, NY, 1988).